How Pac-Man Eats

How Pac-Man Eats

Noah Wardrip-Fruin

The MIT Press
Cambridge, Massachusetts
London, England

This book was set in ITC Stone Serif Std and ITC Stone Sans Std by New Best-set Typesetters Ltd. Printed and bound in the United States of America.

Library of Congress Cataloging-in-Publication Data

Names: Wardrip-Fruin, Noah, author.
Title: How Pac-Man eats / Noah Wardrip-Fruin.
Description: Cambridge, Massachusetts : The MIT Press, [2020] | Series: Software studies |
   Includes bibliographical references and index.
Identifiers: LCCN 2020003046 | ISBN 9780262044653 (hardcover)
Subjects: LCSH: Video games—Design. | Computer games—Design.
Classification: LCC GV1469.3 .W462 2020 | DDC 794.8—dc23
LC record available at https://lccn.loc.gov/2020003046

10 9 8 7 6 5 4 3 2 1

For Max and Zoe

Contents

Series Foreword

Software is deeply woven into contemporary life—economically, culturally, creatively, politically—in manners both obvious and nearly invisible. Yet while much is written about how software is used, and the activities that it supports and shapes, thinking about software itself has remained largely technical for much of its history. Increasingly, however, artists, scientists, engineers, hackers, designers, and scholars in the humanities and social sciences are finding that for the questions they face, and the things they need to build, an expanded understanding of software is necessary. For such understanding they can call upon a strand of texts in the history of computing and new media, they can take part in the rich implicit culture of software, and they also can take part in the development of an emerging, fundamentally transdisciplinary, computational literacy. These provide the foundation for Software Studies.

Software Studies uses and develops cultural, theoretical, and practice-oriented approaches to make critical, historical, and experimental accounts of (and interventions via) the objects and processes of software. The field engages and contributes to the research of computer scientists, the work of software designers and engineers, and the creations of software artists. It tracks how software is substantially integrated into the processes of contemporary culture and society, reformulating processes, ideas, institutions, and cultural objects around their closeness to algorithmic and formal description and action. Software Studies proposes histories of computational cultures and works with the intellectual resources of computing to develop reflexive thinking about its entanglements and possibilities. It does this both in the scholarly modes of the humanities and social sciences and in the software creation/research modes of computer science, the arts, and design.

The Software Studies book series, published by the MIT Press, aims to publish the best new work in a critical and experimental field that is at once culturally and technically literate, reflecting the reality of today's software culture.

Preface

This book tries to answer two questions: *What are the fundamental ways that games work?* and *How can games be about something?* It tries to answer both in the same book, because I believe the two questions are closely related.

These questions matter to many people, from those who already think about and make games to those reading their first book about this increasingly important medium. My hope is that I've written a book that is interesting and accessible to designers, journalists, technologists, scholars, students, and members of the public.

In fields that focus on games, when we talk about "how games work," *mechanics* is the usual foundation of discussion. *Mechanics* is a term with multiple meanings, but commonly refers to things players can do in games—such as jumping and shooting, or harvesting and crafting. But if mechanics are really what games are built on, with no level beneath, some things we see in game creation and play are hard to explain. For example, making things in *Minecraft*,[1] moving material into patterns on crafting tables, feels familiar to people who are experienced in tile-matching games such as *Bejeweled*.[2] The games have very different mechanics—one creates items, the other swaps and removes gems—and yet they share a connection.[3]

This book argues that games have a fundamental level that has not yet been widely discussed, on which mechanics depend. It uses the term *operational logics* to name the elements we find at this level, which have both process-oriented and communication-oriented aspects. Just as we can understand the structure of movies better with knowledge of cuts and pans, knowledge of this level underneath mechanics (which also spans across mechanics, and helps players understand one based on knowledge of another) can help us have a deeper, richer understanding of games.

In particular, if we understand games at this level and look at how these elements combine to support mechanics, we can also get a handle on an aspect of games that has proven surprisingly hard to pin down: how it is that games can be about something. We have many tools for understanding how other forms of media can be about something—looking at them visually, textually, auditorily, historically, and so on. Many games, however, can only be understood if we do something for which we don't have widely used analytical tools. We must see how their systems interact with their other media elements.

This book demonstrates a concrete strategy for doing this: looking at how games create procedural representations of things that happen in their worlds, called *playable models*, of which operational logics are primary building blocks. As we understand the logics and models that are well-developed for games, we can come to appreciate how they support and constrain different things that games might try to be about. And through that we can also come to appreciate the strategies that game creators have used to try to broaden that set and what can be done with it.

Finally, I should note that this book arises from a particular context—that of the University of California, Santa Cruz, where colleagues, students, and friends have been my partners in developing these ideas and often have continued to contribute to their development after moving on to new contexts. This book was written because I'm interested in these questions and think the answers we've developed can be of value. But it was also written because I want to honor and spread the insights of these collaborators, as I discuss further in the acknowledgments.

Noah Wardrip-Fruin

Santa Cruz, California

Acknowledgments

The initial versions of a number of the ideas in this book were developed when I was working on my dissertation. I owe a great debt of gratitude to my dissertation committee—Wendy Chun, Robert Coover, David Durand, George Landow, and Andy van Dam—as well as to Brown University, which provided a creative, welcoming environment and a dissertation fellowship.

Over time, the ideas from my dissertation have evolved quite a bit, with input from many others. In fact, it would be fair to say that the ideas that are in this book arose out of a community—specifically, the community of the Computational Media department at the University of California, Santa Cruz, and within it the Expressive Intelligence Studio (also known as EIS, pronounced "ice"). Michael Mateas founded EIS, and we became co-directors when I joined him at UC Santa Cruz in 2008. This led to many conversations, and eventual publications, working through the ideas that developed into this book.

Or perhaps we could say that the ideas in this book helped lead me to EIS. I remember visiting Mateas in 2005, when I was still at Brown and he was still at Georgia Tech, and having a fascinating, hours-long series of conversations with him about them. Those conversations made it clear to me that there was more to pursue in these ideas and that Mateas would be an ideal partner in the pursuit.

Once we were both at Santa Cruz, we published a joint paper on these topics in 2009, and probably would have continued to pursue them, on and off. But what really pushed the conversation further was work with other members of EIS. In particular, Joseph C. Osborn, Mike Treanor, and Dylan Lederle-Ensign all led research that developed new aspects (and/or revised existing aspects) of these ideas and co-authored publications with us on them.

And beyond formal research and writing, many of these ideas developed through conversation, especially teaching. I am indebted to Melanie Dickinson, Matthew

Balousek, and Joe Rossi, who as undergraduates (two of whom later became graduate student members of EIS) worked with Osborn, Lederle-Ensign, and me to reimagine a large, introductory game design class around the ideas in this book. And I am indebted to the students of that course—CMPM 80K: Foundations of Video Game Design—who have helped develop the ideas, and means of explaining them, through their questions, comments, and creations.

Other members (and alumni) of EIS have also contributed in many ways, from casual conversations to careful, creative reviews of draft chapters. Some of their contributions I remembered clearly enough to footnote, such as those from Aaron Reed, Jacob Garbe, and Adam Summerville. But these ideas have been in development within EIS for more than a decade, and it is only appropriate to acknowledge all those EIS members I have not yet mentioned: Devi Acharya, Bryan Blackford, Duncan Bowsman, Sherol Chen, Kate Compton, Mirjam Eladhari, Cyril Focht, Teale Fristoe, Chaim Gingold, Katherine Green, John Grey, April Grow, Alexandra Holloway, Ken Hullett, Martin Jennings-Teats, Nick Junius, Eric Kaltman, Max Kreminski, Sarah Fay Krom, Larry LeBron, Chris Lewis, Ronald Liu, Heather Logas, Paul Maddaloni, Jordan Magnuson, Chris Martens, Stacey Mason, Peter Mawhorter, Josh McCoy, Wes Modes, John Thomas Murray, Mark Nelson, Marcelo Viana Neto, Elisabeth Oliver, Alexei Othenin-Girard, Adrian Phillips, James Pollack, Allie Riggs, James Ryan, Serdar Sali, Benjamin Samuel, James Skorupski, Adam Smith, Gillian Smith, Benjamin Spalding, Dietrich Squinkifer, Christina Strong, Anne Sullivan, Brandon Tearse, Michael Thomét, and Ben Weber.

The EIS research described in this book was supported by a number of organizations. In particular, I wish to acknowledge those that funded the work that I helped lead and that I describe in some detail (rather than in passing). Each has specific language they prefer that recipients use:

This material is based upon work supported by the National Science Foundation under Grants No. 0747522, 1258305, and 1409992. Any opinions, findings and conclusions or recommendations expressed in this material are those of the author(s) and do not necessarily reflect the views of the National Science Foundation.

This research has been made possible in part by the National Endowment for the Humanities: Exploring the human endeavor (under grant number HD-51719–13). Any views, findings, conclusions, or recommendations expressed in this book do not necessarily represent those of the National Endowment for the Humanities.

This research was supported by a Seed Fund Award CITRIS-2017–0187 from CITRIS and the Banatao Institute at the University of California.

Along the way to the book, as noted above, we made several collaborative conference publications about its topics. I wish to thank the anonymous peer reviewers who asked questions and presented issues that made the work stronger. As this manuscript moved further along, I also made four further publications on its topics. First, during a 2011 trip to visit Cicero Inacio da Silva and Jane de Almeida in Brazil, I took part in the Seminário Internacional Regiões Narrativas (International Seminar Regions of Narratives) event organized by Ilana Strozenberg and Teresa Guilhon. There I met Arthur Protasio, who later invited me to contribute to a book he and Guilherme Xavier were editing that asked authors to focus on their experience of a particular game they'd played. The result was *Jogador de Mil Fases*, to which I contributed an early version of the section of chapter 1 on *Passage* ("De passagem por *Passage*," in Portuguese translation).

Second, drawing on chapters 1, 8, and 9, was "Beyond Shooting and Eating: *Passage*, *Dys4ia*, and the Meanings of Collision." This was first developed as a talk for Shift CTRL: New Perspectives on Computing and New Media, an event organized by Tom Mullaney and Ben Allen at Stanford University on May 6–7, 2016. As I was working on the talk, I had lunch with Wendy Chun (who, as noted above, had helped guide my dissertation a decade before) and she suggested that readers of *Critical Inquiry* might find it of interest. This was exciting to me—and resulted in the publication of a "triptych" of game studies contributions from Patrick Jagoda, Soraya Murray, and me in the Autumn 2018 issue (Volume 45, Issue 1). The revised versions of these chapters have benefited greatly from the feedback of Jagoda, Murray, the *Critical Inquiry* peer reviewers and editorial staff (particularly Hannah Christensen and Hank Scotch), and the Shift CTRL organizers and participants.

The third nonconference publication, drawing on chapter 7 and the conclusion, was "Gravity in Computer Space." This article appears in the December 2019 issue (vol. 1, no. 2) of *ROMchip: A Journal of Game Histories*. The revised version of this chapter was greatly improved by feedback from reviewers and editors Raiford Guins, Henry Lowood, and Laine Nooney. I also appreciate the feedback of copy editor Mary Reilly.

The fourth non-conference publication, drawing on this book's chapter 3 and conclusion, appears as the chapter "You Can't Make Games About Much" in the book *Your Computer Is on Fire: The Politics of Computing and New Media*, edited by Thomas S. Mullaney, Benjamin Peters, Mar Hicks, and Kavita Philip, to be published by the MIT Press in 2021. Both the conclusion and other chapters in this book were improved by a peer review and discussion (with the editors, other contributors, and Jennifer Light) held the day after the February 9, 2018, event "Your Computer is on Fire: Critical Perspectives on Computing and New Media," which took place at Stanford University.

Along the way, some brave souls were also willing to engage the full, in-process manuscript. In particular, I received invaluable guidance and feedback from Nathan Altice, Joris Dormans, Eric Kaltman, Jennifer K Mahal, Robert Zubek, and the anonymous reviewers recruited by the press. I should also thank the anonymous peer reviewers of the book proposal, who pushed me on the questions that resulted in chapter 6.

At the MIT Press, I particularly thank Doug Sery, who always reminds me to focus on what makes the best book and who has supported the idea for this one since I first described it, in snatches, over a group meal near UC Irvine, probably about a decade ago. I also appreciate all the contributions of Noah J. Springer (the "other Noah" in so many email exchanges), Susan Buckley, Michelle Pullano, Elizabeth Agresta, Emily Neiss-Moe, Susan Clark, Yasuyo Iguchi, Mary Reilly, Kate Elwell, and Kendra Millis. There would be no book without them.

I was able to actually finish the book only because Roselle Abraham listened thoughtfully and pursued relentlessly, until I was literally back up on my feet. And it is thanks to Paula Glickman's engagement that I got there metaphorically.

Finally, the inspiration, support, and understanding of my family was essential. My partner (and wife) Jennifer K Mahal, my parents Carolyn Wardrip and Mark Fruin, my brother Nathan Wardrip-Fruin and his family, and my kids Max and Zoe—to whom I dedicate this book.

Introduction

Video games create new worlds, where we learn to see and act in new ways.

This experience can be immensely engaging and satisfying. When we play *Pac-Man*[1] we learn to navigate the maze, finding smart ways to collect the pellets while avoiding the ghosts, wriggling out of tight spots through newly developed reflexes. We come to identify fully with Pac-Man's simple geometric shape—and also to see the wider world of the maze, far beyond what he could perceive, learning the patterns in the movements of the different-colored ghosts.

When we play *Minecraft*,[2] we see the world in terms of materials that can be collected. We learn to craft them into tools that can be used to dig in the ground or chop down trees to collect other materials—which can be stacked and connected and inhabited by flows—allowing us to create elaborate structures for survival, amusement, and even artistic expression.

When we play *Civilization*,[3] at the beginning, we see our small civilization in the context of the wider world that our scouts have discovered. But the space of the map is less important than another space—of potential routes to different kinds of development. Will we prioritize reading and writing, improved farming, better weaponry, or perhaps philosophical and religious development? As the game progresses, will we seek to defeat our neighbors militarily, aim for a different winning condition suggested and accepted by the game, or view play as our own meta-historical experiment, enabled and shaped by the game's workings?

In each game, whatever path we choose, the game world suggests things we might do, provides us the opportunity to try them, and offers a meaningful response that engages our minds and bodies. This process shapes how we see and think about the game world, at levels ranging from abstract consideration of strategies to unconscious, automatic reflex. Over time, our experiences can range from the satisfactions of learning and creating to stark moments of contemplation and regret.

And yet, despite these satisfying and powerful experiences, there are also disappointments. When we play *Star Wars: The Old Republic*,[4] one of the character options is to be a Han Solo–style smuggler. We can imagine ourselves cleverly improvising our way through various situations—but the game never lets us use our quick wits, instead taking us down pre-determined story paths. When we play one of the *Sims* games, we may be interested in romance between the characters (as seen in the popularity of early add-ons such as *Hot Date*[5] and *Nightlife*[6]). We might imagine ourselves building a history of shared trust and important life events with a potential partner—but the game only cares how far we fill a set of relationship meters. And even in games that are explicitly framed in terms of abstract ideas—such as the critique of Objectivism in *BioShock*[7]—the gameplay is generally about the movement of objects and resources, rather than challenging beliefs or changing minds.

This book explains how these satisfactions and disappointments flow from the same source.

In order to do this, it takes a somewhat uncommon approach to talking about video games. Over the last couple of decades there has been great growth in the scholarly study of games. But interestingly, much of what has been written by those of us in the scholarly community has focused on what video games have in common with things in other parts of our culture. We scholars write about the 3-D models and spaces of games—which games have in common with animated film and television, special effects, and architectural visualizations. We look at how those spaces provide challenges that are sometimes focused on human interaction—which are akin to experiences ranging from traffic to *Twister*.[8] We write about the motivations provided by points and goals—which games have in common with report cards and airline rewards programs. We write about how games tell stories—much of which is shared with theater, novels, television, and film. We write about how games invite and structure play—like toys, costumes, and make-believe scenarios. We write about the rules that define appropriate behavior (and opportunities for action) in games—like those in sports or stock trading.

All of this has been useful to me as I seek to understand video games myself and explain things to others. But these writings also generally fail to tackle something fundamental: video games are *systems-oriented media*. That is, video games have two key elements. First, they operate in particular ways. Second, they are designed to communicate certain things. And their essence is that these aspects work together—as game designers have observed at least since Chris Crawford's 1984 statement that a game is a "formal system that subjectively represents a subset of reality."[9]

Many of the scholarly writings about games only fully engage one of these two aspects. But there is other work that has tried to get at this essence, particularly at a high level. For example, Jesper Juul's book *Half-Real*[10] made a splash, in the early days of the field, by explaining how the "real," rule-based aspects of many games can only be interpreted through the fictional aspects they present. Ian Bogost's *Persuasive Games*[11] presents "procedural rhetoric" as a way to interpret, and make, arguments that employ a game's rules together with other communication modes. Mary Flanagan's *Critical Play*[12] describes how players can engage the meaning of game systems critically, and creators can design to foster that critical engagement. D. Fox Harrell's *Phantasmal Media*[13] argues that we can organize the internal structure and operations of systems around the subjective and cultural meanings we aim to evoke and expose. Doris C. Rusch's *Making Deep Games*[14] seeks to guide readers in creating games that have appropriate metaphorical mappings to human experience, both in their operations and in the interpretations and feelings they evoke through play. My prior book, *Expressive Processing*,[15] also contributes to this area, showing how the processes of games (and other forms of computational media) express ideas both through their roles in what audiences experience and in their underlying design.

However, even though all these books contain examinations of specific games, their focus is still at a high level. They focus on things like metaphors and arguments.[16] They are not spending significant time looking below this, at the fundamental level, at the elements with which these metaphors and arguments are constructed.

To finally turn attention to that atomic level of connection between video game system and communication, and the player experiences that such connections support, is the reason I have written this book. It comes out of my work as a researcher, but also out of my work as a teacher, spending more than a decade trying to find ways to explain the essence of video games to my students.

I believe the right approach is to stop talking about system and communication separately, or about the need to connect them. Instead, we should focus on the elements that are fundamentally *both* system and communication at the same time. I call these elements *operational logics* (for foundational elements) and *playable models* (for larger procedural representations, built using logics). To those who are already involved in game design and development, the names of many of the logics and models might be familiar—such as "collision," a logic on which I focus in the second part of this book. My goal is not to introduce counterintuitive new interpretations of games. Rather, I want to cast known elements in a new light and show how to use them to understand our everyday experience of games in a way that I have found helpful in a broad range of conversations.

Many of my example games use the playable models that made video games an international cultural and economic phenomenon: two-dimensional spatial models. These models enabled the arcade hits of the 1970s and '80s, such as *Pong*[17] and

Asteroids[18] (as well as their predecessors in research labs, such as *Tennis for Two*[19] and *Spacewar*[20]).[21] The success of these titles spread video games far and wide: from the niche of barroom jostling with pinball to video game cabinets occupying thousands of dedicated arcades, as well as almost anywhere a business had room to stand one. I remember seeing and playing video games in 1980s grocery stores, gas stations, restaurant waiting areas, pharmacies, and so on.

Two-dimensional spatial models are also the ones supported by the first generations of home consoles, notably the Atari Video Computer System (later renamed the Atari 2600). With consoles, video games spread beyond public spaces into millions of homes. And soon video games, which had been almost unknown a decade before, were the subject of television cartoons, T-shirt designs, and radio hits, and could be seen on store shelves emblazoned across everything from breakfast cereals to tabletop games. While their worldwide spread was certainly uneven, in countries such as Japan and the United States, video games became almost inescapable.

In early examples from this era, video game spatial models were used to represent straightforward spatial things. In *Pong*, a ball bounces off of walls and paddles. In *Space Invaders*,[22] projectiles hit ships and barriers.

But the game that took things to the next level of cultural and commercial impact was *Pac-Man*, which performed a subtle shift. Pac-Man doesn't just run into the pellets in his maze. He *eats* them. The collision between two objects isn't meant to represent them hitting each other, as in *Pong*, but one consuming the other.

And this kind of move—taking a spatial model and using it to represent something more—was the key to game designers beginning to create games on a wider variety of themes, while still using the technology available in arcades and home consoles (which was developed to support spatial models). Looking just at games following in *Pac-Man*'s footsteps (which I'll call "Pac-likes") the most obvious move was to consume something else. We can see this in games like *Mouse Trap*,[23] which replaces the dots with cheese, the ghosts with cats, and Pac-Man with a mouse. But other shifts are possible. For example, *Lock 'n' Chase*[24] turns from consuming to collecting. The dots become coins, the ghosts become detectives, and Pac-Man becomes a thief.

Going further, Pac-like games such as *Make Trax*[25] and *Munch Man*[26] switched from removing something to painting or placing something in each new area. While what they placed didn't do much to expand what games could be about, such expansions are easy to imagine. For example, if someone had wanted to play into 1980s fears that the strange new world of video games was corrupting youth, they could have made a game of being a juvenile delinquent, spray painting graffiti across different areas of town, chased by truant officers.

And things can certainly go farther. One of the strangest Pac-likes comes from Shigeru Miyamoto, Takashi Tezuka, and Koji Kondo—three of the four members of the core team behind genre-defining Nintendo games *Super Mario Bros.*[27] and *The Legend of Zelda.*[28] This game is *Devil World,*[29] in which you play a small dragon named Tamagon who, as the opening screen says, is going to "Attack the Devil's World!" In this game there is a twist on the Pac-like formula: the dots cannot be collected unless Tamagon has touched a power-up. And the power-ups are crosses, which are not consumed, but rather stay in place.

I've only been able to play *Devil World* through an emulator—due to content restrictions that Nintendo of America places on games for its platforms, *Devil World* has never had a US release.[30] But even in a little emulator window on my laptop, it's a fully engaging and remarkably odd experience. The first maze is dominated by massive cross shapes, set off in a different color. The available area of the maze is constantly shifting, as a blue devil in white gloves—with red eyes, wings, boots, and Speedo—directs his one-eyed minions to move a set of boundary walls. As the boundary walls move, they threaten to crush Tamagon between them and the walls of the maze.

Oddest of all are the power-up crosses. They're much more numerous than the power-ups in *Pac-Man* because Tamagon can do nothing without them. When you touch them, rather than disappear, they make another cross appear next to Tamagon (figure 0.1). This appearing cross is nearly as large as Tamagon and travels with him, as though he is carrying it, for the period of his power-up, then fades away. This cross clearly isn't meant as a physical object—it passes through other objects without interaction—but as an indication of Tamagon's powered-up status. And it's odd because that status could easily have been communicated with a color shift, image swap, or other traditional indicator of video game state change. Adding the carried cross made it feel, to me, like an indication that Tamagon's powered-up state is specifically when he "has" faith—it's a spatial metaphor for possessing belief.

Realizing that changed how I saw the power-up crosses. I'm part of a Christian religion myself (I'm a Quaker) and to me it made no sense that literally touching a cross would renew Tamagon's faith.[31] As another spatial metaphor, on the other hand, it made perfect sense. I've heard many people say they need to "get in touch" with their faith, and it fits well for Tamagon to need to do this regularly in order to continue with his task. At the same time, in order to play successfully, I didn't need to think about the metaphors—I needed to think about the physical space, always bearing in mind where the power-ups were and how long it had been since I'd touched one.

In other words, the power-up crosses in *Devil World* must be thought of in terms of literal space, in order to play the game. But they can also be understood as metaphorically

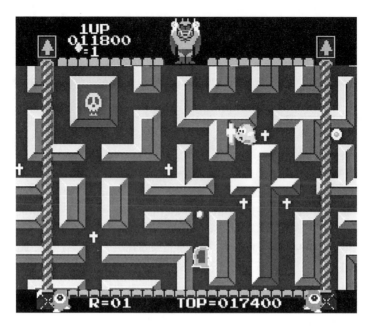

Figure 0.1
Tamagon, carrying his cross before him, with only one dot left to consume. In *Devil World* as
played in an emulator. (Image taken by the author during play on emulator at retrogames.cz.)

reflecting aspects of the game's religious themes. This is not just a step beyond *Pong*'s
simple collision into *Pac-Man*'s consuming and *Lock 'n' Chase*'s collecting—it is a step
beyond these into a further kind of meaning-making with spatial models. This kind of
meaning making was unusual when *Devil World* was released for the Nintendo Famicom in 1984, and these metaphorical meanings may not even have been intended. But
this kind of approach has since become a deliberate, important strategy for indie games
and art games that are pushing to expand game meaning in new directions. Exploring
these kinds of strategies is an important goal for this book.

Specifically, the book is divided into two parts and each part has two goals. Part one
takes a broad view of operational logics and playable models, while part two is more
granular.

In the first section, one goal is to show how we can use the ideas of operational logics and playable models to develop a set of core concepts for the fundamental things
video games do—uniting computational processes with communicative goals. I believe
notions such as "meter" and "rhyme," and examinations of how they work together in
different poetic forms, are helpful for both understanding and crafting poems. I believe

developing a vocabulary of operational logics and playable models—and understanding the different ways in which they are employed—is similarly useful for video games and other forms of computational media. My work toward this begins with an initial laying out of terms (in chapter 1), continues with a more detailed discussion and catalog (in chapter 4), and comes together with terms and concepts that others have used in understanding games—in the context of discussing *Grand Theft Auto IV*[32] and the *Sims* franchise—in the final chapter of the first part (chapter 6).

My other goal, with this book's first part, is to show how game creators push boundaries to communicate new things, and create new opportunities for play, through video games. They do this using three approaches.

One approach is *alternative*, the focus of chapter 2. Alternative work uses an existing logic or model as it has traditionally been used but broadens how games use it. For example, using a model that has been used to support spatial movement, but moving through a type of space that hasn't been included before. Alternative uses may also remove these logics and models from their usual genre context. This might seem relatively trivial, but has in fact been a focus of controversy as games begin to move beyond the limited set of experiences addressed by mainstream games during what I sometimes call the "console era" (to which I'll return later on).

A second approach is *expansive*, which is discussed in chapter 3. In expansive work, an existing logic or model is used to communicate something new. This is how many political games work, for example, by expanding logics and models created for communicating spatial relationships or resource flows to also communicate power, ideology, or social relationships (see figure 0.2).

Finally, a third type of approach is *inventive*, which is the focus of chapter 5. Inventive work is the introduction of new video game logics and models, or new implementations of older logics and models that allow them to be used in new contexts. It is the significance of this kind of contribution, for example, that has led to *Spacewar* often being called the "first video game," even though it was created a decade into the field's history.

Taken together, part one provides a broad view of what operational logics and playable models are, discussing how they are used in different games and various strategies for employing them. Part two, on the other hand, is much more focused. Understanding the origins and potentials of the spatial models behind Pac-likes, other arcade and console games, and today's art and indie games is at its heart. Like part one, part two has two goals.

The first is to trace the history of the development of two-dimensional spatial models for games, particularly by focusing on inventive work on the operational logics that

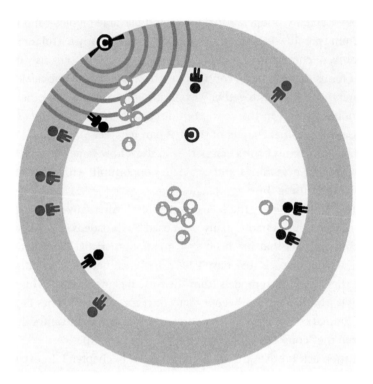

Figure 0.2
In Molleindustria's *The Free Culture Game*, the space in the middle of the circle represents the common, where knowledge is created cooperatively and shared. The gray border of the circle represents the market, where knowledge is commodified and sold. A "vectorialist" (represented by the copyright symbol) moves around the edge of the circle, sucking ideas out of the common to be sold. The player (represented by the upside-down copyright symbol) attempts to keep ideas from the common moving around to the people inside it, so that they keep producing ideas, rather than turning into passive consumers inside the market's circle. This is relatively difficult, because the player has imprecise control and ideas must collide with the heads of the people (rather than just existing nearby) while the vectorialist can scoop up whole areas of ideas at once. In other words, using an expansive approach, the game transforms a complex set of abstract concepts into physical objects in order to make a playable experience. (Creative Commons image from molleindustria.org.) (Molleindustria. *The Free Culture Game*. Adobe Flash. 2008. http://www .molleindustria.org/en/freeculturegame/.)

are key to them. It examines many familiar topics through this new lens—including the games *Tennis for Two, Spacewar, Computer Space*,[33] and *Pong*. These are primarily discussed in chapter 7.

The second goal is to understand the ways that these models have been, and can be, used to bring new meanings to games. One way that part two does this is to dig more deeply into the expansive strategies discussed in chapter 3.

Some expansive approaches are like the way *Pac-Man* employs a logic meant to communicate something physical (things touching) to communicate a different physical action (one thing eating another). I call this kind of approach *refinement* and discuss it in chapter 8—particularly through the examples of Robinett's *Adventure*[34] and *Wario-Ware, Inc.: Mega Microgame$!*[35]

Other expansive approaches are more like the power-up crosses in *Devil World*, which use something physical (touching a cross) both to communicate something in the literal space of the game (you get a power-up) and something metaphorical (you're back "in touch" with your faith). I call this kind of approach *doubling* and discuss it in chapter 9, along with the issue of game metaphor more generally, focusing on *Tax Avoiders*[36] and *Dys4ia*[37] as examples.

Chapter 10, the last chapter in this part, looks at how elements of spatial design combined with particular logics (like the shared structures found in *Pong, Breakout*,[38] and *Kaboom!*[39]) can be understood and assembled even by generative computer software. It also discusses the limits that can be revealed by this strategy.

And it is to this topic, the question of limits, that the book's conclusion finally turns—after touching on it briefly in a number of chapters throughout. While I am excited to celebrate our accomplishments with video games so far, and the potentials of the current moment, I also want to understand this moment's constraints. For example, while game makers such as Molleindustria (who describe their work as "Radical Games Against the Tyranny of Entertainment") have succeeded in using games to communicate a wide range of topics, such games also show the boundaries of our situation. The expansive and alternative strategies cannot get away from the underlying logics they employ. At the same time, the inventive strategy—which is a major focus of the Expressive Intelligence Studio, a lab I run with Michael Mateas—faces all the problems of basic research: from uncertain results to funding challenges.

Creators could instead go the route of many linking-logic games, such as those made in Twine, and move toward games that are less systems-oriented—so that communication happens primarily through traditional uses of static text and images. But this sacrifices the experience of *agency* that is central to the power of many games, as well as other experiences that must be built on system-driven responses. (It is the importance of agency and our limited means for providing it—rather than any inherent cultural conservatism—that I believe explains much of the narrowness in what today's mainstream games address.) By confronting these limits head-on, the conclusion is able to consider a key question: What can games be about?

Throughout the book, I primarily use examples created by small, innovative teams in four overlapping communities: the game industry, the indie game community, the art game community, and the research game community. The *game industry* is presumably a familiar term to readers. But the terms *indie game*, *art game*, and *research game* may require some explanation.

These three communities were marginalized during the console era of centrally controlled video game distribution, mentioned above, but now are flourishing. The console era ran roughly from the late-1980s to the late-2000s in the United States. During this time, the primary cultural idea of video games focused on closed platforms, such as the Sony PlayStation and Nintendo Game Boy, rather than more open platforms (such as home computers). Game distribution was also dominated by physical stores with limited shelf space, making it difficult to reach audiences with alternative visions, even on open platforms. Finally, game development tool kits for closed platforms were tightly controlled and game programming was often quite low-level (commonly done in assembly code) further restricting who could express themselves and reach audiences through games.[40]

The current *independent (indie) game* community began during this era of centralized distribution, often with the creation of games that hoped to be "picked up" by someone with access to mainstream distribution. But now "indie games" is increasingly an overarching term for all those seeking to bring independent visions and voices to video games (much as with independent music and film). The *art game* community also began in an earlier era, often with the creation of games intended for gallery/festival contexts or distributed as "net art" or "electronic literature," but now includes many artists creating games distributed through mainstream game channels. The indie and art game communities have significant intersection and overlap, coming together in venues such as the yearly IndieCade festival and Independent Game Festival. This is also where they have had contact with a third community, what I call the *research games* community.

The research games community—which creates games in contexts such as universities, national labs, and industry or non-profit research organizations—is in many ways the founding game creation community, producing the first video game (Christopher Strachey's 1951 *M. U. C. Draughts*[41]) and many of the games that introduced key operational logics and playable models (for example, *Spacewar*, *Tetris*,[42] and the Crowther and Woods game *Adventure*[43]). It has natural affinities with the indie and art game communities, as all three seek to expand the possibilities for video games through the efforts of small teams with novel visions. Yet these communities seem to be pulling away from each other—with the Independent Games Festival, for example, having taken the unfortunate step of eliminating its "technical" category (between the 2013 and 2014 festivals) removing a natural way for games emerging from technology research contexts to come together with indie and art games.

That said, the connections and disconnections between these communities are only background to the primary concerns here. This book is about the ways that members of these communities have responded to (and created) the "traditional" approaches to the operational logics and playable models of video games. This book is about the work of people seeking to expand the possibilities of games as a medium—as well as what this work shows about what games can mean today, and how they could mean more in the future.

1   Operational Logics and Playable Models

Passage

Jason Rohrer's *Passage*[1] is a strange and powerful game.

The game world is presented to the player as a horizontal strip—with a deliberately simple, nostalgic art style. The first time I played, I went down, scrolling more of the game world into the visible strip. I discovered a familiar-feeling game world of abstract boundaries, shifting backgrounds, and the occasional iconic treasure chest that, when opened, sometimes provided a reward.[2]

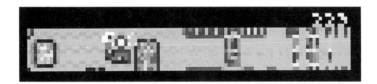

Many traditional game challenges were absent—no gaps to jump, no enemies to fight, no puzzles to solve. Getting the rewards required only locating them in the world and navigating my way to them. Frankly, I began to wonder what the fuss was about—a friend had recommended the game very highly.

Within a minute, a visual shift happened, and I began to notice something strange. The player character—what I've been referring to as "I"—was no longer as far left in the game window. It had moved slightly rightward. And my character's visual presentation had also changed slightly, perhaps looking a bit older.

This was the first of a series of shifts. I continued to move my character through the world, finding my way to treasures and discovering that, after walking my character to the right for long enough, new areas of the game world would be revealed, with different image patterns in the background.

Passage is a brief game, always lasting around five minutes. During my play I sought treasure at times, at others raced forward to find new areas (and to discover whether the game had a destination or goal), and all the while my character kept progressively shifting in a manner beyond my control—taking positions further to the right in the scrolling window and represented by the image of an older and older man. Then, suddenly, I was dead, with the last position of my character replaced by an iconic tombstone.

This was certainly an unusual play experience, but I only began to grasp the full strangeness of *Passage* when I played again.

When I played the first time, I had seen the trace of another person to the right of the first screen—but then never encountered any other people. The second time I walked straight toward the other person. When the player character touched her, they fell in love, the moment marked by a heart (just as the reward from treasure chests is marked by a star).

From there we walked everywhere together, exploring and growing older together. But being together changed the experience of the world. Walking down through the game space, side by side, we could not fit through gaps in barriers I had walked through easily before. Some treasure chests became inaccessible and areas that previously presented no challenge became like mazes.

But we went on, moving together, exploring, and aging. And then, in the moment for which *Passage* is best known, my partner became a tombstone beside me.

I no longer wanted to move. It seemed wrong to leave her behind me. Yet it was no longer her, and there was little point in standing around beside an immobile gravestone. It was an experience of loss and confusion. I paused, then dithered back and forth, moved forward a bit, then mercifully became a tombstone myself.

Perhaps *Passage*'s meaning strategies seem abundantly clear from this description—but as strong as the voices of praise were after its release, there were also critical voices, some dismissive and befuddled. What was the big deal? Critics expressed these views not only in writing, but also in game form, with the release of Marcus Richert's *Passage in 10 Seconds*.[3] In this game, after the player walks the characters across the screen, perhaps opening one or both of the treasure chests presented, the two characters fall dead—and then wild applause breaks out and a monocled audience member proclaims, "Now this is art!"

But the simple appearance of death doesn't get at what makes *Passage* powerful and strange. Or even unusual. Characters die in many games.

It would also be a mistake to think that *Passage* is unusual in representing a landscape of life choices. It has this in common with forms ranging from the role-playing game quest to the Choose Your Own Adventure book.

Rather, what makes *Passage* remarkable is how it works with common meaning-making strategies of video games—in particular, how it takes them apart and reassembles them, so that they are active both in traditional and in new ways, making them visible to us again.

Consider the player character. *Passage* presents us with something we can control in the game. Almost no matter the form such a thing takes—from the nearly abstract graphics of a ship in *Spacewar*[4] to the unnamed textual adventurer of *Adventure*[5]—we quickly, when playing a game, begin to identify with what we control.[6] When describing the game's events we will often refer to this element as "me" or say "then I . . ." for what it does next.

This identification is established through a combination that enables the experience of controlling something external to disappear from how we think about games. One part of this combination is implemented technically, executing algorithms—computation—that alter the ongoing presentation of game state. Another part of this combination is communicative, designed to play a role in how the game is interpreted by players through its ongoing presentation. A fundamental combination of this sort, bringing together algorithm and communication, is *navigation*.

Some of these combinations are so conventional that to describe them explicitly can seem strange. For example, in *Passage*, the player presses the down arrow and the representation of the game world scrolls upward, while the representation of the player character remains in place. The player releases the key and this stops. The player presses the right arrow and the world scrolls left, while the player character remains fixed. As in all computer games, this navigation is enabled by a combination of computational process and media representation, working together with literacies developed while playing other games and analogies with the everyday world, producing in part the identification that causes us to refer to the player character as "me" and "I."

And then *Passage* disrupts this identification. Character aging shifts character representation and screen placement in a manner that is out of player control. When these moments take place—and immediately afterward—we no longer feel comfortable referring to the player character in the unfolding game events as "me." The identification is deliberately breached, opening a space for momentary reflection on the passage of time, also out of our control. Then continued play reestablishes the connection.

Similarly, the events that take place during navigation operate both familiarly and strangely.

It is a well-understood convention of video games, and interactive computer graphics generally, that when virtual objects "touch," the event can have consequences. This is commonly called *collision detection* (for the moment of touch) or *collision handling* (more broadly). Collision detection can be used to represent objects that are solid and cannot pass through each other. This is how it is used with the barriers of *Passage*. Collision handling is also often used, in early computer games of the sort that *Passage* deliberately references, to carry out a wide range of actions in the world—and its range has been further extended over time. Collision is how a *Pong*[7] paddle deflects balls, how Pac-Man eats, how Lara Croft's bullets hit targets, and how Anna Anthropy's autobiographical avatar deflects hate speech (to which I will return in chapter 9).

The conventionality of this wide range of meanings makes every collision with an iconic object potentially rife with meaning. *Passage* takes this a step further. Even collisions with simple, abstract barriers are coded with multiple meanings. They represent the inability to physically move through certain spaces in the game world, while also representing a barrier to making certain life choices. They are not only obstacles that must be navigated to collect certain rewards but also, for example, obstacles that are much more challenging (or impossible) to traverse if moving through life with a partner.

Through these remappings, movements across and encounters with the game world of *Passage* become representations of movement, choice, and action in life at a level more abstract and profound than the momentary level represented by many games. And it is only through this that the sudden stillness of the companion's tombstone becomes potentially shocking and moving.

This is a strategy for producing meaning that is key to computational media. *Operational logics* combine an abstract process and a communicative role, each refined through implementation to drive an ongoing state presentation and play experience. We see examples of this strategy in navigation, collision, and many other operational logics, both conventional and emerging. We see this in how *Passage* combines its operational logics into a *playable model* of space that is at once traditional and, simultaneously, expansive—remapping its structures for use as a model of life's opportunities and choices.[8]

For the casual player of *Passage*, none of this need be said. Players understand *Passage* through expectations and literacies developed over years of playing video games and experiencing other forms of media. But as video games continue to become a more developed and significant cultural form, it is important that some of us begin to examine more deeply how they work with logics and models. This will enable new ways of understanding games, new approaches to game creation, and even new tools to help a broader range of people express themselves through the medium of games. The rest of this chapter sets down the key terms that this book will use in pursuing these goals.

Talking about What Games Are About

I think we need new terms if we're going to get to the heart of the issue: how games are about things.

I coined the term *operational logics* because I needed a phrase for talking about a particular way that games produce meaning.[9] The term was in part inspired by the notion of *cultural logics*—of patterns in the workings of culture, of motifs and structures in how we conceive the world, that can be interpreted critically (see box 1.1, "Operational

Box 1.1
Operational Logics and Cultural Logics

For those with a cultural theory background, the phrase "cultural logic" might be most familiar from the title of Fredric Jameson's *Postmodernism, or, The Cultural Logic of Late Capitalism*.[10] Those with a more technological bent might know it from the title of Seb Franklin's *Control: Digitality as Cultural Logic*[11] (the phrase "motifs and structures" for describing logics, which I use in the main text, is Franklin's). The term is also in use in the social sciences, as seen in titles such as Takie Lebra's *The Japanese Self in Cultural Logic*[12] and John Comaroff's and Simon Roberts's *Rules and Processes: The Cultural Logic of Dispute in an African Context*.[13]

Commonly, whatever the disciplinary background of the authors, the term is employed without much explicit discussion or definition. One exception is Nick Enfield's essay "The Theory of Cultural Logic."[14] Enfield uses the term to point toward the wide range of semiotic and conceptual assumptions that guide the process of interpreting other people. Some of these assumptions are relatively tightly coordinated within cultures, such as linguistic structures. Others, such as ideas of appropriate social behavior, are coordinated more loosely.

A rather different take on the term comes from Nico Baumbach, Damon R. Young, and Genevieve Yue, in the introduction to a special issue of the journal *Social Text*[15] dedicated to the term. They write, "*Cultural logic*: the term is a theoretical provocation." They connect cultural logic with related ideas from Michel Foucault, Raymond Williams, Jacques Rancière, and Bernard Stiegler. They engage the term in the same specifically Marxist context as Jameson's work, writing, "Like these cognate theoretical terms, the term *cultural logic* is not merely empirically descriptive. It is a term of political analysis that is precisely historical: the cultural logic that becomes 'hegemonic,' as Jameson sometimes puts it, under given conditions—that is, the current stage of global capitalism—is also available as a domain of contestation, resistance, and activism, even as it makes the critical distance typically implied by those terms appear outmoded."

What unites both work like Enfield's and work like that in the *Social Text* special issue is the shared intellectual history that gave birth to structuralism. Influenced by linguistics, figures such as Claude Lévi-Strauss and Roland Barthes (before the latter's post-structuralist turn) sought to understand the logic of complex relations that construct culture. While this may have initially been applied to cultures distant from the one from which the author hailed (studying the workings of the cultures of others), in time it was applied closer to home. For example, Barthes's *The Fashion System*[16] looks at descriptions in then-contemporary French magazines to view fashion not as an economic system (which would be more familiar) but as a system of signification, which can be examined to see how it works.

The question might be asked, however, why we need a phrase for talking about ways that culture works—and also why one would choose the word "logic" as part of that phrase.

Box 1.1 (continued)

For those creating and studying video games, which are undeniably both cultural and technical artifacts, the most relevant answers are probably those found in Warren Sack's *The Software Arts*,[17] specifically in its tracing of the story of the term "logic." In chapter 5, Sack points out that, for centuries, "logic" was used as a synonym for "dialectic." Then they went their separate ways, with dialectic continuing as an art of conversation, while logic was folded into mathematics. As a result, for more than a century, we have been living with a gap between dialectic, conversation, and culture (on one side) and mathematics, calculation, and logic (on the other). Before this gap existed, a phrase like "cultural logic" would have been unnecessary—a cultural logic would just be a logic. Now one needs some sort of phrase, to bridge the two sides of this gap, if one is trying to say something about both logic and culture.

My term, *operational logics*, is another such phrase—and Sack also has something to say about the other word I chose. In chapter 3 of *The Software Arts* he distinguishes "operation" from "function" and argues that another split took place. While these both began as terms for "work," the former became connected with eighteenth-century arts and crafts, while the latter became an exclusively mathematical term. Following historian Michael Mahoney, Sack argues that (the protestations of some computer scientists aside) actually existing software is not simply mathematical, but, in Mahoney's words, "an amalgam of mathematical theory, engineering practice, and craft skill." In short, Sack points out that actually existing software is more tied to operations (with all their craft connotations) than to the supposed mathematical purity of functions.[18]

Logics and Cultural Logics"). But the logics of games aren't just ways we think about their worlds (and how they reflect our own). The logics of games are also literal ways game worlds work, through computational operations—the algorithmic workings of computing systems. *Operational logics* is a term for foundational elements that do cultural work, that structure our understanding, and that do so in part through how they function computationally.[19] The next section of this chapter ("Defining Logics and Models") will explore my key terms in more detail.

There are, of course, already many other terms in use for discussing games, and one could question whether new ones are necessary. In chapter 4, I address this question by comparing operational logics and playable models with three widely used terms: *mechanics*, *systems*, and *rules*. Then in chapter 6, I compare this book's approach, which depends on logics and models, with a variety of other approaches for studying games, such as Ian Bogost's "procedural rhetoric" and Mary Flanagan's "critical play."

While greater detail will have to wait for future chapters, let me briefly describe one relationship here, which has in the past caused some confusion—the relationship between the concepts of operational logics and game mechanics. The term *mechanics* is used inconsistently, but most game scholars and creators would agree that "jump" and "shoot" are among the most commonly discussed mechanics. Operational logics are both more and less specific than such mechanics. They are more specific in that logics are the foundations that enable such mechanics: a typical Mario or Sonic jump depends on control, entity-state, physics, and collision logics. At the same time, logics are also less specific. Part of what limits the insight we can get from discussing mechanics is that they seem individual and atomic, in most of our current conversation. But what helps players learn (and designers create) new mechanics is that they already understand much of them from the logics they have in common.

Most of this book will be focused on the human understanding of games. But I've also seen, in the research of the Expressive Intelligence Studio, that operational logics provide an approach to game fundamentals that can be used by software systems. Members of the studio have created software that uses the concept of operational logics to automatically learn game design knowledge, to map game spaces, to generate games, and even to automatically "understand" what will arise from a set of game rules.[20] My hope is that research of this sort will eventually empower more people to express themselves through games, as well as produce currently impossible gameplay experiences.

Beyond the foundational level of logics, I am also interested in how games are about things at a higher level. For this purpose—as mentioned above—I use *playable models*, another term that also provides a different lens from the common vocabulary now used to discuss games. Playable models have a history reaching back, at least, to tabletop war simulations. But video games, and digital computational media in general, have brought them to many more domains, with vastly greater complexity, as well as wider contexts and audiences.[21]

While I coined the term *operational logics*, I did not do so with *playable models*. As with much in this book, this idea and term became part of my vocabulary through my discussions and collaborations with Michael Mateas—who himself builds upon the thinking of others, such as game designer Will Wright. Mateas emphasizes the importance of truly playable models being *learnable* and *actionable*. Though Mateas has mostly explored these ideas in unpublished talks, he contributed the following text to a report from a 2010 workshop:

> To be learnable, a player must be able to make inferences about a game's state and build up a mental image or model of the underlying system as they interact with the rules of the game. This may not mean that they are able to completely reverse-engineer the system. Rather, a learnable computational model is one supporting the incremental development of simplified

and partial mental models that successfully provide guidance for future exploration and inter-action within the game rule system. This exploration is afforded through mechanisms of engagement, that is, a means for a player to affect the state of the game in a manner consistent with his or her desires. To meet this requirement, the game must also be actionable. Defin-ing games as systems that employ such playable models distinguishes them from traditional systems and computational models in other disciplines such as physics or engineering, where cognitive properties of learnable and actionable are not factors.[22]

The operational logics that support playable models are key to their learnable and actionable aspects. The communicative roles fulfilled by logics provide key scaffolding for players to understand what is going on during play. It is the mechanics that logics enable through which players can take actions. But playable models require (and pro-vide) more than logics.

To be specific, playable models are constructed of operational logics (used to support game mechanics) and structuring information. This structuring information allows the logics to compose together (by working on common parts of the game state) in addi-tion to expressing the nature of the domain, such as 2-D or 3-D space. Because playable models are procedural representations of particular domains, they are not as abstract as operational logics—they need to satisfy a more specific and culturally grounded set of obligations to succeed at their communicative role. Through analysis, these obliga-tions can be enumerated, as discussed in the case of combat models in chapter 7.[23] Implementations of playable models also include specific, implemented algorithms for operational logics, as well as data used to support these logics and their game state rep-resentations (ranging from tables of numbers to text, sound, and imagery).

Because models are defined by a set of communicative obligations, models of the same domain can be constructed using different logics. For example, the key logics for *Passage*'s model of space are navigation, physics, and collision. But we can also construct playable models of space with quite different logics. For example, the textual world of the original *Adventure*[24] is navigated through linking logics, connecting one part of the cave system with another. The other important part of the game's spatial model is containment—fluid can be in a bottle, for example, and the bottle can be in the player's inventory. This is also represented by linking logics. A playable model of space is still clearly being constructed (as the many player maps of *Adventure* can attest), but the physics and collision logics found in *Passage*'s spatial model are nowhere to be seen.

Once we begin to look at games through the lens of logics and models, we can see a relatively small fundamental vocabulary, out of which the proliferation of specific game mechanics and game designs emerges. On one level this is useful, because our approaches can focus on this small vocabulary—whether our goal is to understand games or make them. On another level it is disheartening, because the current vocabulary of well-developed logics and models provides few tools for engaging what matters most about being alive. Our models of spatial relation, for example, are much better developed than our models of emotional relation.

Games like *Passage* find ways around this. They engage with a wider range of human experience through innovative uses of the limited vocabularies of games.

Defining Logics and Models

Every emerging media form has elements that set it apart. Film, for example, is set apart from prior media forms by the ways it uses the moving image to communicate. Before the moving image we had photographic framing, theatrical acting, and many other things—but they were recontextualized, combined, and transformed by the moving image.

Similarly, video games are set apart by the ways they communicate using automatic computation—the enactment of processes by digital computers. We had games before video games, just as we had moving images (and sound, and text), but only since the 1950s have we had games or media of any sort driven by modern computers.

Many of the communicative strategies developed for film that depend on the moving image—the cut from wide context to close action, the revealing pan—have become so conventional that we cease to see them except in their most unusual uses. And this is also true for the most conventional strategies of games, such as the ways that navigation, collision, and movement physics are used to create playable models of physical space.

Along a similar vein, the same strategies are used over and over in film, in different contexts. A shot and its reverse are used both to show a character's shock in a war film and a character's tenderness in a family drama. Games also employ the same strategies in many different contexts. The same resource logics are used for military unit production in *StarCraft*[25] and household chores in *The Sims*.[26]

But games are quite different from film in a key way. The moving image always moves the same way. The standardization of projection apparatus and media players depends on it. Computation, however, is constantly shifting—not only in the specifics of its hardware and algorithms, but also through the invention of new high-level processes (more abstract than detailed algorithms). And in games, these processes are often developed specifically to enable new types of communication, modeling, and gameplay.

So to understand the fundamental meaning-making strategies of games we must consider not only what is presented to the audience and the communicative role each element of this presentation plays over time, but also the computational processes that enable the behavior of the elements, and the opportunities these open for play. Just as the cut and pan are inseparable from the moving image, so video game communication techniques are inseparable from the processes that partially constitute them. In other words, to understand how video games make meaning, we need ways to talk about computation and communication together with play.

The concepts of operational logics and playable models provide ways to do this. To be specific, I define operational logics as foundational combinations of *abstract processes* with their *communicative roles* in the game, connected through an ongoing *game state presentation* and supporting a *gameplay experience*. Operational logics are essential building blocks for the construction of playable models, through which games represent everything from physical space to economic systems, social relations, character development, and combat. Though all of these terms will receive greater attention in future chapters, here I will briefly define each concept.

An abstract process is a specification for how a process operates. For example, the abstract process for collision detection could be stated as, "When the boundaries of two virtual objects intersect, declare the intersection." This specification is agnostic as to the specific algorithm and implementation—the method of detecting intersection would be quite different for 2-D and 3-D games, as well as for games using rough bounding boxes versus pixel-accurate methods. Not all implementations of an abstract process may succeed in supporting the communicative role of the logic for all audiences or in all contexts—and, for an emerging or proposed logic, it is possible that no implementation can succeed with intended audiences.

A communicative role describes how the logic is being employed by an author, as part of the larger game system, to communicate something to players. For example, the generic communicative role of collision detection could be stated as, "Virtual objects can touch, and these touches can have consequences." Of course, such communication does not always succeed for all audiences, but the most common logics are widely (if somewhat unconsciously) understood by game-literate players. It is through this understanding that players develop their ability to play—to understand the game world such that they can take action intentionally and interpret its results, an important part of the experience of agency many games provide.

A game state presentation is how players see, hear, and feel the specific behavior of an operational logic in the context of the game. The same logic can require very different data—often called game *assets*—depending on what it is trying to represent.

For example, the only asset specific to the presentation of collision handling in *Pong* is a sound triggered when the ball collides with a wall or paddle. But in *Call of Duty: Black Ops 4*,[27] the presentation of collision for bullets and bodies alone (which takes place in the context of the larger combat model) involves many animation and sound assets, required to present different types and locations of damage with the simulated cinematic feel to which the series aspires. This is a general trend as the sought level of detail rises: more data assets are required for a logic's presentation.[28] At the same time, especially for logics that have been established with relatively abstract communicative roles (such as pattern matching and linking), the crafting and selection of data is a way game creators can suggest more concrete audience interpretations.

The gameplay experience is what happens when a player encounters the logic through the game state and whatever interaction methods are available. This is where the game's creators hope the communicative role will be fulfilled, and also where players may discover possibilities never intended by the creators. Often player understanding and discovery is not immediate and may be imperfect, especially in its details—it takes place through player experimentation. This is especially true of the connections between logics. Even in uncomplicated games such as *Pong* or *Breakout*,[29] the simple movement physics triggered when a ball collides with a paddle can differ depending on where the ball collides with the paddle, and this basic but varying connection (between collision and physics) may take time for players to grasp. Nonetheless, the communication that balls and paddles can collide, and that balls bounce back when this happens, takes place rather immediately in nearly all initial play sessions (confirming the expectations of game-literate players).

As discussed earlier, a playable model is a type of representational practice rising to a new level of cultural significance in video games and other types of computational media. While some games are rightly viewed as largely abstract, many games include procedural representations of domains—ranging from city planning to playing football—that are activated and understood through play. These representations are in part constructed of operational logics, used to support game mechanics. Like any form of representation, playable models are partial (the map is never the territory) and can be used for a variety of purposes: persuasive, educational, escapist, and so on.

The phrase *game mechanics* is widely used but, as mentioned earlier, unfortunately its use is inconsistent. In some cases, it is used for actions that players may take (the meaning I employ in this book); in other cases, it is used for the fundamental operations of the system. There are also other, less-common uses. In particular, I use the term *mechanics* to refer to actions players may take as supported by the game's implemented logics and models. For example, the jumping mechanic in Checkers, a game with a model of discrete space and time, is quite different from the jumping mechanic in *Super Mario Bros.*,[30] a game with continuous space and time. However, they are both jumping mechanics.

The logics discussed in this book are best thought of as families, with different specific logics for different contexts and purposes, but all appropriate to describe with the same communicative role and abstract process. For example, Joseph C. Osborn has identified a family of control logics, which communicate that entities are controlled by particular inputs at particular times.[31] Control logics have an abstract process of mapping potential inputs (controller events, AI intentions, network messages) onto high-level game actions, perhaps grouped onto specific loci of control (for example, one of the ships in *Spacewar*) according to the source (the corresponding controller). The navigation logic discussed in the section on *Passage*, earlier in this chapter, is a member of this family, used to describe control in the context of spatial models.

Knowing the terms we will be working with is important to our discussion of games, but it is only a stepping stone toward my main goals here. This book not only addresses the fundamental vocabulary of how games work but, in particular, focuses on ways to expand what can be said. The next two chapters explicitly explore two strategies to accomplish this.

2 Alternative Approaches

We are seeing profound shifts in the world of video games. The question is how to understand them.

We could look at the changes happening at a technical level. Previously, many games, especially games portraying simulated spaces, were made through low-level programming. The programmers had to include their own approaches to dealing with many of the fundamental elements of games—all the operational logics that weren't already built into each game's target hardware. Now that's changing, with game development being done using tools such as Twine, GameMaker, Unity, and Unreal. As Katharine Neil describes,[1] these tools support high-level programming, and some are accessible even to beginners.[2] They also include explicit support for many operational logics and other elements of well-known playable models.

We could also look at the question of distribution. Previously a handful of physical stores—often part of national chains such as GameStop and Best Buy—determined what games were available in a geographic region. This had obvious impacts, such as a focus on stocking games that buyers for these stores believed would have broad appeal to those already purchasing games. Less obviously, it made it difficult for games to take any form other than a sizable, one-time purchase. There was no way to reach an audience with a game on the scale of a political cartoon, or to produce a game on the model of an ongoing television series.[3] Digital distribution has utterly changed this, both through the "curated" spaces of app stores and Steam-likes as well as through more anarchic spaces such as Newgrounds and itch.io.

These gatekeeping and economic shifts are important. But other shifts have also been underway, sometimes disguised by relatively obvious continuities. For decades we have had games that use playable models of space to enable multiplayer games about shooting each other. Games like *Spacewar*[4] are in our history and games like *Fortnite*[5] are in our present.[6] For decades we have had command and control games focused on resource logics. Games like *Hamurabi*[7] are in our history and games like the *Civilization* franchise are in our present. More generally, we're accustomed to seeing lots of games about the movements of objects and resources.

So how do we understand the fact that we are now seeing games about topics like the fleeting nature of life, callous layoffs driven by the financial industry, beginning to take estrogen as a trans woman, trying to get by while doing precarious service work, wondering what has become of one's family, and more?[8] It wasn't at all obvious that the emergence of new, accessible game tools would lead to this—because the assumptions built into the tools, in the forms of logics and models, are largely derived from games about objects and resources.

To understand what is happening, as suggested in earlier chapters, I believe we need to consider three approaches that independent game makers are taking to logics and models. This chapter focuses on one of these: the alternative approach.

This approach finds ways to evoke new meanings, feelings, and experiences of play using logics and models developed for (and built into tools and platforms to support) very different games. Specifically, alternative uses of models and logics employ the same abstract processes and communicative roles as mainstream uses. However, they employ them in a domain that is novel or unusual and may remove them from common groupings with other logics and models. At the same time, the way we experience the alternative strategy is informed by our experiences with more mainstream games. We can see these phenomena clearly in the 3-D spatial movement game *Gone Home*[9] (figure 2.1).

Gone Home

Gone Home begins on the front porch of a large, suburban, single-family home. It's the kind of upper-middle-class home that we see too much of in most fiction—whether movies, television, stage plays, or novels. But when the game was released in the summer of 2013 this was an unusual place for a video game to begin, and to some extent it still is.

The front porch serves as a tutorial. You have to show understanding of the game's real-time 3-D navigation to move around it. You have to pick up and move objects to find a key. You have to use the key to open the next area of the house. (The main way *Gone Home* restricts movement through the house and shapes the likely order of player discoveries is with successive keys to new areas.)

It's a stormy night and a note on the door indicates no one is home. Once inside, you discover the house is dark and the electricity isn't reliable. When I first played, I soon discovered newspaper clippings pointing to a dark past. All the elements were

Figure 2.1
Lighting, a flickering television, and the stormy night serve to make something spooky out of an everyday space in *Gone Home*. (Image courtesy of The Fullbright Company. *Gone Home* art and imagery copyright The Fullbright Company.)

present for the mainstream game genre that is most likely to choose a contemporary, seemingly real-world setting: horror.

Thus, I moved with trepidation, even though I knew *Gone Home* was created as an independent game aimed at exploring different themes than those found in most games. I walked around corners with hesitancy, thinking something might jump out at me. When the lights flickered, I kept wondering if I might see a ghost in the darkness.[10]

Instead of horror, I discovered what had become of my absent family. I learned about my parents' struggles individually and as a couple. I learned about my high school sister's discovery of her queer identity and of the fateful choices made by her and her partner.

One sense in which *Gone Home* functions "alternatively" is probably clear from this description. The tools it uses are familiar from many games. In fact, many on the game's team were veterans of the *BioShock* series, which also uses documents found in a 3-D environment to tell the stories of those who previously inhabited it. (And as in the *BioShock* games, some of the documents in *Gone Home* are delivered via audio voice-over.) But it uses these spaces and documents in a setting—and to tell a story—which was quite unusual in 2013's games.

Also, as many media works do, it evokes the expectations of genres it does not fulfill. The expectation that it might be a horror game worked to heighten moment-to-moment tension and larger uncertainty about how its plot would develop. Encouraging audiences to wonder "What genre is this?" is a strategy that has been used effectively from Gothic fiction to contemporary movies such as *Happy Accidents*.[11]

But for some audiences it appears to have been most strongly alternative in terms of other genre expectations. To explain this, we must turn briefly to the ways that game genres operate.

Game Genre

If you are familiar with how genre is discussed for most media, or how it is used in library shelving, ideas of video game genre may come as something of a surprise. For example, "science fiction" (or "SF"—also known as "speculative fiction") isn't a genre of games. Rather, some games that take place in recognizably SF settings, such as the *Fallout* series, are categorized as "role-playing games" (or "RPGs"). They share the RPG genre with other games that have settings we associate with other fictional genres, such as the fantasy setting of *Planescape: Torment*.[12] Other games with recognizable SF settings are located in other game genres, such as the first-person shooter (FPS) genre of the *Halo* franchise and the real-time strategy (RTS) genre of the *StarCraft* series.[13]

What games like *Fallout*[14] and *Planescape* have in common with each other isn't their setting, nor is it the plot and character similarities we see in genres like mystery. Rather, it is what they have in common with tabletop RPGs,[15] such as *Dungeons & Dragons*[16] and *Call of Cthulhu*.[17] What unites these physical and digital games is the use of particular logics and models, in particular combinations. Jonathan Lessard calls these patterns of use "game architectures."[18] Some genres are even named after elements supported by their models, such as the "shooter" in FPS.[19]

One odd thing about game genre is how firmly certain logics and models can become associated with the uses and combinations found in particular genres. For example, José Pablo Zagal and Roger Altizer write about how progression logics (and models partially composed of them) applied to characters are often called "RPG elements" when employed in other games.[20] This is despite the fact that progression logics are used in other types of games (from simply unlocking new abilities to complex models such as technology trees) and the fact that RPGs have other logics and models they commonly employ (such as quest models).

But this player reaction could also be seen as a response to an objective fact about games. As scholars Staffan Björk and Jussi Holopainen write, using the language of design patterns, "many of the patterns we identified described characteristics that more or less automatically guaranteed other characteristics in the game."[21] In other words, even if it is theoretically possible that logics and models could appear in many combinations, they have a strong tendency to appear in the groupings that we call video game genres.

Gone Home's Alternative

For the most part, *Gone Home* received a remarkably positive reception. Reviewers praised the way it focused on themes such as coming of age, family tensions, and discovery of queer identity. These are quite different from the themes commonly explored in games (perhaps especially those with playable models of continuous, 3-D space) and reso-nated with the lives of real people.[22] Danielle Riendeau offers a representative perspective, writing for *Polygon*, "I've mowed down thousands of bad guys and aliens and evil henchmen in my 25-plus-year gaming career. And I've enjoyed emotional experiences and fallen for a number of memorable characters in that time. But I never expected to see myself—or such a strong reflection of myself and my own life—in a video game."[23]

But another audience reacted extremely negatively, in a manner that is revealing about alternative approaches to logics and models. For this audience, *Gone Home* vio-lated expectations of game genre in such a way as to not be a game. For a subset of this audience, the best response was to "return" *Gone Home* to the genre's mainstream state.

The genre *Gone Home* was seen as violating, by this audience, was that of the first-person shooter (FPS). This genre combines a playable model of continuous, real-time 3-D space with a model of real-time, largely projectile-based combat. The FPS—especially the games *DOOM*[24] and *Wolfenstein 3D*[25]—introduced the continuous, real-time explo-ration of 3-D spaces to many players.[26] For some players, the FPS is inextricably tied to such models—just as progression logics, used with characters, are inextricably tied to the RPG for some. And even for those who do not subscribe to this tight coupling, for many game-literate players the use of logics and models that are strongly associated with particular game genres does tend to call to mind those genres during play.

Given this, *Gone Home* is actually alternative in two ways. First, it puts its logics and models, which are primarily those used to enable and represent movement through space, toward an alternative use—a kind of space not common in today's mainstream games, used to reveal a kind of story not common in today's games. Second, for those literate in game genre, it is alternative in that it is seen as a refusal.

It is a refusal, specifically, of the first-person shooter genre some saw it as violat-ing.[27] This is a genre with which *Gone Home*'s creators are intimately familiar—as noted earlier, most of the team previously worked on the *BioShock* series, which belongs to this genre. However, the tale of *Gone Home* is told without the projectile-based combat that is central to *BioShock*[28] and other FPS games.

This refusal can be seen as putting *Gone Home* in the category of "anti-games." Melissa Kagen offers this definition of the term: "Anti-games are works that subvert, expand, or otherwise comment on traditional video game tropes, using game conventions to make metacommentaries, offer an alternative way to play, and explore the artistry inherent in gaming."[29] *Gone Home* is now commonly placed in the genre of "walking simulators," and Kagen places that entire genre in the anti-game category.[30] Going further, we can see the use of certain game conventions (those that bridge operation and communication, like *Gone Home*'s real-time 3-D spatial model) to create anti-games as one of a variety of alternative approaches to logics and models.

Gone Home's Reception

At the time of *Gone Home*'s release, in the summer of 2013, the reactionary misogyny found in online spaces such as 4chan had not yet produced the term "GamerGate." But the same elements can be seen in that moment's attempts to police what games can be about, who can make them, and how they can be discussed. One revealing response is *Gone Homo*, a reaction to both ways in which *Gone Home* is alternative—in subject matter and genre refusal. The game remakes *Gone Home* as an FPS, in the *DOOM* engine, with feminists as the enemy (figure 2.2).[31]

While we might see *Gone Homo* as a "disciplining" of *Gone Home*, by remaking it in the form of the genre it refuses, the gameplay is also revealing of how those involved see themselves. The final battle of the game is unwinnable and is followed by a display of *Gone Home*'s positive review scores. So, the player is put in the position of waging an impossible fight against feminism's takeover of games (perhaps on behalf of games with queer topics).

It is almost a parody of the claims (found in many fan communities) that the genres that are most mainstream in media, and most supported by media industries, are actually besieged by formerly marginalized groups. At the same time, it is presumably a real reflection of how its authors feel—revealing some of the emotional core of GamerGate and why the game treats "check your privilege" as a statement of aggression.[32]

Interestingly, there were also less overtly political reworkings of *Gone Home* in the form of the genre it refused.[33] A much more polished version of this phenomenon is "Gun Home,"[34] a video released by the humor site *Dorkly* in January 2014 (figure 2.3). Purportedly an advertisement for a *Gone Home* expansion, "Gun Home" also places a

Figure 2.2
As seen in this screenshot from online video, the final battle of *Gone Homo*—a partial re-creation of the house from *Gone Home*, in the *DOOM* engine—puts the player in an unwinnable fight against "feminists." (Image captured by the author.)

Figure 2.3
Dimly lit closets are a recurring feature of *Gone Home* (see figure 2.1). But they never contain a *DOOM* Zombieman, as is seen in this screenshot of the "Gun Home" video. (Image captured by the author.)

gun in the traditional screen location for an FPS—and populates the house with enemy characters from *DOOM* and *Wolfenstein 3D*. The video shows scenes of killing these enemies, overlaid with voiceover and text boasting of "ex-plode-ration"-based gameplay and "high octane introspection."[35] While "Gun Home" might be seen as a knowing comment on the negative response of some elements of video game player culture to *Gone Home*, a more direct version of this discomfort can be seen in the commentary from online viewers of the video.[36]

In the time since, however, something has happened that might not be expected if we focused only on these initial responses: at least in some quarters, *Gone Home* has become just another game.

One way we see this is in the active *Gone Home* speedrunning community, which Bonnie Ruberg analyzes as "straightening" the game in two ways.[37] First, speedrunning (the completion of games as quickly as possible) for *Gone Home* requires movement in straight lines. Going upstairs at an angle, for example, will slow the player down. So speedrunners train themselves to move through the house in as straight a manner as possible—undercutting both the game's presentation of the house and much comment on the game, which suggest exploratory meandering as the appropriate approach. Second, speedrunners often play *Gone Home* in a way that elides its queer representation. In a speedrun focused only on quickly reaching the end (rather than doing so after collecting all the diary entries) almost none of the game's story is experienced. And discussion of the game among speedrunners, as opposed to elsewhere, makes almost no mention of the queer romance that is at the heart of what the player character discovers in a traditional playthrough. As Ruberg puts it, "These two facets of speedrunning *Gone Home*—what tactics players use and how they talk about the game while playing—shed valuable light on how speedrunning straightens the potential for queer movement in the game, and perhaps in video games more broadly."

It is also possible to see speedrunning in a quite different light. For example, in *Metagaming* Stephanie Boluk and Patrick LeMieux write that "speedrunning investigates the strange games already operating within video games and expands single-player software into a massively multiplayer metagame."[38] And Ruberg's argument goes on to consider that "speedrunning itself could be seen as a form of queer play"—approaching the game in a queer way. Speedrunning connects with ideas of queerness through its resisting the normative time of play, focusing on glitches, and turning the arguably overly neat narrative of *Gone Home* into something partial and strange.[39]

It's also worth noting that *Gone Home* speedrunning includes an active "100%" community. A 100% completion requires collecting all the journal entries—including the "Meow Meow Meow" journal entry from the family cat, which requires playful manipulation of the house's objects.[40] *Gone Home* even appears to encourage such engagement: it includes a "Speedreader" achievement for completing the game, having found all the diary entries, in under 10 minutes.[41]

In whatever way we see speedrunning, from the perspective of this chapter the important thing is that speedrunners approach *Gone Home* much as they would any other game. It is not treated as alternative either in its use of a real-time 3-D playable model for its particular spaces and topics, or in any perceived refusal of the FPS genre.

This acceptance of *Gone Home* as "just another game" should not be seen as unusual or unexpected. Rather, it is the anticipated outcome of alternative approaches. The alternative strategy results in making future games, of similar sorts, less alternative.

Since *Gone Home*, we have seen continued use of real-time 3-D playable models to represent domestic spaces in games such as *What Remains of Edith Finch*.[42] It seems unlikely that games using such models to explore the common settings of middle-class fiction will continue to be unusual indefinitely. We have also seen continued use of such models to tell stories of queer youth in games such as *The Last of Us: Left Behind*.[43] We can hope that this, too, will become unremarkable. And *Gone Home* itself followed games such as *Dear Esther*[44] and those created by artgame studio Tale of Tales in using continuous 3-D spatial models for combat-free exploration and storytelling. The result of this body of work is that the walking simulator has become an established genre— and games such as *Firewatch*,[45] released only a few years after *Gone Home*, have ceased being received with a focus on the absence of FPS combat models.

As a result, just as listening to today's radio makes it hard to hear what was pioneering about early rap and hip-hop, so our ability to perceive works such as *Gone Home* as alternative has already become limited. But this also means such games are doing their work—changing our culture.

Through the lens of logics and models, the work that produces this change might seem quite modest. Characters walk in many games—guided through control logics, as part of spatial models. *Gone Home*'s alternative is not seen in the activity of walking, but seen in where its characters walk, in the story that is revealed through the exploration, and in the lack of a combat model to accompany its continuous, 3-D spatial model. These changes in the domain and genre in which an activity takes place are hallmarks of an alternative approach. And as *Gone Home* shows, such changes can be powerful.

3   Expansive Approaches

While some activities—such as moving through space—are commonly included in games, many activities are nearly or entirely absent. Finding ways to use existing logics and models to make new activities playable is a common expansive approach. More generally, expansive approaches start with an existing logic or model, then seek to add an additional communicative role, one that moves beyond the activities games conventionally make playable through this logic or model. This is a powerful approach for expanding what games can be about.

This chapter explores the successes and limits of a particular kind of expansion: *refinement*, in which the new communicative role can be seen as a more specific version of the conventional one.[1] I explore this by looking at games that use relatively abstract *pattern-matching* logics. These are logics we often first learn through childhood play, in games such as Go Fish and *Connect Four*.[2] Here I will examine games that take refinement to its limit, using such logics to place players in dark roles and disturbing situations.

One general issue with expansive approaches is that there is no additional computational support—no support in the functioning of the logic—for the second communicative role.[3] Even if this role is quite close to the first, it requires consistent use to communicate successfully. This can be seen most clearly in games that employ multiple refinements of the same logic. For example, in many games that focus on *linking logics* (such as games made in Twine) the same logic is refined to play multiple roles, such as spatial navigation, examining objects, and making dialogue choices. These can be employed consistently and marked by some convention—perhaps text styling or screen position, or the more elaborate approaches used in games like *80 Days*.[4] If there is not consistency, the different refinements will become confusing for the player, reducing agency.[5] The projects discussed in the rest of this chapter avoid this issue by pursuing a single refinement of their logics (and doing so consistently).

Papers, Please

Lucas Pope's *Papers, Please*[6] is most effective if you don't have fun playing it.[7]

As the game opens, we learn that the player character has won the October 1982 employment lottery in Arstotzka, a fictional country ruled by an oppressive regime. The prize is to be moved, with one's family, into government housing near a job as a border inspector. The first day, the player examines the papers of those who wish to cross the border, learning how to use stamps to officially approve or deny entry, and learning to follow a simple rule: only let in citizens. The first night, the player learns that (despite some Soviet-style design) Arstotzka is not Communist. Rather, the player is paid for each person processed correctly. With this money, the family must pay rent, food, and heating bills. The first time I played, I wasn't very fast the first day, and we were already dipping into savings the first night.

The next day, people from other countries can also enter, but only if their passport is not expired, and their photo matches their appearance, and their gender appearance matches their document's stated gender, and their papers are issued in one of the cities in which their countries have such offices (figure 3.1). The following day, foreigners

Figure 3.1
Papers, Please highlights a mismatch between a character's gender expression and the gender listed on their visa document, offering the option to interrogate them about it. (Image taken by the author during play.)

also need entry tickets, which also cannot be expired. The following day, those tickets are no longer valid, and foreigners need permits instead, and citizens need ID cards, all with dates, seals, passport numbers, photos, issuing cities, and/or other information that must be checked.

As these changes took place, I didn't feel like I could develop a system. I wasn't methodically checking the number on the passport against the number on the entry permit, then checking the pictures against the faces, then checking the issuing city against the list of valid ones in the book, and so on. I was racing against the clock, trying to read what the characters said and trying to remember the rules, moving documents around on the surface in front of me, running my eyes back and forth trying to find a discrepancy without taking too much time.

I didn't want to make decisions too quickly, because I had also discovered that (in addition to the new requirements slowing the process faster than my skill was increasing) if I made too many errors, my pay was docked. And I also found myself cursing everything outside my control for moving too slowly, from the animation of the visa stamp to the walking animation of the next person in line after I called them. I found the situation, both of my real play and of my fictional character, so off-putting that I started taking breaks, doing something besides playing, between the fictional work days.

And the fictional situation got worse. People pled with me—they needed to get through, to be together with loved ones, to avoid persecution in their home countries— and I had to choose between having the resources to keep my family going (by processing them as the regime required) and doing what I thought would help the people in line. And I could be wrong. A woman tells me that she is afraid that a man behind her in line will force her and her sister into prostitution. I deny him entry, and the next day's newspaper headline is, "Dancers at Grestin Club Found Dead!"

What happened was, in the end, rather predictable. My family's savings were consumed within a few days, and I found myself having to choose between heating the apartment and buying medicine for my sick son. Soon everyone was cold, hungry, and sick. Less than a week in, I couldn't pay the rent. I was sent to debtors' prison and my family was sent home, blessedly all still alive after my "win" of the employment lottery.

The effectiveness of games like *Papers, Please*, which take an expansive approach to pattern-matching logics, depends on the relationship between how we experience the gameplay and how we understand the situation the game depicts. For me, the primary mechanic of *Papers, Please* (having to engage in complex, changing information-verification under time pressure) was quite unpleasant, resonating effectively with the deeply unpleasant situation in which the player character finds himself. And for me, this created a powerful empathy and engagement with the situation. So powerful that I needed breaks from it.

The foundation of the primary mechanic of *Papers, Please* is a particular pattern-matching logic: *informational pattern matching*. This is a logic we experience, for example, nearly every time we play a card game (as when checking, "Do I have two pair? A full house?"). *Papers, Please* adds a second communicative role to the pattern matching: satisfying bureaucratic requirements. The game proceeds whether the pattern is matched correctly or incorrectly, while giving feedback—more like *Rock Band*[8] than a puzzle game.

Just as alternative uses of a logic or model can become conventional over time, so can expansive uses. At one point, colliding with an object in order to collect it (as Mario does with coins) was an expansive use, but now it is conventional—as I discuss further in chapter 9. Becoming conventional seems unlikely in the case of the communication of satisfying bureaucratic requirements through a pattern-matching logic, though not impossible, given the existence of games such as *Jetset: A Game for Airports*.[9]

There are other logics in the pattern-matching family, and the next section of this chapter takes up *spatial pattern matching*. Like informational pattern matching, spatial pattern matching is a logic we often first experience in childhood play with physical objects (as in Tic-Tac-Toe) and also see in video games (as in tile-matching games).[10]

Part of what interests me about the logics discussed in this chapter is that they have often been used in quite abstract games. In many of these games there is little difference between the abstract version of the logic's communicative role (for example, that certain spatial patterns will be recognized) and what the player is meant to experience when playing (certain spatial patterns of arbitrarily colored jewels will be recognized). By showing how a logic familiar from such abstract games can, instead, be used to make games about people—and people in particularly troubling situations—we can understand the power of expansive approaches, particularly refinement.

Two Approaches to Tile Matching

In his 2009 book *A Casual Revolution*,[11] Jesper Juul traces the history of one game mechanic supported by the spatial pattern-matching logic: tile matching. Juul defines this as mechanic as, "the player manipulates tiles in order to make them disappear according to a matching criterion."[12] In a sense, Juul's history begins with the inventive work of implementing spatial pattern matching in a video game context (and developing the initial variations of the tile-matching mechanic it supports) after which a variety of mechanic innovations were developed, producing a small family of logic variations.

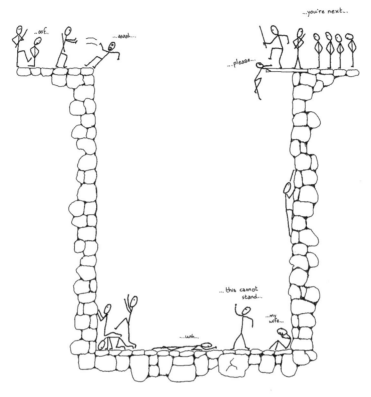

Figure 3.2
In Raph Koster's *A Theory of Fun for Game Design*, he writes: "Consider a game of mass murder where you throw victims down a well and they stand on each other to try to climb out." (Images of Koster's thought experiment are from *A Theory of Fun for Game Design*, 2nd ed. Published by O'Reilly Media. Copyright © 2014 Raph Koster. All rights reserved. Used with permission.)

Juul places *Chain Shot*[13] and *Tetris*,[14] both released in the mid-1980s, at the top of the tile-matching family tree—with later influential games such as the bestselling *Bejeweled*[15] further down. A number of innovative game creators have shown how versions of games like these can be created that represent difficult human situations, within limits. For example, Raph Koster, in his 2004 book *A Theory of Fun for Game Design*, offers this thought experiment (figure 3.2):

> Let's picture a mass murder game wherein there is a gas chamber shaped like a well. You the player are dropping innocent victims down into the gas chamber, and they come in all shapes and sizes. There are old ones and young ones, fat ones and tall ones. As they fall to the bottom, they grab onto each other and try to form human pyramids to get to the top of the well.

Figure 3.3
Koster writes, "The mechanics may be *Tetris*, but the experience is very different." (Images of Koster's thought experiment are from *A Theory of Fun for Game Design*, 2nd ed. Published by O'Reilly Media. Copyright © 2014 Raph Koster. All rights reserved. Used with permission.)

> Should they manage to get out, the game is over and you lose. But if you pack them in tightly enough, the ones on the bottom succumb to the gas and die.[16]

What Koster describes is a horrifically themed version of *Tetris*, in which human beings replace the traditionally abstract blocks (figure 3.3). The game is played exactly the same way, but the player's efficiency is now in the service of a crime against humanity, rather than simply toward a higher score, longer play session, or personal feeling of skill or immersion. Of course, for experienced *Tetris* players, the pull of old motivations would still be present, in conflict with awareness of the task it now serves, as Koster found in 2009 when he played a version of the game implemented by a Brazilian game club:

> I actually didn't finish the first game I played, because of the decapitated heads at the bottom, and then cramming an upside-down person into the gap. Curiously, I started out playing it

just as *Tetris*—and in fact, the tug of doing so was remarkably strong. But the "dressing," the art and especially the sound, was so strong that after a while, I couldn't ignore it, and it made me uncomfortable.[17]

In other words, while Koster's thought experiment certainly shows how an expansive use of spatial pattern matching can open up new subjects for games, there is a fundamental dissonance between the new subject and the feelings created by playing the game. *Tetris* is designed to be fun. Simply "re-skinning" it as a horrible crime—refining the pattern-matching logic to signify death—is an intentionally disturbing idea.[18]

Going further, the re-skinning of another famous tile-matching game shows how this approach can be used for critical ends. *Layoff*[19] was conceived by Mary Flanagan and Angela Ferraiolo of Tiltfactor Lab (at Dartmouth College) and created by Tiltfactor and the Rochester Institute of Technology games program as part of multi-institution research on values in games.[20] It was released in March 2009, at the height of the financial crisis, garnering significant media attention and over a million players its first week.[21]

Layoff employs a version of *Bejeweled*'s gameplay, which takes place in a grid of objects. The player may swap the positions of any two adjacent objects, as long as the result is at least one "match" of three or more objects of the same type. Matched objects disappear; the player scores points (and may receive additional bonuses, for matching more than the required three objects); and the remaining objects move down the grid (to be replaced by more coming in from the top). *Bejeweled*'s objects are colored jewels, with the colors being arbitrary (there is no reason for players to prefer one color over another) and with no distinction made between individual jewels of the same type (except that some occasionally carry bonuses).

Layoff, in contrast, refines the pattern-matching logic to present something much more specific. Each object is an individual worker. Mousing over a worker reveals a capsule story about them—their name, age, what they do, and so on. The player is put in the position of trying to match the workers for "workplace efficiency adjustments." These make the matched workers disappear, as well as adding to the group of people milling around the unemployment office shown at the bottom of the screen. In between the grid of workers and the unemployment office is a text ticker, displaying messages such as: "The American economy lost 2.6 million jobs in 2008, but the average performance-based bonus for 132 of the largest US companies increased to $265,594."

The unemployment office and text ticker are not among the elements that are usually displayed together with *Bejeweled*'s object grid. But they leave its fundamental gameplay unchanged, just as Koster's thought experiment does with *Tetris*. Crucially,

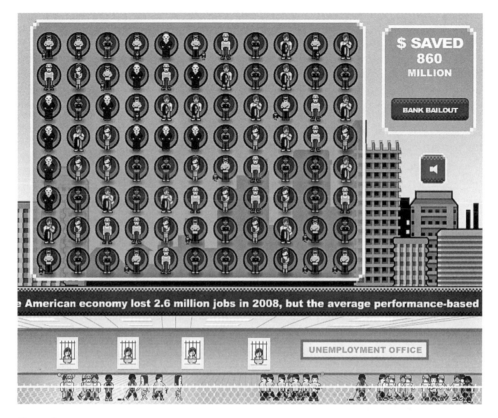

Figure 3.4
Layoff is played like *Bejeweled*, with matched characters falling into the unemployment office at the bottom of the screen—unless they are suit-wearing workers, as along the left of this image. (Image taken by the author during play.)

Layoff then goes further, introducing a new kind of object—suit-wearing workers (figure 3.4). When these workers are moused-over, no biography is revealed. Instead, the player sees a quote that appears to be from the suit-wearing worker's perspective, such as: "Customers of the new merged corporation should feel secure. Your investments are safe in our hands." And, most importantly, suit-wearing workers cannot be matched. They can only be moved to make the layoff of another type of worker possible, and they can never be laid off—even when the movements of other workers result in a match. Given this, successfully playing *Layoff* eventually results in a grid dominated by suit-wearing workers, above a very full unemployment office, with no further changes possible. In short, *Layoff* becomes less fun, because its pattern-matching logic becomes harder to employ, as the consequences of the player's actions are revealed.

How you think about this gameplay seems to depend on where you sit. Writing on games site *Kotaku*, Michael McWhertor says: "It's not only educational and entertaining, it's also depressing."[22] On the other hand, Cindy Perman, writing on the business-oriented site *CNBC*, suggests:

> . . . it's a fun way to pass the time. And, the next time you're in a bookstore or drugstore and there are a gaggle of employees behind the counter but it's still taking a ridiculously long time, just close one eye and with your thumb, line them up and lay them off.[23]

Perman and McWhertor, in their own ways, point to the same experience with *Layoff* that Koster reports with extermination-themed *Tetris*—it is possible to make games about people using spatial pattern matching, but in these games, we treat people inhumanely. *Layoff* makes its point more effectively, by also ensuring that the gameplay, over time, ceases being fun (as the space becomes dominated with suit-wearing workers). But both still begin with gameplay that is designed to be enjoyable, in which we carry out acts that the game creators do not endorse.

And while it is certainly possible to imagine, for example, a human tile-matching game with a less depressing theme (for example, romantic matchmaking) it would still boil down to treating humans in the impersonal, instrumental fashion supported by the abstract process of the spatial pattern-matching logic. This reveals one of the key limitations of expansive approaches to logics and models—their underlying characteristics do not go away. A game like *Layoff* can refine the communicative role of spatial pattern matching (creating the experience of matching employees), but it cannot fundamentally change it.

Broader Context

In *Layoff*, the only thing to do is lay people off. You see the negative effects of your actions—and you feel the game becoming less fun to play. But the only alternative to laying people off is ceasing to play the game.

Papers, Please offers a different approach. Just as mousing over a worker in *Layoff* presents their story, so those who approach the immigration checkpoint in *Papers, Please* have their stories. But while *Layoff* provides only the options of pattern-matching gameplay, *Papers, Please* lets us refuse that gameplay. We can instead decide to simply let people through.

If we step out of pattern-matching gameplay, however, we step into the part of *Papers, Please* that is governed by resource logics. We don't get paid for people we don't process correctly. And if we process too many incorrectly then our pay is docked. And we may already not have enough funds to cover the basic needs of our family.

Encountering this, one thing we see is that the alternative and expansive approaches to logics and models can coexist in the same game. The approach to pattern matching in *Papers, Please* is expansive, communicating something through the logic (satisfying bureaucratic requirements) that it does not conventionally communicate. On the other hand, the approach to resource logics uses them to communicate economic transactions, which is common in games. What makes their use alternative is the domain for these transactions, which is uncommon: a family struggling, and often failing, to get by under an oppressive regime that dictates the terms of employment but will only provide them what they can pay for.

Peter Mawhorter explains what makes this combination of pattern matching and resource-oriented play so effective.[24] As he puts it, the gameplay of *Papers, Please* appears to have the structure of a classic dilemma. On one hand we have a very important goal, pursued through the pattern-matching gameplay: doing what is morally right, letting through those who need to get through. On the other hand we have another very important goal, pursued through the resource gameplay: taking care of our family, who are under constant threat from cold, disease, and a precarious living situation.[25]

And then, as Mawhorter explains, *Papers, Please* undermines this dilemma. It introduces uncertainty about our moral choices. We try to help the dancers, but they end up killed. We have people come to the checkpoint who are obviously lying to us, leading us to wonder who else is lying. As we play, we come to realize (probably unconsciously) that we are choosing between one high-priority goal that we are uncertain to achieve (doing what is right) and another high-priority goal that we are certain to achieve (if we can play the pattern-matching game well enough). So, the rational choice is to take care of our family—to do what the regime wants.

In terms of Mawhorter's "choice poetics,"[26] we can then see the structure of *Papers, Please* as positing, "dilemma + doubt → complicity."[27] To choose something other than complicity becomes the harder, more unlikely choice.[28] This, in the end, is what *Papers, Please* is about.

This is one way around the limits of refinement. Even if the underlying logic gives us no way of dealing with human beings other than as objects, we can place this activity in a context that gives the player an alternative. We can then use other logics, and fictional context, to make choosing this alternative a meaningful choice.

Another option is to create a broader context that isn't a game—and thereby change the framing and motivation of play. This is the strategy of *Parable of the Polygons*[29] and other projects described as "explorable explanations."[30]

The underlying logic of *Parable of the Polygons* is nothing new. It performs spatial pattern matching for a particular spot on a grid, based on the spots that neighbor this

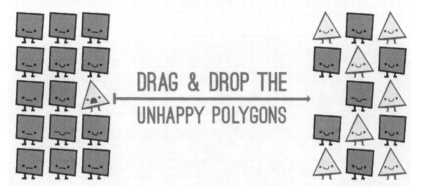

This is a story of how harmless choices can make a harmful world.

These little cuties are 50% Triangles, 50% Squares, and 100% slightly shapist. But only slightly! In fact, every polygon *prefers* being in a diverse crowd:

DRAG & DROP THE
UNHAPPY POLYGONS

Figure 3.5
Parable of the Polygons introduces its cellular automata-style spatial pattern matching. (Image taken by the author during play.)

grid. This is familiar from cellular automata experiments such as Conway's Game of Life.[31] It is also familiar from its use in games, such as the original *SimCity*.[32] But it is expansive in what it is communicating through play: the workings of segregation.[33]

Parable of the Polygons is a long webpage, created by Vi Hart and Nicky Case. Its structure combines three elements. First, short passages of text. Second, small "tutorial" examples that demonstrate (often by asking the player to take action) how its pattern matching functions in a tightly designed scenario. Third, larger simulations that offer more opportunities to explore the potentials of the system—but with a prompt given to guide player exploration. The beginning, just after the title section at the top of the page, introduces the first two elements (figure 3.5).

Positioned as players, we follow the tutorial instructions. We see the triangle get happier, once we move it from left to right, as it is no longer surrounded "only" by squares. We also see the squares around that triangle's former location, which used to be smiling, take on the flat "meh" expressions of the others on the left. They would prefer a more diverse environment (though they're not made actively unhappy by its absence).

From there, *Parable of the Polygons* introduces its initial rules: 1) Only unhappy shapes can be moved, and 2) "I wanna move if less than [one-third] of my neighbors are like me." Then the first larger simulation is introduced (figure 3.6).

Harmless, right? Every polygon would be happy with a mixed neighborhood.
Surely their small bias can't affect the larger shape society that much? Well...

drag & drop unhappy polygons until nobody is unhappy:

(just move them to random empty spots. don't think too much about it.)

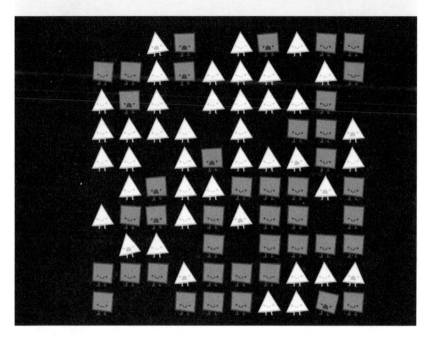

Figure 3.6

Parable of the Polygons invites players to enact a model of segregation based on its pattern-matching
logic. (Image taken by the author during play.)

While experimenting with this simulation, the player discovers that the rules lead,
inevitably, to a highly segregated society. Building upon this realization, *Parable of the
Polygons* introduces a simulation that runs on its own so the player can try it several
times, seeing different specific movements but the same pattern emerging. Further
simulations enable turning bias higher and lower—eventually leading to a demonstration that even zero bias, if starting with a segregated society, leaves us with segregation.

This would seem to be the depressing endpoint of the argument. But then *Parable
of the Polygons* goes a step further. It asks, "What if shapes wanted to seek out just a
lil' more variety?" In the final simulations, in addition to wanting to move if too few
neighbors are of the same shape, the shapes can want to move if too many are the

Box 3.1

Critical Games and Alternative Approaches

Using expansive approaches to make critical games (such as *Layoff*) can be limited by the central metaphorical move of the expansion. A closer examination of the metaphor may not reveal more about the subject and may even reveal unintentional messages—as Mike Treanor identifies[34] with Molleindustria's *Kosmosis*.[35]

Making a critical game through alternative approaches can avoid this problem. For example, Molleindustria's games also include a number that use common design patterns with resource logics to create alternative simulation games. Just as walking is a conventional communicative goal with a control logic, but alternative games let us walk in new contexts, so profit-producing resource allocation is a conventional communicative goal with playable economic models, but Molleindustria's games put this in a new context. As Paolo Pedercini, the force behind Molleindustria, explains:

> Games like the *McDonald's Videogame* or *Oiligarchy* embrace tropes and conventions of the genre: players manage a production process trying to maximize profits, they are presented with an objectified nature ready to be exploited, they invest resources according to numerical trends and feedback, etc. But instead of portraying these activities as natural and neutral, these games introduce elements of criticality that subvert players' expectation: the exploitation of the environment has troubling consequences, the attempts to exert control over workers, consumers, and indigenous populations cause backlashes and protests, and so on. In a nutshell, the so-called "negative externalities" of a production process and the capitalist conflicts are included in the simulated world, sometimes at the expenses of playability and elegance in design.[36]

The advantages of this kind of alternative approach are that such games are often easier to make (leaning on existing design knowledge) and, when players think more deeply about their play experience, there often is something more to learn about the game's topic (as opposed to many games using an expansive approach, like the re-skinned *Tetris* games discussed in this chapter). The disadvantage is that it's impossible to make a game about anything other than the few topics for which we have well-developed logics and models (such as spatial movement, economic systems, and pattern-matching puzzles and performances). What is exciting about the expansive approach, even if it has its limits, is that through applying logics and models to new domains and using them metaphorically it can open the door to talking about more topics and talking about current topics in new ways.

same.[37] Hart and Case create scenarios that show, as we play them, that even if this number is quite high (the initial value is 90%) the result is emergent desegregation.

This "happy ending" is certainly quite different from a game like *Layoff* or *Papers, Please*. But even earlier, when we are enacting simulated segregation, it feels different. The question is why.

Parable of the Polygons isn't different because it lacks play. Its experience hinges on play, builds on the design traditions of video game tutorial sequences, and is founded on a logic well known in games. But it does position the player differently.

In a game like *Layoff* or *Papers, Please*, we are positioned as actors in a fictional world, making something happen in that world. In a game like *Tetris* or *Bejeweled*, on the other hand, we are positioned outside the game world, making a system operate for the ("autotelic") pleasure of operating it. We can think of this as a spectrum, with *Tetris* a bit more abstract than *Bejeweled* and *Layoff* more abstract than *Papers, Please*. Players can move along this spectrum as they play, not staying where the game seems to position them, as Koster reported with playing the horrifically rethemed mass murder *Tetris*.

What *Parable of the Polygons* does, instead, is take us out of the position of simply being players. We are no longer on that spectrum. It invites and structures play, and it builds upon the practice many of us have with using playful experimentation to understand how systems work, but our motivation for play is different. We are not "enacting segregation" in a fictional world when we play, nor are we simply manipulating a system for its own sake. We are playing in order to understand how a system works, while actively considering it as a metaphor for something in our larger world.[38]

Of course, this is effective because *Parable of the Polygons* expands a pattern-matching logic as part of building a considered portrayal of segregation, one that can be understood more deeply through play. In contrast, we cannot develop a deeper understanding of corporate human resources through playing *Layoff*, or of crimes against humanity through Koster's re-skinned *Tetris* thought experiment (see box 3.1, "Critical Games and Alternative Approaches"). These re-skinnings function more in the momentary mode of political cartoons—in contrast to the deeper drawing of a fictional situation in *Papers, Please* and the approach of playing to understand a system in *Parable of the Polygons*.[39]

Playing to understand, and consider as a real-world metaphor, is a way that a player of any game can choose to engage. It is one meaning of Flanagan's term *critical play*, which I will discuss further in chapter 6. But *Parable of the Polygons* is deliberately designed to place players in this mode of engagement. In doing so, it presents an exciting future possibility for expansive approaches to operational logics.

4   Six Questions about Logics and Models

Before we can consider the invention of new logics and models, which is the subject of the next chapter, we need to consider six questions about them more broadly. Each section in this chapter expands a question and then offers an answer.

Are Logics and Models Natural?

One reason it can be challenging to discuss operational logics and playable models is that they can seem obvious and natural. When collision detection allows me to eat a dot in *Ms. Pac-Man*[1] or prevents me from making a life choice in *Passage*,[2] it feels normal. It takes effort (as shown in the discussion of *Passage*) to take a step back and see that what is going on is not natural, but something constructed that I have learned to interpret.

This sense of naturalness persists even though, in these games, I see the same logic (collision detection) used to represent very different things (eating and decision making). It is also true in the opposite direction—when I see the same activity being represented through different playable models, employing different logics. For example, when I play *XCOM: Enemy Unknown*,[3] I take my time, each round of combat, to position my characters in one of the discrete locations they can occupy and choose who they will attack and with what. I know a simulation engine will determine my success based on the numerical properties of my character, their weapon, who they are attacking, the cover the enemy is behind, and so on. When I play *Uncharted 2: Among Thieves*,[4] I play only "myself" (the player character, Nathan Drake), and everything keeps happening all the time—there is no pause between rounds to make careful plans. My success or failure is based on how quickly and accurately I can run, take cover, aim, shoot, and carry out other actions in the continuous 3-D graphical world of the game. These two models for combat are quite different. And yet, during play, they both seem like natural ways of making the experience of combat playable.[5]

The existence of these two models is not happenstance or the result of clever game designers doodling on whiteboards. Rather, each of these models is the result of long-term, well-funded efforts to create playable models of combat for use in military training. The model employed by *XCOM: EU* was first developed as part of tabletop *Kriegsspiel* games by European armies and was further developed and made into software in the twentieth century by the RAND Corporation and others.[6] The model employed by *Uncharted 2*, on the other hand, was the result of the development of 3-D computer graphics pushed forward by military funders, for purposes such as creating fighter pilot training simulators. This is not simply history, but also the foundation of ongoing connections between game development and military investment.[7]

So, when today's game developers find well-developed operational logics for certain purposes built into their game engines, or certain playable models well understood in the craft wisdom of their field, this is neither natural nor accidental. And it should be no surprise that so many games are made in which combat is central. Had a similar level of investment been made in developing logics and models for other areas of human life, the game industry would likely have built upon those.

Are Logics and Models Inevitable?

We might also ask the question: once we have decided to pursue the development of logics and models in a particular area, is the result inevitable? To put it another way: are certain logics and models the ones that would always emerge, once we turn our attention to some domain? As a guiding example, let us consider *pathfinding*. This is a common behavior logic for characters in graphical games, allowing them to find their way from their current location to a desired location.[8] There are a number of well-known technical implementations of pathfinding, and versions are built into common game-making tools such as the Unity and Unreal engines. This is because pathfinding is useful to so many commercially proven types of games, including arcade games such as *Ms. Pac-Man*, strategy games such as *XCOM*, and action games such as *Uncharted*.[9] And this, in turn, makes it much easier to produce future games of the sorts that feature pathfinding and other widespread logics.

But it seems unlikely that the centrality of pathfinding was inevitable, once we began to develop logics for autonomous movement in space. For example, Craig Reynolds identified a set of related "steering behaviors" for characters in graphical environments in the 1980s and '90s.[10] These include a number that are arguably more common and fundamental in everyday life than pathfinding, such as *pursuit, evasion,* and *obstacle avoidance*. But implementations of them are not nearly as widespread and easily available as pathfinding, despite Reynolds's creation of the "OpenSteer" library to help encourage their dissemination.[11] One reason might be that, by the time of Reynolds's work, the commercially dominant game genres of the era were already established, based on the logics and models that were already available, and the risk-averse game industry of that period proved infertile ground for experimenting with alternatives. Another reason might be that, as Andrew Fray has argued, the common implementations of these logics are not robust, or at least not sufficient on their own.[12] Or, as Robert Zubek has argued, it might be that steering behaviors are too low-level, given what we expect from game characters.[13] The result may have been due to all of these factors, and more, but it remains the case that it is not necessary or natural that many in-development games can easily use a pathfinding logic but would require much more effort to use an obstacle avoidance logic (or to use both).[14] We could easily imagine the history of games having played out a different way, pursuing a different set of "fundamental" logics for autonomous movement.

How Are Logics and Models Implemented?

There is another sense in which our available logics and models are not natural or inevitable: the actual implementation of a logic or model, in a specific game we can play, depends on the answers to questions on three topics: how the logic will operate, how players will understand this, and how this will fit into the game's design.

First, how will this logic or model operate? What is our guiding theory for how it should function? How will we implement that theory? This might seem obvious in the case of, for example, movement physics—but it isn't. At a historical level, we might argue that it took a lot of thinking to come up with the theories we now use in the everyday world. But at a more practical level, it's also the case that games rarely employ even something as straightforward as movement physics by simply following a previously existing, everyday world theory. Instead, games are designed so that characters like Mario can easily jump higher than their own heights, and sometimes can jump in mid-air, which is quite different from any existing theory of the physics of people in our world. So, these questions of theory must be considered.

And for a logic or model that is new to games (rather than well-trod ground like physics) the questions are, of course, more challenging to answer. Further, we have to consider how the theory will be implemented—how will the abstract process be not only made concrete, but made to function in the particular context? Particularly on constrained platforms, there may be significant distance between the abstract process and how we would describe the details of its particular implementation.[15]

Second, how will players understand this? How will we communicate the operation of the logic or model? Again, in cases such as physics and collision this might seem obvious, but it isn't. Game developers don't, for example, simply move the image of a jumping character upward, then move it back down until it touches something. They use communication tools from the field of animation, exaggerating movements and environmental responses (such as a character crouching down on impact, with dust rising around her feet, and perhaps, when landing after a long fall, shaking the "camera" looking at the scene). They use tools from sound design, signaling character actions and types of spaces (such as a different landing sound on dirt or metal). And they use tools that aren't available in most media, such as vibrating the controller in the player's hands.

Third, how does this fit into the game's design? In what different circumstances will the logic or model be used, toward what different types of communication and play? How does the player take action? How do we want that action to feel? For those doing mainstream game design, there is a substantial body of craft wisdom and experience to draw on in answering these questions. For example, the book *Game Mechanics*,[16] by Ernest Adams and Joris Dormans, is a good introduction to the different ways that resource logics and economic models are used, while a comprehensive primer on "game feel" (for games using movement physics) can be found in Steve Swink's book by that name.[17] The essence of expansive approaches (see chapters 3, 8, and 9) is to move beyond the conventional communicative roles for a logic or model, though in these cases one can still in part be guided by conventional uses. But as the next chapter will discuss, when a logic or model is being invented, no such guide is available, and experimentation with use and feel is a key part of the inventive work.

Now, one might argue that these questions don't have to be answered until an actual game is made—that a logic or model could be invented on its own, first, and then employed in games later. But it doesn't work that way. A logic or model is only invented through a process of repeated use and refinement in actual audience experiences. Just as there is no way to see if a literary trope actually has an impact on audiences (so that we know it actually functions) without creating a piece of literature, there is no way to create new logics or models without the messy work of trying to create specific games—or other works of computational media—that use them.[18]

Finally, there is one further aspect that is revealed if we look closely at what happens when we make things: we see that the implementation of a logic or model in a particular game is always situated in a much larger context, with the creator(s) having less control than we might imagine. For example, Dylan Lederle-Ensign led an investigation into the phenomenon of "strafe jumping" in games that use engine technology from id Software (idTech).[19] In these games, such as *Quake*,[20] players discovered a mechanic that allowed them to far exceed the normal movement speed. This mechanic was not intentionally included in the games in which it was first discovered, and it was only possible because of an error in the implementation of the physics logic.

As Lederle-Ensign demonstrates, this case is revealing for our thinking about logics in three ways. First, as mentioned above, it is a reminder that many game creators build upon already established approaches to logics—particularly those built into game engines. John Carmack, the lead developer of the idTech engines, brought forward the key piece of code, implementing this part of the physics logic, through multiple generations of the engine. Other games that used the engine, and even other engines derived from engines of id's (such as Valve's Source engine), "inherited" versions of the implementation of the logic and the mechanic it enabled.

Second, it demonstrates that game developers have less control over what emerges from their logics than we might assume. Carmack viewed the behavior that enables strafe jumping as a bug and attempted a fix that is still visible in the engine code (which has been released open source). But as he noted in a public ".plan" file, he was unhappy with how the fix changed the feel of the game's running mechanic. Changing the implementation of a logic can change many mechanics that depend on it, and not always in predictable or desirable ways.

Third, the case of strafe jumping reminds us quite clearly that, like other technologies, game technologies are socially negotiated. Carmack might well have pushed forward and found a more complex fix for the engine's physics logic, preserving the feel of running while eliminating the strafe jumping mechanic. But strafe jumping already had many vocal proponents in the player community, and the engine technology was already licensed to a number of other companies who were aware of its popularity among players. Not only was Carmack eventually forced to walk back his plans to "fix the bug" that enabled it, but id Software's own level designers embraced the mechanic, creating gameplay situations in *Quake III Arena*[21] designed to reward player knowledge of how to carry out the difficult actions the mechanic requires.

In short, while developers must answer the three questions outlined in this section in order to implement a logic, we will misunderstand their work if we simply think of this as "authoring." The implementation of logics and models happens in a much wider context, of which we should not lose sight.

Are Logics or Models Another Name for "Mechanics" or "Systems"?

In game studies and game development there are already a number of terms in common use for discussing games, such as "mechanics," "systems," and "rules." It's reasonable to ask whether one of these terms (or another) covers the same territory as "operational logics" or "playable models"—so that we don't introduce new terminology needlessly. But the common terms are both too narrow and too broad for discussing some of the key issues.

The term "mechanics" has been useful in discussing relatively low-level aspects of games. For example, in the context of the "Mechanics, Dynamics, Aesthetics" (MDA) framework it has helped illuminate how the low-level aspects of games (mechanics) shape the resulting gameplay (the dynamics) which in turn shapes the potential high-level player experiences (the aesthetics).[22] But as I mentioned in chapter 1, what precisely is meant by "mechanics" in game design and game studies is unclear. Even in the first academic publication on the MDA framework,[23] it is given two rather different definitions: "Mechanics are the various actions, behaviors, and control mechanisms afforded to the player within a game context" and "Mechanics describes the particular components of the game, at the level of data representation and algorithms."[24] And this kind of slippage is common, with "mechanics" being used to name very different kinds of low-level elements of games.

Perhaps for this reason, a number of alternatives have been offered. An especially rich time for this was the 2000s, when we saw an upwelling of formal accounts in the game design community. This upwelling is described by Katharine Neil, in an excellent review of game design tools, as the community's first moves from Christopher Alexander's "unselfconscious" to "self-conscious" design.[25] She follows in the tradition of Ben Cousins, who used the same distinction as the basis of an August 2004 blog post.[26] Cousins went on to coin the term "primary elements" in an article in October of that year[27]—a renaming of his earlier term "ludemes," which was published only on a private game design forum (in summer 2003).[28] In parallel, Raph Koster and Rod Humble, in the context of a discussion of *EverQuest II*, developed the idea of game "atoms"—with Koster publishing an essay on this idea to the same private forum in June 2004[29] and then making an influential conference presentation titled "A Grammar of Gameplay" in March 2005 (in which he also uses the term "ludemes").[30] Dan Cook, writing about the "Chemistry of Game Design" in 2007, extended the idea of "atoms" to focus specifically on "skill atoms."[31]

So, we might ask if one of these might be used, rather than the term "operational logics." Unfortunately, this runs into problems in each case. Koster's conception of atoms/ludemes, for example, is explicitly "fractal"—when we look closely at each game atom, we find deeper games within it, until we reach the level of players figuring out how to perform the physical actions that translate into control events. One of Koster's layers may be a near relative of logics, but it would be mischaracterizing his concept to use it to specify one level of games.

As for the conceptions of Cousins and Cook, these—like the "player actions" notion of mechanics—name units that are significantly broader than operational logics. They have this in common with their ancestor, Chris Crawford's notion of game "verbs."[32] For example, "jump" or "shoot" would qualify as a primary element, skill atom, verb, or mechanic.[33] But from an operational logics perspective, a mechanic such as "jump" (within a game like *Super Mario Bros.* or *Quake*) involves at least four logics, each functioning and being communicated to the player.

First, the jump is triggered by a control logic, which may also play further roles as the jump continues (depending on whether the length of a button press matters, whether double-jumping is allowed, and so on). Control is communicated to the player through animation (perhaps crouching and springing up), sometimes sound, and often the physical feel of a controller button depressing. Second, an entity-state logic shifts the character into a "jumping" state, which changes the available actions (it is no longer possible to walk, as it was a moment before). The new state is communicated by changes in the sprite or animation used to represent the character, different ways the character may respond to collision, and different responses (or non-responses) to control events. Third, the jump's trajectory is determined by a physics logic, which (as discussed above) may operate in a way closer to or further from the physics of our everyday world, shaping the parabola of the jump, and often taking into account the speed and direction of movement happening before the jump (which can be particularly important if a complex multi-jump pattern, like strafe jumping, is being attempted). Physics is communicated to players through the shape of movement, and perhaps changes to movement under different circumstances, so that players learn to have a sense of its operations over time. Fourth, the jump concludes with a collision logic—often the character's feet touching down on the ground or a platform, which in turn changes the entity state. But the jump-ending collision might also be falling through the bottom of the level, or running into the side of a ledge (or hitting the player character's head on the bottom of a block) that converts the jump into a fall (a different change in entity state). The shape and speed of a collision-activated fall state is also determined by physics. As discussed above, collision is communicated many ways, including animation, sound, and controller vibration.

In short, operational logics are a way of talking about a fundamental level on which games communicate what is happening to players and offer opportunities for play. They support game mechanics—and the things named with other, related terms. In this way, logics are more specific than mechanics.

But logics are also broader than mechanics, in a different sense. Discussions of mechanics generally treat them as stand-alone: jumping, shooting, running, collecting, building, trading, and so on. From such a perspective, it's hard to see what unites them—what players bring from one mechanic to the understanding of the next. Without considering the level of abstraction which is the focus of operational logics, it's hard to see that physics logics play a role in jumping, shooting, and running—while resource logics are key to collecting, building, and trading.

For some readers, this broader view of operational logics may place more emphasis on another terminology question: whether the term "systems" could be used instead of "logics" in this book. After all, it is not uncommon to talk about the "physics system" of a game, which is employed by many mechanics. But at the same time, it would be less common to talk about the "resource system"—and very uncommon to use the term system to name other common logics, from pattern matching to linking. This is because "system," when used to describe parts of video games, does not name the same level of abstraction as operational logics. Instead, the term *system* is generally used to mean something like, "a significant subset of the game's processes," often one used repeatedly to handle similar game situations. Sometimes this coincides with logics, but it is not the same.

"System" also shares with "rules" (or "rulesets") another distinction from the idea of operational logics. Logics are specifically communicative, algorithmic, and connected to play—each one names a way that games procedurally represent their worlds to players, operate internally (at a high level), and have opportunities for state change and interaction. Systems and rules, on the other hand, simply name things that exist in the game, or are true about the game, which need not make this kind of connection. *Spacewar*,[34] for example, had an entire system dedicated to producing a realistic starfield background, which had no influence on how the game was played.[35] And the rules of a game can be almost anything, from "The player starts with three lives" to "The poisonous toadstools are purple."

Finally, one can also imagine substituting the term "systems" for "playable models" (rather than as an alternative to "operational logics"). After all, it is common to talk about "crafting systems" and "combat systems"—referring to what are clearly playable procedural representations. But similar objections would apply as in the case of using "systems" rather than "logics." In discussions of games, a "system" can name something at almost any level of abstraction, which may or may not be representational or directly enable play—people talk about everything from "particle systems" to "natural language understanding systems." (The term "systems" is sometimes even used as a synonym for "mechanics.") A "playable model," on the other hand, is specifically a procedural representation that people come to understand and manipulate through play. It gives us a way to talk specifically about "how games are about things through play"—something I believe we need to talk about more.

What Logics Are There?

When we identify a logic or model, we are making an argument—we are offering an interpretation of how games work. For some aspects of games, no one has yet attempted to even catalog the foundational logics. (Probably the most notable such area is AI behavior.) More broadly, ideas continue to evolve, and people disagree.[36]

That said, I believe a project led by Joseph C. Osborn created a well-developed initial catalog of operational logic families found in games (see box 4.1, "Identifying Logics").[37] This collection has shown strong interpretive value, providing a vocabulary that explains the fundamental communication/computation pairings that underlie the experience of games from a wide range of genres. It has also shown strong value in technical research, providing a knowledge representation approach that has been useful in contexts ranging from automatically extracting game maps to modeling character jumps in action games and creating an intelligent game design system.[38]

In this book I use a modified version of Osborn's catalog, in which I gather together all pattern-matching logics into one family—much as both he and I gather together all resource logics into one family. Within each family there is much further work that could be done to catalog the types of logics we see in games, to describe their operations, and to outline knowledge about their effective use. Joris Dormans's foundational work on the Machinations framework is an example of doing something like this within the domain of resource logics.[39]

A Catalog of Logics

This book's modified version of Osborn's catalog includes the following major families of operational logics: camera, chance, collision, control, entity-state, game mode, linking, pattern matching, persistence, physics, progression, recombinatory, resource, and selection.

For each of these logics I will describe things that happen in games, which depend on the logic. Then I will briefly give a version of the logic's communicative role and abstract process.[40]

Camera logics. Many games—from 1980s arcade cabinets to contemporary mobile phone games—show the entire space of play on the screen at all times. At other times the world is larger than what we see on screen, as when we can turn around while

Box 4.1

Identifying Logics

Just as logics themselves are not obvious or natural, the identification and interpretation of logics and models itself is not natural. The decision to name, describe, and analyze a logic or model is an act of interpretation. Games do not come with a list of their key logics and models—and it is entirely appropriate to disagree about what they are, what roles they play, and how our thinking about them is best organized. For example, I talk about collision detection as a separate logic from movement physics, because of the primacy of collision to some games I discuss, and because their abstract processes are to me quite different. But others have suggested (in conversation) that collision is a component of physics—in our physical world, and sometimes in game implementations—rather than existing at the same organizational level. In other words, for them, that objects can collide is both part of what is communicated by physics and part of the abstract process of physics. Thinking in this way is most appropriate for the arguments they wish to make.

As for what makes a compelling argument for the identification of a logic more generally, Joseph C. Osborn explains the process behind his catalog in section 3.2 of his dissertation. His process begins by looking closely at games, trying to explain observed phenomena using existing logics. In the case of awkward fits, or failure to reflect both the abstract process and communicative role of a logic, he considers a new one:

> For example, a full resource pool inhibits the addition of new resources in a similar way as a collision logic inhibits the movement of objects into occupied space; but this blockage is hard to interpret successfully as *collision*, being more adequately interpreted as *saturation* or *exceeding capacity*. To detect a redundancy, fulfilling the abstract process is important; but I only have a truly redundant set if the communicative role—broadly construed—can be readily expressed by other logics.[41]

Further, his goal is to use the category of logics for fundamental elements of games—with other aspects being considered ways of using logics, or types of models, or simply other things games can do or communicate. He writes:

> I would prefer to work with a collision logic, but not a logic of space; a physics logic, but not a logic of driving or running; a resource logic, but not a logic of growth. While collision logics may be used to model space, and physics logics may be used to communicate running, and resource increase may be used to model personal growth, the latter set of concepts do not qualify as *primary* or *fundamental* logics: one can find other logics that model space, running, or growth equally well using completely different game state presentations and abstract processes. The "growth" of an object increasing in size is quite different from the "growth" of a character's strength statistic increasing.[42]

Osborn goes on to explain how he decided to include a camera logic (as in the moving viewport of *DOOM*) but not a vision logic (as in the roving eyes of NPCs in *Metal Gear Solid*[43]). Crucially, much "vision" in games is readily explained by collision logics (NPC vision cones) or resource logics (time-limited torches), whereas showing the player a moving sub-region of a game level is not explained by other logics in the catalog. Generalizing from this, Osborn identifies one of the two questions he asks "when attempting to explain

Box 4.1 (continued)

a modeled concept and determine whether it justifies the introduction of a new operational logic." It is: "does this candidate logic have a distinctive role?"[44]

Osborn's second question is whether a candidate logic has an implementable or usefully concrete abstract process.[45] Osborn provides scheduling as an example of a candidate logic excluded on these grounds:

> Games often have *scheduling*: for example, the turn order of a role-playing game or the alternation between players in a turn-taking game. But the abstract process this suggests—"determine who goes next and whose turn it is, and give the current player control"—is at once too generic and too specific. A good operational logic has a process which is abstract but puts constraints on possible implementations, and at the same time does not over-constrain its set of abstract operations and limit the contexts in which the logic can be used (recall that abstract operations describe the sorts of game state transitions that the logic enables). A scheduling logic phrased as above excludes the possibility of simultaneous turns, and if it expands any further to incorporate that it morphs into a version of the more general *control logic* ("different entities are controlled by different inputs at different times").[46]

Neither Osborn nor I would argue that the catalog included in this chapter is complete and definitive. But these families of logics provide good coverage of the phenomena observed in the games that we and collaborators have studied, while avoiding redundancy. Many of the logic families would benefit from more in-depth study—and this might result in arguments that they should be broken into smaller groups. Similarly, attention to games beyond those we have examined would likely lead to the proposed introduction of additional families of logics.

---

playing *DOOM*,[47] or survey a large geographic area in *SimCity*[48]—with different modes revealing different information (such as patterns of pollution or crime). In these cases, games use camera logics to communicate that the player has a potentially mobile viewport (or more than one) onto the game world. The main operation of these logics is to present a projection of the world space in a portion of the player's screen space (or occasionally into another portion of the world space, as with in-world surveillance systems). As with all logics, these can also provide operations that are specific to the larger model and game design—such as panning, zooming, and selective rendering—which are driven by their integration with other logics (such as control or entity-state logics).

Chance logics. The 20-sided die of *Dungeons & Dragons*[49] has become emblematic of the way that some tabletop games foreground randomness and its consequences. For computer games, randomness is often not communicated effectively to players—instead taking place as a hidden process from which they only see the results, which they may misattribute. When randomness is communicated in a way that players can understand, this is a chance logic. The communication could use approaches familiar from tabletop games (for example, a tabletop or computer solitaire game in which you "shuffle" and show a dwindling card deck) or through computationally specific techniques such as dynamic interface elements (perhaps exposing percentage chances or possible ranges).

Collision (Detection/Handling) logics. This is how Pac-Man eats. It is also what happens when one Chess piece takes another. More generally, this is a key way games communicate that objects occupy space—they can touch, and those touches can have consequences. The abstract process declares the intersection when the boundaries of two objects intersect, potentially triggering a reaction, as long as they are of types that should collide (there is no collision when, for example, Mario intersects with a cloud or when two *Candy Land*[50] characters are located at the same space).

Control logics. While there has been some amusing discussion of "zero-player games,"[51] a fundamental aspect of games is that they are played. This requires player control of game elements, and communication of that control. At the same time, other aspects of the game could be controlled by the game itself, or by other players, and that control could then be communicated in some way. The abstract process of control logics maps control events (button presses, wiggling in front of a Kinect camera, AI intentions, incoming network packets with actions of other players) onto the available high-level actions of the appropriate game entities.

Entity-State logics. When your game character switches from walking to running, jumping, or standing, and perhaps back again, it's a game entity changing state. We see this when many types of characters change size, change stance, gain abilities, and so on—potentially including more than one active state at the same time, with each being communicated in different ways. And it's not just characters that change state. Even simple moving platforms are operating in terms of this logic. The abstract process governs a limited, differentiated set of states for each entity, altering the game state presentation and operations of other logics when a new state is entered.

Game Mode logics. Just as a game character can change state, so the larger game can change how it operates. Perhaps we "pop out" to a menu that allows saving and quitting—or maybe "dive in" from a broad map view of the world to an encounter with a non-player character. When the game changes modes in this way, it is not only what we see that changes, but often what it is possible to do—perhaps navigation was possible previously, and now options for conversation or combat present themselves—and these changes are communicated. The abstract process is in some ways quite similar to entity-state logics, but it governs large subsets of the game's operations, activating and suspending a limited, differentiated set of game modes.

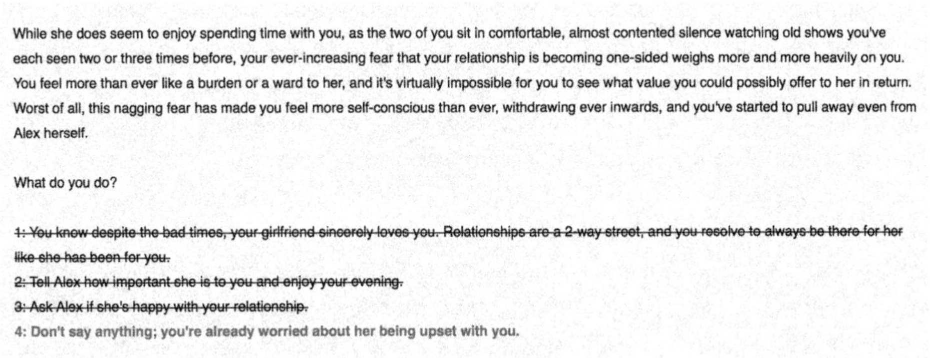

While she does seem to enjoy spending time with you, as the two of you sit in comfortable, almost contented silence watching old shows you've each seen two or three times before, your ever-increasing fear that your relationship is becoming one-sided weighs more and more heavily on you. You feel more than ever like a burden or a ward to her, and it's virtually impossible for you to see what value you could possibly offer to her in return. Worst of all, this nagging fear has made you feel more self-conscious than ever, withdrawing ever inwards, and you've started to pull away even from Alex herself.

What do you do?

1: You know despite the bad times, your girlfriend sincerely loves you. Relationships are a 2-way street, and you resolve to always be there for her like she has been for you.
2: Tell Alex how important she is to you and enjoy your evening.
3: Ask Alex if she's happy with your relationship.
4: Don't say anything; you're already worried about her being upset with you.

Figure 4.1
In *Depression Quest*, links can only be followed if their associated depression level is not exceeded. Unavailable links are struck through but remain legible, so that the player and character can consider what might be possible if things were different. (Image taken by the author during play.)

Linking logics. When we approach a cave entrance in a *Zelda* game and Link transitions to a new space, a linking logic is at work. The same is true when we click on a highlighted word in a Twine game and are brought to a character memory associated with that word. The same is true in games like *Ticket to Ride*,[52] which directly expose their link-based graph structures to the player. Linking logics communicate that things are connected to each other—in manners ranging from the literal to the metaphorical. Other logics (in a larger model) may govern whether links can be traversed, such as resource logics that determine whether the player has enough experience points to proceed to the next node in a skill tree or has too many depressive thoughts to select particular actions in *Depression Quest*[53] (figure 4.1). As Susana Pajares Tosca notes, when we can't see both sides of a link, "links force us to make meaning before and after travelling them"[54]—interpreting a highlighted word or cave entrance both before we traverse the link and after. The logic's abstract process is to follow or activate the currently available directed connections between game entities, perhaps performing some additional action through another logic (for example, traversing map links in *80 Days*[55] costs money, so a resource logic is involved).

Pattern-matching logics. We see pattern-matching logics in simple, human-operated games, such as Tic-Tac-Toe. We also see them with elaborate audio and visual effects, as with the special matches in *Bejeweled*.[56] Finding the correct way to match the pattern can be an intellectual challenge, as with a Rubik's Cube. Or knowing what patterns work can be key to successful play, as with the crafting table in *Minecraft*.[57] Some pattern matching is quite abstract, representing nothing but itself, as in playground hand-clapping games or hands in Poker. Other pattern matching can be seen as a stylized representation of something in the game world, such as personal grooming quicktime events in *Heavy Rain*,[58] special moves in *Street Fighter*,[59] or *Monopoly*'s[60] color-coded neighborhoods. And some pattern matching is comparatively unabstracted, as when the player must mimic on-screen moves in *Dance Central*[61] or when finding and checking all the elements of the current document pattern on the messy desk of *Papers, Please*.[62] In each case, the communicative role is that particular patterns can have effects—patterns which are often signaled through real-time prompting and feedback (as seen with the scrolling prompts of games like *Guitar Hero*[63] and *Rock Band*[64]) but not always (as in *Heaven's Vault*,[65] which allows, and has story content to account for, incorrect translations of its rune patterns). The abstract process is to enable or trigger events when objects enter, leave, or fail to match currently active patterns (arrangements, sequences, etc.).

Persistence logics. Many things can change in games. In the physical environment, doors can be opened and bridges lowered, crates and pots smashed, walls broken through or even blown apart, and so on. Characters and creatures can be talked with, traded with, and fought—sometimes leaving corpses on the ground. But if we walk out the door, or scroll the camera view over, or save the game and then return or reload, or change levels or lives, some of the changes may be undone. For example, when you get eaten in *Ms. Pac-Man*, the ghosts immediately respawn as your next life begins, no matter their prior state—but the current maze's consumed pellets and your score persist. Persistence logics communicate, generally by example, what things will stick around (the treasure chest remains empty, its contents remain in your inventory) and what will not (bullets are gone when they fly off screen, the battle carnage will be cleaned up as soon as you turn your back) within different game contexts. The abstract process preserves, resets, or disposes of game state data, based on changes at various context scopes (for example, the visible area or the current level).

(Movement) Physics logics. In *Portal*,[66] if you want to get up to a platform, you can position one side of your portal on the wall above the platform, the other on the ground, and then jump down through the ground to get up to the platform. Or you might miss, having too much momentum and flying past the edge of the platform and back down to the ground, maybe even back into the same portal you placed, picking up more momentum. In *Pong*,[67] the physics governing the movement of paddles and balls is much simpler, with no role for changes in momentum. Without a computer, the tabletop game *Momentum*[68] uses tile placement and human-operated rules to cause "dropped" marbles to push others off the board (figure 4.2). But all three games use their specific physics logic to communicate that entities can move in space and time,

Figure 4.2
While we associate movement physics logics primarily with video games, tabletop games like *Momentum* can also make stylized versions of physical laws a focus of gameplay. (Image courtesy of Néstor Romeral Andrés.)

obeying some version of physical laws. The abstract process is to update physical properties (position, velocity) based on the laws governing physics for that entity (which may be as simple as the scripted movement of a platform or include complexities of fluid dynamics, competing gravitational fields, or whatever else serves the model and game design).

Progression logics. In many games, quests and missions give players things to do, and track their progress at doing them. Player progression may unlock whole new areas of the game world or radically change the appearance or behavior of familiar areas. On a much smaller level, a non-player character may simply say, "Hello again" on your second interaction. Games often have multiple models incorporating progression logics, such as character skill progression (with associated perks) together with developing quest lines in *The Elder Scrolls V: Skyrim.*[69] Progression logics communicate that player actions can move the state of the game world forward, using tools ranging from triggered cutscenes to updating the player character's journal. While persistence logics communicate and govern what changes stick (rather than being reset), progression logics are about what changes matter, moving the game forward along pre-defined sequences. The abstract process, then, is to track and check measures of progress, potentially parameterizing the operations of other logics in the model (for example, changing the active set of links in a dialogue tree).

Recombinatory logics. While playing a game like *Rogue*[70] or *Diablo*,[71] even though the layout of each dungeon is uniquely generated, the rooms can start to be familiar. This is when we understand that a recombinatory logic is at work, communicating that some parts of what we experience are created out of smaller, potentially recognizable elements. A recombinatory logic is also at work in games and other forms of computational media (like Twitter bots) that use natural language generation systems such as Tracery[72] or Expressionist.[73] It is here that Osborn's catalog of logics most closely connects with AI techniques, and we can see where this becomes potentially troubling: the examples that seem most successful at producing engaging results (whether levels, language, items, bosses, or something else) may be those where the recombination becomes less apparent. The communication may drift from recombination to "intelligence," "emergence," or something else that could perhaps be addressed with processes that are not primarily recombinatory. In any case, the abstract process of a recombinatory logic is to build a structured object from a fixed set of elements, following a set of rules and constraints.

Resource logics. Games use many resources, not all of them the same. Every hit point, gold piece, or experience point is like all the others. But every property in *Monopoly* is unique, with its own name, location, and cost to develop. And many elements of games are in-between: resources that are not undifferentiated but also not unique. For example, to create something in *Minecraft*, you don't need a number of "crafting points" but rather a collection of different types of items (and any items of those types will do). Resource logics communicate that this wide range of resources can be acquired, held, and used—as appropriate for the model and game design—using communication strategies ranging from simple health bars to complex inventories that can be managed (sometimes represented using other logics, such as collision) and even to social wearables on the bodies of LARP players.[74] The abstract process creates, destroys, and moves discrete quantities of tangible or intangible resources (to use Dormans's terms[75]) between concrete or abstract locations, on demand or over time.

Selection logics. In the first phase of *Darfur Is Dying*,[76] we see the members of a family lined up across the screen (figure 4.3). As we move along the line (using a control logic) each one can be selected to try to gather drinking water, with the current selection shown with a highlight. If one of them is captured or killed while trying, it is no longer possible to select them. This is a simple selection logic, working together with control and resource logics. (Making the family unique members of a resource pool is more disturbing, in my experience, than if the resource was generic "lives.")

Figure 4.3
In *Darfur Is Dying*, the player uses a selection logic to indicate that Jaja will forage for water next. The faded images of Sittina and Poni indicate that they cannot be selected, having been lost to the militia during previous water collection attempts. (Image taken by the author during play.)

We see more complex selection logics when choosing a set of real-time strategy (RTS) game units to move, or a set of role-playing game (RPG) enemies on which to cast a spell, or a set of items to move to or from our inventories. Selection logics communicate that some things are available to be selected, that some subset of them is selected, and potentially that multiple different types of selection are active—with highlighting, icon placement, and sound effects being common communication strategies. The abstract process tracks sets of selectable and selected objects, updating them based on other logics and making them available to others.

How Do Logics and Models Work Together?

Many of the things that happen in games depend on logics working together—including the jumping mechanic example discussed earlier in "Are Logics or Models

Another Name for 'Mechanics' or 'Systems'?" as well as a number of other things mentioned in this chapter's logics catalog. A ball bouncing off a paddle requires physics and collision working together. Using a crafting table connects at least control, selection, resource, and spatial pattern-matching logics.[77]

These momentary connections are complemented by more long-lasting ones. Game characters, for example, are ongoing connection points for logics. A game character collecting a power-up in mid-flight is enacting an entity-state transition, triggered by collision, on an entity that remains under physics control the entire time. When the power-up expires, the same character should change its entity state, and perhaps become newly vulnerable to damage that reduces its health resource.

Osborn has suggested three ways that these combinations should be understood.[78] One he calls "communication channels." Here everything involved in the game state presentation, including visual and interaction design, comes into play. For example, when a bar is placed over a character's head, moving along with that character, visually literate (and especially game literate) players understand that the bar is associated with the character. If the bar progressively "empties" over time (losing color from one end), but "fills" again when the character collides with food, we may come to understand that it represents a "hunger" resource logic. The relationship between the collision logic and the resource logic is made apparent to players by using the character and the space around it (which holds the bar) as a shared communication channel.

When collision with food causes the hunger bar to fill—as when collision with a power-up causes the entity state to change—we can think of this as a direct connection between logics. Many game rules (or "mechanics" in the broader sense) are made up of these kinds of connections, with one logic having to act on a fact determined by another logic. Osborn terms these types of connections "operational integrations."

Finally, there are also compositions of logics that refer to some entity—some part of the game state—in common. It could be physics and entity-state logics knowing they should act on the same character over time. Or it could be the different parts of a crafting system knowing to act on the same character's inventory.[79] In these cases the "same" character or inventory must be unified across logics with different abstract processes and communicative roles. Osborn calls this "structural synthesis."

These kinds of connections can be discussed as enabling compositions of logics, as supporting the mechanics players use to play, as the foundation of the broader rules of the game world, and in many other ways. But I am particularly interested in the way logics come together in playable models—the concept of Michael Mateas's that is foundational for this book and much of the related research it describes.

As discussed in contrast with the term "systems" earlier in this chapter, playable models are a way of representing how something works in the game world, which players explore and come to understand through interaction. As described with combat, at the start of this chapter, for each thing we might want to represent in a game, there are a variety of combinations of logics that might enable the representation. This is different from operational logics, which have relatively stable combinations of less-specific communicative roles and abstract processes. Instead, for playable models we want to think about what is necessary for a model to serve as an interactive representation of something. Then we can consider how different logics and other game elements are, or could be, employed to provide those necessary things—or, to think about it another way, to meet those communicative and procedural obligations.

The different choices developers make in composing a model can create very different opportunities for designers, enable different experiences for players, and make different statements (consciously or unconsciously) about what is important about the thing being represented. For example, imagine that we are creating a playable model of conversation. We could decide, as a starting point, that any such model must support players being able to choose things to say as well as non-player characters (NPCs) offering responses.

One common way to meet these obligations is through linking logics. This type of model is called a "dialogue tree." The possible things the player could say are each linked to the appropriate NPC response, creating a tree-like structure of dialogue choices and replies. For game creators, a dialogue tree model offers the opportunity to choose the things that players might say. This means that writers can craft clever options, which provide both characterization and choices that map onto available game actions. On the other hand, writers *must* provide all the options, which quickly becomes an overwhelming authoring problem unless conversations are very short or the tree "folds back" on itself. The second of these options (foldback) is the one chosen, in practice, by most games using a dialogue tree model—and it quickly creates two kinds of problems. One problem emerges when the exact same lines are repeated, which works better in a Beckett play than when players return to "hubs" in what is supposed to be an ongoing conversation flow. The other problem is that the dialogue choices players make cannot necessarily have consequences that are incorporated into future nodes of the tree structure itself, because many choices lead to the same point later in the tree.

A solution to the second of these problems is to create a model that integrates an additional type of logic. A common choice is to add progression logics to the linking logics, creating a more complex dialogue tree. This can be used in simple ways, such as having one way an NPC will greet the player character the first time they meet, as well as a different one if they have met before. More complexly, player dialogue choices can shape the progression of character traits, making other dialogue options or in-game actions available (as with the "Paragon" and "Renegade" options in *Mass Effect*[80] dialogue). Or dialogue choices can lead to progression in quests or missions, including accepting them, completing stages of them, or choosing options within them. Alternately, dialogue trees can be augmented with resource logics, ranging from the simple getting and spending of currency through conversation to uses such as *Depression Quest*'s, discussed earlier. All of these are ways to provide consequence to dialogue tree options even after the player's traversal of the tree folds back to join a path also used by players who chose other options.

Of course, greater complexity also creates opportunities for breakdown. In *Expressive Processing*[81] I wrote about how the ambitious link-based progression structures of the dialogue and quest models for *Star Wars: Knights of the Old Republic*[82] were prone to breakdown when faced with the player's ability to move through space and trigger encounters in many orders. There is also the common problem of misalignment in progression structures, as when the world of a game (such as an *Elder Scrolls* RPG) allows the player to develop their character in many ways, but the progression structures of the dialogue trees all expect player characters to begin at a certain point—so that, for example, your powerful mage (who has been roaming the countryside, finding and exploring dangerous ruins) is assumed to be a callow beginner when you return to the dialogues for the main quest line.

But however one chooses to augment a dialogue tree model, and use the opportunities it presents for game creators, it may be that it doesn't present the right opportunities for *play*. If you want to create a game about dialogue, maybe you want to provide players the ability to choose things to say (to meet that obligation for a playable model of conversation) in some other way than selecting from a menu. Maybe imagining possible things to say, and exploring the space of possible system responses, is the key experience you want for players. The simplest conversation model that enables this kind of play is the one found in *Eliza/Doctor*[83] (which I also discuss in *Expressive Processing*). This uses a recombinatory logic to, in effect, translate anything a player might write into a response from the system. Like a dialogue tree model, it provides opportunities and presents pitfalls—but they are quite different ones. There is greater opportunity for play in what to say, but less coherence in responses, less structure of conversation flow, and less guidance in how to make meaningful moves in the wider game. Of course, the addition of more logics to the model can change these things. (For a different approach, see box 4.2, "Metaphorical Conversations.")

Box 4.2

Metaphorical Conversations

Most playable models, when they are implemented in a particular game, include relatively direct representations of the activity they enable players to engage in. Combat models include representations of specific attacks and defenses, while conversation models represent particular statements and replies. But it is also possible to represent an activity metaphorically, through an expansive use of a playable model of a different domain. For example, a game could represent conversation simply as reciprocal action, as seen in the "conversation *Pong*" examples in chapters 9 and 10. These don't provide opportunities for players to choose what to say, but this may be desirable for a particular game.

In a similar vein, the game *Florence*[84] shows conversation between the title character and her partner Krish as the reciprocal completion of speech bubbles. The bubbles contain no language—instead, they must be filled with colored puzzle pieces before they enter the conversation stream. Batu Aytemiz, Nick Junius, and Nathan Altice note how this is used to effectively communicate the act of conversation becoming easier for Florence during their first date:

> Initially, the player must drag eight different fragments to form a complete sentence bubble. This number shrinks to six, then four, and so on, until the player only needs to drag one puzzle piece to form a thought. Dragging one piece is seamless compared to fumbling with eight pieces, signaling that similar change has happened in Florence's conversation.[85]

However, such metaphorical approaches to conversation also run the risk of leading players to believe that the opportunities for play are different from those actually available. I found this in later chapters of *Florence*, in which Florence and Krish argue. The game animates putting together Krish's speech bubbles, with the pieces snapping quickly and sharply into place, each making an "impact" sound as they land, effectively communicating that the speech is produced in anger. This made me, playing as Florence, feel that I should be able to defuse the situation by putting my speech bubble together gently and slowly (figure 4.4). I tried and tried, but my pieces made the same impact sound however gently I moved them into the bubble—and however slowly and carefully I completed a bubble, it continued the argument. Because of course there's no actual connection between the way the control logic is used to take spatial pattern-matching actions and a social interaction model. The dialogue progresses angrily when you complete the pattern, and otherwise it just waits.

On some level this communicates the inevitable tragedy of the scene. But on another it's a headfake, leading to false expectations that pushed me out of the game for a while. And this type of tangle, of success and miscommunication, is far from unique to *Florence*. Rather, it is hard to avoid with metaphorical uses of playable models, as I discuss further in chapter 9.

Box 4.2 (continued)

Figure 4.4

By this stage in an argument in *Florence*, the connections between the puzzle pieces are sharp points, and the pieces are lined up to make an angry statement easy to assemble. But while the animation of Krish's statement construction also expresses emotion through the movements used to put the puzzle together, the player cannot change the expression in this way. (Image taken by the author during play.)

Stepping back from dialogue models—returning to the more general question of how playable models are constructed—for each of the logics integrated into a model, a game must have answers to the three questions discussed above: How will this logic operate? How will players understand this? And how does this fit into the game's design?[86] The answers often come from unexamined sources: through inheritance from a game engine, common game design practices, and so on—but not always. Answers are often considered anew (and new answers given) when a game is being designed with novel mechanics. The combined answers to these questions help players understand (consciously and unconsciously) how the game is representing the subject of the model, which is often something that also exists in our world, such as combat or conversation.[87] Osborn puts it this way:

> How can a designer construct a playable model for some real-world system? How can they ensure that they produce a system which both models a concept and makes that model playable? Simulations are built out of rules, and these rules are enacted by computation; but playability requires that these rules are communicated in a way that helps players understand the operations of the system. From an authorial standpoint, operational logics provide the building blocks of readable rules, and for the player their literacies in operational logics give them a *ladder* which they can climb to understand the model.[88]

Further, operational logics provide not only the building blocks for readable rules, but also for the opportunities for play that reveal the structures that the rules operate over and within. For example, exactly the same image could appear on a player's screen in a game like *Myst*[89] (with a spatial model founded on linking logics) or a game like *DOOM* (with a spatial model founded on movement physics logics). When the player uses a control logic to navigate the space, both the nature of the model and the shape of the space are revealed. Some aspects of this happen immediately, as when a spatial model based on movement physics is shown to be operating in two or three dimensions. Others happen over time, as when we learn whether the game's spaces operate the way our world does. For example, in Tamiko Thiel and Zara Houshmand's *Beyond Manzanar*,[90] it is possible to enter an internment camp building from the California desert landscape in which it sits, then walk out of that building into a Japanese garden, which we experience through its control and linking logics (figure 4.5). Alternately, in experiences like Alexander Bruce's *Antichamber*[91] and Jun Fujiki's objective locative environment (OLE) coordinate system prototypes (which formed the basis of Sony's *echochrome*[92]) we must learn to think in terms of Escher-like spatial structures, through particular uses of camera, physics, and control logics.[93]

Finally, to complete the picture, smaller models provide building blocks for larger ones, which players come to understand individually and in their connections. For

Figure 4.5
Encountering ghosts in *Beyond Manzanar*. Through the windows, we can see the California desert from which we entered the building. But if we exit through the far door, we find ourselves in a Japanese garden instead. (*Beyond Manzanar*, large screen virtual reality projection, Tamiko Thiel and Zara Houshmand, 2000/2017.)

example, the connected dialogue trees and quests of an RPG are generally the core of the game's narrative model. These are often connected to other models, such as a model of the player character (with skill progressions, a health resource, an inventory model, etc.), a model of space, a model of combat, and so on. Growing to understand these models and their connections is how players understand the broader game.

These connections between playable models are also an exciting—and under-discussed—site of game meaning. As outlined in chapter 3, the power of *Papers, Please* depends on the connection between its pattern-matching and resource models. The choice of whether to attempt correct pattern matching (which produces payment for the player character and results in the suffering of others) is given context and consequence by the family's precarious resource situation—a connection designed to produce complicity. Further, the connections between models do not have to be as direct as one producing what is needed for another. For example, Paolo Pedercini writes about the contrasting experiences of *Cart Life*,[94] which combines a resource model (of precarious service work) with a story model (in part inherited from its platform, Adventure

Game Studio). As Pedercini puts it, "In *Cart Life* the numeric, formalized, computational core of the game is exposed in its harshness while the loose, narrative, player-driven component outlines an enticing world of qualities—possibly, even a different way of living."[95] A related comparison could be drawn between the graphical model gameplay (of drone strikes and a video game-within-the-game) and link-based dialogue/story model gameplay (discussions with a co-worker, a spouse, a child, and the player character himself) of Pedercini's and Jim Munroe's game *Unmanned*,[96] discussed in chapter 7.

5   Inventive Approaches

Beyond Metaphor

Passage[1] can be a powerful experience, but what if you wanted to go further? What if you wanted courtship to be more than a moment's touch? Or partnership more than walking together? What if you wanted to include other characters, perhaps children, and wanted your actions with one to shape how others saw you?

For some of these ideas, an approach like *Passage*'s could continue to work.[2] Perhaps a compelling courtship game could be created as a series of playful, mutual touches.

But for other ideas, a different approach would be needed. Imagine multiple characters interacting, with changing attitudes toward each other, informed by a shared history, and expressing their motivations in a way players can understand, over an extended period of time. At our present moment, to make such a game would require an *inventive* approach.

An inventive approach uses one or more operational logics and/or playable models that aren't in the common vocabulary of video games.[3] From the 1950s through the 1970s, inventive approaches introduced the key vocabulary of logics and models for objects and resources that is still in wide use today. Some of the inventive work since has been primarily technical, such as the work to bring real-time 3-D spatial models to personal computers, enabling the FPS genre. Other inventive work has been primarily design-oriented, as seen in the development of the computer RPG genre—from importing of the model of character progression found in tabletop RPGs to developing the dialogue tree model of conversation.

Inventive efforts continue anywhere there is work to bring new logics or models to games. These logics or models might be based, in part, on computational processes already in use for related purposes elsewhere—perhaps running as part of non-interactive simulations or on supercomputers far beyond the reach of most game players. Or the processes might be new, invented for the purpose of enabling new kinds of video game play. Or the processes might have already been tried in a previous game, but the new game introduces or develops a new approach to their core elements or implementation—the incremental inventive work that is key to new logics and models eventually creating meaningful new play experiences.

Chapter 7 takes a look at the invention of the common "graphical logics"—collision detection, control/navigation, and movement physics—that are at the heart of the visual, continuous spatial models of many games. In this chapter, instead, I want to look at a much less established area: playable models of social interaction that enable richer relationships between game characters (including with player characters). This is an area of video games in which a new set of logics and models is struggling toward birth. Specifically, I examine *Prom Week*,[4] a game I helped make, and our struggles to develop a particular, key model: social volition.

Games and Social Models

Most video games have no model of social relationships. For example, in a *Medal of Honor* game you may have squad mates, and in the fiction of the game they may be presented as the most important people in the world to the player character, but there is nothing the player can do to shape those relationships in any way. They move along according to the game's script, just as they would in a war movie.

Some games are exceptions to this. In some simulation games (such as *The Sims*[5]) and some role-playing games (such as *Dragon Age: Origins*[6]), character relationships can change over time. Some of the potential relationship elements are binary, on/off, such as the player character being in a romantic relationship with a non-player character (NPC). Some potential relationship elements are variable numbers, able to grow and shrink over time, such as a feeling of closeness between characters. These can be related. For example, a high feeling of closeness might be a necessary condition for starting a romantic relationship. Also, these elements can be used cleverly. For example, as a relationship value gets higher it could become harder to move upward, so that a player can't "grind" their relationship with an NPC up to its top value by giving an ongoing series of small gifts.[7] Rather, something bigger may be required, such as completing an NPC-specific side quest.

But fundamentally, these are impoverished models of relationships, lacking context and history. They are unable to represent the richness of social connection we find in media that tell us something about being alive. A Sim may be sad because of her grandmother's death or angry that her father did something insensitive, but if she doesn't, and her father doesn't, and the game doesn't understand those reasons for her sadness and anger as part of an ongoing relationship, they can't be used to create a more compelling, meaningful experience—and may instead create a nonsensical one.

However, it also isn't obvious how to move beyond this, as the rest of this chapter will explore.[8] As noted above, my primary focus will be on the game *Prom Week*, developed at the Expressive Intelligence Studio of UC Santa Cruz, a lab that Michael Mateas and I run together. We see the role of the university in games as a place to take risks and push boundaries, so our explicit goal was to explore ideas not covered by previous work in the area. In particular, we wanted to cover territory not explored by the previous highwater mark in playable models of social relationships: the game *Façade*,[9] which Mateas created with collaborator Andrew Stern and released in 2005.

Façade is an interactive drama, in which the player sees a troubled couple (Grace and Trip) from the perspective of an old college friend. The NPCs speak and interrupt in real time, as does the player character, and it is possible to move around the apartment and interact with people and objects (figure 5.1). This offers a lot of channels of communication. The characters' expressions change from moment to moment. They have many different things they can say, and different ways they can say them, based on the current topic and their feelings of affinity for the player. Where they stand and look is meaningful. And they pay attention to all these things as the player does them, as well as to everything from objects the player picks up to physical gestures made by the player (such as hugging and kissing) and patterns in what the player says over time.

Given all these means of communication (and concerted effort to make character motivations legible) *Façade* is quite successful at helping players retrospectively understand social volition, which I believe is a key element for games with social models. Trip fixes a drink because the player asks for one. Grace turns her back on Trip because the tension between them is high. Trip reveals his feelings of class anxiety, in comparison to Grace's parents, because the player keeps returning to related topics of conversation. And this retrospective understanding helps players develop their forward-looking, prospective ideas of what the characters might do—which are further improved by replaying the game and learning what sorts of social actions are possible.

But *Façade*'s social volition is implemented in such a way that it is "baked in" to the specific characters and the specific actions that take place between them and the player. That is to say, *Façade* doesn't have a general notion of the ways characters can feel about themselves and each other, the kinds of social actions that they are likely to initiate as a result, the different forms those actions may take, and the possible responses they are likely to give to the actions of others. It doesn't have a separable model of

Figure 5.1
In *Façade*, the player reassures Grace and Trip about the apartment's decorating, while neither meets the player's gaze. The characters' blocking, facial expressions, gestures, language, and vocal delivery are all used to communicate their current emotional states, feelings toward each other and the player, and reactions to events. This creates a context for interpreting why they do what they do and projecting what they might do next. (Image courtesy of Michael Mateas.)

social interaction. And that is perfectly fine for the experience it aimed to create—an "existence proof" of the possibility of interactive drama.

Our goal with *Prom Week*, then, was to push in exactly the directions where *Façade* didn't try to go. We wanted to create an experience of "social physics," in which players could learn how the social model worked, through experimentation and feedback— and then use that knowledge to push a wide cast of characters, in a variety of scenarios, in many different possible directions, seeing satisfying results. Among other things, this required actually implementing social volition as a defined model (rather than baking it into the larger system, as with *Façade*'s dynamic script), taking an approach that could be learned from and improved upon by future games. Given our resources, it also required backing away from the many expressive channels of communication in *Façade*—foregoing *Façade*'s real-time dramatic interaction (supported by voice acting and more complex animations) for written text and simple animation, delivered in short scenes.

We chose as our game's setting the week leading up to the graduating students' final dance in a US high school. Each "level" is a play-through of that week focusing on a different character, with a variety of goals for that character that players can choose to pursue, ignore, or subvert. Achieving different goals in different ways creates different endings, shaping player imaginations of the lives that characters will go on to lead after high school. At the end of each level, the world resets to the same state, so that players can build and use knowledge of the world (including its backstory) as they play further levels. *Prom Week*'s creation was led by UC Santa Cruz graduate students Josh McCoy, Mike Treanor, Ben Samuel, and Aaron Reed, with contributions from around twenty additional graduate students, undergraduates, and even people outside the university. It was first released on Valentine's Day in 2012, with a major update that October.

Social Volition in *Prom Week*

Work toward *Prom Week* began before I arrived at UC Santa Cruz, though none of us knew it at the time. Mateas was deep in discussions with McCoy (who as an undergraduate had studied both computer science and social science) about playable models of social interaction.[10] The first small system they built focused on ideas of social stigma. But increasingly their attention (and, after I arrived in 2008, mine) turned to the idea of social performances or "games"—which we eventually came to call *exchanges*—that could be carried out differently by different characters, in different situations, but would serve the same goals.[11] This is an idea that runs through the social science literature in different forms, from academically influential work such as Erving Goffman's *The Presentation of Self in Everyday Life*[12] to mainstream bestsellers such as Eric Berne's *Games People Play*.[13]

From a certain perspective, this wasn't an entirely new idea to video games. Many games do something similar with animations. An animation is created and then *retargeted*, allowing different characters (with different models and sometimes different bone structures) to use the animation in their own way.[14] This allows each character to have a much richer variety of animations than the team could create if they were specific to each character. Our goal was to extend this to social exchanges.

Of course, something had to motivate these exchanges, provide ongoing context for them, and otherwise define "how the world works." Further, we needed a way to expose these things to the player, a context for the player to learn about them, and a situation in which the player could exercise that knowledge. In other words, we needed to develop both our model and a game, so we asked who in the lab would be interested in joining a team to pursue both.

McCoy named the model *Comme il Faut* (or "CiF") which roughly translates to "being in accord with conventions or accepted standards," because our initial vision was to define the world in terms of social norms, the often-invisible shared expectations of behavior that are noticed most when they are violated. This meant that, by default, characters would be motivated to do the same things. Only their differences of personality or situation would motivate acting differently from what the default norms would suggest—and so the only thing needed to define a character would be these differences. The question was what they should be. A number of potential answers presented themselves, both from the social science literature and from our own thinking about media focused on relationships.

In parallel, we considered a number of different potential scenarios for the game that would become *Prom Week*. At first we considered a dinner party, perhaps in Victorian or Regency Era England. But in the end we decided, following common fiction writing advice, to choose something "closer to the bone" for our student team—settling on the high-stakes social moment of the high school prom.

Our first prototype was a failure, but one from which we learned a lot.[15] In it two factions—"goths" and "emos"—were socially maneuvering for the favor of the DJ at the school's "alt prom." This version of the game was created as a paper prototype, but incorporated computational assistance. Gameplay happened on a tabletop, with the results of each tabletop action determined by running a version of CiF on a nearby laptop (figure 5.2). In that version of CiF, the key motivations of each character were determined by adapting the sixteen "basic needs" from the recently published book *The Normal Personality* by Steven Reiss.[16]

As a set of ideas, it all made perfect sense. The players could activate needs for the characters. The drive to satisfy those needs would lead to characters initiating social exchanges. The exchanges would have fallout in the social world, which the DJ would like or dislike.

It was meant to be a very simple scenario in which to explore initial ideas, but even we couldn't play it. Despite the fact that we all knew exactly how the system worked, as an approach to volition it was quite opaque. Satisfying a need for "power," "honor," or "independence" didn't match how we thought about characters. We didn't know, when playing, what type of exchange it would spark for a particular character in a particular situation, and even in retrospect it wasn't always clear (without looking at the software) why a character had made a certain choice.[17] As a result, we realized that our approach to social volition might lead to interesting, unpredictable social storytelling, but it wasn't a good match for enabling social play.

Figure 5.2
Puzzled players of the "alt prom" prototype, in which character actions were driven by sixteen "basic needs" from *The Normal Personality* by Steven Reiss. The prototype combined printed materials and software. Pictured, from left to right: Gillian Smith, Noah Wardrip-Fruin, Michael Mateas, Ronald Liu, and Josh McCoy. (All individuals pictured appear by permission.)

We also learned important things from asking other members of the lab and outside players to talk aloud about their thinking as they tried the first prototype. People talked a lot about relationships—who felt friendly toward each other, or admired each other, or were attracted to each other. They talked about events that had happened in the game, and how they might leave characters feeling and acting (such as embarrassed). They talked about how those historical events, current feelings, and long-term personality traits might influence choices of what to do.

It became clear that, rather than a focus on internal needs or drives, the elements coming up in these conversations should be the ones driving social volition. For the next version of CiF, we supported the common-sense social reasoning we'd heard, along lines like this: "He won't ask her out, because even though he's attracted to her, he's introverted, and the last time he talked with her he ended up embarrassed."[18] We also later added "triggers," so that the social state could be further changed after a social exchange (for example, if a character starts dating during an exchange, but they are already dating someone else, a trigger rule will give them the status of "cheating"—something to which their first partner might have a great desire to respond).[19] In early 2010 we put together a demo called *Promacolypse* (in part to have something to show off at the upcoming Game Developers Conference) using this common-sense social reasoning approach. It had a body of rules that would raise and lower the amount characters wanted to do something—their volition for a particular social exchange—based both on norms for what people "should" generally do in the high school and on ways that someone with particular personality elements, in particular circumstances, might act differently.

To be specific, I'd say we arrived at a particular volition model, which combined two types of logics.[20] First, the model includes a *rule-evaluation logic*. This determines things that are true about the world (some of which are exposed to the player), including what social exchanges are possible for characters to initiate (actions have "preconditions" that may or may not be met), when the triggers mentioned above are activated, and so on. One can imagine building a social volition model entirely with logics of this type—perhaps with each game character, at each time step, carrying out the first exchange found with preconditions that are all true, or choosing among them randomly, or presenting them as a list to the player.[21]

But the social volition model for CiF instead combines this with another logic. We might call this something like a *ranked-choice logic*: of the many possible exchanges that characters might initiate, a few types are selected as the most appropriate and exposed to the player, and of the possible responses to each exchange, one is selected as part of the enactment of the exchange. In the CiF social volition model, such rankings are populated through connection with the rule-evaluation logic. Many of *Prom Week's* social rules are written so that they increase or decrease the likelihood of characters initiating types of social exchanges, or the likelihood of accepting or rejecting what other characters attempt through social exchanges—or to guide the selection of the most appropriate specific exchange to enact, within a particular type.[22]

All of these rules can take into account, and thereby work to reveal, the structures shared with the larger social model. Most key to these are the structures used for defining characters: long-term personality elements, short-term statuses, and current feelings of relationship and history with other characters.

This volition model, as part of the larger model of social interaction, enabled a new kind of gameplay. Players were able to form goals for the social world and explore a variety of different paths to pursue them, each of which would send differently shaped ripples through the life of the high school. For example, imagine the player notices that two characters—Nicholas and Kate—are in a relatively loveless relationship (they have low feelings of romance for each other). The player decides to instead get Nicholas together with his "frenemy" Oswald. Even though they have some negative history together, they also have a lot more romantic passion for each other.

The player could try to have Nicholas or Oswald ask the other out. But perhaps Oswald is opposed to cheating—he won't want to ask Nicholas out, and he'll decline if Nicholas asks him out. It might seem that Kate and Nicholas will have to break up first. But even though Kate and Nicholas are not that interested in each other, neither one currently wants to break up. The player will have to find ways to change the world until they do. Right now they don't want to do anything negative with each other.

One option might be to have Nicholas flirt with Oswald. Even if Oswald doesn't respond, it could still bother Kate enough to make a negative social exchange rise to the top group in her choice ranking. But the player might notice a different option. Perhaps one of Nicholas's friends, Monica, has a history of putting Kate down—so Kate is pretty mad at her. Maybe it's time for Kate to finally tell Monica how she feels. If she does this, Nicholas, who has a strong friendship with Monica, will likely be mad at Kate. This could be the moment that destabilizes the Nicholas/Kate relationship that the player has decided to end.

Each of these options will change the larger high school in different ways. If Nicholas flirts with Oswald, perhaps he might even build up their mutual feelings of romance until he can overcome Oswald's resistance to being in an unfaithful relationship. But in the process he'll get a reputation as a cheater and Oswald will get a reputation as a homewrecker, which will factor in as other characters decide what they want to do with them (and how they will respond to the things they initiate) in the future. If Kate unloads on Monica, it could provide the inciting incident for a breakup between her and Nicholas—but all of Monica's friends will remember Kate's actions, and potentially respond to her differently, not just Nicholas. And, of course, there are many other options that might present themselves, each with different potential repercussions. Maybe the player instead decides to build up Kate's relationship with Doug, bonding over their shared love of skateboarding, setting the stage for a budding romance that might give Kate a reason to walk away from her current, passionless match.

The *Prom Week* Interfaces

We were proud of the *Promacolypse* demo, in part because of the approach to social volition and the gameplay it enabled. We could tell there was a compelling experience there. The characters and social world felt real and ongoing, but also like they could be deeply shaped by players in intended directions. And so we began to think, and continued to think, wrongly, for the next two years, that we were about six months away from finishing *Prom Week*.

What made us so wrong? We were missing one of the key elements of inventing new models, and new versions of logics to work with them. We had a theory we'd implemented for the operations. We had a compelling use in gameplay that opened exciting opportunities for players. But we were not yet communicating the operations of the logics and model successfully. As a result, other people still couldn't have a strong experience of play.

Part of the issue was a challenge we had set for ourselves. In fiction writing, or dramatic acting, or *Façade*, the social state is revealed retrospectively by social action. Characters say things, have facial expressions, or take broader actions in the world that let us know, looking back, the most important parts of how they're feeling. We instead wanted to create a game in which players could look forward in the social world, understand what is most important to characters, and then shape social action before it takes place. We needed a way other than action to communicate how characters are in a social world.

Our initial instinct was to focus on the three social "networks"—friendship, romance, and coolness—that we had chosen to connect all the characters. The team was doing in-depth analysis of media about high school (such as *Mean Girls*[23]) and other media focused on social relationships (such as *Sex and the City*[24]), which was informing the writing of rules for social behavior, and such networks played an important role in the emerging body of rules.[25] In the *Promacolypse* demo such networks could be overlaid on the main view of the game, once an active character and network were chosen (figure 5.3).

The interface also had a bar that showed what the character most wanted to do, offered the option to learn more about their personality, and so on. It took a long while, as well as experimentation with a lot of interface elements, to realize that we had things backward. Here's what we eventually realized: Just as characters in fiction best reveal themselves through the actions they take, characters in a game like *Prom Week* best reveal themselves through the actions they *wish to take*. It is when a player wonders *why* a character wishes to take an action that access to information about social connections, underlying personalities, current statuses, and interpersonal history becomes important. In other words, we needed to emphasize the outcomes of the ranked choice logic—making that the gateway to exploring the workings of the rule-evaluation logic and the model's structuring information.

Figure 5.3
The width of directed bars running between characters shows social network values in the *Promacolypse* demo. Here we see Karen's romantic feelings toward Edward and Simon. (Screen shot taken by the *Prom Week* team.)

You can see us slowly learning this lesson through the interfaces that followed. By 2011, we had moved social networks to the top of the screen, which makes them less central but also makes them constantly visible (figure 5.4). The actions the active character most wants to take with the selected character appear in the main view, but there is no way to dig more deeply into why they are desired—as soon as one is selected it is carried out. And the networks are brightly colored, while the desired actions are muted.

By the time of the game's beta and initial release, in early 2012, the actions characters wish to take are finally given major prominence. But we haven't fully abandoned our earlier ideas. For example, when the interface is expanded, we are still displaying arrows for network values relatively prominently (figure 5.5). Also, we haven't found a good way to take the detailed information we had about why characters desire certain actions and integrate it into the display of actions—but at least it is possible, once an action is chosen, to dig deeper into the social volition behind the character's desire to perform it (through the interface at the bottom of the screen).

Finally, in conversation with Eric Loyer and others, Treanor and Samuel spent the time before *Prom Week*'s appearance at IndieCade 2012 developing the last version of the interface (figure 5.6). We realized that many players would recognize the thought

Figure 5.4
In a 2011 version of *Prom Week*, we see the actions that Naomi most wishes to initiate with Cassie—but in muted colors, arranged around Cassie's head. At the top of the screen, in bright colors, we see the social network values (with strength now indicated by line length, rather than width) and an icon indicating that they are friends. (Screen shot taken by the *Prom Week* team.)

balloon as a convention from comics, and this allowed us to strip away much interface complexity, instead putting key information into such balloons.

In this interface, the active character can quickly switch between "thinking about" other characters in the scene. A small thought bubble appears next to each of them, indicating their network values with short phrases (rather than line length or thickness), and showing whether they have one of the three types of relationships that other characters recognize (key structuring information and current values for rule evaluation). A much larger thought bubble lists the social exchanges the active character most wants to try with the selected character (results of ranked choice). These provide a strong window into the character's social volition and, next to each, an "information" icon allows the player to delve deeper into the reasons the character desires to take that action (results of rule evaluation and a window into the nature of the specific rules, the structures over which they operate, and current values).[26] Players can also choose

Figure 5.5
By early 2012, the interface for displaying the social network values (and digging further into character motivations) has moved to the bottom of the screen, while the actions characters wish to take are displayed in brighter colors. (Screen shot taken by the *Prom Week* team.)

to use a resource to reveal, ahead of time, how characters will respond to an attempted exchange—and this, too, is revealed textually, using language that gives a sense of how far they are from changing their minds, and offering the opportunity to dig into why. In the process, an interested player can discover more about character histories, personalities, influences from the feelings of other characters, and much more. This reveals not only what motivates that particular potential action, but also contextualized information about how the broader system works.

Of course, even once we were satisfied with our approach to social volition and its communication, the question remained: Would this work for a broader audience, not just the friendly play-testers we had recruited?[27] If it did, we hoped they would react to the social relationships in *Prom Week* in a way quite different from the relationships in other games. We wanted players to feel responsible for what happens in a way they don't with pre-scripted social relationships like those in a *Medal of Honor* game—and

Figure 5.6
In the final *Prom Week* interface, the most prominent information is what characters wish to do with each other, and social network values are expressed in language. (Screen shot taken by the *Prom Week* team.)

to feel that social actions mattered in a way they don't with the weightless characters of *The Sims*.

My belief, based on the responses we saw (though many of them came before the final version of the interface) is that we took an important step toward these goals. For example, here is part of what Craig Pearson wrote on the games-oriented site *Rock, Paper, Shotgun*:

> I was looking for anything to exploit: a rumour I could spread, more friendship bonds to break. But then I genuinely started to worry about what I was thinking about. After the grim social strategies I'd been considering, did I deserve to be Prom King? Think back to how you acted as a teenager? Every devastating thing you said to a friend, just to cause trouble. I never liked the me that grew up in Glasgow. I wanted to get away from my teenage years, from those cruel, unnecessary barbs I slung. Yet I was here, hovering a mouse over a teenage girl, looking to see how I could bend her emotions to my will. I decided to make no more moves and skipped to the story resolution. I'd take a lose over actively attacking any more of Zack's confidence.
>
> Then Naomi announced Zack and Lil were Prom King and Queen. I'd won.

The reason why had nothing to do with the theatre of cruelty that I'd just directed: over the course of the night, I'd made friends with Naomi, and she was looking out for me when the votes were in: everyone had voted for themselves, and because we were nice (to her) and she knew how much it meant to Zack, she'd given me the crown. I didn't need to be cruel, which made me feel even worse. I just saw horror and cruelty when the opportunity arose. I presumed I'd need to be nasty, but that route got me nowhere. Not that it wouldn't have worked, and horribly it makes me want to see if I could destroy Buzz, but I won the game by accidentally being nice and friendly.

So now I feel bad and impressed, and want to play it all over again.[28]

Writing from a different perspective, Alastair Stephens (then best known as co-host of the StoryWonk podcast), reviewed *Prom Week* with a focus on story, rather than gameplay:

The genius of *Prom Week* isn't that it stitches a myriad of disparate stories together seamlessly— that's an admirable technical achievement, certainly, but it's less immediately important than you might think. Rather, the triumph here is the evocation of the heroism and heartache of a high-school prom. The complexity of these relationships is absolutely, intricately mechanical— but like all successful stories, it swiftly moves beyond the mechanical, beyond the ludic, to the personal and emotional. The temptation to manipulate these characters is enormous, but crossing that line feels . . . wrong. It's all to[o] easy to stop guiding, to stop storytelling, and to start puppeteering. In the end, I stopped playing *Prom Week* because I didn't like the person I felt like when I played it, and I can think of no greater compliment than that.

But I'll be back tomorrow, Simon. You and me, buddy. You and me.[29]

I realize it might seem odd to quote two authors who both felt bad after playing the game, but in some ways the potential for them to feel bad is an illustration of what we were seeking.[30] For these players to feel bad they needed to understand the social model well enough to be manipulating it intentionally (to feel responsible for the outcome) and they also needed to feel that the characters were real enough that shaping their lives wasn't entirely meaningless. To put it another way: Players often set Sims on fire for fun. If some players of *Prom Week* felt bad just manipulating emotions, something succeeded. Players understood characters' social volitions enough to work with them, and these desires were portrayed in a way that could actually evoke human empathy.

Two Directions for Social Models

At the moment I am writing, I believe we have two choices of how to pursue future playable models of social interaction for video games.

The game *Redshirt*,[31] released the year after *Prom Week*, points in one possible direction. The game's creation was led by Mitu Khandaker at the same time that she was pursuing a PhD at the University of Portsmouth, based on a completely different games-focused project, a remarkable feat. Set on a space station with some familiarity to *Star Trek*[32] fans, *Redshirt* doesn't feature exciting encounters with alien civilizations (in fact, "away missions" are handled minimally) or even the ability to explore the space station itself. Instead, almost all interactions take place through Spacebook, the station's social network. This allows the game to leverage widespread familiarity with social network interfaces and behaviors—both as scaffolding for interactions and for purposes of parody. As *Prom Week* co-creator Reed argues, "The genius of this as procedural rhetoric, of course, is in presenting a story world where there is no distinction between making real human connections and performing them on social media: the act and the online representation thereof become one and the same."[33]

Redshirt works with science fiction tropes in an amusing way. The player character's first job is as a "Transporter Accident Cleanup Technician," and the descriptions and simple animations of what happens at work are cheerfully gruesome. And this aspect comes together with the engagement of social issues in a number of ways. For example, if you choose to play a member of the Asrion species (who appear as green- or light-blue-skinned females, no matter what the player chooses on the gender slider or skin color selector) you will be bombarded with Spacebook flirts, even from beings you don't know (figure 5.7). This recapitulates something familiar to those who have watched the original *Star Trek* series (or played the *Mass Effect* games), but it also was uncomfortably unexpected for some players, leading to a mini-controversy after Khandaker explained that this behavior could be avoided.[34] When I played as a member of this species, my character's boyfriend regularly said he "saw me flirting" with other characters, even though I had taken no such action—and I had no way to respond. It left me feeling frustrated, unable to manage how others saw me and my actions, which I think is exactly what was intended.

In general, *Redshirt* is quite successful with this kind of social volition—characters taking actions that enact tropes of social network interaction and its SF setting. But *Redshirt* has a harder time with volition in the ongoing social world. When I played, I had old friends begging to spend time with me—and then, without explanation, not showing up when I invited them to do things. I had someone steal my girlfriend—and then feel "jealous and neglected" that I didn't invite him to hang out in my quarters. I asked someone else to be my girlfriend (via a Spacebook relationship request, as with all social interactions) and she didn't respond. Instead the game told me she was feeling bad we hadn't interacted, when I'd just interacted with her in the most consequential way the game includes.

Figure 5.7

When playing an Asrion in *Redshirt*, the player character is constantly accused of flirting with other characters, no matter the actions of the player (unless the bigotry setting is reduced from the default level). Here, my character, JO2 SPACEMAN, is accused by her boyfriend, NOF VIJEN, twice in quick succession—as seen in the right-hand interface elements, halfway up the screen. (Image taken by the author during play.)

While the details of *Redshirt*'s social model aren't available, my experience of it left me with no ability to get past the Spacebook interface to actually understand the motivations of the characters. Without understanding their volition, without understanding why they did what they did, I didn't feel empathy for them. I don't know if the underlying model was as simple as the interface suggested, but for me it might as well have been.

And creating simple social models is certainly one direction we could pursue as a field.[35] But then the most effective design and play strategy—the one, in fact, that I pursued when playing *Redshirt*—will be to focus on the player treating the NPCs like objects. That is to say, we will be closer to the experience of games such as *Layoff*[36] (discussed in chapter 3) than to the goals discussed earlier in this chapter. Or perhaps it might be even better to treat the characters as enemies—as seen in the delight players find in manipulating the social relations of Orcs in *Middle-Earth: Shadow of Mordor*.[37]

The other path we might pursue for the future of playable models of social behavior is exemplified by *Blood & Laurels*,[38] released in 2014. The game was created primarily by Emily Short (a well-known author of interactive fiction) and uses the Versu tools that Short created with Richard Evans (an AI expert best known for his work on *The Sims 3*).[39] The development of Versu was funded by Linden Lab, creators of the virtual world *Second Life*.

Rather than the individual actions of CiF's social physics, Versu is organized around multi-stage "social practices," many of which can be active simultaneously. *Blood & Laurels* takes place in ancient Rome at a time of grain shortages, unrest, and bad omens. The player's character navigates through this world by making choices that are sometimes quite small scale (whether to eat, where to look, and how to feel about things at a meal) but that add up to massive consequences, including putting oneself (or someone else) on Rome's throne. As with *Prom Week*, it encourages players to explore its world repeatedly (for example, with "achievements" for a wide range of narrative outcomes), but replaying as the same character rather than from another's perspective.

Versu's social practices describe recurring social situations, some of which go through multiple stages (a conversation begins with a greeting) or even repeated stages (a card game goes through its round structure multiple times). Each social practice can make multiple actions available to characters, such as a dinner party making available eating, drinking, commenting on the food, and so on. A dense social situation could include the player character simultaneously involved in a party, a main conversation, side flirtations, and more, creating many potential actions to consider (figure 5.8).

When I first played *Blood & Laurels*, the long list of available actions sometimes felt overwhelming. I had a hard time understanding which actions would be consequential. I also had a hard time understanding the motivations of the other characters and what was happening in the wider world of the game. But that is also exactly the situation that the main character, Marcus, is meant to occupy at the start of the story. And everything the characters did made sense retrospectively, allowing me to build an understanding of the particular characters and of how the world worked. As I played repeatedly, I was able to use my greater understanding of social volition, and other elements of the model, to successfully become emperor and then explore a number of other narrative pathways. In short, I developed a sense of agency that paralleled that of the character in a very satisfying way.

Blood & Laurels makes some quite different game design decisions from *Prom Week*.[40] Players see the world from the perspective of a single character, rather than being able to switch between characters. What the player character wants to do is presented as a long list, and the only further information available about why these actions are desired

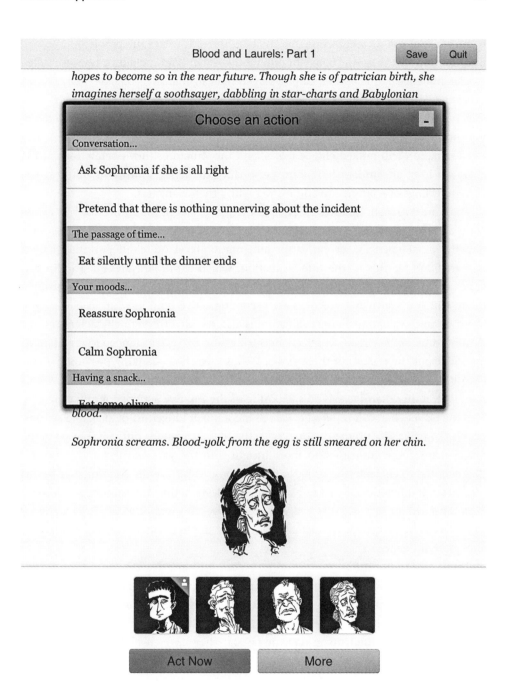

Figure 5.8
The first of two screens of actions available to the player character at the present moment in *Blood & Laurels*, organized by their social practices. (Image from Jason Dyer, "Review: Blood and Laurels," *Renga in Blue*, June 13, 2014, https://bluerenga.blog/2014/06/12/review-blood-and-laurels/.)

is the name of the social practice that includes them. It solves the problem of how to include "outside the norm" behavior differently—*Prom Week* includes a resource called "social influence points," which allows players to push characters outside their comfort zones, while *Blood & Laurels* has a player character who is much less constrained by social norms than NPCs. But despite all these game design differences, in its underlying social volition model Versu's approach is quite similar to CiF's. It includes both rule-evaluation and ranked choice logics, and the structures they operate over at the character level are similar: long-term personality elements, short-term statuses, and current feelings of relationship and history with other characters.

There are two main differences. First, at the process level, the connected rule evaluation and choice ranking take place in the context of a different structure for actions: ongoing social practices. Second, at the presentation level, quite different information is shared. We see this in the rule evaluation, which is primarily revealed indirectly. For example, player choices are shown grouped by the social practices that contribute them, which reveals what practices are becoming active (and moving to new stages) based on rule evaluations. Rule evaluation is also revealed through character portraits at the bottom of the screen, which change expression and can be tapped to reveal information about the reason for their mood. We also see choice-ranking providing different information. Non-player characters reveal their ranking only through the actions they take, rather than *Prom Week*'s exposure of the top five actions for any character. And the player character of *Blood & Laurels* has a much longer list of available actions, which can make identifying the ones with the highest volition difficult, but gives the player many more choices—and more insight into the various rules and structures that can lead to characters desiring to take actions.[41] I believe the consequence of this second set of differences is that it takes longer to develop the understanding of *Blood & Laurels* needed for strategic play but, as noted above, this is appropriate for a narrative game focused on a player character who initially doesn't understand the world well enough to influence it.[42]

That said, fundamentally *Prom Week* and *Blood & Laurels* use similar logics, working with similar structures, to determine and expose character volition. It could be that this convergence means that we have found a key approach on which others will be able to build successfully. There is some evidence for this, such as the work of Pedro A. Santos and collaborators at the Universidade de Lisboa. They have created CiF-successor systems and used them to demonstrate that such social models don't need to be the main focus of gameplay to increase player enjoyment. For example, one project shifted the experience of an RPG merchant from a human-shaped vending machine to an actual character—which 93% of players preferred, in their study.[43] Another project compared player interaction with a set of three NPCs around a bonfire, situated within a larger game with many other gameplay options. A study of this project found that 72% of players preferred interacting with the NPCs driven by a CiF-style social model and that the mean time at their bonfire increased more than half, as compared to NPCs driven by the traditional dialogue tree model, even though the dialogue tree NPCs had professional writing and voice acting.[44]

At the same time, there is clearly much inventive work left to be done. For example, one significant challenge in creating *Prom Week* was the tuning of the rules so that the "right" actions would be the ones most desired by characters. The creators of Versu note the same challenge with their system.[45] Perhaps finding a way to address this tuning challenge, or avoid it, will be an important contribution of a future project.

In the meantime, we need to make it easier for others to get started. The Versu effort seemed to hold out great hope for that, as Linden was rumored to be planning to open its tools to the public, just as it did with tools for creating 3-D objects in *Second Life*. Instead, after a change in leadership, Linden suddenly shut down the entire Versu project. Not only are the tools not available, but the games (including *Blood & Laurels*) have been removed from sale and have not been updated to run on current operating systems.

Those of us who created *Prom Week* are working to address this. We have taken the lessons learned from work that followed it (including a social RPG prototype led by Anne Sullivan and April Grow,[46] an anti-bullying game created as part of an EU project, and a still-confidential collaboration with a major game publisher) and used them to produce an updated version of CiF, called Ensemble.[47] The students who led *Prom Week*'s development have now graduated (McCoy, Treanor, and Samuel have gone on to faculty jobs—at UC Davis, American University, and the University of New Orleans—while Reed co-founded the startup Spirit AI with Khandaker, Short, and others) and have contributed further developments, including Versu-like social practices created by Treanor, McCoy, and Sullivan.[48] As I write this, a basic open-source release of the core Ensemble project has just taken place, based on code from Samuel, Reed, and Paul Maddaloni. It is being maintained by Max Kreminski and Melanie Dickinson, who aim to expand it with documentation, examples, and extensions over time.[49]

Our hope is that this will make further inventive work in this area easier, both for those who build directly on Ensemble and for those who simply experiment with it, finding inspiration for their own projects. I look forward to seeing new approaches developed for characters to decide what to do in complex and changing social worlds. Even more, I look forward to seeing new approaches for helping players understand character volition—building both our mental models and our empathy. Building our mental models of character volition is necessary for us to experience agency in social game worlds, because we only have agency if we understand the world well enough for informed speculation about the consequences of our actions. But beyond that, such innovations will also set the stage for new kinds of emotionally resonant experiences with game characters, ones that prompt us to reflect, sometimes critically, on how our agency is used.

Finally, I hope that we will see more groups taking an inventive approach to logics and models, over time. I believe inventive work can open paths to creating games that address new topics, through play, in powerful ways. Opening these paths can't be done through pure design research work or pure technology research work—it requires that they be brought together. At the same time, in bringing them together, it creates many challenges. The work can only be done by groups (or individuals) who combine both kinds of abilities. And it combines the risks from both types of research—the technology may not perform as hoped, the experience may not come together in a way that matters to audiences, and the funding may be hard to come by. These challenges are worth taking on because the inventive approach is the only way we are going to get video games that enable us deep, meaningful opportunities for playful agency on topics such as human relationships, beliefs, and stories. The power and potential of video games is too great for us to settle for the logics and models we have now.

6   Understanding Games through Logics and Models

There are many ways of playing video games. There are many ways of understanding video games. But unless we take an approach that ignores the specifics of how games are experienced and how they function—perhaps, studying games only with the tools we'd use for research on stamp collecting or movie watching—logics and models can help ground and guide our understanding.

While I am most interested in how a focus on logics and models helps us understand innovative games made by small teams, they are also at the core of our experiences with mainstream games made by hundreds of people across multiple companies. Consider, for example, the *Grand Theft Auto* (*GTA*) franchise.

I remember the opening moments of *GTA IV*.[1] The player character is introduced as Niko, now at the end of a trip from Serbia to Liberty City, after having seen and done some bad things during and after the war. He steps off the boat, waiting a moment before his cousin, Roman, drives into view (figure 6.1). Then, because Roman is clearly too drunk to be driving, the first interactive section of the game is the player driving, while Roman gives directions to his apartment and spouts childishly sexist fantasies.

When I begin playing, it becomes quickly apparent that my Niko's not a very good driver. He probably didn't have much opportunity when he was growing up. Plus, I've never been great at driving games. That is to say, as soon as interaction begins, I start to understand my experience of *GTA IV* as an interplay of the game's fictions, its systems, and myself as a player.

In these first interactions I learn that *GTA IV* has a model of driving that enables and rewards play. The model employs control/navigation, movement physics, and collision-detection logics, as well as supporting animations, sounds, and dynamically applied tire tracks. Driving takes place in an urban environment that includes cars and pedestrians that try to get out of my way (for the cars, often unsuccessfully), a wide range of objects that my car can damage (the wreckage of which my car may plow over or get caught in), and patrolling police who don't care about speeding or red lights, but don't like to be sideswiped.

Figure 6.1
Roman (right) welcomes Niko (left) to Liberty City. (Image taken by the author during play.)

I also think I understand, as I play more, that the condition of vehicles is handled by a less complex resource logic. While damage to the car appears, cosmetically, in the position where an impact happened, as far as I can tell a vehicle's driving condition seems to move steadily toward general inoperability as it is increasingly damaged (rather than specific damage in a particular area causing a specific type of inoperability). In fact, it is much more complex, but this is something I will only learn after a colleague (Adam Summerville) points it out to me, rather than through my hours of gameplay. That is to say, the model of driving is more learnable and playable than the model of vehicle condition.

And the contrast with learnability and playability of driving is even more apparent for character interaction. Some characters move out of the way as I drive, some cars honk, and Roman will sometimes complain if I crash the car into something—"Man, stop that. I'm going to puke!" But if Roman is in the middle of one of his scripted monologues, he won't stop delivering it even if I drive us both into the river—as I discover through restarting the game to experiment, amazed he didn't pause after a head-on crash (figure 6.2). And choosing something to say to him is not one of my options for this drive, or any other. In fact, the only detailed interaction I can choose to have with another person is combat.

Figure 6.2
Even as you drive Roman's cab backward into the water, he doesn't interrupt his juvenile mono-loguing about women's anatomy. (Image taken by the author during play.)

Through playing, I develop my own version of Niko, interacting with the game's fiction and systems. He goes to the stores and comes out dressed as I want. When he needs to fight, engaging the game's combat model, he does so as I prefer—using his fists when he can avoid gunplay. When he needs to regain his health (resource), he goes to the restaurants I think fit him best. He makes a priority of spending time with his cousin and girlfriend, going out when they call to suggest it, and raising the simple "like" or "fondness" value that *GTA IV* tracks in its affinity (resource) logic for each of these characters. He explores the available areas of Liberty City, following my curiosity and engaging in solo and pair activities ranging from bowling to watching cabaret acts—all of them pre-scripted after selection, except in their physical interactions. And my Niko becomes a much better driver, given he has to drive before, after, and during most of these activities.

At the same time, mixed in with all the things I choose to do, those around Niko make certain events feel inevitable, via the game's mission structure. Niko needs to do things to help his cousin Roman, to bring in money, or to curry favor with members of the community. One set of missions comes from Vlad, an unpleasant Russian mobster

Figure 6.3
The *GTA IV* interface, explaining how to execute the unarmed Vlad. The box in the upper left
reads: "To perform an execution on Vlad, lock on to him and fire. When locked on, the reticule
will flash if an execution can be performed." (Image courtesy of Nathan Wardrip-Fruin.)

to whom Roman owes money. These involve driving, and some fighting, and a little
thuggery. I have lots of choice in how I drive, some choice in how I fight, and one
choice in the thuggery—when I chase down Ivan. Vlad tells me Ivan was planning to
rob Roman, but as I chase Ivan up to and over rooftops, he says he was set up. At the
end of the mission, Ivan is dangling from the side of a building and the game gives me
the choice of killing or sparing him. There's no question—especially after the war, the
Niko I'm playing would never execute someone defenseless.

Or so I thought. Eventually, it is revealed that Vlad is sleeping with Roman's girlfriend. Niko and Roman go to confront him—leading to fighting, vehicular chasing,
and finally cornering Vlad at a construction site beneath one of the city's towering
bridges. As I approach Vlad, the game instructs me in performing executions (figure
6.3). But whatever murderous things Niko said in voiceover as I chased after Vlad were
out of my control. The Niko I'm playing would not do that. I try waiting, but Vlad
keeps walking around, waiting to be executed (figure 6.4). I try walking away, but come
back to find the situation the same.

GTA IV will let me play a Niko who drives almost any way I could imagine. I could
learn to drive precisely and tightly or be wild and destructive. I could decide to drive

Mikhail Faustin thought of me as a brother. He will get revenge.

Figure 6.4
Vlad waits around for death no matter what Niko does. You can break line of sight, climb around on the scenery behind him (seen here), or even leave the area entirely. *GTA IV* will not progress until the player directs Niko to execute Vlad. (Image courtesy of Nathan Wardrip-Fruin.)

everywhere backwards—the acceleration and steering work in reverse, and I can swing the camera to point in the direction I desire. In any case, the game will respond in a fluid and satisfying way. But if I want to play a character—specifically the character of a killing-weary war veteran I feel the game's fiction has suggested to me—*GTA IV* can only respond minimally, on occasion.

And at the moment I am forced to execute Vlad or stop making progress, the sense that I am playing my own version of Niko is lost. I never go any further with *GTA IV*.

Understanding *Grand Theft Auto IV*

Talking with people who don't play them, most discussions of the *GTA* games focus on things we might say if each game were a movie. We might talk about the demeaning depictions of women, from Roman's fantasies to the interactions (including violent interactions) available with female prostitutes. Or we might talk about the sympathetic depiction of Niko, an undocumented immigrant who is forced by circumstance into a life of crime.

Talking with people who do play them, most discussions of the *GTA* games focus on non-obvious elements of the games' spaces and systems. We might talk about where to find hidden pieces of body armor, weaponry, and health boosts, or unusual cars, and so on. Or we might talk about how to get achievements and trophies, hidden features or cheats, or alternate possibilities that arise from the game's few story choices.

But if we look at what the game's models and logics support richly, at the experience where players have the most agency and opportunity for expression, we see a game about something else. Not surprisingly, given the series' full title, *Grand Theft Auto IV* is a game about urban driving and fighting. It is a procedural representation of urban life, primarily as seen from behind the wheel of a car. This procedural representation operates through the specific ways its logics and models have been implemented technically and the specific 3-D models, animations, and sounds created for those logics and models to communicate.

We can only understand this procedural representation if our discussion engages its full specifics. We can't ignore the game's systemic and play-driven elements, as statements from non-players often do. We can't ignore the game's larger communicative and cultural elements, as statements from the game's players often do.

Some elements of the procedural representation connect to models and logics in obvious ways. For example, the apathetic police, ignoring all driving infractions except when the player's vehicle damages theirs, are clearly responding to the collision logic that is key to the game's model of driving and using it to represent an idea of urban policing.

But thinking about the game's models and logics is also important to our understanding of other elements of the game. If we examine *GTA IV*'s pedestrian population in isolation, for example, it might seem very odd. Why would a simulated city's sidewalk population include many different types and ages of characters, but no children or even teenagers? We can connect this back to the wide range of driving styles the game's model supports—presumably it was seen as unacceptable (by the developer, or perhaps for the deliberately provocative developer's place in the wider culture) to have players with wild, destructive driving styles run down children. In a game without as much focus on driving, or as much player choice in where and how to drive, or even in a game that rewarded activities other than destruction with more interesting responses from its models, this would not be necessary.

This kind of attention to logics and models, within the wider context of the game, provides a foundation for understanding games in ways that connect game systems, media, and player experiences. This can be done with a focus on the game's most central, complex, and player-engaging models and logics—as I believe is important when trying to understand what a game is about. But it can also be done by contrasting particular examples of a game's models and logics, then looking at the interactions between them.

For example, as mentioned in chapter 4, in the book *Expressive Processing*[2] I look at the game *Star Wars: Knights of the Old Republic*,[3] contrasting the freedom provided by the game's spatial movement model with the limited choices of its story models. *KotOR* is in many ways an admirable game, pushing its story models to their limits, giving the player some sense of responsibility for story events and character relationships. But this same act of ambition also leads to breakdown, as the much more flexible spatial movement model interacts, through play, with the brittle story models.

A similar comparison for *GTA IV* reveals story models providing almost no meaningful choice, perhaps working to absolve the player of any sense of responsibility for the harrowing acts Niko carries out in the story.[4] Together with the fact that the game's models and logics offer more opportunity for meaningful interactions with vehicles than people, we might see this as giving license—or even encouragement—to explore the violent, antisocial behavior (especially directed at non-story characters, from pedestrians to prostitutes) enabled for players by the driving and combat models. This, in the end, is the sense I came away with of what *GTA IV* is about.

GTA IV is a procedural representation of urban life focused on enabling players to explore the pleasures of destruction and violence without empathy. The models enable such actions, the wider game environment rewards them, the mission structure requires them, and the unreality of the game's other people (they can really only be interacted with as crash dummies, punching bags, gun targets, and vending machines) removes any sense of consequences. While *GTA IV* dresses itself in the appearance of a crime drama, it is not about what drama is about—the tensions and evolutions of human relationships. Instead, the catharsis it presumably aims to provide, through players' explorations of destruction and violence, is closer to the genre of unreflective action, or even titillation horror.

In the end, the elements of *GTA IV* that had humanized Niko—and that had led me to feel I was playing a particular Niko—just made it taste more rotten the further I played. For me, it would have been much more enjoyable as a cartoony playground of destruction, rather than a set of actions presented as carried out by a real person, especially one that I identified with.

Part of my interest in logics and models is in considering new ways they can be used (and inventing new logics and models) that will allow games like *GTA IV* to move beyond the choice of being disconnected from our world or offering dehumanizing procedural representations.

Related Approaches

Of course, we might interpret *GTA* games somewhat differently, while still being grounded in logics and models. For example, along related analytical lines to the above, we might look at a game like *GTA IV* through the lens of Michael Mateas's approach to the idea of agency, which will be discussed in more detail in this book's conclusion.[5] We might note that almost everything the game's story and world suggest that a character like Niko might do while driving is supported for the player. But only a very narrow subset of the things they suggest he might do when interacting with other characters is supported. This creates an agency mismatch—powerfully experienced in one area of the game, but almost absent in another—because of the nature of the game's models and logics.

Why is this a problem? To continue along lines similar to the above, we could argue it is because *GTA IV* is even further along the trajectory that Gonzalo Frasca noted[6] between *GTA III*[7] and *GTA: Vice City*.[8] As the games progressed—from *GTA III* to *Vice City* to *San Andreas*[9] to *GTA IV*—the games moved from a comfort with, and emphasis on, being urban driving simulations (Frasca likens *GTA III* to a flight simulator) to an increasing emphasis on their stories and mission structures. The mission structures are even enforced, denying whole areas of the game's space and activity to players who do not meet milestones in the mission progression. As Frasca writes, *GTA III* encourages seeing its "people" as nothing more than parts of the environment. By *GTA IV* the series succeeds in partially humanizing both the other people and the player character—through the more realized and required story and missions—while not providing anything of the agency with people that one feels with the driving model. In fact, it requires inhumane actions toward and by its characters, making its play, to me, feel more grotesque.

Alternately, we might also interpret games such as *GTA IV* by looking at models and logics that are more peripheral and simpler, rather than the central models of driving and combat. Ian Bogost demonstrates this in the book *Persuasive Games*[10]—looking at the model of bodily health and its connections to the wider game in *Grand Theft Auto: San Andreas*. The model is composed of a number of simple resource logics, most notably numbers for the character's health, fat, muscle, and stamina. Unlike *GTA IV*, in *San Andreas* the player character must eat or he will lose fat (if there is any), muscle, and health, eventually leading to death. The player character—Carl "CJ" Johnson—lives in inner-city Los Santos. There, the only available food is fast food. Most of the menu items are unhealthy (adding to CJ's fat, which can reduce his abilities and his appeal to other characters) and the more healthy options cost more money (connecting to another important resource logic). Especially early in the game, the player may simply be unable to afford to eat anything but unhealthy food. As Bogost observes:

The dietary features of *San Andreas* are rudimentary, but the fact that the player must feed his character to continue playing does draw attention to the limited material conditions the game provides for satisfying that need, subtly exposing the fact that problems of obesity and malnutrition in poor communities can partly be attributed to the relative ease and affordability of fast food.[11]

Bogost goes on to interpret elements of *San Andreas* as reproducing both progressive and conservative ideological frames. Despite the game drawing attention to the poor nutritional options in the environment (a progressive framing), CJ is able to keep healthy if he works hard at the gym or does in-game activities that produce money (a conservative framing). Bogost goes on to a wider interpretation of the game's overall structure of activities and representations, along similarly conflicted ideological lines. As mentioned in this book's introduction, he calls his interpretive practice for this work "procedural rhetoric" and characterizes operational logics as the "tropes" that undergird the construction and interpretation of procedural rhetorics.[12]

The models of policing, which players cannot engage directly, are also revealing in these games. The police not only respond to acts in the driving model, but also in the combat model—such as those that result in the deaths of other characters. David Leonard describes the racism inscribed in this portion of the policing model for *San Andreas*:

> *San Andreas* elucidates the role (or lack thereof) of the state in protecting and serving communities of color. Throughout the game, the police ignore the murder of other "gang members," often intervening only in moments where violence is directed at the "innocent." In other words, Carl can, at times, kill rival gang members in front [of] (or close to) police without consequences. Killing an innocent citizen brings the police swiftly and with the full force of the law. Furthermore, as these individuals lie in the street in virtual wait for medical attention, the paramedics rarely arrive. The murder of the innocent in the game frequently leads to not only a quick ambulance response but also the resuscitation of these characters. *San Andreas*, thus, concretizes hegemonic ideologies regarding criminality and the state's role in only protecting the "innocent."[13]

Some might defend the developers as parodying, or calling attention to, injustices of policing and emergency medicine in poor, Black communities. But for many players, inscribing them into the game's models, so that they are learned through play, is likely a way of normalizing and teaching these ideas. As Leonard puts it, "although video games and popular culture in general are sources of entertainment, they are sites of education, where common sense ideas of race and dominant discourses of racism are constructed and disseminated for mass consumption."[14] For games (and popular culture generally) this is most often discussed in terms of surface representation, but it is at least as powerful, and in need of confrontation, at the level of logics and models.

Another example of understanding ideology in the *GTA* franchise through the lens of logics and models can be drawn from Nick Dyer-Witheford and Greig de Peuter. In the "Imperial City" chapter of their book *Games of Empire*, they examine three titles in the series. For each, they draw out "the relation of its virtualities to . . . the systemic patterns of inequality and marginalization inherent to global capital, of which violence and crime are often only symptomatic."[15] They identify these patterns within the operation and communication of the models through which play takes place. For example, they write of *Vice City* and the connections between its economic model and spatial model:

> This is a world where access to, mobility in, and knowledge of urban territory are complexly tied to accumulation's advance: how much city there is for you as [a] player depends on how much money you have. But what makes *Vice City* properly neoliberal is that, as your financial tally rises, there is not a hint of labor, just the abstracted, increasing magnitude of accumulated capital.[16]

We might also pull back from a focus on specific models and logics, instead looking holistically at the larger procedural representation built upon them. For example, when *GTA V* was released—around the same time as D. Fox Harrell's book *Phantasmal Media*[17] was published—MIT News pointed out that no one needs to tell *GTA V* players that its Los Santos is a stand-in for Los Angeles.[18] (Similarly, no one needs to tell *GTA IV* players that its Liberty City stands in for New York City.) This is because of the effectiveness of the *GTA* cities in prompting what Harrell calls "phantasms"—blends of cultural, ideological ideas and sensory imaginations. By connecting process, communication, and interaction, logics and models can help us investigate the specifics of how these phantasms are prompted. Further, I believe there is a complementary relationship between Harrell's work with morphic semiotics and the ideas of models and logics presented here, as I discuss in chapter 9.

On the other hand, some might argue that all these interpretations are misguided. Perhaps the key moment in my play of *GTA IV* was when I restarted, repeatedly, on the docks at the beginning of the game—experimenting with driving, and destruction, and Roman's range of reactions. Perhaps the mission structures, Niko's character, CJ's eating, and much else of what I have discussed in relation to the GTA games are mere distractions.

Rule Breaking and "My Trip to Liberty City"

The voiceover begins, "Mm-kay. This is just some of the video from my trip to Liberty City." We hear Jim Munroe narrating, while we see footage from the game *Grand Theft*

Figure 6.5
The "Canadian Tourist" skin from "My Trip to Liberty City" by Jim Munroe. (Composite image designed by Patricio Davila, Canadian Tourist character skin by Marc Ngui. Courtesy of Jim Munroe.)

Auto III, as we begin the video "My Trip to Liberty City."[19] One of the first things that Munroe's character does is refuse the game's mission system. He's asked to "introduce a bat" to the face of another criminal, and Munroe reflects: "You know, I just didn't feel like it. It was a great day, it was beautiful out, the sun was shining. And I don't even play baseball. Much less, you know, want to kill someone with a baseball bat."

He changes the game's avatar into a "Canadian Tourist" skin, so as not to confuse anyone else by having a thuglike appearance (figure 6.5).

Next, Munroe's character refuses driving. While everyone's heard of all the cars in *Grand Theft Auto*, he feels like the best way to get to know a city is to walk around on foot. He demonstrates the beauty one can find by walking up to a rooftop—pointedly ignoring the valuable hidden package spinning at its top—and takes in the almost-setting sun and the street scene below. Then he notices a distant stand of trees that may be a park.

Back at street level he tries to "ask directions" to the park but finds an impolite response from everyone he meets (as *GTA III* players know, there is no way to ask anyone anything, only a way to bump into them). He tries to take in the natural beauty, but falls in the water and ends up at the hospital. On the way home he tries to catch a cab, but they all pull away (as *GTA III* players know, it is because he refuses to engage the carjacking mechanic), leaving him behind.

The next day, to make up money from his unfortunate hospitalization (no Canadian socialized medicine in Liberty City), he decides to try some street busking. This involves "miming" by triggering the animations of the combat model, but without a target, while wearing a custom "Attack Mime" avatar skin simulating white pancake makeup. He elicits a range of reactions from fellow pedestrians, especially the one he accidentally strikes. Finally, when a nearby pedestrian is hit by a car, he tries to help but can't—even after changing into a "Street Preacher" skin—so gathers up some of the money the pedestrian dropped (for his medical bills) then runs away as he hears a siren growing nearer.

Obviously, "My Trip to Liberty City" is a performance. But it could also be seen as a distillation of how players are seen in a particular approach to understanding games—as by far the central element, trumping game rules and other systemic elements. For example, Thomas Malaby argues that "games are grounded in (and constituted by) human practice and are therefore always in the process of becoming. This also means that they are not reducible to their rules."[20] In a related vein, Miguel Sicart, in his "Against Procedurality" article, positions "creative play as the privileged way in which games act as rhetorical artifacts" and argues "pla[y] cannot be codified; it cannot be limited and bound to the processes delimited by arbitrarily created rules dictated by distant designers."[21]

For these authors, game players are most interesting when they are not doing what game designers expect of them. They opt out of the apparent rules or attempt to change them. They invent new, creative modes of playful engagement with games.

But what are video game players doing when they opt out of designer expectations? What is Munroe's character doing when he refuses *GTA III* missions, and cars, and packages? What is he doing when he stands on the roof, admiring the view, or falls in the water, or "mimes" on the street? What was I doing, when I restarted *GTA IV*, over and over, exploring the limits of Roman's car and his persistence in delivering voiceover? What are other *GTA IV* players doing when they discover that there are playground swings that will launch vehicles into the air?[22]

In each case, even if players are ignoring the high-level rules and expectations built into aspects of the game design, even if players are refusing the core mechanics that are meant to be at the center of the gameplay experience, these same players are deeply engaging the game's logics and models. Munroe's rooftop visit is a celebration of *GTA III*'s spatial movement model, while refusing to be motivated by the "rewards" meant to entice movement. His miming exploits aspects of the combat model, while refusing to employ the mechanics it supports. In short, while—as his article's title suggests—Sicart and others with similar views may see their position as opposed to procedurally oriented approaches to video games, the player activities they celebrate can only be understood through lenses (such as that of logics and models) that take the computational, procedural nature of video games into account.[23]

As Soraya Murray puts it, writing of *San Andreas*:

> In this imagined space, the conventional social contract is suspended; however, this is not to say that what results is a lawless space. Rather, games such as *Grand Theft Auto* represent rule-based, problem-solving environments that require creative solutions within a defined set of parameters.[24]

Even if we choose not to address the problems the designers imagined us solving, or choose to deliberately subvert them, our play is always grounded in the rule-based environment defined by the logics and models.

Critical Play, Complicity, and *The Sims*

Mary Flanagan's writing on *The Sims*[25] can help us further develop ideas of creative, subversive, and critical video game play and their relationships with logics and models. In her book *Critical Play*,[26] Flanagan situates her discussion of *The Sims* within a wider discussion and history of domestic, household, and doll play. Drawing on a variety of sources, but especially Miriam Formanek-Brunell's *Made to Play House*,[27] Flanagan investigates such play as a cultural practice. While it is often seen by adults as training in normative behavior and "feminization" for girls, there is much historical evidence that doll play has long been approached as a critical, subversive practice—and that such practices have been widespread enough to, in turn, shape the products of the toy industry. Flanagan quotes Formanek-Brunell's observation that "for some, a doll's worth was determined by its ability to subvert convention, mock materialism, and undermine restrictions."[28]

Flanagan outlines three kinds of critical play enacted by Victorian girls with dolls:

> In doll play, *unplaying* manifests in children abusing their dolls, "killing" them, or some other revision of the "care giving" framework of expected play. . . . [In *re-dressing* or *re-skinning*] Players make alternative arrangements and disguise their dolls for subversive roles, altering the appearance or the presentation of dolls in a way that allows dolls to enter the forbidden scene. . . . [Through *rewriting*] those involved in the manufacture of dolls and doll culture (including children, as they wrote letters to such publications) could constantly revise or rewrite the narratives surrounding dolls.[29]

Like traditional doll play, *The Sims* focuses on domestic life. But because it is a video game, rather than a set of physical objects, its play is built on a foundation of logics and models. One can imagine a wide variety of possible logics and models that might be employed for such play and a wide range of ways they might be implemented. A domestic game might employ a mission model, founded on a simple progression logic, that places players on the traditional trajectory of a rags-to-riches story. Or it might instead focus on simply maintaining a household that constantly threatens to fall into chaos, perhaps using pattern-matching logics to force players to remember what will mollify different children in different situations, and presumably to do so under increasing time pressure (perhaps as additional children are born). And because such a video game is not a physical object, it might come with a small number of pre-set families, rather than just one—presumably all White, able, upper middle-class, and heteronormative—but no options for employing alternatives or making alterations.

Yet this is not what was done in *The Sims* or later entries in the series. Instead, as Flanagan points out, while by default the game seems to suggest quite mainstream ideas and engagement, it also enables the same types of critical play she identifies with Victorian dolls. In *The Sims*, the models of character health, house construction, and house operation allow for unplaying—it is common for players to deny Sims a place to urinate, trap them in doorless rooms, set them on fire, and otherwise subvert the framing of caregiving. The communicative aspects of logics and models are deliberately implemented in ways that allow players to replace elements of them—to re-skin Sims and their environments—with more sophisticated tools for this provided by the developers for each successive title. And because Sims games are not primarily shaped by a linear mission model, but rather by a numerical simulation model built primarily of resource logics, players are able to rewrite the expected narrative of material progress, telling a variety of types of in-game stories with their Sims—and through practices such as machinima and fan fiction, telling many more.[30]

Such options have doubtless contributed to the popularity of the series, with the *Sims* games by far the most successful of their type (and among the most successful PC games of all time). Given this, we could certainly dismiss the efforts of Maxis (the studio that initially created the games) as no different from Victorian toy makers, who converted critical play into a capitalist opportunity through "packaging their fashion dolls to appeal to such subversion."[31] But what players have experienced with the Sims games, through their openness to critical play, isn't so easy to dismiss.

Of course, we don't have access to what most players experience. But we have access to many rewritings (both more and less radical) as quite a few players do share stories of their play sessions, through various means. One of my favorite *Sims* stories is "Alice and Kev"[32]—a playing of *The Sims 3*[33] told through a screenshot-heavy blog by Robin Burkinshaw.

Rather than engaging in the wealth-accumulating household fantasy that *Sims* games seem to suggest, Burkinshaw gave a two-Sim household an empty lot, with two park benches. Rather than sending the Sims to climb one of the game's simulated career ladders, Burkinshaw made Kev, the father, jobless and mentally ill. Alice, the daughter, is clumsy, with low self-esteem, and also is too young to work—so she gets somewhat-regular meals from the school cafeteria.

After that, Burkinshaw mostly lets the logics and models of *The Sims 3* determine what will happen next. In a sense, this is turning most play decisions over to the Sims' "volition" model—which lets characters determine what they want to do next, by seeking to improve their happiness.[34] Sims have a number of simple, numerical resource logics that are important to this—measuring things like how much energy they have, how clean they are, how much their social interaction needs are met, and so on. *The Sims 3* also includes long-term and shorter-term wishes, as well as some awareness of appropriate behavior in different contexts, which can be powerfully motivating in choosing the next action.[35]

What happens next is, mostly, predictably depressing. Alice doesn't sleep well on the park benches at her "home" (they do little to re-fill her energy resource) and she doesn't get along well with her father (his interactions are mean, lowering her social resource level, rather than raising it), plus he tends to wake her up. The need for rest is urgent. So, she sleeps on other people's benches and in other people's homes. They disapprove—because she doesn't have a shower (no means to raise her hygiene resource), so she doesn't smell good, and because Sims know it's impolite to sleep in someone else's bed without permission. Sometimes she takes their food, because she simply must eat.

A question hangs over all this. It goes unasked as Alice finishes her short, unhappy childhood—becoming a teenager who can have an after-school job and perhaps with it some change in the sad and desperate life with her father. Finally, a version of the question arises in Burkinshaw's narration of the moments after Alice's first day of work:

> When her shift at the supermarket ends that evening, she has 100 hard-earned simoleons, but she is as exhausted as it is possible to be. She wobbles slightly after walking out the door, and only just manages to stop herself from losing consciousness there and then.
>
> But she doesn't want to rest now. She's just come up with a new wish. It's a wish that would be easily fulfilled, but the idea scares and horrifies me. I don't want to grant it to her.
>
> But it's her life, and her choice. I reluctantly let her do it.
>
> She takes all of the money she has just earned, places it into an envelope, writes the name of a charity on the front, and puts it into a mailbox.[36]

The question is one which Burkinshaw's narration has mostly avoided—by discussing Alice's and Kev's actions as though they are autonomous characters, living in a world outside the player's control. But, of course, that is not the case. And with this moment of acknowledging the player's presence and power, of wanting to deny Alice her wish, Burkinshaw's hand is tipped.

The real question of "Alice and Kev" is "Why are you letting this happen?" That is, the real question of "Alice and Kev" is about complicity, about letting suffering continue when we have the power to stop it, and about going along with the actions of a system that produces and perpetuates it.[37] And this, of course, is also the nature of the real questions—outside of video games—about actual homelessness, hunger, and untreated mental illness. Many games only offer us a potential distraction from this, while "Alice and Kev" shows that the opportunities for critical play in *The Sims 3* might offer us an opening for reflection on it.

Of course, "Alice and Kev" works because it is a story about resources, reflecting on suffering brought on by distribution of resources, told through a game with logics and models that are squarely focused on resources. In contrast, while the ability to re-skin individual Sims might also offer opportunities for critical play around (for example) gender roles and performances, setting the simulation loose is not going to produce an interesting story on this topic. And while, by default, characters in *The Sims 3* can do things that are very important to people and communities—like fall in love, or die— again, the simulation does not guide us toward interesting experiences around these topics. The characters would need to view their own histories (and be able to offer reflections on the past and on possible futures) in ways that are quite different from the largely historyless characters and icon-based speaking the series features.[38]

In other words, the critical play that Flanagan draws our attention to—like all the other types of video game play (and understanding) we have discussed so far—rests on a foundation of logics and models. It succeeds when it engages them creatively, and we can only understand it by taking them into account.

Why Logics and Models?

As this chapter has outlined, however we seek to understand video games—whether we embrace procedural rhetoric, expressive processing, anti-procedurality, critical play, or other approaches—we need concepts that help us see and discuss the connections between play, systems, and media. But perhaps there are other concepts, already available, that are better suited to the task than logics and models? Or, to put it another way, given the wealth of lenses for looking at video games—and computational media more broadly—one might ask why colleagues, students, and I have invested energy in developing the ideas of logics and models.[39]

Many of the most influential writings about games emphasize the connections between games as systems, as media, and as play experiences, often calling attention to these in pairs.[40] Jesper Juul's 2005 book *Half-Real*[41] foregrounds the connections between a game's rules (system) and its fiction (media). Similarly, the "Mechanics, Dynamics, Aesthetics" framework, which emphasizes the connections between systems and play experiences (and which is discussed briefly in chapter 4), has for years been at the core of the Game Design Workshop offered at the Game Developers Conference—and has become widely cited since the 2004 MDA writeup by Robin Hunicke, Marc LeBlanc, and Robert Zubek.[42]

Our question is how to follow through on what these ideas recommend: that we think, at the same time, about how games function, how they communicate, and how this shapes play experiences. While other frameworks give names to the different categories one must think about (such as Juul's "rules" and "fiction") they do little to develop the terminology they use for discussing what exists across categories (such as Juul's "virtual" and "simulation"). One approach would be to get concrete in thinking about the elements of games and how players come to understand them and their interactions. This interesting direction has been pursued by the "formalist" end of game design thinkers (also discussed briefly in chapter 4) and especially by those engaged in attempts to create diagrams, grammars, or notations as resources for explaining and understanding game designs. For example, Raph Koster's work to develop "A Grammar of Gameplay"[43] (first presented at the 2005 Game Developers Conference) emphasizes the nested, "fractal" nature of game experiences. In his ongoing work on this topic,[44] he describes how each fractal level of games—from the physical actions required for basic control through the high-level game outcomes—includes a set of key elements: player intent; affordances within the game for taking action; control inputs that allow taking action; the game action itself, which feeds into a "black box"; the resulting changes in the game, presented via feedback; and the resulting changes in the player's model of the game, through which new intents are formed.

On one level this is very similar to a logics and models approach—we can imagine "physics," "pattern matching," or the names of other logics filling in the "black box" for a particular layer of games, and perhaps the names of models doing so for other layers. At the same time, Koster's approach is different in a couple of key ways.[45] First, from a psychological perspective, Koster's atoms are richer than logics and models, in that they explicitly include players, especially their mental models and intents. This is in line with the priority Koster has put on understanding player learning, as seen in his influential *A Theory of Fun for Game Design*.[46] Second, however, Koster's work explicitly brackets how games are experienced as media.[47] It would be out of scope to talk about the various things collision can be used to express or what ideas about communication are embedded in different dialogue models.

And this second distinction is also true for most other work in this tradition, such as Joris Dormans's Machinations diagrams (see box 6.1, "Machinations and *Monopoly*").[48] On one level, Machinations diagrams are very close to the perspective of this book—arguably, they are tools for illustrating (and simulating) how playable models are constructed from resource logics. On the other hand, they explicitly leave out discussion of what such models are meant to procedurally represent. This does not mean they are useless—any more than a building's engineering diagrams are useless because they don't give a full sense of how the building will appear and be experienced. But it does mean that they can't fulfill the purpose of logics and models, which is to bridge these concerns.

A different, but related sort of bridge is built by work in this tradition from Stéphane Bura. Bura created an approach to game diagramming in 2006 (inspired by Petri nets) that in some ways anticipated Machinations, and Bura actively encouraged Dormans's work in the area.[49] But then in 2008 he published a quite different formal take on game design.[50] Drawing on Nicole Lazzaro's work describing the different types of emotions that arise from gameplay,[51] Bura attempts to drill down into the specifics of gameplay patterns that can (when paired with appropriate writing, music, imagery, etc.) evoke targeted player emotions. For example, Bura describes this possible pattern for evoking hope:

> If you reduce the number of choices a player has at the cognitive level—which means that he may have the tools and plans to face a challenge but is overmatched or doesn't have the opportunity to use them—and maintain him in this state (Low Freedom at the System level), you may drive him to despair. But if you then give him an opportunity (Increase), suddenly there's a way out. Suddenly, there's hope.[52]

This work certainly bridges how games operate and what they communicate, but in a different way. Just as a playable models approach might look at the different patterns that are used to procedurally represent different domains (from cooking to combat) so an approach like Bura's might look at the different patterns that are used to procedurally evoke momentary emotions (such as hope or shame) or longer-term emotional experiences (such as developing a nurturing instinct or feeling one is being hunted). Again, this can complement a logics and models approach, but does not serve the same purpose.

Alternately, rather than focus on the cosncrete, we could look at a much more abstract level. For example, arguing that game players must understand game systems algorithmically to succeed, Alex Galloway calls for us to interpret these algorithms—to

Box 6.1

Machinations and *Monopoly*

Joris Dormans's Machinations diagrams are the best-developed way of illustrating the resource logics and economic models at work in games. The basic vocabulary of these diagrams is shown in figure 6.6. *Pools* hold resources, distributing them when triggers fire or at particular rates. *Gates* are pools that immediately redistribute. *Sources* create resources. *Sinks* make resources disappear permanently. *Converters* change one resource into another. *Traders* cause resources to change ownership. These are "node" types, and resources flow between them along "connections" shown as arrows (to indicate the direction of flow). There are also dotted lines, which indicate changes in state, such as a shift in the chance of something happening or a transition to the end of the game.

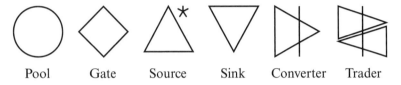

Pool   Gate   Source   Sink   Converter   Trader

Figure 6.6

The core vocabulary of Machinations node types. (Image created by the author with the browser-based Machinations tool at machinations.io.)

One strength of Machinations is that the economic models of games can be diagrammed at different levels of abstraction. As an example, let us consider four diagrams of the tabletop game *Monopoly*[53] (discussed in more detail in the conclusion). These are drawn from *Game Mechanics: Advanced Game Design*,[54] Dormans's book with Ernest Adams. In the first diagram (figure 6.7), the game is very simply represented: the chance of another player's money moving from their pool to your pool is random, but increased by owning property.

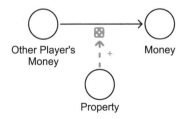

Other Player's Money   Money

Property

Figure 6.7

A simple view of *Monopoly*, with the die indicating randomness and the dotted line with a plus sign indicating a positive influence on the random outcome. (Diagram courtesy of Joris Dormans.)

Box 6.1 (continued)

A more complex diagram (figure 6.8) shows that paying rent takes money out of the player's pool, that passing Go and rental income are money sources, and that money can be converted into property, which increases the chance of rental income. Here the positive feedback of *Monopoly* begins to become clear: you need money to buy property, which in turn increases your chance to get rent income (which is money).

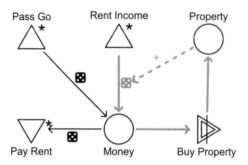

Figure 6.8

A more complex view of *Monopoly*, in which the game's positive feedback is apparent. In Machinations diagrams, asterisks are put on entities that activate automatically, every turn. Shapes with double outlines (as with the "buy property" converter) represent player actions and fire in response to them. (Diagram courtesy of Joris Dormans.)

A more complex diagram (figure 6.9) adds the second player, showing that each player's property adds to a percentage chance that money will move from the other player's property to theirs. Here the rates are specified along the connections, with single numbers indicating amounts that move every turn, while numbers with a slash indicate an amount that moves every time the number of turns on the right side passes (for example, from passing Go, two resources move every six turns). This diagram also shows the initial percentage chances and the changes to those chances based on resource levels. The stacks of tokens on top of resource pools indicate resources within the pools. Since there is no source that can add to the pool of available properties, this diagram shows that the number of properties in the game is finite. The result is a diagram that can simulate a simplified game of *Monopoly*, making it possible to observe what emerges (and potentially experiment with changes to the economic model).

But the real key to the positive feedback in *Monopoly* is property development. A final diagram (figure 6.10) includes buying houses, solidifying what in Machinations is called the "dynamic engine" pattern—more resources flowing to those who have converted resources into upgrades. However, the positive feedback is too dominant, with no way to ameliorate it if the diagram is left at that. So, a "dynamic friction" pattern—consuming resources based

Box 6.1 (continued)

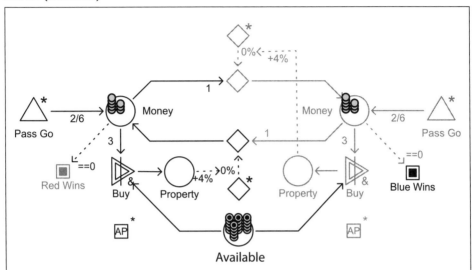

Figure 6.9

This diagram of *Monopoly* adds a second player. "AP" indicates an "artificial player." With two artificial players, this Machinations diagram could run its simulation independently, providing a quick way to see a range of possible game shapes and outcomes. Adams and Dormans, in their book, show how this diagram can be used to study the effects of luck in the traditional *Monopoly* and in potential variants. (Diagram courtesy of Joris Dormans.)

on the game state—is also added. This initially removes zero resources through property tax every six turns, but with the number increasing based on properties owned and houses built. This is different from the actual property tax mechanism in *Monopoly*, which does much less to keep the positive feedback of the dynamic engine in check. The lack of real dynamic friction in *Monopoly* is part of why it is a frustrating game.

If we take *Monopoly* as Hasbro presents it, the lack of real dynamic friction may seem puzzling. We might wonder if this is an artifact of an earlier game design era, before we grew accustomed to the "rubber banding" that tries to keep games exciting to the end by putting obstacles in the way of leaders and/or by giving boosts to those behind. But in fact it is a different type of artifact, as I discuss in the conclusion. *Monopoly*'s frustrating end-game—a combination of positive feedback and chance-driven events—arises from features inherited from the playable model of the game it rips off: Elizabeth Magie's *The Landlord's Game*.[55] Digging into the model helps us see what *Monopoly* remains about, even without meaning to: the deep problems of unchecked capitalism, as intended by the creator of its playable model.

Box 6.1 (continued)

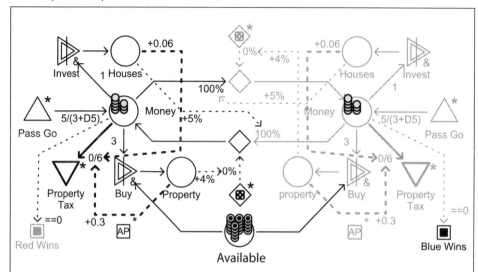

Figure 6.10

This diagram includes buying houses, which is key to the positive feedback of *Monopoly*. At the same time, it also includes property tax with a more powerful design than in traditional *Monopoly*—rather than being a space that players may land on randomly, it happens every six turns and drains an amount based on owned properties and built houses. This property tax design makes it possible to tune *Monopoly*'s economic model, ameliorating or even removing the advantages from property ownership and development. (Diagram courtesy of Joris Dormans.)

discover the "allegorithms" of games.[56] McKenzie Wark expands this notion, relating the "allegorithms" of games explicitly to algorithmically infused life in our everyday world, and focusing on the gap between them.[57] This is related to Bogost's notion of the "simulation gap" between a rule-based representation of something and our subjective experiences of it.[58] Interpretations in these veins could be supported by the concepts of logics and models, allowing a focus on the specific elements that build up "allegorithmic" experiences—but no writings in this area provide any concepts or vocabulary at anything but a quite abstract level, so they provide no alternative to logics and models.

The approaches of semiotics—from a variety of traditions—seem likely to help address this in the future. And the influence of semiotic thinking on the concepts of logics and models, and work that has been done with them, is undeniable.[59] But for now even the most games-focused semiotic approaches tend to bracket the actual systems of games, instead focusing on game processes (to the extent they do) only as experienced by the player. For example, William Huber's 2012 dissertation, building on the tradition of Peircean semiotics, makes the argument that "the basis of the player's engagement with the digital game is the interpretation of a stream of signs."[60] Whether we accept this or not, such a framing leaves no space for talking about the operations of the game system. Similarly, approaches that adopt a "pattern language" approach to thinking about games also tend to bracket consideration of processes, exclusively focusing on player experiences.[61]

Logics and models address this lack. On a detailed level, looking at a logic (such as collision detection) names a general strategy (how it combines an abstract process and a communicative role) and gives a way of talking about how a particular game, or part of a game, employs the strategy (the specific algorithmic implementation and game state representation) opening possibilities for player experience. At a broader level, looking at a playable model (such as of movement through a continuous, two-dimensional space) encompasses the logics that allow the model to operate, as well as the structuring information for the types of domains the model is designed to represent and enable play in terms of.

Certainly, my goal is not to argue that operational logics and playable models are the only useful lenses for thinking about games—or computational media generally. Rather, they provide a vocabulary for thinking about elements that are simultaneously process-oriented, communication-oriented, and play-oriented. This nicely complements existing vocabularies, which often urge us to think about the connections between process, communication, and play, but which provide concepts that organize them apart.[62]

Sunset Valley and Liberty City in the Rearview Mirror

For big-budget, mainstream games, I find it valuable to look at them in terms of logics and models even to answer simple questions—for example, where the opportunities for play actually are and how they are shaped. The opportunities for play matter both for understanding games individually and for understanding our wider culture. As Murray argues in *On Video Games*,[63] big-budget, popular games are an important part of culture and are as ideologically revealing as the most popular television or music.

Returning to *The Sims 3*, it presents itself as a game about suburban life—about friends, neighbors, and family, as well as homes, furniture, and appliances. But if we look at the logics and models, the playable representations of interpersonal attitudes, relationships, and histories are actually pretty shallow. The deep, central logics and models are, instead, found in the game's representations of resources—with possessions being just one aspect of this. And it is the playable model of life resources that enables players to explore resource-focused issues, such as the homelessness explored in "Alice and Kev." It would be impossible for a player to set up a similar situation around a relationship-focused social issue (say, marriage equality) and watch the game's logics play themselves out as a simulation of it, because little related to the issue would happen. The game's opportunities for play are about resources much more than they are about relationships.

Similarly, *GTA IV* presents itself as the story of a war-weary immigrant trying to make his way in an unforgiving city, together with the traditional *GTA* opportunity for players to experiment with rule breaking. But if we look at the game through the lens of logics and models, we see it is an odd hybrid. Its most developed logics and models are in support of play as an urban driving simulation, and they enable a lot of player experimentation and expression. These are fused, however, with story logics that aren't about role-playing the main character and aren't about rule breaking, but rather are about compliance. We have to agree to carry out the criminal acts dictated by the story, including executing unarmed people, if we want to continue to expand the possibilities for play in the driving simulation. It can't help but make one wonder what would happen if these logics were removed from the game or at least stripped of their gating function.

And with *GTA V*, players have answered that question. Using mods like FiveM, with custom additions, they have set up dedicated multiplayer servers for role-play.[64] They're creating worlds of interacting characters—journalists chasing stories, law-abiding cab drivers, police officers pulling over criminals, helpful ambulance drivers, and, of course, criminals racing gleefully from robberies, lining their own pockets faster than any of the other in-game occupations allow.[65] In throwing off the strictures of the *GTA* story logics, and creating their own world of rule following and breaking, the players might seem to be engaging in the same kind of open-ended doll play that Flanagan discusses.

But if we look again, we see that the movements of these dolls aren't through the puppeteering we remember from childhood. Rather, they're in terms of the emotes and other animations built into *GTA V*. And if we look at the activities being role-played, the driving that is the central playable model for *GTA V* remains central to most of them.[66] In other words, we see a hybrid of open-ended role-play (as in what the characters say) and deep, ongoing engagement with the logics and models of *GTA V*. Using what is built into that game as both a constraint and a creative prompt, the players are answering the question posed by Stephanie Boluk and Patrick LeMieux: "What if video games were not considered games in the first place, but equipment for making metagames?"[67] Using *GTA V* as equipment, role-players have created something like an ongoing, multiplayer "My Trip to Liberty City"—with the live streaming of Twitch now opening the ongoing show to a vast audience.[68]

Like Jim Munroe's Canadian tourist, they are in the world of a *GTA* game, and the actions they perform require intimate familiarity with how the game's logics and models operate—but through their play, they can make the game about something more.

Part II

7 Inventing Graphical Logics

The word "video" appears in "video games" for a reason. Even though text-only games have a fond place in my heart, and certainly sound-only games exist, there is no denying the central place of video screens. It is on video screens, and using other elements of television technology, that video games came to prominence in our culture. The public space of the arcade and the private space of the television-connected home console were where a new generation of games reached a broad audience—and where designers did the most work to bring new experiences to that audience.

David Sudnow's *Pilgrim in the Microworld*[1] is an early book about getting deeply connected to game screens. It describes Sudnow—an academic phenomenologist and passionate jazz pianist—bringing his skills of keen observation, critical thinking, and dedicated practice to the world created by the video screen, its computationally driven objects, physical game controls, and his own actions. As Sudnow discusses, that world is not inside the screen. Rather, as he learned to play, and as each person learns, "we traverse the wired gap with motions that make us nonetheless feel in a balanced extending touch with things."[2]

What happens when we traverse that gap? Sudnow describes the virtual paddle controlled by *Breakout* players (figure 7.1) as like a part of a player's body, akin to a knuckle or the fully physical extension of a baseball bat:

> When you've got the paddle properly in hand it's a different kind of thing, not really a thing at all, but an extension of your fingers. You bring the so-called second section of the paddle beneath the ball in the same way you can move the back of your hand toward a cup in front of you so the knuckle of your index finger touches it. You don't have to look at that knuckle. . . . When a paddle or a bat is incorporated by the body, becoming a continuation of ourselves into and through which we realize an aim in a certain direction, such implements lose all existence as things in the world with the sorts of dimensions you measure on rulers. They become incorporated within a system of bodily spaces that can never be spoken of in the objective terms with which we speak of objects outside ourselves.[3]

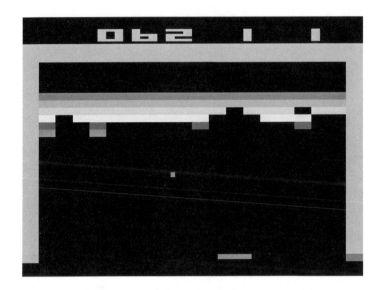

Figure 7.1

In *Breakout*, the player controls a paddle moving across the bottom of the screen, bouncing a ball against a wall at the top of the screen. Each bounce removes a brick from the wall. Each color-coded layer of the wall, when reached, makes the ball bounce faster than the layer before. Eventually, successful play requires that paddle positioning be done by reflex, operating the controller and the spatial model through the "system of bodily spaces" Sudnow describes, rather than through conscious planning. (Image of *Breakout* taken by the author during play on the Stella emulator, version 5.0.2.) (Atari, *Breakout*, 1978.)

What Sudnow is describing is the experience of having deeply learned the playable model of space in a game. Once it is learned, we cease to think about it, instead thinking of the actions we wish to take within it.[4] When it is learned, much of our ability to play within it is transferred from that game to similar games, just as most of our ability to drive transfers from car to car.

Once we can play within a game's model, that becomes the foundation of further experiences. Most books about game design focus on introducing challenges and goals to push players past what they can easily do within models. Later chapters of this book will instead discuss what additional meanings have been, and can be, layered atop the experience of virtual space.

But this chapter will look beneath the surface. It will examine the operational logics that form the foundation for the playable models of space we see in most games.[5] It will look back at how these logics were introduced into video games. In the process, it will tell a story that is familiar to many with an interest in the history of video games. Yet by telling the story differently, through the lens of logics and models, I believe we can shed additional light on four topics.

First, this chapter will trace the development of continuous, two-dimensional spatial models in video games—not to engage in a fetishization of "firsts" but for what their development can expose about the importance of aspects of these games that have commonly received less attention. The tracing reveals the importance of gravity, an aspect of these models that is little discussed. Second, through this process, this chapter emphasizes something too often forgotten: the work of game design innovation is not the exclusive province of sketchbooks and software but also of wiring diagrams and electric relays, and the latter's affordances and limitations have shaped our history. In particular, I recount two attempts to develop video game designs for wide audience–oriented hardware (comparatively inexpensive television technology), versions of which designs had previously existed in research labs (where they could employ computers far more expensive than could be deployed to wide audiences). This will not only provide another chance to discuss inventive approaches to logics—covered earlier in chapter 5—it will particularly be an opportunity to look at the importance of implementation to invention. Third, this chapter will call into question one of the most famous "just so" stories[6] of video games: that of *Computer Space*[7] flopping due to its complication, whereas *Pong*[8] succeeded due to its simplicity.[9] Finally, this chapter will offer a specific example of what is required to construct a playable model, discussing the combat models that so often accompany real-time continuous spatial models.

Continuous Spaces and Graphical Logics

Of course, games of the sort Sudnow describes are not the only ones that are played in a virtual space. The very earliest video games, decades before arcades and home consoles—such as Christopher Strachey's 1951 *M. U. C. Draughts*[10]—presented spaces of some sort. But like the tabletop game Strachey emulated (known in the United States as Checkers), the spaces in these games were *discrete*. They were divided up into non-overlapping spaces, and each game action involved moving a piece from one discrete space to another, with no in-between position available or meaningful.

The works that introduced games as a cultural force, instead, had models of space that felt *continuous*. The first hit video game in the computing subculture—*Spacewar*[11]—created the experience of smoothly flying a ship through space.[12] The first game well-known by broader culture—*Pong*—allowed players to smoothly move paddles to intercept a ball that, itself, moved smoothly through the space.

For this feeling of continuity to exist not only requires that there be many potential positions in the virtual space (so many that moving between them creates a feeling of continuousness) but also that time is ongoing.[13] Games like Strachey's, on the other hand, also operate in terms of discrete time—one player moves, then the other moves. And this sort of spatial model, with discrete space and time, is not only common in video games that emulate board and card games. It is also commonly seen in genres such as strategy games, simulation games, and puzzle games.

For us to understand the core mechanics of games—the key actions that players take—we have to understand the logics and models that are their foundation. For example, "jumping" is a core mechanic in many games. But the possibilities for player action and game response make jumping fundamentally different in a game like Strachey's (with a discrete spatial model, built using appropriate versions of logics) and a game like David Crane's *Pitfall!*[14] (with a continuous spatial model and different versions of logics).[15] Though Crane's game came three decades after Strachey's, the importance of this difference made it possible for *Pitfall* to become a highly influential early entry in the platformer genre.

Which brings us to the title of this chapter. There are three key *graphical logics*: *collision detection*, *movement physics*, and *navigation* (the last being another name for control logics, when used in spatial models). Each of these could be implemented in many ways, including as part of discrete spatial models. But I (and others) use the phrase "graphical logics" to refer to these logics when they form the foundation of continuous spatial models, presented visually. This is now usually done with the tools of computer graphics—such models are, in a sense, "computer graphics made playable" (though, as this chapter will describe, they have not always been implemented this way).

These logics are key to many of the experiences that have defined video games as we know them. In particular, they undergird the continuous, two-dimensional spatial models upon which video games grew into an important cultural and economic force, as with coin-op games of the 1970s such as *Pong*. Expanding the uses of such models, as described in chapters 8 and 9, has been central to the work of those pushing the meanings of games in new directions. And, of course, these models have an essential role in conventional games today, as seen in mobile phone titles such as *Angry Birds*,[16] which have made video game play ubiquitous.

Collision, Movement, and Physics: *Tennis for Two*

The history of computing is a funny thing. Innovative hardware and software are made up of reusable parts, or made for machines with other uses, and then may be disassembled or overwritten without leaving a trace. What history we know of video games, like other areas of computing, is the result of the happenstance of preservation as much as deliberate archiving and investigation.

Raiford Guins is probably the person who has spent the most time investigating the history of the game now commonly called *Tennis for Two*.[17] As Guins discusses in his 2014 book *Game After*,[18] it's not even clear how the game got that name—which seems to have appeared about four decades after the last time anyone played the original. Luckily, the game was also investigated in the 1980s, as part of a long series of video game lawsuits initiated by Magnavox, which itself created greater interest, leading to the preservation of documents and conducting of interviews that have helped us understand some of its history. As Guins reports,[19] these documents include diagrams of the original plans for the circuits, as well as notes indicating that the plans were revised in practice, but do not include any documentation of the revisions. So the original game cannot be entirely recovered. Still, we know things about it, both from documents of the time and from attempts to re-create it since.

Tennis for Two was certainly not the first video game. I currently believe that honor belongs to Strachey's *M. U. C. Draughts* (which I have given that name because I believe its lack of a name is part of why it has not been credited more widely).[20] But I also believe that *Tennis for Two* holds a very important place in the history of video games: it is the first video game with a continuous model of space, and it introduced versions of the key operational logics of collision detection and movement physics that are appropriate for building such models.

Tennis for Two was created by William Higinbotham, Robert V. Dvorak, and David Potter as a demonstration for the 1958 visitors' day at Brookhaven National Laboratory (BNL).[21] It presented a simplified side view of a tennis court on an oscilloscope screen, with a visible ball, net, and groundline but invisible racquets. Two players used simple controllers, each with two inputs: a button for determining when to hit the ball and a dial for determining the angle. In footage from the documentary *When Games Went Click*[22]—taken of a re-creation led by Peter Takacs, Gene Von Achen, Paul O'Connor, and Scott Coburn[23]—when the ball hit the net or ground it would bounce back (figures 7.2 and 7.3).

This bouncing is particularly important, because it is here that we see the collision-detection logic at work. All the elements of a logic (as discussed in chapter 1) are in place. The game state is presented on the oscilloscope, showing the ball colliding and responding to that collision. The display is controlled by analog computation, carrying out the abstract process—"when the boundaries of two virtual objects intersect, declare the intersection"—enabling the response.[24] The gameplay experience is of being able

Figure 7.2

Scott Coburn, Peter Takacs, and Gene Von Achen who, together with Paul O'Connor, reconstructed the retrospectively named *Tennis for Two* for its fiftieth anniversary in 2008. As Diane Greenberg reports, "Using Higinbotham's original plans, Takacs and his colleagues rebuilt the game with vintage parts, including mechanical relays and germanium transistors that first became commercially available in the 1950s. The original 1950s model analog computer that was made from vacuum tube circuits had to be simulated using modern integrated circuit chips." (Image courtesy of Brookhaven National Laboratory.) (Greenberg, Diane. "Celebrating *Tennis for Two* with a Video Game Extravaganza." *The Bulletin, Brookhaven National Laboratory*, October 31, 2008. https://www.bnl.gov/bnlweb/pubaf/bulletin/2008/bb103108.pdf.)

Figure 7.3

In a re-creation of *Tennis for Two*, the ball, net, and ground are visible, but the racquets are not. Re-created for the New York Historical Society Museum's exhibition, "Silicon City" (2014–2015). Re-creation consisted of a simulation of an oscilloscope displaying an emulation (by Ben Johnson and Peter Takacs), reconstructed controllers (by Adelle Lin), and exhibition design that "enlarges" the original oscilloscope (by Jeanne Angel, working with the show's exhibition and graphic designers, John Esposito and Kira Hwang), with consultation from Raiford Guins. (Image courtesy of Raiford Guins; Raiford Guins, "*Tennis for Two* at the NY Historical Society Museum," *Raiford Guins* (blog), November 19, 2015. https://raifordguins.com/2015/11/19/tennis-for-two-at-the-ny-historical-society-musuem/.)

to drive the game's collision detection over and over, learning how it operates in the spatial model of *Tennis for Two*. Taken together, these clearly fulfill the communicative role, "Virtual objects can touch, and these touches can have consequences."

Interestingly, as Nathan Altice pointed out to me in conversation,[25] it is less clear that collision detection supports the key mechanic (or gameplay "verb") that it will in future *Pong*-like games. This mechanic is returning the ball when it is served or returned by the other player. Because the paddles are invisible, it is hard to argue that collisions with them are communicated, so the logic is unfulfilled. It is this that most strongly gives the sense that *Tennis for Two* is not yet a mature version of a *Pong*-like game.[26]

The other logic introduced by the game (in a version appropriate for playable models of continuous space) is movement physics. This logic communicates that virtual objects move according to physical laws, sometimes in ways beyond the direct control of players. The abstract process evaluates the rules that apply in order to determine future positions of virtual objects. Of course, in the case of *Tennis for Two*, these rules were not written down mathematically or as software, but rather assembled in physical components. For those interested in understanding the logics of video games deeply, looking at early games is helpful, in part, because it broadens our thinking about how logics can be implemented. Electric relays can be where an innovative game designer does her work, not just lines of code.

One interesting thing about *Tennis for Two* is that it doesn't have objects that players can move around the visual space. Rather, every movement shows players an example of what happens when the ball moves with particular force at a particular angle. The game state presentation is always showing how the forces of physics are shaping the arcs, bounces, and remaining momentum of the ball. And this is key to the player learning the spatial model and developing the ability to effectively use the game's two key mechanics: serving the ball and returning the ball.[27]

Tennis for Two also illustrates another important idea about operational logics: they can be implemented in different ways, which shapes the resulting gameplay experience and playable model. For example, the movement physics logic in *Tennis for Two* is implemented in a way that includes gravity and wind resistance, which are often absent from later games (like *Pong*). The implementation of these forces threads through all aspects of the logic. For example, in *Tennis for Two* (and many other games) the implementation of gravity adds an abstract process: all unfixed elements not attached to a fixed element, or not on the "opposite" side of a fixed element, have attraction toward a point or region of the space, of which there may be more than one.[28] The communicative role is that one or more elements (the bottom of the screen in *Tennis for Two*, the central star in *Spacewar*) is a source of gravity. This issue will become key in our discussions of *Spacewar*, *Computer Space*, and *Pong*.

Tennis for Two's innovation was not in using analog computation to present images on the screen, or even in using collision detection and physics. As BNL's account tells us, "The computer's instruction book described how to generate various curves on the cathode-ray tube of an oscilloscope, using resistors, capacitors, and relays. Among the examples given in the book were the trajectories of a bullet, missile, and bouncing ball, all of which were subject to gravity and wind resistance."[29] But using these elements to construct video games' first playable model of continuous space and designing the first example of a *Pong*-like game (which would go on to great commercial success) were certainly very significant innovations.

Higinbotham and his collaborators also employed an inventive approach to implementation—particularly, implementation of the visual display. Versions of this approach would later become very important to game developers in other resource-constrained contexts, such as the Atari VCS (as described by Nick Montfort and Ian Bogost in *Racing the Beam*[30]). This approach is using a single visual output to draw multiple objects on screen, by changing its position quickly. BNL employee Peter Takacs, who led the re-creation of *Tennis for Two*, describes this: "Higinbotham used the transistors to build a fast-switching circuit that would take the three outputs from the computer and display them alternately on the oscilloscope screen at a 'blazing' fast speed of 36 Hertz. At that display rate, the eye sees the ball, the net, and the court as one image, rather than as three separate images."[31]

Tennis for Two's gameplay was novel and compelling enough that visitors lined up to experience it. However, it seems unlikely that serious thought was given to opening up the experience to a wider group. The game was composed of a large, heavy amount of hardware, driven by an analog computer. This was before the spread of digital computation made such experiences much easier to distribute—because they could travel as software for machines already configured with display screens, rather than as schematics for assembling and configuring an analog computer and additional hardware. That moment of software distribution for a landmark game came, instead, with *Spacewar*—the game that introduced the fundamental combination of a continuous spatial model, a combat model, and scenario/level design to the computing world.

Navigation, Combat, and Scenario Design: *Spacewar*

In 1961, Digital Equipment Corporation (DEC) occupied an unusual place in the computing landscape. Though it was a sizable company selling very expensive machines, it was also seen as a radical upstart, challenging the computer orthodoxy overseen by the dominant International Business Machines (IBM).[32] DEC was selling a vision of interactive computing, or working directly on a computer, that now seems everyday, but was an abrupt break with the tradition of delivering programs to computer operators (perhaps as trays of punch cards) and then waiting patiently for a reply after the scheduled run of one's program. What DEC was selling wasn't brand new, however. It was an experience pioneered in universities, government labs, and other research organizations—such as the MIT labs that were home to the legendary Whirlwind and TX-0 computers.

In the summer of 1961, the three people who conceived of *Spacewar*—Steve "Slug" Russell, J. Martin Graetz, and Wayne Wiitanen—were all working in the IBM computing paradigm (at Harvard University's Littauer Statistical Laboratory).[33] Then Graetz was hired at MIT by electrical engineering professor Jack Dennis, a recent PhD who was in charge of the department's computers, and Russell returned to MIT's Artificial Intelligence Group.[34] Dennis gave students and staff remarkable latitude in using the computers,[35] including the TX-0 and, particularly, the PDP-1 computer donated by DEC in September of 1961.[36] Russell, Graetz, and Wiitanen came up with the concept for *Spacewar* while brainstorming what to do with the Type 30 Precision CRT display that was scheduled to be installed a couple months after the PDP-1. They wanted to outdo the existing demonstration programs for the Whirlwind and TX-0, which included a bouncing ball, a mouse that would traverse user-constructed mazes, a tic-tac-toe game, and Marvin Minsky's generative animation program Tri-Pos (better known as the "Minskytron").[37]

The first version of *Spacewar* was completed by Russell in February 1962. Two visually distinct ships could rotate and thrust to move across the screen in a manner governed by relatively realistic physics (momentum is key to playing *Spacewar*). In creating this much, Russell had already introduced another key logic for playable spatial models: navigation. Further, the two ships could fire projectiles at each other and destroy each other when there was a collision between a projectile and a ship—introducing video games' first mechanics of combat in continuous time (figure 7.4). The wedding of these two experiences—of continuous spatial movement and combat in continuous time—became an extremely important, almost dominant, approach as video games developed further.

Focusing on *Spacewar*'s introduction of the navigation logic, we can see what an important difference it makes that the racquets in *Tennis for Two* are invisible. For a model of any domain to be playable, it must support interaction.[38] That is, there must be a control logic available to players that changes the state of the model in a way that

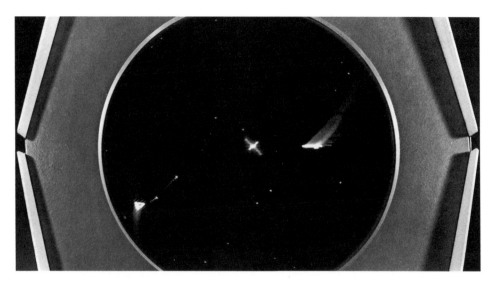

Figure 7.4
In a game of *Spacewar*, the "Needle" ship approaches the central star (right) while the "Wedge" ship fires two photon torpedoes, shown as dots brighter than the background starfield (left). Screenshot showing DEC PDP-1 display during Computer History Museum PDP-1 restoration project, as featured in "Story of *Spacewar!*" (Courtesy of the Computer History Museum, image number 102695600.) (Plutte, "Story of *Spacewar!*")

is presented to players. For continuous spatial models, the key control logic is navigation. Even a game as simple as *Pong* gives players the ability to navigate paddles up and down the screen. But because of the nature of *Tennis for Two*'s paddles, the introduction of navigation to continuous space video games fell to *Spacewar*.[39]

The abstract process for navigation in this type of model could be stated as moving one (or more) virtual object(s)—and/or the rest of the virtual space apart from the object(s)—so that all the elements of one are progressively offset relative to the other, based on a player-controlled input, for as long as that input is in effect. The communicative role could be stated as the player controlling the type, and/or direction, and/or timing of the movement of a virtual object with which she identifies. (Both the abstract process and the communicative role would be different for a navigation logic in a different sort of spatial model—such as the first-person 3-D spatial model of *DOOM* or the link-based, textually represented model of the Crowther and Woods *Adventure*.)

The implementation of navigation requires that some process is "listening" for input from the player and, also, that some process can make a representation of something under the player's control change position in the space of the model. Of course, the player's control can be partially indirect, as when the player acts together with a physics logic. This is the case in *Spacewar*, where the player's primary mechanic for movement is thrusting. The player holds down the thrust control for differing amounts of time, and the ship is rotated to different angles to provide input to the physics logic that (together with the other forces already in effect) determines where the player's ship will navigate. Indirect control is also present in other types of games. For example, in platforming games players can often let go of (or walk off of) ledges, with the expectation that physics will take them "down" in the model's space.

Learning to perform navigation, both directly and indirectly, begins with players identifying what represents "them" in the game state presentation, then experimenting with interface controls to learn how the navigation mechanics operate. As players become more fluent in navigation, they are increasingly able to choose actions to take in the game's spatial model (ones that they desire and ones that the game supports) and anticipate the potential results. Player understanding may initially be considered and deliberate. But as Sudnow and others discuss, in most cases it quickly becomes a bodily understanding, with the things that represent us in continuous space games (and the interfaces that bridge our actions and theirs) coming to feel like extensions of our own bodies and "decisions" about how to act made at a preconscious level.[40] If we fail to make this transition, many games (including *Spacewar* with a competent opponent) move far too quickly for us to succeed. Brendan Keogh—building on the work of Sudnow, N. Katherine Hayles, Henri Lefebvre, James Ash, and others—writes of this as "embodied literacy."[41]

At this point in *Spacewar*'s development it might have been considered complete—except for one glaring problem. Over time, it wasn't a very compelling experience. It was an exciting demo, but not something with depth, something that would pay off players' investments of time and consideration. As Graetz writes:

> Up to this point, *Spacewar!* was heavily biased towards motor skills and fast reflexes, with strategy counting for very little. Games tended to become nothing more than wild shootouts, which was exciting but ultimately unrewarding.[42]

Spacewar lacked an interesting gameplay scenario, what is often referred to as *level design* (though games such as *Spacewar* obviously are not divided into levels). It didn't lack primarily in terms of the logics it implemented for play, though the further development of one of these was key to its next step. Rather, *Spacewar* lacked an interesting situation for play. It lacked a selection and arrangement of elements that would matter in terms of its models and mechanics, shaping patterns of play, opening new strategic possibilities and new skills needed to exercise them.

The solution was twofold. First, Dan Edwards expanded the physics logic of *Spacewar* to include gravity. Second, a large star was introduced in the middle of the play area, with a gravity well encompassing the entire area.[43] Colliding with the star, like collision with a projectile, caused immediate death (which would happen relatively quickly if players applied no thrust to their ships at the start of a game). As Graetz explains:

> The star did two things. It introduced a player-independent element that the game needed; when speeds were high and space was filled with missiles, it was often sheer luck that kept one from crashing into the star. It also brought the other elements of the game into focus by demanding strategy. In the presence of gravity, both ships were affected by something beyond their control, but which a skillful player could use to advantage.[44]

The first fruit of this new scenario was a maneuver called the "CBS opening"—because the paths of two ships executing it resembled the television network's eye-shaped logo (figure 7.5). Skilled players, rather than immediately thrusting away from the star, would fire short blasts directing their ships to fall into the gravity well and whip around the star. This proved to be the fastest way to build up all-important momentum.[45]

Spacewar was complete by the end of April 1962 and was first shown publicly at MIT's Science Open House in May. Its creators expected a crowd, and they got one. By summer the group that completed it was drifting away from MIT, but the game had taken on a life of its own. As Graetz reports, "Program tapes were already showing up all over the country, not only on PDP-1s but on just about any research computer that had a programmable CRT."[46] Unlike *Tennis for Two*, which could not be distributed as software, *Spacewar* was on its way to becoming the world's first hit video game.

But *Spacewar*'s rapid spread wasn't simply due to labs sharing tapes with each other. As historian Henry Lowood writes, the game "was shipped by DEC with PDP computers as a test program to verify their operation after new installations. *Spacewar* became a fixture in university and industrial laboratories of the 1960s and 1970s."[47] *Spacewar* was a perfect demonstration of the vision of personal, interactive computing that DEC was selling—so DEC not only distributed it, but selected it to be one of the first things seen after each successful DEC computer installation.

Further, as a testament to the depth of strategy and skill that could be brought to the completed *Spacewar*, Stewart Brand (of *Whole Earth Catalog* fame) organized a "*Spacewar*

Figure 7.5
Whipping around *Spacewar*'s central star, through the use of momentum and gravity, creates a
shape reminiscent of the US CBS network's logo in this time-lapse image. (Image from Graetz,
"*Spacewar!* Real-Time Capability of the PDP-1.")

Olympics" at the Stanford Artificial Intelligence Laboratory (SAIL) in 1972. The event
was sponsored by *Rolling Stone*, and Brand published his account both in that magazine
and in his later book, *II Cybernetic Frontiers*.[48] This not only served to document the
game's popularity after a decade of play but also brought that popularity to another
level of public consciousness.[49]

Yet there appeared to be no easy way to bring *Spacewar* to that public. The very fact
that made it almost omnipresent in the computer culture was what blocked it from the
wider culture: it was software for digital computers. Such computers were simply too
expensive for any sort of commercial public deployment of games, even a decade after
Spacewar's creation.

Combat in Games

In video games that include combat, the combat models are most commonly designed to work with continuous spatial models (supported by graphical logics) and resource logics. For example, in *Spacewar* shooting torpedoes obviously requires movement physics and collision-detection logics for their flight (together with a control logic for determining when to fire). Less obviously, there is also a resource logic involved. Though *Spacewar* does not treat the amount of damage that each ship can take as a resource except in the most basic sense (a single collision with a torpedo destroys the ship) the number of torpedoes a ship can fire is a time-limited resource. As Graetz writes, "There was a fixed delay between shots 'to allow the torp tubes to cool.'"[50]

But this sort of observation does not give us a broader sense of how combat models operate in video games. And in fact such a broader sense is not often put into words, even if we "know it when we see it"—as Joseph C. Osborn, Dylan Lederle-Ensign, Michael Mateas, and I discovered when we worked to explore this question.[51] While it is generally taken as a given that combat is modeled by many games, we were able to find no discussions—in game design, game studies, or elsewhere—that tried to be specific about what this means across game genres.[52] So we began with a close examination of how particular games implement combat, especially *Super Street Fighter II*[53] and *Final Fantasy*.[54]

Looking for the common ground of combat between them, the traditional way of talking about game design, through focusing on mechanics, offers no help. In terms of mechanics, there is almost no overlap between the real-time, physically detailed punching, kicking, crouching, jumping, and special moves of *Super Street Fighter II* and the turn-based, physically abstract melee attacks, magic casting, potion drinking, item using, and running away of *Final Fantasy*. Another popular way of discussing game design, in terms of genre, is equally unhelpful. One of these is considered a fighting game and the other an RPG.

But we were able to look at how each game implements and composes operational logics to form a model of activity that players interpret as combat. (In chapter 4 I referred to this as meeting the "communicative and procedural obligations" to be understood as a playable representation of something.) First, at a relatively abstract level, the combat models of games involve multiple agents who are able to carry out violent acts toward one another in some space. The same logics may be used in other situations, as when players attempt to destroy inanimate objects, but this is not interpreted as combat.

At a more detailed level, combat models include means to determine what actions agents may take, whether they succeed, and to what extent. Different games satisfy these requirements using different logics, implemented and connected in different ways. *Super Street Fighter II*, for example, uses a "stance" entity-state logic—the player's character standing, crouching, or jumping—to determine which attacks are available. It uses collision detection to determine whether normal attacks are successful but uses a temporal pattern-matching logic for special moves. It uses the state of the opponent— who may be blocking (also the stance logic), simultaneously completing an attack of greater strength, or in some other relevant state—to determine the extent of damage to the opponent's health (a resource logic).

Final Fantasy, on the other hand, has different logics determining the availability of different types of attacks. A mage, for example, can only cast a spell that they know (a resource logic with differentiated items, similar to many inventory logics), can only cast it if they have enough magic points left (a resource logic with undifferentiated items), and can only cast spells at all if they are in an appropriate entity state (for example, not in a silenced state)—whereas different considerations would come into play if the mage attempted a melee attack. Similarly, rather than the success of melee attacks being determined by visible collision detection (and largely driven by player skill) as in *Super Street Fighter II*, the success of *Final Fantasy* attacks is determined by largely invisible chance logics (parameterized by character attributes, which can change over time)—making player skill in *Final Fantasy* battles more akin to skill at Blackjack than skill at Basketball.

These are two different approaches to deciding what actions agents may take, whether they succeed, and to what extent. In addition, to complete a combat model, a game must implement its logics such that combat actions have observable effects, must define the circumstances under which characters enter and leave combat, and must define how instances of combat themselves come to an end.

This outline of combat in games helps us know what we should examine when trying to understand a game's combat model and when comparing it to the models of other games. And it also helps us understand when what we are seeing is not combat. For example, consider Molleindustria and Jim Munroe's game *Unmanned*.[55] This game stands out for both employing and interrogating combat. The player character is a drone operator who lives in the western US but remotely pilots military drones located in the Middle East. The game seems to be built on two models: a link-based dialogue/ story model and a combat model of the sort just described. The dialogue/story model drives the experience of the operator talking to himself, his co-pilot, and his wife and son. The rest of the game consists of two representations of mediated violence: using the drone for tracking and shooting targeted people in the Middle East (figure 7.6) and playing a modern warfare-themed video game at home with the character's son.

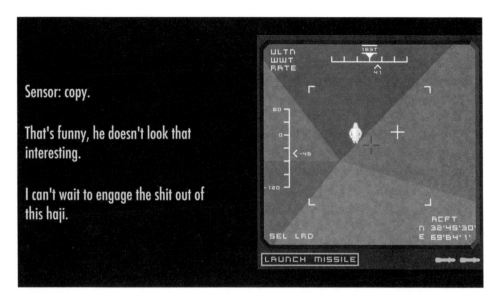

Figure 7.6
In the split-screen game *Unmanned*, the two panes are used to show different types of gameplay, as well as dialogue, character portraits, landscapes, and more. Here the left side displays choices in the link-based dialogue/story model and the right side displays missile targeting in what we might call its "hunting" (rather than combat) model. (Creative Commons image from molleindustria.org.)

But if we examine *Unmanned* using the idea of a combat model described here, it becomes immediately clear that only one of these activities actually represents combat. While the game-within-the-game employs such a model exactly, the drone operation portions have only one agent capable of taking violent action: the player character. This is therefore not a model of combat, but rather a model of something else—perhaps *hunting*. Only the state is capable of committing violence in this circumstance (of course, this asymmetry is the norm for state violence). *Unmanned* uses a combat model in its game-within-the-game precisely to emphasize what most military-themed games elide: the model of combat in games is not the model of much of the violence carried out by the US military—despite the rhetorical stance of games like *America's Army*.

The Importance of Implementation: *Computer Space* and *Pong*

Lowood's excellent article "Videogames in Computer Space: The Complex History of *Pong*"[56] tells the story of what happened after *Spacewar*'s unprecedented spread through the 1960s computer culture. He traces the converging paths of commercial video game pioneers Nolan Bushnell and Ralph Baer, and in doing so tells the story of how certain approaches to continuous spatial models—and the game designs they supported—became dominant in the early video game arcade machines and home consoles.

Bushnell's story is the more famous. He graduated in 1968 from the University of Utah, where he later claimed to have played *Spacewar*, and moved to California to work for the technology company Ampex. This was not far from Stanford University, the future site of SAIL's *Spacewar* Olympics and the likely site of Bushnell's actual first exposure to the game.[57] Working with fellow Ampex employee Ted Dabney, Bushnell sought a way to commercialize *Spacewar*—but the great expense of even stripped-down digital computers (such as the Data General Nova) made it seemingly impractical. Two others actually did this, but only in a limited manner, as Lowood reports: "[A] recently graduated SAIL student, Bill Pitts, and his friend Hugh Tuck built a coin-operated (coin-op) computer game, *The Galaxy Game*, for the newly released PDP-11/20, DEC's first 16-bit computer. . . . [They] converted the PDP-10 version of *Spacewar* for this machine."[58] With a total expense of $20,000 (including computer, display, cabinet, and controllers) it was clearly not a route to reaching the broader public.

What Bushnell and Dabney came to realize was that the only practical route was to attempt to implement the key operational logics in hardware—using television technology—rather than in software for general-purpose digital computers. In pursuing this route, they were able to reproduce a good number of *Spacewar*'s key elements in innovative new implementations. For example, as Lowood writes:

> [A] small number of diode arrays connected to logic gates produced the rotating images of rockets seen on the screen; the rocket images were clearly visible even in the pattern of diodes on one of the PC boards. . . . Bushnell's rockets were essentially hardwired bitmaps that could be moved around the screen independently of the background, a crucial innovation that made it possible to produce screen images efficiently.[59]

This enabled the logic of navigation. However, other elements had to be stripped out, most notably reducing the physics logic to remove gravity—and with it *Spacewar*'s central star scenario design (figure 7.7). The result, *Computer Space*, was released in August 1971 by Nutting Associates. *Computer Space* failed to become a hit, while *Pong* was a great success the following year. This is one of the most discussed pairs of events in video game history, and the outcome is generally attributed to the complexity of *Computer Space* as compared with *Pong*'s simplicity.

For example, Mark J. P. Wolf writes, "The first arcade video game, Nolan Bushnell's *Computer Space* (1971), failed commercially, because players found its controls difficult to understand and use, and it was not until Bushnell's second effort, *Pong* (1972), which had a single control and simplified graphics, that the videogame as a commercial entity

Figure 7.7

Computer Space had the dueling spaceships of *Spacewar*—both in the original single-player version and a later two-player release—but without gravity and the central star. This was previously found to be a less-than-compelling experience when the original *Spacewar* was being developed at MIT. Unfortunately, Bushnell and Dabney do not appear to have known this, and Bushnell later blamed the limited success of *Computer Space* on its complexity. Image of *Computer Space* from a cabinet repaired by Ed Fries. (Image courtesy of Ed Fries.) (Fries, "Fixing *Computer Space*.")

finally found success."[60] John A. Price offers a similar comparison, writing that Bushnell and Nutting Associates "released the world's first commercial video game under the title of *Computer Space* in 1970. Only 1,500 of the machines were sold, in part because the game was too complex and too difficult to play. Determined to come out with a game that was not too complex, in 1972 Nolan Bushnell started the Atari Company. Their first game was a Ping-Pong game called *Pong* for the arcades. Pong was highly successful and it was widely imitated."[61] Montfort and Bogost tell the story in similar terms, observing that Bushnell sought a way to bring an experience like *Spacewar* to the public, and the result "was *Computer Space*, which arcade game manufacturer Nutting Associates released in 1971 to very limited commercial success. Complexity of play was part of the problem—the general public wasn't accustomed to arcade games. . . . *Pong* solved the problem that plagued *Computer Space*—ease of use—partly by being based on the familiar game table tennis and partly thanks to the simplicity of its gameplay instructions."[62]

Interestingly, the common version of this story offers no source for the idea that it was over-complication that led to *Computer Space* not becoming the first hit video game. Those that do cite a source indicate that Bushnell may be a contributor to (or even the originator of) the idea. Wolf writes, in a different book from the earlier quote, "Bushnell attributed the lack of success of *Computer Space* to be partly due to the complexity of the game's instructions and its gameplay mechanics."[63] Lowood quotes Bushnell as saying that "'the typical guy in the bar' was completely baffled."[64] Steven L. Kent writes in *The Ultimate History of Video Games*, "Bushnell admits that the instructions were too complex: 'Nobody wants to read an encyclopedia to play a game.' He also blames Nutting for marketing the game badly."[65] Tom Sito offers the same Bushnell quote, in his *Moving Innovation: A History of Computer Animation*, "the instructions were too complicated. 'Nobody wants to read an encyclopedia to play a game,' Bushnell confessed."[66] Sito writes this despite noting, on the previous page, that the more complicated *Galaxy Game* (discussed earlier) was being played by the "coffeehouse habitués" on the Stanford campus, only a few miles away from where *Pong* would become a hit.

There are, of course, many other reasons one might imagine for *Computer Space* not catching on as *Pong* did. Perhaps it was the fact that it was a single-player game at first, with a two-player version not introduced until 1973. Maybe the issue was cabinet design—as Guins notes, the wood grain design of *Pong* (as opposed to the fiberglass cabinet of *Computer Space*) was such that it would fit into many more contexts.[67] Maybe it was a game scenario that, while compelling in the computer subculture, didn't resonate with the broader public.

But a different explanation is suggested by the facts already discussed in this chapter. The design of *Computer Space*—essentially, *Spacewar* without gravity and the central star—was already known to lack compelling gameplay in February of 1962 when the game was still in initial development at MIT. While complexity may have been an additional issue, it seems likely that the key reason for the limited success of *Computer Space* is that the versions of its operational logics that could be implemented in commercially viable technology could not support a compelling version of *Spacewar*-style game design. As former Atari employee Jerry Jessop commented to the *New York Times*, "The game play was horrible."[68]

Matt Barton's account, in *Vintage Games 2.0*, is the only one I have found that directly discusses the gap between Bushnell's preferred story and the realities of *Computer Space* gameplay:

> Bushnell concluded that the game was too complicated for gamers accustomed to pinball. "The lesson was," said Bushnell, "keep it simple."
>
> However, Computer Space's failure is probably owed more to its dull gameplay than dull-witted players—as later, more successful efforts show.[69]

As Barton suggests, should we require further evidence that a game of *Spacewar*'s complexity could be a success outside the lab, we need only look at the story of *Space Wars*,[70] a 1977 version developed by Larry Rosenthal for Cinematronics. As Barton and Bill Loguidice write, "Rosenthal's key innovation was developing a special processor, which was cheap to make yet still sophisticated enough to run the full version of *Space-war!*, complete with the gravity well and two-player dog fighting that made the original so compelling."[71] Rather than turning off audiences with its complexity, "it was a wonderful adaptation of *Spacewar!* and earned rich profits for Rosenthal and Cinematronics," Barton and Loguidice conclude.

Looking again at the hardware for these early games may help clarify why *Computer Space*'s development resulted in its particular design. Lacking Rosenthal's specialized processor, it appears that the implementable spatial models, and the gameplay they could support, were significantly determined by available television technology. Ralph Baer's story, running in parallel with Bushnell's, helps illustrate this. As Baer reports in *Videogames: In The Beginning*,[72] in 1966 he was working at Sanders Associates and, while waiting for a bus, returned to previous musings about using home televisions as game devices. After some unofficial work by himself and Bob Tremblay, Baer got approval to pursue the project further, bringing in Bob Solomon, Bill Harrison, Bill Rush, and others. The team developed technology prototypes and games at the same time, including games with player-controlled objects chasing each other, "pumping" games in which players tried to raise or lower color levels (for example, one player trying to raise blue water behind a screen overlay of a burning house, while the other tried to lower red fire from the top of the screen), and multiple-choice games. But nothing seemed compelling enough to justify a home unit's likely cost.

When Rush suggested a third, machine-controlled object (in addition to the two player-controlled ones) the Sanders Associates team quickly found themselves converging on the types of Tennis/Ping-Pong games that Higinbotham had pioneered (though Baer's team was likely unaware of *Tennis for Two*). This might seem like a doomed project, given the discussion here. After all, gravity was as central to the design of *Tennis for Two* as it was to *Spacewar*—maybe even more so, because the fundamental gameplay of *Tennis for Two* was lobbing the ball back and forth, choosing the right moment in its parabola to hit the button and "return" the ball to the other player along another gravity-controlled arc.

The Sanders team didn't invent video games (as Baer and others have suggested). But they did come to a crucial realization: that a compelling *Pong*-like video game could be created without gravity implemented in its physics logic. What this required was (literally) a different perspective from that pursued by the BNL team. Rather than the "side view" of *Tennis for Two* (as though sitting near the umpire, looking down the line of the net), the Sanders team adopted a "top-down view" (as though looking at the game from above, with the net stretched from top to bottom of the screen). When seen in this way, the gravity-defined arcs of the balls in such games would become much less salient, such that they could be abstracted away while still having the video game be interpretable as a procedural representation of the physical world gameplay.

This sort of gameplay turned out to be compelling. And without the need for gravity, it could be supported by relatively low-cost television technology. As a result, the Sanders team had an appealing game using components that could potentially be sold in a home consumer unit. This led to a licensing deal with television manufacturer Magnavox—which then produced the groundbreaking Odyssey, the first home video game system, released in 1972.[73]

The Odyssey system was first demonstrated in spring, but not released until summer—a gap that proved important. Bushnell attended an early demonstration and, shortly afterward, Bushnell and Dabney separated from Nutting and founded the company that would become Atari. They were soon joined by another ex-Ampex engineer, Al Alcorn, who Bushnell assigned to create a simple Tennis/Ping-Pong game—which he characterized as the simplest game he could think of. However, as Lowood writes, "When he tasked Alcorn with a ball-and-paddle game, his suggestion must have been influenced by what he had seen from Magnavox."[74]

Alcorn's top-down view game, christened *Pong*, was launched in a tavern later in 1972 and—as noted in multiple accounts quoted earlier—became an immediate hit, initiating the arcade era of video games. It presumably even helped drive sales of the Odyssey, which for a time was the only way to play a *Pong*-like game at home. In becoming such a great success, *Pong* demonstrated to the world that Tennis/Ping-Pong games are a design "sweet spot" for the kinds of simple, continuous spatial models that could be implemented with television technology. Many similar games from competing companies were launched in both the arcade and home markets in the coming years. (And it was Magnavox's decision to sue these companies, Atari, and others, that led to the rediscovery of *Tennis for Two*.)

Logics and Models as a Historical Lens

With the launch of *Pong*-like games, the initial invention of playable models of continuous space (in continuous time) for video games was completed. Of course, significant inventive work remained to be done, and would shape the future of games when it arrived. For example, the rise of the FPS genre would only take place after the invention of the implementations that would allow for real-time 3-D spatial models on consumer-level hardware. As with *Spacewar*, pairing with a combat model would be important to the success of the FPS and others. And as noted in chapter 4, the underlying technologies and design practices would benefit from long-term military investment—some of it indirect—as seen in this chapter with the prominence of BNL and MIT's TX-0 lab, both of which depended on military funding.

My main interest here is not simply to retell the story of these games, which is often told. Rather, it is to tell it with attention to the specifics of the versions of the operational logics that were actually implemented for these early games, how they were implemented, and what playable models and gameplay scenarios these enabled. Doing this here has revealed that one of the most widespread game history stories—of the complexity that kept *Computer Space* from *Pong*-like success—is at the very least partial, and more likely simply mistaken. By engaging the limitations of the television technology with which *Computer Space* was implemented, we can understand why its physics logic lacked gravity. By looking at the importance of adding gravity to the physics logic of *Spacewar*, and how it achieved compelling gameplay only after this addition, we can understand that it was likely a lack of compelling gameplay that led to the fate of *Computer Space*. We can't know for certain how the story of *Computer Space*'s overcomplication became so widely accepted—but we can speculate that Bushnell, the source most often cited, would have been happier to have

Computer Space known for overestimating its audience than for being uninteresting at its core.

At the same time, this chapter's tracing of gravity's role in early spatial models for games has revealed something further. While gravity was part of the physics logic of the earliest known *Pong*-like video game (*Tennis for Two*), it was established by the Sanders team that such designs could succeed without gravity through a change in gameplay perspective. *Pong*, the first hit video game, lifted this changed perspective from the in-process Magnavox Odyssey. In short, the story of *Computer Space* versus *Pong* is actually of one game design known to fail without gravity as part of its physics logic versus another game design known to succeed under such circumstances—the circumstances that faced all parties at the launch of the coin-op game era.

We need to start telling these stories differently. And it is my hope that we can also begin to use attention to the specifics of logics and models—and their implementations, even when these stretch beyond the comfort zone of software implementations—to reconsider other widespread stories about game history. That said, this book will not continue to focus on the history of inventive work with graphical logics, the playable models they supported, and the game genres those enabled. Rather, it will turn to the expansion of how the underlying logics were used, and the creation of models of space that are also meant as models of more.

8   Refinement

Now it is time to return—with more depth—to a question raised in this book's introduction: How does Pac-Man eat?

More specifically, how is it that millions of people around the world have moved Pac-Man (and other Pac-folk) around mazes, encountering dots, and unproblematically thought of the removal of those dots from the screen as them being "eaten"? How have players come to think of themselves, on some level, as the entities that are eating? (Thinking, "I did it!" after successful play.)

Using the vocabulary of this book, one might give the answer, "collision detection." But as the previous chapter discussed, the early uses of collision detection in video games were to create experiences of quite literal collisions. *Tennis for Two*'s[1] ball hits a net. *Spacewar*'s[2] ship hits a star.[3] *Pong*'s[4] ball hits a paddle.

And yet when playing *Pac-Man*,[5] I experience such a collision as eating. Clearly we have the ability to interpret logics in multiple ways. This goes beyond our ability to see eating in other media, when it isn't "really" going on. (Cookie Monster doesn't actually consume cookies, even on set.) With these broader interpretations of logics, we can come to take action in terms of, and feel agency to undertake, things that not only are not literally happening, but also are not what the logics were used for when they were invented.

As discussed in chapter 3, I call the introduction of new communicative roles for existing logics and models an "expansive" design approach, and it has been key to broadening what games can address through play. This chapter begins by looking at a game released the year before *Pac-Man*, through which we can see how expansion was being employed by game creators at that time. And by considering the context, in this chapter and the next, we can suggest an answer to another question: If collision is the answer to the question of *how* Pac-Man eats, *why* is that?

Adventure and *Adventure*

The 1970s gave us two highly influential games with the same name. The first *Adventure*[6] was developed by Will Crowther and greatly expanded by Don Woods, using DEC PDP-10 computers in 1975–1977.[7] Also known as *Colossal Cave Adventure*, it is based on the experience of exploring a real cave system in Kentucky. As you might expect, a spatial model is key to this *Adventure*, but not the continuous, graphical sort described in the previous chapter. Instead, each space is described textually. Movement between spaces happens when the player types a command such as a direction (perhaps "down" or "west") or a more specific move (such as "climb" or the name of the room to enter). See figure 8.1.

While the spatial model that supports play clearly works in terms of discrete space and time, it is also clear that it cannot operate on a grid, like Checkers or Chess. Caves are not arranged in regular, geometric patterns. This is fine, because the foundation of the spatial model is a linking logic—enabling different parts of the cave system to be connected to varying numbers of other parts, in a variety of ways. Players engage in exploration, maze-like navigation, object collection and manipulation, puzzle solving, and simple combat—specifying their actions, and receiving game responses, in text. One advantage of this type of game is that it can be played without a graphical terminal. A paper teletype will do, and these were easier to come by in 1970s computing environments.

The computer game tradition that *Adventure* founded is now commonly called "interactive fiction" (or "IF")—a not-uncommon alternate name is "text adventure." *Adventure* itself was hugely popular in the computing culture of the 1970s, and the genre[8] it spawned included some of the best-selling software of the 1980s.[9] The commercial era of IF produced a series of notable titles from dedicated studios such as Infocom, as well as one-offs such as *Mindwheel*,[10] written by future US poet laureate Robert Pinsky.[11]

In what would seem to be an almost-unrelated area of the gaming world, in the late 1970s home consoles had moved beyond machines with a fixed number of pre-installed games (or a fixed set of components that could be connected). Instead new games were written after the consoles were already in players' homes. The new games were packaged as cartridges, which players inserted into the consoles. By 1978 the most successful of these cartridge-based consoles was the Atari Video Computer System (or "VCS"), later renamed the 2600.

Warren Robinett wanted to bridge the gap between these two areas of games, creating an experience for the Atari VCS inspired by the original *Adventure*. As Nick Montfort and Ian Bogost discuss in *Racing the Beam*,[12] Robinett faced a massive challenge.

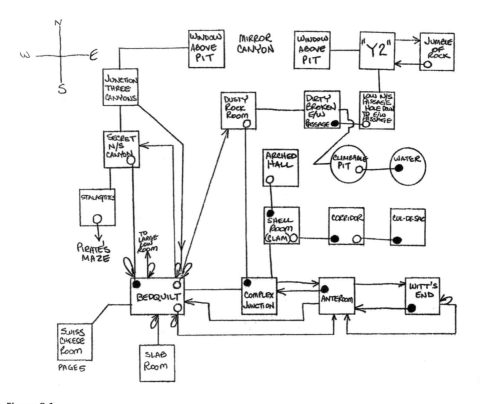

Figure 8.1

Hand-drawn map of a portion of *Adventure*—attributed to Edward Wright, from a group of maps created January 1979 to May 1980. The link-based structure is visible in the lines, which by default represent two-way links at the same "level" of the cave structure. There are also arrows, representing one-way links; arrows that return to their origins, representing looping links; filled circles, representing upward movement via links; and empty circles, representing downward movement via links. (From a file preserved at the IF Archive, a public service of the Interactive Fiction Technology Foundation. Partially reconstructed by Jennifer K Mahal. Original located at http://www .ifarchive.org/if-archive/solutions/maps/Adventure_Maps.pdf.)

The experience of the original *Adventure*, like the original *Spacewar*, was created on a general-purpose computer far too expensive for use in homes. In attempting to create an analogous experience for the Atari VCS, Robinett's task was similar to what Bushnell and Dabney attempted (and arguably failed) in emulating *Spacewar* with the limited resources used for *Computer Space*,[13] as discussed in the previous chapter.

This was because the Atari VCS, even though it had a stripped-down microprocessor within it, could only be used effectively by offloading much of a game's logic and presentation to a proprietary Television Interface Adapter (TIA). The TIA embodied many of the lessons Atari had learned with *Pong* and its arcade successor *Tank*.[14] In particular, the key operational logics of navigation and collision detection were implemented by the TIA *in hardware*.[15] As Montfort and Bogost explain regarding collision detection:

> Collision detection is a common feature of graphical video games, but it is often a bit tricky to code up. Thanks to the TIA's provision for collision detection in hardware, it is easy to implement things such as shooting or being shot by missiles, running into a wall, or consuming something. All the program has to do is read from a set of memory-mapped registers reserved for collision.[16]

This had the impact for Robinett—and for every other programmer and designer seeking to bring a new video game experience to the vast VCS audience—of making spatial models of the sort pioneered by *Pong* the overwhelmingly obvious choice for making playable almost anything they sought to represent. But it was not at all obvious how to do this for a spatial model like *Adventure*'s. Robinett's approach was to make a virtual world of many interconnected screens, with movement "off the edge" of one triggering a move to another. This may seem familiar and trivial to us now, but it was a very influential innovation in the era of single-screen games. Further, the games for which the VCS was designed didn't actually have to keep track of the locations of objects in an absolute coordinate space (the programs could simply move objects relative their previous positions and respond to collisions). Robinett had to alter the implemented model to trigger an event, rather than wrap around the screen, when the edge of the screen is reached.[17]

Moving from screen to screen is a very different implementation of a linking logic, one that has lived on in many games. It is not only what players would later experience when moving off the edge of the screen in games such as *The Legend of Zelda*. It is also the logic behind *Zelda*'s within-screen cave entrances and the pipes in *Super Mario Bros*.

With exploration in a virtual world possible, Robinett was left with the question of how to create gameplay analogous to the original *Adventure*'s many experiences of finding, transporting, manipulating, and employing objects—in order to gain access to new areas, collect treasures and objects useful in future areas, and defeat enemies. In addition, the virtual world needed to include walls—for basic navigation, for access-restriction puzzles, and for maze-like experiences. Only one of the TIA's primary hardware-implemented logics remained for this collection of tasks: collision detection. Further, the standard VCS joystick offered only two controls: the directional pointing of the joystick and a single button.

Figure 8.2
Collision detection is used to create walls that limit navigation in Warren Robinett's *Adventure*. The small square is the player character. (Images of *Adventure* taken by the author during play on the Stella emulator, version 5.0.2.)

As a result, in the *Adventure* game Atari released in 1979,[18] collision detection is used to create walls that limit navigation (figure 8.2). And collision is also used for picking up objects (figure 8.3). And collision, while holding an object, is used for the simple puzzles (figure 8.4). And collision, while holding a sword, is also used for simple combat (figure 8.5).

The expansion of collision detection to this range of uses and meanings may seem unremarkable now. Most of us who have played video games have become culturally accustomed to interpreting collisions in a wide variety of ways—much as viewers of film have become accustomed to interpreting cuts as transitions across a wide range of shifts in space and time. But at the time even using collision to collect objects was in need of explanation, with *Adventure*'s manual telling prospective players:

> Scattered throughout the Kingdom are certain objects to help you in your search for the Enchanted Chalice. To pick up an object, all that is necessary is to touch it. You will hear a sound that will notify you that you have the object in tow.[19]

Soon this era would pass. A great number of game programmers and designers (who were, at the time, largely the same people) would find ways to expand collision

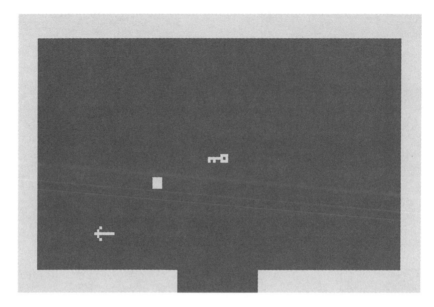

Figure 8.3
Collision is used for picking up objects in *Adventure*. The joystick's button is used to put down objects.

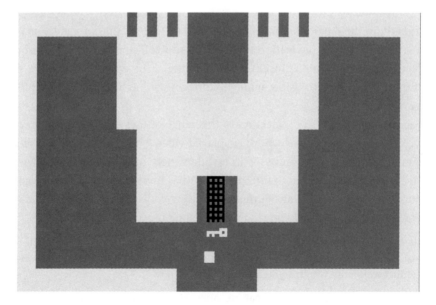

Figure 8.4
Collision, while holding an object, is used for the simple puzzles in *Adventure*. Castles of different colors can only be opened using keys of corresponding colors.

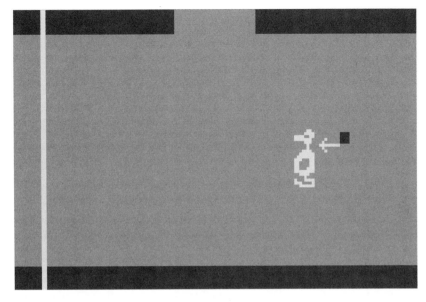

Figure 8.5
Collision, while holding a sword, is used for simple combat in *Adventure*. This may not look like it to a modern eye, but here the player fights a dragon.

detection. In the arcade, *Pac-Man* would soon communicate eating and *Dig Dug*[20] would soon communicate digging. On the Atari VCS, even odder experiences would appear, such as *Tax Avoiders*,[21] which I discuss in the next chapter.

As this took place, certain expansions became conventional, such as *Adventure*-style collection, combat, and object use. They no longer required explanation. And more generally, the use of collision to represent nearly any kind of physical interaction seems to have become increasingly expected for audiences familiar with video game conventions.

This history helps reveal something. Our experience of a second communicative role for a logic or model sits somewhere on a spectrum. At one end is "refinement"—the subject of this chapter. This is when the second role is experienced as a more-specific version of the first. At the other end is "doubling"—the next chapter's subject. This is when the first and second role are understood as totally separate. One interesting thing about the history of game design, as shown in the example of *Adventure* and what follows it, is how it has created an audience that is accustomed to expansive approaches to certain logics and models. This familiarity leads us to experience these expansions as closer to the refinement end of the spectrum (and potentially as conventional, as discussed in the next chapter).

Eventually, the use of collision to represent nearly any kind of physical interaction became so well established that it could be parodied in game form.

WarioWare, Inc.: Mega Microgame$

WarioWare, Inc.: Mega Microgame$[22] is a 2003 game presented as the nefarious Wario's attempt to cash in by creating a video game company.[23] Wario and his friends create games that use collision and control/navigation in many ways familiar to video game players: spaceships shooting, characters collecting coins, athletes catching balls, characters jumping over obstacles and onto enemies, cars dodging other cars, athletes skiing around obstacles, a customer catching a drink as it slides down a bar (reversing the situation of the *Tapper*[24] arcade bartending game), and so on. However, these are presented with much greater variety and in quicker succession than in most games, with generally short timers for completion, creating a sense of disorientation even from these familiar tropes. Part of this disorientation comes precisely from the way that the learning process—so important to navigation and the identification and agency it produces—is disrupted. As Chaim Gingold observes in "What *WarioWare* Can Teach Us about Game Design":

> Sometimes a *WarioWare* micro game will start, and I'll understand the fiction, goal, and controls, but fail to map myself into the right object. My goal is to keep a creature under a spotlight, and I often guess incorrectly as to whether my directional buttons move the spotlight or the creature. If I were consistently mapped to a particular character, such as Mario, there would be no such confusion.[25]

Further, in *WarioWare* the logics of collision detection and navigation are also used in situations that are perhaps no more unusual than in the microgames that reference past games, but that are unfamiliar as game representations and thereby reveal a certain absurdity even in the more traditional uses with which they are intermixed. These include a character catching falling clothes to get dressed (figure 8.6), a racecar fleeing from giant soccer balls, a finger picking a disembodied nose, a character falling on a diamond to mine it from the ground, pieces of a robot falling and stacking as an assembly process, and an anime-style character sniffing mucus back up her nose (the mucus is navigated across a background featuring a lighthouse, dark ocean, and starry sky). This gameplay experience emphasizes both the flexibility with which we are accustomed to interpreting these logics, as well as the continuity of the Nintendo Game Boy Advance (the 2003 game's platform) with the models of space and interaction in earlier generations of game systems, such as Atari's VCS. This formula was so successful that it continued on a variety of other Nintendo platforms, with *WarioWare: Touched!*[26]

Figure 8.6
Collision with falling clothes as a way to get dressed, in *WarioWare, Inc.: Mega Microgame$*. (Image taken by the author during play on emulator at emulatoronline.com.)

performing a similar approach to the touch screen interaction of the Nintendo DS and *WarioWare: Smooth Moves*[27] undertaking this for the Nintendo Wii's motion-sensing remote.

One way of looking at the first *WarioWare* is that it humorously pushes the expansion of navigation and collision to its limits. But from another perspective, it serves to reveal the limiting boundaries of common approaches. The scenarios *WarioWare* presents are all versions of physical interactions, which are precisely the kinds of interactions it had already become conventional to represent with collision and navigation. Given this, even the novel *WarioWare* interactions are experienced (by game-literate players) as closer to the refinement end of the expansion spectrum, or even as alternative uses of the logics.[28] A different group of games has, instead, explored the power of doubling, as discussed in the next chapter.

9 Doubling

There is a distance between a ball hitting a paddle in *Pong*[1] and a key being used to unlock a gate in Robinett's *Adventure*.[2] But perhaps it is not a huge distance—both are physical actions involving touch. Robinett's move may have been surprising to players initially, but for today's players it would be unremarkable.

There is a greater distance when considering the events of *Passage*[3] that depend on the same collision logic. These events, such as becoming partners or being blocked from life choices, are still unexpected for players today—and they seem unlikely to become commonplace, the way other expansive uses of collision have.

This is one of the key differences between the *refinement* of logics (the subject of the prior chapter) and their *doubling* (the subject of this one). When doubling takes place, one operational logic fulfills two distinct communicative roles. This chapter discusses the phenomenon of doubling and the *overloading* of playable models that accompanies it. Through looking at particular games, and more broadly at ways that we might understand the metaphorical relationships at work in games, this chapter also begins to trace some of the power and limits of expansive approaches.

Tax Avoiders

Tristram Shandy[4] is an odd book. It has a self-aware, thoughtful playfulness about the conventions of storytelling and the physical book. In this it is nothing particularly odd, since we are familiar with authors ranging from Jorge Luis Borges to Robert Coover to Kathy Acker. But it is odd in the context of certain histories of fiction, which describe this kind of playfulness as having its roots in the twentieth century (perhaps starting with Dada or Surrealism) and truly flowering with postmodern fiction after the Second World War. This is because *Tristram Shandy* was published in the 1700s.

We might see *Tax Avoiders*[5] as occupying a similar place in the history of video games. Though I know of no serious attempts to track down the specifics of its history, the mere fact of its existence was brought to greater attention by Ian Bogost's 2007 book, *Persuasive Games*.[6] Apparently published for the Atari VCS in 1982, we can see it enacting an expansive approach to logics and models that is more commonly associated with contemporary independent and art games: a doubling of the logics as part of an overloading of the models.

While playing *Tax Avoiders*, as the days of the game's year tick by, the player character navigates a four-level space in which green dollar signs and coils of red tape appear, disappear, and move left to right. Colliding with the dollar signs adds to income, while colliding with red tape reduces it. Four times during the year the player character is moved to another screen (figure 9.1) of ladders and box-shaped platforms, on which a non-player character is alternating between three states. One state is as a black-colored IRS agent who, upon collision, performs an audit that players always lose, costing income. Another is as a green-colored investment advisor who, upon collision, provides the best tax-sheltered investment currently available. The third is as a pink-colored CPA who, upon collision, provides a more valuable tax-sheltered investment

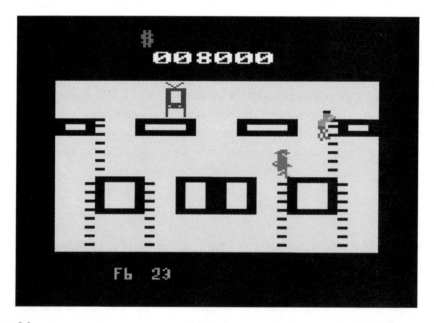

Figure 9.1
The player character in *Tax Avoiders*, scrambling onto a ledge, while the non-player character follows. Colliding with the television set (top left) will collect a tax-sheltered investment in computer software and video games, causing it to disappear and the portfolio briefcase to appear. (Image taken by the author during play on the Stella emulator, version 5.0.2.)

than currently available, for a fee. Once character collisions make investments available, the player character must collide with the investments to collect them and then collide with a briefcase to put them in his portfolio before "tax time" ends. Bogost considers *Tax Avoiders* through the lens of procedural rhetoric, which he describes as "a practice of using processes persuasively. . . . persuading through processes in general and computational processes in particular"[7]:

> *Tax Avoiders* mounts an interesting and relatively complex procedural rhetoric about tax avoidance strategies. The fact that these techniques are mapped onto movement, a graphical logic, is perhaps not ideal, but it is also not detrimental to the argument. The player must run around to collect income, literally *avoiding* red tape. Likewise, he must avoid the IRS agent while racing to *catch* investment opportunities before their window of opportunity closes. These metaphors of locomotion correspond quite well to the abstract processes of work, investment, and taxation.[8]

By using the operational logics built into the VCS's Television Interface Adapter in this way, *Tax Avoiders* creates an experience that is at once both spatial and not spatial. The player character's movement is not through the sort of space simulated in *Adventure* (or *Spacewar*[9]) but through a metaphorical space we might call a "financial landscape."[10] The player character's collisions are not meant to represent actually touching anything, but rather taking individual financial actions, being caught in bureaucratic situations, and even carrying out transactions with other people. At the same time, the player character is literally moving around the space of the screen and is literally colliding with other on-screen objects, with ensuing effects. As a result, the logics of navigation and collision are used with two different communicative roles and contribute to the construction of two different playable models—one spatial and one financial.

This brings us to two questions. First, how do players experience taking actions within two simultaneous playable models? Second, how should we best understand that experience?

Experiencing Overloading

When I play *Tax Avoiders*, I don't try to remember how to take advantage of investment opportunities in the financial model. I see them in the visual space and move toward them with the spatial model's controls. When I play *Passage*, I notice there are areas I can't pass through when the two characters are together (creating a larger, combined object for me to navigate). Only after noticing this do I consider that, in the game's model of life choices, there are directions that are cut off if one has chosen to have a partner.

In other words, in *Tax Avoiders* and *Passage* I experience the playable model of space as primary. The primary communicative role of collision is virtual objects touching. The primary communicative role of navigation is moving the object with which I identify. The other meanings of these logics, in the context of the other playable model, are secondary to my moment-to-moment experience.

At the same time, however, when I play *Tax Avoiders*, I avoid touching the color-changing character until it provides benefit. In *Passage*, I didn't find the experience of play emotionally moving until I tried having a partner and she passed away. In other words, my forward-looking goals and backward-looking understanding are shaped more by the second playable model.

I call this experience of playable models (accompanied by the doubling of what operational logics communicate) *overloading*. Our moment-to-moment experience is determined by, and happens in terms of, a first playable model or set of playable models (for example, a spatial model and a combat model). But our broader motivations and understandings are in terms of a second domain, and our actions in the first model(s) can be seen as actions in this second domain, allowing us to understand play in its terms. Most games that take this strategy present the second, overloading domain as the important one—as what the game is about.[11] As Nick Montfort writes, "*Passage* is about life, about how your movement through a virtual space using video game conventions maps to our experience of moving on, living together or alone, growing old, and dying."[12]

How can we understand this experience? Using everyday language, we could say it is "metaphorical"—one thing being seen as representative of something else. In overloading, the way we play in the domain of the first model (spatial movement in *Passage*) is understood as representative in the domain of the second model (life choices in *Passage*).

But it's worth digging deeper. Overloading is one of the primary ways that innovative video game designers are working to expand what games can address through play. The more deeply we understand it, the better we can learn it and teach it, and the better we can understand its strengths and limitations.

Conceptual Metaphors

Doris C. Rusch's book *Making Deep Games*[13] dives into metaphorical approaches to game design.[14] She examines games that obviously take metaphorical approaches at a larger, structural level—such as *Passage* and *Papo & Yo*[15]—as well as the workings of metaphor in portions of more literal games such as *God of War II*[16] and *Angry Birds*.[17]

She argues "that the salient aspects of what it means to be human reside in the realm of abstract concepts (rather than what is physically tangible) and that, in order to make the abstract concrete . . . we need metaphors."[18]

To understand the workings of metaphor, she turns to some of the most influential ideas on the topic: the writings of George Lakoff and Mark Johnson. This work famously rejected the prior theory of metaphor, which saw metaphor as an unusual, linguistic, and primarily literary phenomenon. Instead, this work sees metaphor as key to much of our everyday thought. As Lakoff puts it in a 1993 review article:

> In short, the locus of metaphor is not in language at all, but in the way we conceptualize one mental domain in terms of another. The general theory of metaphor is given by characterizing such cross-domain mappings. And in the process, everyday concepts like time, states, change, causation, and purpose also turn out to be metaphorical.[19]

This is sometimes referred to as Conceptual Metaphor Theory, or CMT. In CMT, we think of the two domains as a "target" and a "source." The target is the domain we are meant to understand through the metaphor. The source is the domain that will help us understand. For example, in the metaphor "love is a journey," love is the target and a journey is the source.

Rusch focuses on two specific ways that games operate metaphorically. One she calls *structural metaphors*—when players are meant to understand that the game system (source) operates in the same way as the aspects of the life experience being addressed (target). The other she calls *experiential metaphors*—when the game system (source) produces a feeling, through play, that players understand as similar to the feeling of a life experience (target).[20]

The examples I have discussed for overloading pursue both of these. In *Tax Avoiders*, I find myself wondering when I should attempt to interact with the pink-colored CPA (spending time and money to make a better investment available in the future) and when I should attempt to interact with the green-colored investment advisor (to take the best investment available now) given the quick passage of time. This tradeoff works to express ideas about how the financial world operates (structural metaphor). It also produces an experience of wondering how to spend one's resources, and sometimes feeling regret or pleasure at the result of a closely timed choice, that mirrors the feeling of someone who puts a high priority on avoiding taxes and takes a risk that succeeds or fails (experiential metaphor). Rusch discusses Rod Humble's *The Marriage*[21] as an example of a game that only pursues one type of metaphor—structural, but not experiential—saying something about marriage from the perspective of an outside observer, rather than a participant.

Rusch also helpfully provides a number of case studies of her own work, often with groups of students, to develop games that embody these types of metaphors. What is revealed, reading these accounts, is that the metaphorical approach to design—seeking an appropriate overloading—is quite difficult. For example, she tells the story of the group that would eventually make the game *Akrasia*.[22] They had a set of concepts that most attracted them: "identity, memory, inner demons, and love." But the group didn't end up making a game about any of them, because "it was very hard to reach an agreement about the experiential core of any of these concepts."[23]

The team then decided to make a game about addiction. They chose as their approach the overloading of a spatial model. Interestingly, Rusch doesn't present this as a choice, instead stating, "Games are predominantly spatial."[24] Their first design made addiction the space of a racetrack with the goal to get off the track. But they had not mapped dependency into the spatial model in any way (and had made the interesting spatial activity the one players should reject). Their second design made addiction the space of a maze, adding a dragon to be chased (for a drug-induced high) and rewards when the dragon was caught. This was too successful at getting players to chase the dragon, so they added a resource system representing health, which lowered when the dragon was caught. But then it was easy to ignore the dragon, so they added a demon that chases the player, representing withdrawal. They were tempted to make the demon also cause health damage, but they realized this didn't make sense to them metaphorically, so instead the demon changes the navigation controls when it catches the player. The team stopped there, but even this final iteration is problematic, which Rusch admits freely.

At each step, the team proposed something that would work as a linguistic metaphor, such as addiction as a trap from which it is difficult to escape. But when they translated this into something spatial and familiar from the practices of game design, such as a racetrack, the specifics of gameplay produced neither structural nor experiential metaphor for players. In short, their design process revealed that overloading the playable model of a game is not the same as the sort of metaphor we use in everyday speech.

We can understand why by returning to CMT. One notable feature of this theory is that not everything in the source domain is applied to the target domain. For example, if our metaphor is that a theory (target) is a building (source), we may talk about "constructing" the theory or how "well-founded" we find the theory. But we are very unlikely to ask about the stairwells or HVAC system of the theory.

Raymond W. Gibbs, Jr., in his overview of the evidence supporting CMT, explains why CMT proponents believe this happens:

CMT does not maintain that *all* aspects of the source domain are mapped onto the target domain in metaphorical expressions or conceptual metaphors. One proposal within CMT, named the "invariance hypothesis," states, "metaphorical mappings preserve the cognitive topology (that is, the image-schematic structure) of the source domain" (Lakoff, 1990, p. 54). . . . Image schemas are not propositional in nature, but are highly abstract or schematic (Hampe, 2005; Kovecses, 2006).[25]

In other words, when "a building" is our metaphorical source, we are not mapping all the specifics of a particular building but a highly abstract or schematic notion of a building.[26] This abstract idea of a building doesn't contain stairwells or HVAC systems. If someone starts elaborating a metaphor at that level of detail, they're clearly violating the usual way it is employed, and we may see them as belaboring the metaphor.[27]

A game is not like this. In *Passage*, every aspect of the spatial model and the world it is being used to navigate is concrete and immediate. It is the primary thing we experience. No element of it is abstracted away. In other words, games that work metaphorically do not operate like conceptual metaphors.

Game Metaphors

Given that no aspects of a metaphorical game are abstracted away, game developers have a few options. One is to create extremely simple games, so that they are close to the abstract sources of CMT. *WarioWare, Inc.: Mega Microgame$*[28] demonstrates that it is possible to create very simple games and sequence them into a compelling experience. But as odd as they are, *WarioWare*'s microgames are also experienced rather literally. Later in this chapter I will discuss *Dys4ia*,[29] a game that takes up the challenge of metaphorical overloading in the context of microgames.

Another option is to create games that are more complex, but still small scale, and aim to correspond every detail in the source domain to something in the target domain. This is different from the kind of metaphor that is the focus of CMT, in which an abstraction of a source (such as the idea of a building) is connected with a target that is itself often quite abstract (such as the idea of a theory). Rather, this kind of overloading is two things. First, it is a metaphorical connection between two models, created through different procedural representations driven by the same set of logics—the specifics of the primary one driving the immediate gameplay, and the overloading being a way of interpreting that play. Second, it is a metaphorical connection between ways of seeing the elements of the scenario design (such as a game level)—both in the immediate, specific terms of the primary model and the interpretive terms of the overloading model.

We can see how this works by returning to *Passage*. In his statement about the game, the creator, Rohrer, presents it as autobiographical and as a *memento mori*—a reminder of mortality. But the game's primary playable model is spatial. And the scenario design largely appears to be that of a traditional spatial game, in the same vein as a *Zelda* title.[30] There is a large world to explore, with simple walls to navigate around and treasure chests to locate, which provide varying rewards. How is it that, as Rusch put it in a 2008 article with collaborator Matthew J. Weise, "living is translated into screen navigation"?[31]

Somehow games that overload their primary model must signal the secondary model. In *Tax Avoiders* this is done in a quite straightforward manner: the objects that the player character can collide with include dollar signs and images of red tape. In *Passage*, this is more subtle. For example, the first time I played (when I did not encounter the potential life partner) one of the strongest signals was the interruption of the navigation control logic. When the image of the player character was removed from my control, placed in a different screen location, and replaced with the image of an older man, it was clear the game was doing something different from a traditional spatial game. When I played again, and gained a life partner, and then found areas I had been previously able to enter were now too small for the combined object of the two of us, it became clearer. I began to understand that the game was about the passage of time and the choices we make in life. That is, I began to see the second playable model, overloading the first. This cast new light on my larger pattern of play: would I focus on seeing the world or gathering treasure? And it was also this that allowed me to see how the logics were being doubled, to see what it meant when my partner and I couldn't move in a particular direction, which then brought more metaphorical meaning to my immediate play.

I believe this is how the overloading of models and doubling of logics function more broadly. Consider a game with a spatial model presented using textual characters, such as *Rogue*[32] or *Dwarf Fortress*.[33] In such a game, a character could collide with a dollar sign, just as in *Tax Avoiders*. But in such a game I would not interpret that collision as being doubled—as representing both a physical touch and a financial transaction—unless I had been signaled to do so. A dollar sign might as easily be a monster, a stream of water, or a simple piece of currency. But once I suspect that the primary playable model is overloaded with another, I am prepared to understand the communicative roles of logics as doubled, as I do with the dollar sign collisions in *Tax Avoiders*.

So, rather than the schematic metaphor of CMT, this is how games with this design approach operate metaphorically. We experience a specific playable model and scenario and then build an understanding of a second playable model (which may be signaled more or less directly and immediately) overloading the communication of the first. This understanding of the overloading model supports an interpretation of the logics as doubled, which brings the metaphorical meaning to our moment-to-moment play.

If we want a more formal way of understanding this kind of metaphorical overloading of a very specific source (a game's specific playable model[s] and scenario), CMT is not the right approach. D. Fox Harrell, in his book *Phantasmal Media*,[34] presents a more appropriate alternative. Harrell provides a detailed account of *Passage* that shows how each aspect of the implemented, playable version of the game maps onto ideas the game is expressing metaphorically, using an approach he calls *morphic semiotics*.[35] This approach is intriguing not only because it accounts for the specifics but also because it can be expressed quite formally—so that computing systems can, for example, blend together metaphors expressed in this form. Harrell has demonstrated, through his own creative work, some of the exciting possibilities this opens.

But Harrell's analysis also reveals part of what makes *Passage*'s design approach challenging, especially for more complex games. As Harrell notes, "Every element and action in the game reflects an underlying metaphor involving abstract ideas about the passage of time and one's (both Rohrer's and the player's) eventual death."[36] This means that every time a new element is added to a game, we must understand its role in terms of both the primary and overloading models, down to the level of logics.

To make this more concrete, when Rusch and her students add a dragon, they must ask: "Why does it choose to move that direction?" "Why does it do that much damage?" "Why is it that much slower than the player?" They must ask these and a host of other questions and come up with answers that work both at the immediate and metaphorical levels. In practice, if games fail to make all elements correspond, we experience things in the immediate model that do not correspond with anything on the metaphorical level, or that muddle the metaphor (for example, if Rusch's group had included the withdrawal demon damaging the player's health resource).

As a result, there is a limit on the complexity that it makes sense for a metaphorical game to have, at least for a particular portion of play. More complex metaphors are harder to construct and can be experienced as belabored.

Alternately, of course, game designers can also approach metaphor in a less totalizing way. Only a portion of a game might operate metaphorically. Or a game might be more loosely metaphoric. For example, the game *Journey*[37] (which Rusch discusses as "allegorical") can be seen as a metaphor for life's journey, like *Passage*. But running into a wall when playing *Journey* is just running into a wall—the collision logic isn't doubled to represent the inability to make a life choice (or anything else). There is really only one thing being expressed through *Journey*'s spatial model: movement through space. The space suggests a second interpretation as a life journey, but not with the specificity that would be needed to create a second playable model, allowing us to take spatial actions that we interpret as non-spatial life decisions.[38]

Finally, game designers can also take a different view from Rusch's, "that the salient aspects of what it means to be human reside in the realm of abstract concepts"[39] which must be approached metaphorically. For example, the game *Cart Life*[40] uses an alternative approach to resource logics to create a compelling experience of precarious service work for players. Team-based shooters such as *Overwatch*[41] create experiences of excitement and camaraderie through conventional uses of spatial and combat models. In other words, we don't need to overload game models with metaphorical meanings to create games that address important human experiences. And while we do need to acknowledge the limits of what current models can address, we also need to acknowledge the limits of what can be done metaphorically with these models. After all, even with someone like Rusch as their leader, the *Akrasia* team could not find a way to overload a spatial model to explore any of their first four choices for game topics.

But designers can find successful ways to overcome these challenges, perhaps especially when limiting game complexity, as another game demonstrates.

Dys4ia

Not only is it challenging to construct complex game metaphors, we may also wonder if audiences will be able to interpret them, especially if they stray beyond the mainstream. After all, *Tax Avoiders* presents a well-known conservative vision of personal finance, as one finds in media ranging from the high seriousness of the *Wall Street Journal* to the broad humor of CNBC's *Mad Money*. Similarly, *Passage* presents a well-known heteronormative model of romantic relationships and the tradeoffs between pursuing material reward, broad life experience, and partnership. These examples leave open the question of whether game design approaches such as theirs can be used to communicate and explore ideas that may be unfamiliar to audiences or that present an alternative to the easily recognized tropes of mainstream culture.

Anna Anthropy's 2012 game *Dys4ia* serves both as an answer to this question and as an example of alternative and expansive approaches—at the levels of logics, models, and broader game designs. *Dys4ia* is built from a series of microgames, much like *WarioWare* (discussed at the end of the previous chapter). But while *WarioWare*'s microgames avoid metaphorical overloading, *Dys4ia* embraces it while also employing both refinement and alternative uses. *Dys4ia* also explores something not yet discussed in this chapter—what happens when metaphorical overloading is used in the context of a familiar game design.

Dys4ia does these things in a context very different from *WarioWare*'s. While *WarioWare* is presented with a minimal frame story (and a knowing wink), *Dys4ia* tells Anthropy's specific story of beginning, as a transgender woman, to take estrogen. This is obviously a complex topic, of the sort that might result in a belabored metaphor if taken on as a single-mode game using an expansive approach. *Dys4ia* shows how it can be addressed successfully as a series of microgames, often by taking approaches familiar to players of *WarioWare* and employing them in a new way.

One aspect of this is repetition. *WarioWare*'s microgames are often repeated (at higher speeds) and sometimes combined into "boss" games that mimic traditional game genres. These combinations are interesting formally, as Chaim Gingold notes,[42] in that they illustrate how microgames are in some sense decompositions of game elements familiar from larger games—a point I will return to in the next chapter on *logic structures*. But in the context of *WarioWare*'s deliberately disposable fictions, the return of previous games (in their original forms or as combinatorial transformations) offers little emotional resonance. *Dys4ia*, in contrast, uses transformed repetition as a key element of its emotional communication.

The strategies of these repeated microgames include both alternative and expansive approaches to spatial models and graphical logics. Take, for example, the three microgames of "walking home" that *Dys4ia* presents. These are examples of ways *Dys4ia* uses spatial models in an alternative mode. As discussed in chapter 2, alternative uses of models and logics employ the same abstract processes and communicative roles as mainstream uses. However, they employ them in a domain that is novel or unusual. In the case of *Dys4ia*'s walking home microgames, spatial models are used to represent space—but an everyday space containing emotional and physical challenges not usually represented in games.

In the first phase of *Dys4ia*, titled "Gender Bullshit," we play in the initial state of the world, before Anthropy's hormone therapy. A character that serves both as a representation of Anthropy and as the player character (for this microgame) walks past three characters that call her "sir" (in a large speech bubble of contrasting color) and she replies with an ineffectual correction to "ma'am" (in a small speech bubble close to the background color) (figure 9.2).

Evelyn C. Chew and Alex Mitchell write about this as an example of "unchoice," highlighting the fact that Anthropy and the player have no choice but to continue through a deeply unpleasant situation. We could see this as a form of Rusch's "experiential metaphor." As Chew and Mitchell write:

Figure 9.2

The first of three versions of a "walking home" microgame in Anna Anthropy's *Dys4ia*. The player character's responses to being misgendered are ineffectual and almost invisible. (Image taken by the author during play.)

> Players must move the character along a straight line toward "home," bearing with nonplayer characters who address the player character as "Sir." The life protagonist's unease with the situation is conveyed by the feeble correction "Ma'am" that emerges in response to each "Sir," while the player, much like the protagonist, has no choice but to continue along the same path, as there is no other.[43]

This microgame next appears, in a different form, in the third phase of *Dys4ia*, titled "Hormonal Bullshit." We play in the world after Anthropy has started taking estrogen from a medical provider who requires that she also take blood pressure medication. The walk home is solitary and initially seems to the player as though it is without obstacle. But the farther the player character walks, the slower the speed of physics becomes, with the final steps greatly drawn out. A text appears, telling players, "These blood pressure meds are really draining my energy" (figure 9.3). Here, altering the walking mechanic's relationship with the physics logic is another strategy for

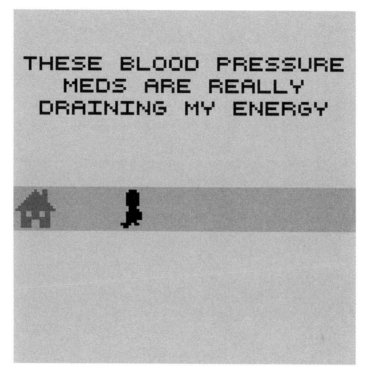

Figure 9.3
The second of three versions of a "walking home" microgame in Anna Anthropy's *Dys4ia*. The speed of walking slows progressively as the player character gets closer to her destination. (Image taken by the author during play.)

placing the player in an experientially metaphorical relationship with Anthropy's situation. As Naomi Clark writes in *A Game Design Vocabulary*, a book co-authored with Anthropy:

> The player moves a pixelated character toward home while the text explains that medication has made her exhausted. The system shows this as well, creating more and more resistance to the player's movement across the screen, slowing it to a crawl, and making the experience of exhaustion tangible.[44]

Finally, in *Dys4ia*'s fourth phase, titled "It Gets Better?," we play in the world after Anthropy has been on estrogen consistently, without the blood pressure medication. Here we revisit the walking home experience again, but rather than altering the relationship with physics (walking stays at a consistent speed) *Dys4ia* offers an altered, expansive presentation of collision. When a single character refers to the

Figure 9.4
The last of three versions of a "walking home" microgame in Anna Anthropy's *Dys4ia*. The walking speed remains steady, while the response to being misgendered pushes the other character off screen. (Image taken by the author during play.)

player character as "sir," the reply of "ma'am" is not only much larger and more apparent but is presented as colliding with the other character and pushing it off screen (figure 9.4).

A similar pattern of repetition is seen in revisiting other *Dys4ia* microgames that work with spatial models in an alternative way, including a series of shaving games that appear to give a visual nod to *WarioWare*'s personal grooming microgames.

Meanwhile, interleaved with the microgames that treat spatial models in a mostly alternative manner, other microgames operate in an expansive mode. One set of these introduces and further develops the idea of speech bubbles as physical objects. In the first microgame of this series, appearing in the "Gender Bullshit" phase, two pairs of flapping lips project speech bubbles containing male (Mars) symbols across the screen, representing "feminists" not accepting Anthropy as a woman (figure 9.5).[45]

Figure 9.5
The first of three versions of a *Pong*-like conversation microgame in *Dys4ia*. Speech bubbles are hurtful whether intercepted or not. (Image taken by the author during play.)

The player character is represented by a shield that moves up and down the screen, like a *Pong* paddle—and, as in *Pong*, the off-screen space is also important to the player.[46]

Collision between the speech bubbles and the shield causes it to strobe visually, an indication of "taking damage" used in many games, and unlike *Pong* the collision does not cause the objects to bounce back. Speech bubbles that get past the shield cause new speech bubbles containing iconic swearing to appear from that side, analogous to the other side scoring a point in *Pong*. Tellingly, there is no way for the player's/Anthropy's side to "score points" in this conversation—either in the literal space of the *Pong* variant or in the metaphorical space of the gender accusation.

A transformed version of this microgame appears in the third phase of *Dys4ia*, "Hormonal Bullshit." The shield representing Anthropy and the player has moved to the right-hand side, where the aggressor lips appeared in the previous version. Now a single

Figure 9.6
The second version of a *Pong*-like conversation microgame in *Dys4ia*. Speech bubbles bring a tear
if intercepted, no response if not. (Image taken by the author during play.)

pair of lips, representing Anthropy's girlfriend, appear on the left-hand side, projecting
speech bubbles containing question marks (figure 9.6).

In this version, collision once again does not result in the speech bubbles bouncing back. Instead, the shield sheds a tear, and text on the screen informs the audience,
"Everything my girlfriend says makes me cry." But the other element of gameplay calls
this assertion into question. If the player fails to move the shield to collide with the
speech bubbles—the situation that would correspond with failure in *Pong*—it appears
that nothing happens. In other words, if the player/Anthropy exerts effort to converse,
the experience is painful. But without effort, or with failed effort, the worse result is no
response to the girlfriend's attempts to reach out.

The last version of this microgame appears in the final phase of *Dys4ia*, "It Gets
Better?" The shield representing Anthropy and the player has returned to the left side,
and two pairs of lips again project speech bubbles containing male symbols—the same

Figure 9.7
The third version of a *Pong*-like conversation microgame in *Dys4ia*. Speech bubbles bounce back if intercepted and sometimes even when not. (Image taken by the author during play.)

characters still saying Anthropy is a man. But now, if the shield collides with one of the bubbles, it bounces back and is transformed into a speech bubble containing a female (Venus) symbol (figure 9.7). When these transformed symbols collide with the lips, the lips strobe as the shield did in the first microgame (taking damage). And when the speech bubbles projected by the lips aren't intercepted by the shield, the results are curious. Sometimes there is no response—the gender accusations no longer seem to impact Anthropy/the player. But at other times the gender accusations bounce back, and are transformed, on their own—they no longer always require effort from Anthropy/the player to be rebutted.

A number of other microgame progressions in *Dys4ia* also use expansive approaches to spatial models. As with the *Pong*-like conversation microgames, these are often explicitly modeled on elements of well-known games. A particularly striking example features a *Tetris*[47]-like piece and a *Breakout*[48]-like wall. At the start of *Dys4ia* the player is

Figure 9.8
In *Dys4ia*, a *Tetris*-like piece shifts through a wide range of shapes and colors, moving toward a wall that has been opened enough (through earlier play) to admit many of them through. (Image taken by the author during play.)

asked to move the piece through the wall, but discovers it is impossible (piece-blocking collision is unavoidable) and text tells us "I feel weird about my body." During the "Hormonal Bullshit" phase, the piece reappears, rotated, with one square dangling and shifting position—passage through the wall is even more clearly impossible. But in the final phase of *Dys4ia*, two related microgames appear. In the first, a visually similar wall is opened through *Breakout*-style gameplay. And the second is the final moment of gameplay, featuring a *Tetris*-like piece shifting through a wide range of shapes and colors, moving toward a wall that has been opened enough to admit many of them through (figure 9.8).

In these microgames that use spatial models expansively, *Dys4ia* is in some ways operating similarly to games like *Passage*. Navigation and collision detection are doubled, each with an unconventional second communicative role. This supports two simultaneous playable models—a primary spatial one and an overloading one representing another aspect of Anthropy's experience (such as conversation or body image). But there are two key differences. The first is the rapid succession of different microgames. The second is using elements of well-known games as the basis of many of the microgames with expansive approaches to spatial models.

Dys4ia's succession of microgames supports a metaphorical complexity I will discuss later on. At the same time, its rapid switching between microgames, each of which can have initially uncertain rules and roles for the player, produces some of the same disorientation that players experience with *WarioWare*. And because many of *Dys4ia*'s microgames are simultaneously building two playable models, players are sometimes asked to quickly reorient in two domains, rather than just one. Yet, at other times, *Dys4ia* is using spatial models in an alternative way, so that a player who has been keeping two models in mind must collapse back down to one—or vice versa—as the gap between two models is opened and collapsed in rapid succession. This is another manner in which *Dys4ia* succeeds in putting its audience in a situation that is an experiential metaphor with that of its protagonist, increasing the potential resonance, and frustration, of its play. As Elise Vist describes it in "Cyborg Games":

> This disorientation is incredibly frustrating for players who are used to games that encourage a one-to-one relationship with the avatar; you "are" the avatar, or, at the very least, you are the person who controls the avatar, the player-character. In *dys4ia*, however, Anthropy controls you, while you attempt (and fail) to control the ever-shifting avatar.[49]

Simultaneously, *Dys4ia*'s use of elements from well-known games as the basis of many of its microgames follows a strategy that is not only familiar from *WarioWare*, but also from many independent and art games (such as Mary Flanagan et al.'s *Layoff*,[50] discussed in chapter 3). As Alexei Othenin-Girard explains in "Bodies, Games, and Systems," for *Dys4ia* this is not only an effective means of shaping player expectation (helping scaffold some of the agency and identification that discontinuous microgames undermine) but also provides players with a familiar situation on which to map the (potentially) unfamiliar situation Anthropy communicates through the game:

> The familiar nature of the vignettes as game-objects serves both to guide and remap player expectations, such that the experience of playing a vignette serves as an analogy to Anthropy's corresponding experience. Most of *Dys4ia*'s players will not know what it is like to have to fight for their preferred gender identification, but most of them will be familiar with the systemic elements of *Pong*. Since the "lose" condition in *Pong* mirrors the "failing to protect yourself from hurtful assertions made by others" condition in *Dys4ia*, players can quickly make the emotional analogy between the two. It is important, of course, that Anthropy has chosen the rhetorics of her vignettes carefully.[51]

As a result, *Dys4ia* strongly illustrates two aspects of the potential for overloading of playable models. The first of these is present in all expansive uses of logics and models (when the abstract process remains the same while also serving a second, unconventional communicative role). In these cases, as discussed above, while the overloading communicative role may be successful, the original is never entirely effaced. We see this clearly in *Passage* (the spatial model is always legible spatially, as well as the model of life choices) and in *Dys4ia* (the spatial models are always legible spatially, as well as the models of conversation, body image, and so on).

What separates *Dys4ia* from the previous examples is that it is organized as a series of microgames. This allows *Dys4ia* to take an approach different from Rusch's, of trying to create a single space that contains compatible metaphors for all elements of a situation—such as escaping addiction, chasing a high, the pressure of withdrawal, and so on. The spatial metaphors in the "conversation *Pong*" microgames are incompatible with those of the *Tetris* piece moving through the *Breakout* wall. In the current design, each is simple, stands on its own, and serves to deepen the overall experience. If they were combined in one screen, rather than combined through sequence, the result wouldn't work spatially or metaphorically. By reducing what needs to be communicated at any particular moment through the overloading of playable models, *Dys4ia*'s design shows an important way forward for expansive approaches.

Second, *Dys4ia* shows how overloading can be used with familiar game designs, producing a doubling of the communication of aspects beyond the logics. The intended audience understands how the referenced game operates at a high level—the player goals, the failure states, and so on. Players know how to play and, unless and until it is demonstrated that they should not (or cannot) play in this manner, they will attempt to. At the same time, as Othenin-Girard suggests regarding *Dys4ia*, players will also interpret elements of the referenced game in terms of the second, expansive playable model. For example, in the second and third iteration of *Dys4ia*'s "conversation *Pong*" microgames, we might not interpret the lack of response to speech bubbles moving past the shield as meaning anything if we did not already know that this is the circumstance that players work hard to avoid while playing *Pong*.

Taken together, *Dys4ia*'s strategies show that the microgame approach and remapping of familiar game elements have strong potential for communication regarding a wide range of topics—including the autobiographical and political. (The next chapter describes a strand of work that takes this potential as its starting point.) However, *Dys4ia* (like *WarioWare*) also leaves open the question of how, and whether, these strategies can be used in games that allow for greater player experimentation, creativity, and discovery. Each of *Dys4ia*'s microgames is played so briefly that players do not uncover or enact anything beyond the immediately obvious even to the extent they do in *Pong*, much less to the extent of *Spacewar*, *Adventure*, or *Passage*. This too will be discussed further in the next chapter.

Lyric Games

That said, it is also worth questioning whether it is appropriate to apply the common values of game design to experiences like *Dys4ia*. In order to allow for greater player experimentation, creativity, and discovery, the microgames in *Dys4ia* would have to be quite a bit larger, experienced for longer. It may be that the short nature of their gameplay is not something we should view as a defect, but rather something that they have in common with another generally short artform—the lyric poem. As Jordan Magnuson writes, "the fact that lyric poems are short is not an accident, or a failure at the level of entertainment, but rather a characteristic which positions them within a tradition of lyric works, works that beg you to pay attention, to consider their every word, every line break, every sound and image."[52]

Magnuson writes about lyric poems both as an inspiration for his mode of game creation and as a lens through which we can understand the games of others.[53] He calls out a number of key elements shared between the lyric tradition and games such as *Dys4ia* and *Passage*—not just that lyric poems are short, but that they are subjective, that they are bound to metaphor and ambiguous imagery, that they employ poetic address, and so on. Looking at games in this way can provide a different perspective on topics already discussed in this chapter and the prior one. For example, when writing about poetic address, Magnuson draws our attention to the "complex apostrophe" of the game *Seasonal Mixtape* by dino (formerly nina) which incorporates quotes from Ali Smith's *Seasonal Quartet*. Through text, imagery, and interaction, the autumn scene of *Seasonal Mixtape*[54] produces a situation in which "as players we find ourselves uncertain about whether we are addressing a leaf on the wind (whether via text or interaction), or whether someone is addressing *us* as a leaf on the wind." Though *Seasonal Mixtape* differs from a game like *Dys4ia* in that it is not built around microgames, the uncertainty Magnuson describes could be seen as analogous to the experience created by microgame-based approaches—which address the player over and over, with a succession of new scenario designs and control schemes, so the player must enter each new microgame uncertain and become accustomed to identifying with something new at every turn.

In other words, we do not have to view the doubling of playable models as a difficult game creation technique that often fails to scale to the length, complexity, and opportunities for player experimentation we "normally" expect from games. Rather, we can see short, metaphorical games as operating in a different mode. Magnuson makes a compelling case that an analogy with lyric poetry is a powerful way to understand this mode.

What Can Become Conventional

Chapter 7 traced how key graphical logics, supporting spatial models, were introduced into video games. It also brought us to the technological moment when particular implementations of those logics and models became widespread in public arcades and private homes.

This chapter and the prior one have traced some of the ways designers have worked to expand the things that play can be about when supported by these logics and models. At first designers worked to push these boundaries, at least in part, because they were the only logics and models available—general-purpose computers capable of running and displaying video games were in very few hands. In time, as years of innovative game development produced knowledge about a wide range of compelling gameplay possible with these models and logics, this game design knowledge also made them attractive for expansive uses. And for today's independent, art, and research game developers, these models and logics are attractive for expansive uses for a variety of additional reasons, including cultural currency, widespread player literacy, developed toolsets, and personal nostalgia. Together these have led to a large number of games that employ these models and logics in expansive ways, resulting in audiences that have come to expect such uses. Further, uses like those in *Pac-Man*[55] and Robinett's *Adventure*, which were once expansive, have now become conventional.

One question I have not addressed is whether uses like those in *Dys4ia*, *Passage*, and *Tax Avoiders* could themselves become conventional. Could certain doublings of the communicative role of collision, for example, become widely understood among game players? Could this either change how we experience the meaning of collision or become the foundation of a new logic? In 2009, Michael Mateas and I wrote about *Passage* from this perspective, emphasizing the role that expansive approaches could have in the potential establishment of new logics:

> In this game, graphical logics are used as the basis of spatial mechanics associated with metaphors about life. For example, collision detection is used to determine whether the character's journey will take place with a partner or alone. This isn't just part of the fictional world—solo characters can explore parts of the world that couples can't . . . One can imagine such currently unusual uses of graphical logics eventually becoming well-understood, to the point that the

underlying abstract processes become recognized as participating in two kinds of operational logics: both the current graphical/spatial logics and another in which the shifting position of elements on the screen is actually understood as the making of non-spatial life decisions. This seems unlikely in the specific case of *Passage*, but it explains part of what seems unusual and full of potential about the work.[56]

It now seems clear to me that this is one of the key ways we can distinguish between refinement and doubling. Both of these are expansive approaches, giving an additional communicative role to an existing logic, but we experience them differently as they become more familiar. For example, the refinement of "touch" to "collection" that Robinett's *Adventure* pioneered is now conventional—with the joyful Mario collecting coins mid-air, while tough-as-nails soldiers walk over health packs to collect them in their apocalyptic battle zones. This is because the actions communicated remain physical—the playable model remains spatial. The model is not being overloaded to communicate something further.

Doubling operates differently. When I interpret touch as "responding to a gender accusation" in *Dys4ia*, I can only do so because the spatial model is overloaded. This doesn't become conventional, as we see moments later in *Dys4ia* when the spatial model is being overloaded to communicate about body image, rather than conversation. Overloaded models can be, and are, used to communicate about many incompatible domains. This is their power. But the result is that the stability that would be needed across games for doubling to become conventional is absent. Even for experienced players, they can only slide a little way toward the "refinement" end of the expansion spectrum.

New logics are, of course, born. The inventive work described in chapter 5 is focused on enlarging the options for logics and models available to game creators. But they are born through new work on abstract processes, communicative roles, gameplay experiences, and implementations, not simply through the layering of an additional communicative role. This is a difficult path. The next chapter will explore, instead, how far we can push the limits with an approach that cuts across alternative and expansive uses of graphical logics and spatial models.

10 Logic Structures

Imagine a video game made by the US Democratic Party, in an earlier political era, making its case to the American people. A simple version might look like figure 10.1.

In this game, the Republicans are constantly trying to do things to harm "ordinary" people—rolling back health care, undermining unions, removing drinking water protections, militarizing police, and so on. The Democrats position themselves, via the player-navigated donkey icon, as the defenders of the people, stopping these attacks before they can do harm.

Now imagine a video game made by the Republican Party during the Obama administration. It might look like figure 10.2.

In this game, the Obama administration is constantly trying to throw away the money of the American people—on Keynesian stimulus spending, controversy-stoking arts programs, assistance for the undeserving, research into abstruse subjects, and so on. The Republicans position themselves, via the player-navigated elephant icon, as the agents of thrift, the preservers of financial sanity.

Or imagine a game made by people who think video games are destroying childhood, turning after-school time into an unhealthy virtual (rather than wholesomely physical) experience. It might look like figure 10.3.

The school bus releases children who will fall into the clutches of game systems unless something is done to prevent it. The player-navigated sports equipment can save the day by diverting the children into outdoor activities.

Finally, imagine a video game made by someone who sees sin as the key element of Christian theology—the game equivalent of a Chick tract. It might look like figure 10.4.

The devil is constantly producing sin, which hurts those it touches. The ordinary people at the bottom of the screen are in for a lot of suffering, unless the player-navigated Jesus intercedes, taking that suffering on himself.

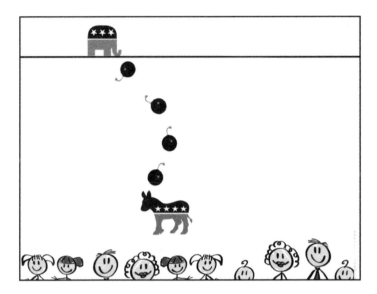

Figure 10.1
A design mockup for a Democratic Party political game, created by and courtesy of Mike Treanor. (Treanor, Mateas, and Wardrip-Fruin, "*Kaboom!* is a Many-Splendored Thing)

Figure 10.2
Mike Treanor's 2010 design mockup of a Republican Party game.

Figure 10.3
Mike Treanor's design mockup for a video game in which players try to keep kids away from console and handheld video game systems.

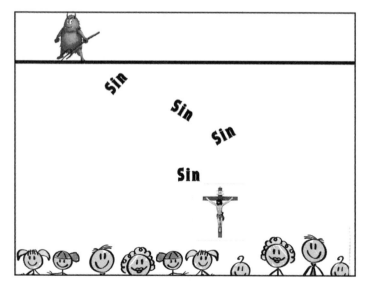

Figure 10.4
Mike Treanor's design mockup for a game in which sin emanates from the devil.

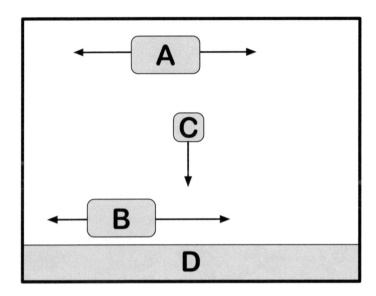

Figure 10.5

A diagram of the key elements of *Kaboom* (after the figure 5 diagram in Treanor, Mateas, and Wardrip-Fruin, "*Kaboom!* is a Many-Splendored Thing").

As most readers will recognize, these games share a fundamental design. Though not as famous as *Pong*,[1] this design is also based on a popular video game: Larry Kaplan's *Kaboom*.[2] And each game above is a sketch selected from an investigation led by Mike Treanor into the question of what a game can mean.[3]

Treanor reduced *Kaboom* to a diagram like figure 10.5. Something moves across the top of the screen (A), dropping things (C), that the player-navigated object (B) can intercept, before they hit the bottom of the screen (D). This design can be used to create games that enact, through play, views about politics, video games, and even religion. And yet the only thing that differentiates these games, at a formal level, is the images for A, B, C, and D. And what those images do is prompt us to understand which elements can do harm and which can be harmed.

Specifically, in Treanor's imagined Democratic game, the ordinary people at the bottom of the screen (D) would be harmed if they were hit by the falling objects (C). But the Democrats (B) are unharmed, so they can *protect* the people. The design of the sin-oriented game is almost exactly the same, except that Jesus must suffer (can be harmed) to protect ordinary people from sin, so the result is *self-sacrifice*.

A different approach is taken in the other two games. In these, the falling objects (C) are things that can be harmed, rather than harmful things, and the bottom of the screen (D) is something that would harm them. In the imagined Republican game, it would be wasteful for the money to fall into the fire, so we are saving the money, enacting *preservation*. In the game about children, they want to collide with the video games—too much—and we must *divert* them to more healthful activities.

If we consider the possibility of actively beneficial collisions, other potential games open. For example, Treanor sketched an anti-taxation game in which the ordinary people (A) are trying to drop their money (C) into their savings (D), but a player-navigated Uncle Sam (B) intervenes. Because the collision between the money and the savings (represented by a piggy bank) would be positive and is prevented by the government, the government's actions are presented as negative.

I call the structures that will be the focus of this chapter *logic structures*. They are larger than a single logic, such as control/navigation or collision. But they are not as detailed as full game designs. For example, a common graphical logic structure is a game entity that moves via *physics* (perhaps with player *control/navigation*) toward another entity, then *collides* with it, and the result of that collision. For this logic structure to become part of a full game design, it would probably be combined with other logic structures, often with shared entities between their structures, and the entities would need to be arranged in space.

For example, in *Kaboom*, there is the logic structure of the falling object (C) that moves toward, and collides with, the bottom of the screen (D), and then disappears—as well as the logic structure of the player-navigated object (B) that can collide with the falling object (C), which then disappears (and, through this, interferes with the operation of the first logic structure). These entities generally need to be skinned (or at least labeled) in a way that allows players to interpret their logics, through which they may refer to general or specific things in culture.

This chapter also tells the story of a direction of research mapped out by Michael Mateas before my arrival at UC Santa Cruz, to which I have contributed in more recent stages. This research program, which includes Treanor's explorations, seeks to help authors create meaningful games—or even find ways to autonomously generate games. Through pursuing this goal, these projects have undertaken some of the most concrete work on how games communicate meaning, including the most significant prior thinking about graphical logic structures. As it turns out, trying to understand logic structures with the level of formality required for this goal is quite useful both for discovering the strengths of such an approach and for uncovering the limitations.

Rhetorical Affordances

As mentioned earlier, Treanor's investigation is one way to the question: What can a game be about? Not just any game, but a particular game. Looking beyond *Kaboom*,

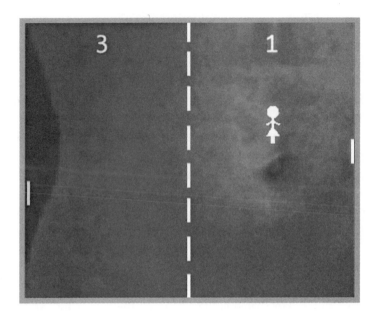

Figure 10.6
Two men, represented by paddles, pass a woman back and forth in Natalie Bookchin's *The Intruder*. As Jim Andrews writes in "Videogames as Literary Devices," "The story is the Jorge Louis Borges piece *The Intruder* with a few changes. The female in the story is 'the intruder.' She is as a possession of the two closely bonded miscreant brothers enmeshed in a hopeless triangle of psychosexual possession with homoerotic undertones." (Andrews, "Videogames as Literary Devices.") (Image taken by the author during play of the Internet Archive's online record at https://web .archive.org/web/20090427161342/http://muse.calarts.edu/~bookchin/intruder/.)

why has *Pong* been used as the design template for games about conversation—not just in *Dys4ia*,[4] but also in games ranging from relatively direct presentations of dialogue like *Conversation Pong 1.0*[5] (by Hanna Fidelis Siecke) and *Pongversation*[6] (by Nick Alexander et al.) to stranger presentations such as the partner-sharing sequence of Natalie Bookchin's *The Intruder*[7] (figure 10.6)? And why has *Pong*, to the best of my knowledge, never been used as the design template for games about much more common game topics, such as building structures, matching patterns, or allocating resources?[8] Why does even the *Tetris Pong* variant of Pippin Barr's *PONGS*,[9] which presumably pushes *Pong* as close to *Tetris*[10] as possible, fail to include the pattern matching that is fundamental to *Tetris*? On a more theoretical level, why does Bonnie Ruberg, writing about the original, abstract, arcade version of *Pong*, suggest that it "embodies some of the key structures through which desire, agency, power, and queer intimacy are formed"?[11]

In Treanor's terminology, these are questions about the *rhetorical affordances* of games. We might assume that a particular game design is only suited to framing play in one particular way, but the history of game skinning (including Koster's *Tetris* thought experiment) shows that this is not the case. On the other hand, we might assume that, through clever skinning, a particular game design might enable play that communicates almost anything. However, the work that has already been done—the way *Pong*-like games have been used for conversation, but not for more common domains— makes this seem unlikely. To dig deeper into this question, to understand a design's rhetorical affordances, we need some method.

To create his sketches, Treanor didn't try to imagine a set of different games based on *Kaboom*. Instead, he systematically went through all the possible permutations of harmful, beneficial, and neutral collisions between the objects in his simplified design. He also considered other elements that he thought might be important to our understanding of each game, without changing the core structure, such as whether the image at the top of the screen (A) was dropping the objects (C) deliberately, whether the game would come to an end, and whether the game was winnable. Treanor describes his work as inspired by the semiotic approach of *paradigmatic analysis*, looking at a series of signs and imagining what the author did not choose for inclusion in it.[12]

His choice to focus on *Kaboom* was inspired by *Kabul Kaboom!*,[13] Gonzalo Frasca's game critique of the initial rhetoric of the US war in Afghanistan (figure 10.7). In October 2001, as the United States was bombing the country, US public relations liked to focus on the air dropping of aid packages and the goal of freeing the civilian population from the rule of the Taliban. In Frasca's game there are a number of differences from Treanor's basic *Kaboom* design. First, no entity (A) is shown at the top of the screen—things simply fall from it—though, for those aware of the original game, the design places the United States in the role of the Mad Bomber. Second, the falling objects (C) are of two types—bombs and food. Third, because the objects are of two types, the player object (B, a mother holding her child, sampled from Picasso's famous anti-war painting *Guernica*) responds to them differently. Fourth, there is no impact on the game when the falling objects hit the ground (D).

During play, the first collision with a bomb brings instant death, revealing a photograph of Afghan civilians looking at a bombing's rubble, body parts of the *Guernica* figures scattered across it. Before this, bombs and food fall from the sky together, quickly. While a player might "rationally" want to collect the food, the only smart strategy is to try to avoid everything falling from the sky, and even that will only delay death for a short time. In terms of Ian Bogost's procedural rhetoric, we might say play becomes the enactment of a *procedural enthymeme*,[14] completing the game's argument that dropping

Figure 10.7
Gonzalo Frasca's *Kabul Kaboom* confronts players with rapidly falling hamburgers and bombs.
(Image courtesy of Gonzalo Frasca.)

bombs and food on the same population is irrational, rather than praiseworthy. It also shifts the play experience from the engaging, rewarding one of the original *Kaboom* to one that is frustrating and short, aligning player affect with the message of the game.

Looking at *Kabul Kaboom* clarifies why Treanor thought issues like winnability could be key to the meaning of a *Kaboom* variant. *Kabul Kaboom*'s omission of the dropping entity (A) also reveals that not every element of *Kaboom*'s design is necessary for certain meanings. Treanor's sketches suggest something similar. For example, if the school bus was removed from the anti-video game sketch, it would lose its "after school" framing, but it would still communicate diversion from one activity with another.

Further, *Kabul Kaboom* reveals the potential power in adding a small bit of complexity—specifically by having two different types of objects in one of the logic structures. If the falling object represents something that is happening (such as literal objects falling, or money being metaphorically thrown toward a fire) then having two types of objects (C) can communicate more than one thing happening (such as bombs and food falling). Similarly, we can imagine that a change in (D) could communicate more than one kind of potential result of the thing happening, such as money sometimes landing in a helpful place, sometimes in a wasteful place. Or a change in (B) could communicate more than one kind of potential response to the thing happening—perhaps the player-navigated object is made up of two politicians, one who successfully intervenes when colliding with (C), while the other fails.

But even with this added potential complexity, we still have a pretty good sense of the rhetorical affordances of *Kaboom*. The falling objects (C) communicate something happening. The collisions with the bottom of the screen (D) communicate what will happen without intervention. The collisions with the player-navigated object (B), which make the falling objects (C) disappear, communicate the possible intervention. If an entity appears at the top of the screen (A) it communicates the reason the thing (C) is happening. If the falling objects are too numerous, the results of collision with both the player-navigated object and the bottom of the screen are communicated as inevitable. If the falling objects are too hard to catch, the chances of intervention are communicated as unlikely, perhaps impossible.

Building on this, we can return to the question of why *Pong* has been used to communicate conversation, but not other, more-common game subjects. In the original design of *Pong*, a collision between the bouncing object (ball) and the player-navigated object (paddle) is evaluated positively, while collision between the bouncing object and the side of the screen is evaluated negatively. So far, this is essentially the same set of logic structures as *Kaboom*, oriented horizontally rather than vertically. But because the result of a positive collision (by player one's paddle) is to knock the object back toward an object for which collision with the object is also evaluated positively (player two's paddle), and the result of that collision is to knock it back again toward the other object (player one's paddle), it has rhetorical affordances for conversation. In conversation, replying (successful collision) is a social obligation, and not replying (failed collision) is failing to keep up one's side of the conversation.

We could argue that, more generally, *Pong* has rhetorical affordances for turn-taking activities and perhaps other kinds of reciprocal action. Something is happening (the moving object[s], C, as in *Kaboom*); two parties have equal, alternating obligations to intervene (the player-navigated object[s], B, as in *Kaboom*); and something will happen without the intervention (the screen-edge object[s], D, as in *Kaboom*). Because the ball is shared—and what will happen without intervention is good for one side and bad for the other—the player-navigated objects in *Pong* could be seen as taking the role, for the other player, of the top of the screen object (A) in *Kaboom* (figure 10.8).

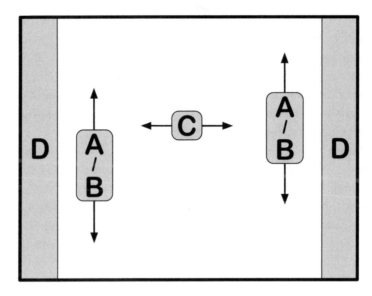

Figure 10.8

A diagram of the key elements of *Pong*, with labels matching the diagram of *Kaboom* seen in figure 10.5.

Of course, there are many other kinds of conversation beyond this most generic one which *Pong* could be skinned (or altered at a gameplay level) to represent. When knocking something skinned negatively back and forth, *Pong* can be seen as trading accusations or insults, with those missed (un-replied-to) "hitting home." With changes to the results of collision—as in *Dys4ia*, when colliding with an accusation does not cause it to bounce back—it is possible to represent activities such as one-sided conversations.

And the reciprocity between the paddles, the "connection at a distance" that can be skinned to represent conversation, is at the heart of Ruberg's interpretation, mentioned at the beginning of this section. Ruberg—in a reading resonant with Bookchin's skinning in *The Intruder* (figure 10.6)—views *Pong* through the lens of Eve Kosofsky Sedgwick's *Between Men: English Literature and Male Homosocial Desire*.[15] Sedgwick reinterprets eighteenth- and nineteenth-century English novels in which men pass women between them (for example, as romantic rivals) to focus not on the direct heterosexual relationships between men and women, but rather the indirect homoerotic intimacy between the men. Ruberg sees the relationship between *Pong*'s paddles as resonant with the relationships between men explored by Sedgwick, writing:

> Technically, the paddles cannot touch, or even approach each other; the game only allows players to move up and down, never closer to their opponent. Instead, the ball serves as a

go-between—the material object that they both touch in place of touching each other. . . . In *Between Men*, straight relationships act like a conduit through which the spark of homosociality and homoeroticism travels, facilitating the creation of queer intimacy at a distance. Similarly, in *Pong*, the ball is the object through which connection is transferred: the mediating surface, like a skin that both players touch.[16]

From this broader perspective, we can imagine skinnings of *Pong*, and perhaps changes to its collision results, that could be used to make games about many kinds of reciprocal connection and/or failed reciprocity. Yet it is hard to imagine any results of collisions, or any other changes to gameplay, that would give *Pong* the rhetorical affordances necessary to communicate the other activities mentioned earlier, such as building structures or resource gathering, through the spatial play. Rather, these would have to be shown as side effects of the play (much as the score is a side effect of play in the original version).

From this we can see that it is possible, analytically, to characterize the rhetorical affordances of a simple game design. We can also imagine some of the range of potential variations on such designs, as when an optional object is portrayed as responsible for the thing happening (A in *Kaboom*) or when the collision that should result in intervention instead fails (the *Pong*-like paddle "taking damage" in *Dys4ia*) or when an object is made more complex (the two types of falling objects, with very different collision results, in *Kabul Kaboom*). And we can see how logic structures can be assembled into larger configurations—such as the two reflected versions of the *Kaboom* structures that make up *Pong*—and what they can communicate.

Given these thoughts, there are a number of ways that one might go further. One of the most challenging, but also most potentially rewarding, is to create computational tools to enable further exploration. This is challenging because every assumption must be stated explicitly for any part of the exploration carried out computationally. It is rewarding because the computational tools then become immediately responsive partners for analysis, brainstorming, and creation.

In 2006, Mateas and Mark J. Nelson were moving from Georgia Tech to UC Santa Cruz—Mateas for a faculty position, Nelson to continue his PhD research with Mateas. They decided to pursue the creation of computational tools for this kind of investigation, building on insights from the arts (game design), humanities (game studies), and engineering (artificial intelligence). As Treanor and others continued this work, it would help point toward answers to the questions that motivate this chapter: What are the potential strengths of communicating non-spatial ideas using graphical logics and spatial game structures? And what are the weaknesses?

Game Structures and Spaces

Treanor actually offered one *Kaboom*-based design sketch that is even simpler: a game about self-destruction. In this, a celebrity (B) tries to catch drugs (C) falling from the sky. This might be the simplest possible structure to extract from *Kaboom*. It is a logic structure with one thing navigating relative to, and colliding with ("catching"), another, or not. We could also imagine the falling thing being beneficial to the catching thing (healthy food falling in a child's mouth), or the falling thing needing to be caught (a baby falling into a bassinet), or the two objects needing to come together (the two sides of a broken peace symbol), and so on. Or we could imagine the most common version of this gameplay structure: the player-navigated object tries to avoid a harmful thing (a spaceship tries to avoid a missile).

We could sit down and try to enumerate all the different communicative roles of collision (or other logics) for a particular structure, as Treanor did. And we could also try to break down well-known game patterns into smaller elements, looking for the basic structures. But while Treanor-style imagining of different communicative roles can be a creative and interesting activity, it is difficult to work from there toward more general theories of what a structure can communicate. And while it would be potentially productive for us to break down spatial game patterns into smaller structures, we don't need to start from scratch, because that work is already begun—most famously in a game already discussed in chapter 8: *WarioWare Inc.: Mega MicroGame\$*.[17]

In fact, as Chaim Gingold argues,[18] *WarioWare* can be seen as an explanation, in game form, of how games are made out of smaller structures. He gives the example of "Galaxy 2003," the game presented at the end of *WarioWare*'s Dribble level. "Galaxy 2003" is a standard top-down shooter, of the sort pioneered by *Space Invaders*[19] and *Galaxian*.[20] To game-literate players, there might be nothing new to notice—except for the fact that *WarioWare* players will have earlier played three microgames that each present one of the basic structures that "Galaxy 2003" combines.

WarioWare's "Dodge!" microgame has a player-navigated car avoid collisions with other cars. The "Collect!" microgame has a player-navigated character collect coins by colliding with them. The "Attack!" microgame has a player-navigated spaceship at the bottom of the screen trying to launch a projectile at the right moment to collide with another spaceship moving at the top of the screen. The three of these combine in "Galaxy 2003" to enable the activities of a top-down shooter: navigating across the screen to dodge incoming projectiles and enemies, collect power-ups, and attack enemies with projectiles.

From this we can see that *WarioWare* can provide us with some of the basic structures that are worth investigating—and that it is possible to (re)combine them. But we also can see that *WarioWare*'s "Attack!" microgame has nearly the same structure as one of the *Kaboom* variants we discussed. So, clearly this structure can be used to communicate that its gameplay is about attacking, but also that it is about other things. And as we have seen with *Kaboom*, what communicates this is a combination of the logic structures, the spatial arrangements and behaviors, and the skinnings of the objects that tell us how to interpret the logics.

Nelson and Mateas[21] came up with a clever approach to investigating these kinds of possibilities: a system that automatically skins *WarioWare* microgame structures. People play two roles when interacting with this system. The first role is the normal one: playing microgames and interpreting what they communicate. The second role is an unusual one: defining rules for the system to use, when skinning a structure, to produce a microgame to communicate a particular activity.

Nelson calls the construction of such rules the definition of a "game space"—a set of possible games meant to communicate something. It's hard to know how to define a game space in a way a computer will understand. Skinning is the kind of "common sense reasoning" task that is notoriously difficult for AI techniques, but also impossible with other techniques. Nelson's approach is to have people build diagrams of game spaces. Figure 10.9 is a part of his diagram for the "Avoid" game space.

This specifies that a game in this space must contain an "Avoider" and that there are two constraints on what can be the Avoider. The constraints are constructed using two outside sources for common-sense knowledge: Princeton's WordNet and MIT's ConceptNet. WordNet[22] is a carefully constructed hierarchical database of English words, grouped by words with similar meanings (rather than similar spellings). More-general words (and sometimes concepts, like "animate thing") are "hypernyms" in WordNet, while more-specific ones are "hyponyms." The left side of the image in figure 10.9 specifies that the Avoider must be a hyponym of "animate thing" in WordNet.

ConceptNet is a much wider ranging "semantic network" of common-sense knowledge. It contains the types of relationships that are in WordNet (and in its current version uses WordNet as one of its knowledge sources) but also relationships such as "CapableOf," "CapableOfReceivingAction," "PropertyOf," and "UsedFor." This wide range is possible, in part, because ConceptNet's foundations are in crowdsourced knowledge, starting with the Open Mind Common Sense project.[23] But it also means that ConceptNet has historically contained errors and omissions, which Nelson used WordNet in part to address. The left side of figure 10.9 specifies that the Avoider must be, according to ConceptNet, CapableOfReceivingAction for one of the attack verbs chosen by Nelson (these are: shoot, attack, damage, chase, injure, and hit).

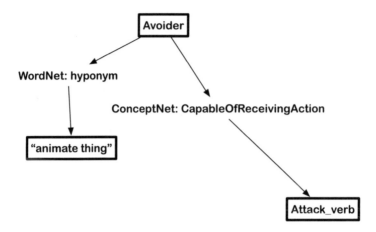

Figure 10.9
A partial diagram of Mark Nelson's "Avoid" game space. (After figure 3 in Nelson and Mateas, "An Interactive Game-Design Assistant.")

We can see how both of these constraints are important for a microgame about avoiding an attack. For example, a wall is capable of being hit, but it's not good at avoiding being hit, because it isn't animate. Similarly, a ghost is animate, but it doesn't need to avoid things, because it isn't capable of receiving most attacks.

Part of what is interesting about constructing game spaces as graphs, tied to common-sense knowledge sources, is that it forces us to make our assumptions explicit. Then these assumptions might turn out to be wrong, when we see the games that result. A simple version of this occurred as Nelson was constructing the full "Avoid" graph, seen in figure 10.10.

We might expect the right side of this graph to be much simpler. Surely the "Attacker" only needs to be CapableOf one of the attack verbs? But when Nelson tried this,

> it turns out to preclude many games that we think of as canonical in the avoider game design space. Something trying to avoid a bullet, for example, is excluded because a bullet isn't itself *CapableOf* "shoot": A bullet doesn't shoot, but is shot, and therefore isn't *CapableOf*, but rather *CapableOfReceivingAction* shoot. We informally expect it to serve in the role of attacker and perhaps anthropomorphize it as "chasing" the Avoider, but those notions are too subtle for the common-sense databases that currently exist to capture. To take these cases into account, we've added an alternate possibility for fulfilling the last constraint: If an Attacker is a projectile (according to WordNet), then we check whether the Attack verb can sensibly act on *it*, rather than whether it can sensibly act out the Attack verb.[24]

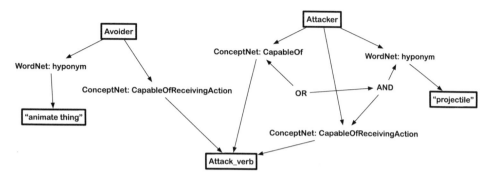

Figure 10.10
A full diagram of Mark Nelson's "Avoid" game space (after figure 3 in Nelson and Mateas, "An Interactive Game-Design Assistant").

Once a game space is defined in this way, a set of rules can map it to one of the five *WarioWare*-style microgame structures the system knows. In addition to "Collector" and "Attacker," these include: "Dodger," in which a dodging object tries to avoid one or more attackers; "Shooter," in which objects move across the screen and can be shot by moving crosshairs and firing; and "Pick Up," in which a navigating object tries to gather a stationary one, with obstacles in the way. Each of these combines one or more logic structures and a specific spatial arrangement of objects.

As with *WarioWare*, the player might play either role—the attacker or avoider. The final structure can be realized differently depending on the player's role and the specific nouns chosen for the attacker and avoider. For example, using the Dodger structure, if the player is the avoider and the attacker is a projectile, the attacker will move in a straight line. But if the attacker is also animate, it will chase the player.

Interestingly, Dodger isn't the only structure that can communicate the "Avoid" game space. It can also be mapped onto the Shooter structure. Figure 10.11 shows two microgames generated by Nelson's and Mateas's system, both of which have chosen to have a duck avoid being shot by a bullet, but which use two different structures (and one different image).

The same is true of the other game spaces Nelson investigated. For example, Nelson constructed an "Acquire" game space. He found that the results can be mapped onto the Pick Up structure (as one would expect) but also onto the Dodger structure.

In short, Nelson and Mateas developed a method for investigating more rigorously and specifically what I have discussed in a broad way. The same spatial game structure can be used to communicate that play is about multiple things. The three keys to that

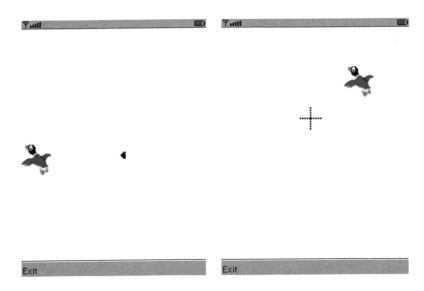

Figure 10.11
Two games from Mark Nelson's and Michael Mateas's *WarioWare* game generator. They characterize these as "Two games generated for the noun 'pheasant' and verb 'shoot.' A duck is in both
since it is the closest noun to 'pheasant' for which the generator has a sprite. Both are Avoid
games with Attacker-verb 'shoot,' Avoider-noun 'duck,' and Attacker-noun 'bullet.' The left game
is implemented by the Shooter concrete mechanic and has the player trying to shoot the duck;
the right game is implemented by the Dodger concrete mechanic and has the player, as the duck,
trying to avoid bullets." (Nelson and Mateas, "Towards Automated Game Design.")

communication are the logic structure(s), the spatial arrangement and behaviors, and
the skinning of the objects. The skinning of the objects draws in our cultural ideas of
what, for example, is capable of attacking or acquiring something else.

One way of thinking about Nelson's and Mateas's system, then, is as a prototype of
a scholarly and pedagogical tool. Such a tool could be used to propose and evaluate
theories about game spaces and structures. We can also imagine this kind of approach
being used more broadly, in trying to understand other forms of computational
media.

Another way of thinking about such a system, that Nelson and Mateas propose,
is as a brainstorming partner for novice game designers. There are lots of systems to
help people create games once they already have an idea of how to map their ideas
into game structures, but none of them help with that initial mapping. And again we
can imagine this being undertaken for other kinds of computational media. (Anne

Sullivan pursued this in the area of role-playing game quests to create the QuestBrowser system.[25])

Further, we could imagine this system as the basis for an endless, generative version of *WarioWare*, as Nelson and Mateas also propose. Such a game wouldn't just be generative in the spaces it constructs (in the tradition of *Rogue*[26]) but in what it is *about*. In the decade since Nelson's system was created, much further work has been done in the area of game generation—in research, indie, and mainstream games—but largely with much less attention to the topics of games.

That said, there are also real limitations to this approach. Consider, for example, the conversational *Pong* variants in *Dys4ia*. A gender accusation is not something WordNet believes is animate. A shield might be something that can be attacked, but it is not something that ConceptNet thinks has a gender. While Nelson's and Mateas's ideas offer much to those wishing to explore games that use spatial models in conventional and alternative manners, either another approach is needed for exploring expansive uses or a specific diagram would have to be created for each type of expansive game space—seeking a way to use existing commonsense knowledge sources to capture its nuances.

This problem goes away, however, if we shift the role of the human participants. Such a shift is at the heart of a different system, which builds on the work led by Nelson and Treanor.

Game-o-Matic

Game-o-Matic[27] is a proposal, in the form of a system, for a radical vision of media creation: making media by specifying what it is about.

When using most video game creation tools, you start by specifying spaces, objects, and behaviors. Tools aimed at novices make this process easy—for example, making it possible to drag and drop common logics (collision, navigation) onto objects. But the process of making a game begins with constructing the elements that will eventually appear in the final product. Obviously, at some time before this, you need to have figured out how your ideas for the game's topic will translate into spatial behaviors and structures.

In Game-o-Matic, instead, the first stage is to tell the system what play will be about. Then you never need to construct spaces and objects. The system itself produces a wide range of proposals for possible games that might communicate, through play, the situation you specify. You browse through them and tweak them—perhaps replacing their abstract shapes with specific images.

For novices, this approach makes the creation of video games possible. Even the most friendly game-creation tools are still a challenge for novices to use to create a complete game. This is at least in part because of the difficult translation process—moving from an idea about the world to spatial play that communicates it. Game-o-Matic performs this process itself.

For experts, a tool like Game-o-Matic could be a brainstorming partner. It could also be part of creating complete games, if they could be carefully adjusted and polished after the system produces the initial sketch. The first stages of game creation, even for simple games, are time-consuming for everyone.

The question, of course, is how a vision like Game-o-Matic's is possible. The team behind Game-o-Matic—made up of faculty and students from UC Santa Cruz and Georgia Tech, including Mateas, Bogost, and Treanor—proposed a particular answer. It begins with diagrams similar to those Nelson suggested for defining game spaces. But rather than trying to draw on common-sense knowledge sources like ConceptNet, these diagrams depend on the knowledge of the person creating the game.

For example, in Treanor's dissertation[28] he describes the process of creating a simple game about the Occupy movement. The initial diagram looks like figure 10.12.

While this looks like one of the game space definitions created in Nelson's system, it is in fact operating at a higher level. Each of the arrows specifies one of the verbs that

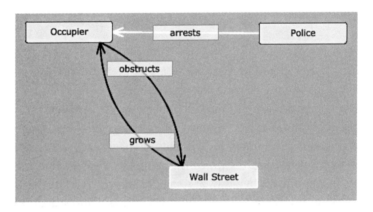

Figure 10.12
A reconstruction of Treanor's Game-o-Matic diagram for creating a simple game about the Occupy movement. (Image taken by the author during Game-o-Matic interaction, after figure 8 in chapter 2 of Treanor, "Investigating Procedural Expression and Interpretation in Videogames.")

the system knows, the equivalent of Nelson's game spaces. Each of these verbs can be mapped to one or more of the logic structures the system knows, which the Game-o-Matic team call *micro-rhetorics*.

The nouns, on the other hand, the system treats only as labels. Because they are not connected to outside sources of common-sense knowledge, the system would not be able to suggest other skinnings for them. But this also means that the system has no problem with creating games that operate metaphorically, or in other expansive ways. The expansive understanding comes from the human being who creates the diagram.

Once such a diagram is created, Game-o-Matic begins the process of creating a series of games for the user to consider. In each game a different combination of micro-rhetorics can express the verbs. For example, Game-o-Matic has micro-rhetorics for both "obstruct" (when, upon collision, one object stops the movement of another object) and "redirect" (when, upon collision, one object causes another object to bounce off of it). Game-o-Matic classifies both of these logic structures as communicating obstruction.

For the particular example game that Treanor describes, Game-o-Matic chooses a "take custody" micro-rhetoric for the Police arresting the Occupier, which operates similarly to its "obstruct" logic structure. It chooses the similar "obstruct" logic structure for the Occupier obstructing Wall Street. Finally, it chooses a "grow" logic structure for Wall Street growing the Occupier, which causes the Occupier to get larger when it collides with Wall Street.

The result Game-o-Matic gives Treanor is compelling, expressing an idea about the Occupy movement that wasn't obvious in the diagram. The player controls the Occupier, at first racing to avoid Police on the way to Wall Street. The player's goal is to defeat ("collect") Wall Street ten times. In Treanor's play of the game, the player catches Wall Street, which begins to shrink out of existence while the Occupier/player grows. This larger size makes it easier for the Occupier to catch the next Wall Street, but also makes it easier for the Police to catch the Occupier. As a result, the Police immobilize the Occupier when it is already in contact with the next Wall Street, causing it to grow again. The Occupier can no longer move, but now it is so large that it catches the following Wall Street as soon as it spawns. As Treanor puts it:

> As the Occupy movement grows to fill the screen, overwhelming the police forces, removing Wall Street happens without any actions from the player. And this is just the first game generated![29]

In short, this game suggests an idea about the larger situation, which arises through play: If the Police bottle up Occupy where it is in contact with Wall Street, it will only

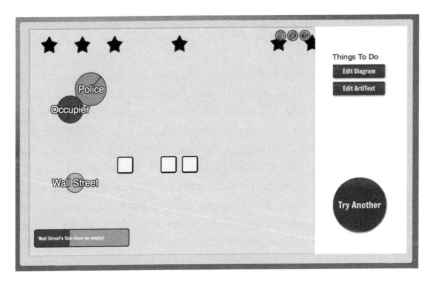

Figure 10.13
An Occupy-themed game generated by Game-o-Matic, based on the diagram in figure 10.12. (Image taken by the author during play.)

get stronger. This idea depends on the micro-rhetorics but is not immediately obvious from the original diagram. And, further, this game demonstrates an answer to a question raised earlier in this chapter. It shows that it is possible to take logic structures drawn from multiple games and combine them in a way that preserves the communication of each.

Of course, the game Treanor reports is only one of many that Game-o-Matic is capable of producing based on his diagram. I decided to make the same diagram and see what else it would generate. The results were telling.

In my first game I played the Police (figure 10.13). This game had only one Wall Street and, when it shrank too small, I would lose. It shrank when it was in contact with Occupiers, of which multiple were created, and each Occupier would head straight for Wall Street. I had a goal zone (marked by stars) and I needed to drag the Occupiers away from Wall Street and into the goal zone.

When played, this game, as one might expect, expresses ideas very similar to the game Treanor describes, but it does so from the point of view of the power structure. The Police must get Occupy away from Wall Street and into the distant jail. Wall Street is damaged, and Occupy is made stronger, by every moment they are in contact.

Then my second game was very odd. I was given the role of the Police, again. But this time my goal was to make more Occupiers before the time ran out. I wasn't sure, but it looked like I was, as the Police, meant to grab the Occupiers and take them to Wall Street in order to get them to reproduce. Needless to say, this didn't strike me as a sensible game about Occupy.

These three games show us some of the weaknesses and strengths of Game-o-Matic's focus on logic structures, and the ways it tries to build full games from that foundation. We can see this more clearly by describing its process.

After a diagram is created, the first thing Game-o-Matic does is look for ways to interpret the diagram that go beyond the explicit arrows. It has three strategies for this. Through *augmentation*, it can find additional relationships. For example, if A attacks B (in the diagram) and C protects B, Game-o-Matic will infer a relationship like that in Treanor's Democratic Party version of *Kaboom*: C protects B from A. Through *synthesis*, Game-o-Matic looks for ways that two of its simple verbs might be better communicated by a more complex micro-rhetoric. For example, Treanor tells us that, "If a protester 'informs' a citizen and the citizen 'joins' the protester, the protester 'mobilizes' the citizen and a micro-rhetoric written for 'mobilize' is used instead of the two mechanics for the original verbs."[30] Finally, through *decomposition*, a single verb can be broken down into two, such as "repair" being replaced with "touch" and "heal."

These micro-rhetorics are similar to Nelson's game spaces in that they are not tied to concrete game structures. For example, just as Nelson's avoider must be animate, something that Game-o-Matic has given the role of an avoider will be assigned an abstract behavior "_moveInAnyWay." These abstract behaviors (which the Game-o-Matic team calls "non-terminals") are kept open to broaden the possibilities considered while a complete game is constructed.

Game-o-Matic then builds a complete game for every combination of micro-rhetorics it can derive from the diagram. And what this requires is key. Game-o-Matic's work with micro-rhetorics represents a set of compelling extensions to our understanding of how graphical logic structures can communicate about topics that aren't necessarily spatial. But even after the core structures are specified, based on the diagram, the result may be missing important elements for a spatial video game: an object for the player to navigate (and a type of navigation), something for the player to attempt to achieve or prevent, and objects placed in sensible positions (for example, a game that is trying to communicate about something challenging shouldn't start out with objects in their goal positions).

Game-o-Matic uses a set of *recipes* to try to convert the collections of partially specified logic structures (which it calls "micro-rhetorics with non-terminals") into complete games. Some are structure recipes, based on common ways games are arranged. For example, if one type of object is trying to navigate to a goal and another type of object is meant to make this challenging, the goal could be put on one side of the screen, the navigating object on the other side, and the objects that present a challenge in the middle (as in games like *Frogger*[31]). Other recipes focus on win and loss conditions, for example, making sure that, if the player's goal is to remove an entity from the screen, it is actually possible for it to be removed. As these recipes are applied, non-terminals are resolved in ways that work with them, and even already-determined design elements can change. For example, in Treanor's Occupy game, a point-scoring win recipe was selected. When this was applied, a collision between the Occupier and Wall Street shifted from stopping Wall Street's movement to removing Wall Street from the screen. As Treanor notes:

> This rhetorical leap enables *Game-o-Matic* to give novel interpretations of the system represented in the concept map, but [it] can sometimes significantly change the message being expressed. For example, in this case, the idea of the Occupier obstructing Wall Street is replaced with something that might be more interpretable as the Occupier destroying Wall Street.[32]

All of the recipes are individually sensible. Each one is applied based on thoughtfully considered rules, which account for the current state of the in-construction game. These rules decide the recipe to use—based on policies for which are appropriate in the current circumstances and a ranking of those that are found appropriate. But none of these have any access to what the game is trying to communicate at a higher level. And as a result, we get games like the one in which the Police are trying to make more Occupiers.

Given this, Game-o-Matic teaches us two things. First, as already noted, it teaches us that we can draw logic structures from multiple games, then combine them in novel ways, and have them communicate as intended. In fact, it also shows that unforeseen implications of the relationships between these structures can emerge positively in the gameplay, saying something further about the topic (as shown in Treanor's Occupy example). Second, however, it shows that logic structures require placement in an appropriate wider context. In order to design, to interpret, and (certainly) to generate games, we need to consider not only how structure and communication work together at a small level but also at larger ones.

The Limits of Spatial Structures

How would one move beyond Game-o-Matic? How could we enable people who are not experts to make games that express their ideas about the world, through a tool that suggests structures, arrangements, and behaviors that are appropriate both at the level of individual interactions and the level of wider context and goals? For example, imagine a student who wants to make a game about the impact of debt on students' lives. They could make a diagram that says:

1. Students need money.
2. Tuition takes money from students.
3. Loans give money to students.
4. Loans grow tuition.
5. Loans harm the future.
6. Students need the future.

For the system to propose sensible games about this situation, it must be able to do things that Game-o-Matic cannot. For example, it must be able to understand that students (after they understand the game) will try to avoid taking loans as long as possible, in order to avoid the growth of tuition and harm to the future. The game elements must behave, and must be physically organized in the game space, in such a way that players are able to engage with an attempt to avoid the losing conditions (rather than, for example, losing happening immediately or the outcome feeling arbitrary).

Mateas and I have been working on a project that does this—together with postdoctoral scholars (Chris Martens and Ben Samuel) and graduate students (Adam Summerville, Joseph C. Osborn, Sarah Harmon, Melanie Dickinson, and others).[33] Our system is called Gemini, and it is a framework for logical rules that derive consequences from small game facts.[34] For example, we derive consequences such as "the player will attempt" actions that (a) create favorable conditions for the player and (b) are under the player's control. More complexly, we can also derive consequences such as the fact that a collision between two objects will increase a resource and that this has the potential to move a resource above (or below) a threshold, creating a winning (or losing) condition. Putting these together for the example game above, we would derive that students interacting (perhaps colliding) with loans will not only lead toward a losing condition but also be necessary to avoid another losing condition, so that the player will take the action, but only if necessary.

The system is called Gemini because it has "twin" approaches. It can examine a game and attempt to interpret it—or it can be given a desired interpretation of a game and attempt to generate games that communicate such things about the world. I think an approach like Gemini's will be powerful for uses such as Game-o-Matic's, when the goal is to create a small game that communicates something pointed about the world through play. Looking further, one of our hopes for Gemini is to be able to generate microgames that communicate through simple logic structures with appropriate spatial arrangement and behavior—as in games like *Dys4ia*—but to perform that generation based on prior actions of the player. This could enable some of the exploration of wide possibility spaces that is key to larger, more simulation-oriented games, while retaining the ability to communicate in multiple domains seen in overloaded microgames.

At the same time, however, being part of this research has led me to believe that there are limits to what graphical logic structures can communicate about things other than space. We see a hint of this already in Game-o-Matic's Occupy games. The growing and shrinking of Occupy and Wall Street are certainly spatial, and they influence what takes place via logics like collision and navigation. But the growing and shrinking are also resource-oriented, with game-winning resources transferring from one entity to another.[35]

This becomes even clearer when considering the hypothetical student loan games that Gemini might generate. First, it would be awkward and unnecessary for Gemini to reason about such games purely spatially. The underlying approach to the system understanding such games—that include things needed, given, taken, and grown—should engage with resource logics, not only graphical ones. Second, while such games could be represented to players in ways that straddle spatial and resource communication strategies (such as growing and shrinking shapes), there is no reason to restrict the games to such strategies. The resource levels and transfers could also be shown using numbers, partially filled bars, changing colors, and other common video game communication strategies.

In other words, while it is certainly possible to use graphical logic structures and spatial arrangements to communicate about ideas that aren't primarily spatial, it's not always the best strategy. That is part of why graphical and resource logics are so often used together in human-designed games, and why we have established strategies for communicating resource states and spatial states at the same time.

So, this is the first issue: There are well-understood logics that aren't graphical logics, and there are well-understood structures of other logics (as explored with resource logics and source/sink models in books like Michael Sellers's *Advanced Game Design*). There are situations in which it is more appropriate to use these logics, including in games meant to be presented visually. That is why we have game design conventions for visually combining and communicating the states of multiple types of logics and models.

The second issue is one of visual complexity. This is something that tools like Game-o-Matic can help us investigate, allowing our work to be more grounded than if it were pursued only through abstract thinking. For example, I tried using Game-o-Matic to produce somewhat more complex games about Occupy. I created one with new entities labeled "the Public" and "the Media." I connected them with new verbs, including Wall

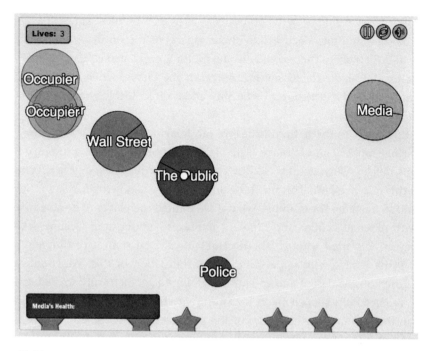

Figure 10.14
An Occupy-themed game generated by a more complex Game-o-Matic diagram.

Street "buys" the Media and the Media "influences" the Public. The resulting games are hard for me to interpret, even though I created the diagrams from which they were generated. And the problem isn't something that a smarter system, like Gemini, could address. Figure 10.14 is an example.

The problem is that there are too many visual relationships. With only a few entities, it was possible to see things that could happen—the Police bottling up the Occupier in contact with Wall Street (which will help the Occupier) or getting it away from Wall Street (which will hurt the Occupier). But with more entities, how do we interpret the Police dragging the Occupier away from Wall Street but toward the Media, or the Public? What does it mean for the Occupier to collide with Wall Street and the Public at the same time, especially when these collisions might have different effects—or one of them might have no effect?

In short, with more entities and relationships, it is no longer possible to identify and interpret the intended logic structures. The spatial field, and the play it enables, has become a hindrance to understanding the ideas that motivated the creation of the game. If we want to use graphical logic structures to say something more complex about Occupy, we would be better off doing so in a series of microgames, like *Dys4ia*'s. There could be multiple small games about aspects of the on-the-ground actions of Occupy and the Police. There could also be multiple small games about how Occupy depends on the Media for its message to reach the Public, while at the same time the Media is shaped by the direct ownership and indirect ideology of the one percent (including Wall Street).

And this brings us to the third issue. We can imagine some of these Occupy microgames using graphical and resource logics. Perhaps public support is a resource which, at first, is quickly generated by Occupy's actions. But then ideology intervenes and reduces this resource flow. This much could work fine. Taking further steps, however, is difficult to imagine. For example, what if we wanted the player to be able to experiment with different actions and different messages coming from Occupy—then see how they are distorted through the different ideological stances of different media outlets? Perhaps we can imagine some spatial translation of this. We could make a game focused on the design and careful navigation of geometrically shaped messages through geometrically shaped media pathways, with the shapes of the messages changing when they collide with the sides of the pathways. But at some point we will be better off seeking an approach beyond this kind of expansive use of graphical logics— striking out in an inventive direction, attempting to create logics and models that are designed to communicate about ideology, rather than trying to expand the uses of graphical logic structures to express that message.

The Necessity of Other Art Forms

There is one remaining, vital issue we must consider in the relationship between logic structures and game meaning: How much meaning is "in" logic structures, or arrangements of structures, or even full game designs? To put it another way, how much do the rhetorical affordances of structures shine through to players in the absence of significant contributions from other artforms? Clearly it is possible to arrive at interpretations like Ruberg's of *Pong*, even in the absence of anything to tell us what the paddles or balls represent (no images or textual labels on the shapes), with minimal animations to suggest how the balls or paddles respond to their collisions (merely physics-based redirection), and with only abstract sounds. At the same time, what makes Ruberg's interpretation notable is that it is novel—to my knowledge, no one has suggested such an interpretation before.

This ties into an influential discussion that has been taking place in game design and game studies. Rod Humble, for example, claims that "the rules of a game can give an artistic statement independent of its other components."[36] Humble's *The Marriage*[37] is a game with no sound and with imagery limited to colored circles and squares. Many players do successfully understand the game to be communicating ideas about a human relationship. This aligns with what we might call a "strong" interpretation of Bogost's notion of procedural rhetoric. One definition Bogost offers for this term is "the art of persuasion through rule-based representations and interactions, rather than the spoken word, writing, images, or moving pictures."[38] The strong interpretation focuses on the "rather than" in this definition—on what games can communicate through how they operate in the absence of other art forms or without considering the contributions of other forms.

This idea has also been widely challenged. For example, in the case of *The Marriage*, Jesper Juul argues that Humble's game only communicates its ideas "if the player understands that the game represents a marriage at all."[39] The game's title does significant work in this regard, employing the power of language.[40] Further, even the colors employed for the abstract shapes in *The Marriage* are culturally loaded—blue for male, pink for female—as Jason Begy notes.[41]

One way to investigate this question further is through the tools of psychology. Barrett R. Anderson and Christopher R. Karzmark pursued this approach,[42] having players experience three games:

- First, *September 12th*,[43] a game by Frasca and collaborators that portrays through its systems the arguments that missile strikes inevitably lead to civilian casualties and that civilian deaths inspire terrorism. These systemic expressions are made apparent to players in a context that also uses the tools of traditional visual arts (explosions flattening pedestrians, mourners huddled over them) and auditory arts (the sounds of explosions and weeping).

- Second, *LIM*,[44] a spatial game by merritt k (formerly Merritt Kopas) in which players navigate a color-changing block through a maze. Single-colored blocks will attack (collide with) the player's color-changing block—shaking the game's camera and impeding progress—unless the player holds down a button before other blocks react to them, which allows their block to assume the color of the local blocks and "pass" as one of them. But holding down the button also causes the game's camera to zoom in, progressively narrowing the field of view and eventually also causing the camera to shake, making spatial understanding and progress impossible.

- Finally, *Threes JS*[45] is a JavaScript version of a game by Asher Vollmer and collaborators in which players match number tiles on a grid, attempting to achieve a high score before further moves become impossible. It is an abstract puzzle game, which was a precursor to, and conceptual inspiration for, the better-known game *2048*.[46] While it is possible to interpret any game rhetorically, *Threes JS* was included in the study to serve as a control in comparison to the other two intentionally rhetorical games.

September 12th is a game that uses a range of artforms to make its point. *LIM*, on the other hand, can be seen as a more pure example of Humble's rules-only stance than *The Marriage*. As merritt k puts it, "I wanted to convey things with as little verbal language as possible and as little specific imagery as possible."[47] For most players, the title does not suggest a particular game situation—and unlike the culturally loaded colors used for the shapes in Humble's game, the blocks that take action in *LIM* are colors such as brown and indigo. It is likely for these reasons that *LIM* has been described by Samantha Leigh Allen as "a classic example of procedural rhetoric at work: it is a sparse, abstract game which conveys a powerful message to the player through its systems alone."[48] On the other hand, it cannot be denied that the attacking blocks and camera effects are making some connection with players' understanding of the arts of animation and cinema.

Anderson and Karzmark found some things that should reassure those who believe in the power of systems-based expression. Most importantly, both *September 12th* and *LIM* were seen as making an argument by players, while *Threes JS* generally was not— though more players understood this for *September 12th*. (90% for *September 12th*, 60% for *LIM*, and 5% for *Threes JS*.) Further, the player interpretations of *September 12th* agreed with the common interpretations of experts in game design and game studies. Specifically, all the categories of player response touched on some interpretation aligned with expert interpretations, with the largest group (59%) focusing on civilian deaths in the "War on Terror."

On the other hand, *LIM* was not as well understood. Experts describe *LIM* as a "response to the violence and dread and suffocation of being a woman who doesn't conform to society's popular image of a woman" (Porpentine[49]) and discuss the violently shaking camera (when the button is held) as enacting the point when the player's square is "unable to maintain the psychic labor of passing" (Shira Chess[50]). But the largest group of player responses had the opposite interpretation: 44% of players said they thought the game was about the necessity, or even the benefits, of conformity— offering interpretations such as, "you need to blend in to get through certain parts of your life."[51] In other words, while the largely abstract game was able to communicate that it was necessary to use its color-matching mechanic to make progress, and that this color-matching was mapped by players onto real-world situations demanding normative behavior, without sufficient support from other artforms, the game was deeply misunderstood by many players.[52]

We have also used Gemini to explore questions in this area, with Dickinson and Osborn leading our part of a collaboration with Jill Denner and David Torres at ETR Associates.[53] In this case, rather than investigating a few expert-designed games (as Anderson and Karzmark did), we looked at groups of games generated by varying the instructions given to Gemini.

At first, we used traditional playtesting approaches. At the time, we were using Gemini to generate minigames that were played alongside (and framed by) a dynamic, choice-based narrative about climate change.[54] The games had instructions; the objects in the games had labels; and players generally seemed to figure out how to play them and interpret them as we intended, in a broad sense.

Beyond this, we also wanted to understand if the games made sense on their own, without the framing of the narrative. When we popped them out and presented them on their own, potential players were totally confused and resistant to engaging them. So, what we settled on was presenting the games with a list of "things to try" (potential game mechanics). Then, afterward, we would ask the players what mechanics they thought were present, what larger gameplay patterns they identified, what ideas they had about the game's meaning, and, finally, which possible interpretations of the games they played (interpretations provided by us) made sense to them.

For Gemini, the good news was that players were able to figure out how the games were played—which was not guaranteed with an AI system that, when we were initially developing it, created many games that even we found totally alien and unplayable. But for those who believe in the inherent communicative power of systems, the bad news is that most players were not able to offer their own interpretations of what the games were about (let alone appropriate interpretations). Further, most players were not able to figure out, thinking back on their play experience, which interpretations provided by us were appropriate or inappropriate for the games they played.

This was true even though one of the game and interpretation pairs we provided—an abstract game meant to represent a beach cleanup—was one that players had shown no trouble interpreting when the game and its theme were presented together. In this Gemini-created game, players drag red triangles together and each pairing clears a bit of the background color. We had shown this game (figure 10.15) to players during our pilot studies with the title "Beach Cleanup" and instructions such as: "Red triangles represent people trying to clean up a beach and save a crab population. They can be dragged around with the mouse." With that framing, players made comments such as, "It made me proud that a series of small changes became something good" and offered

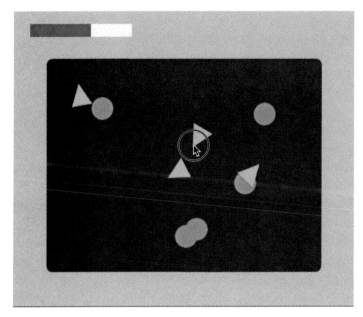

Figure 10.15
In this game, generated by the Gemini system, triangles can be dragged together, resulting in "clearing" an area of the background color beneath them. Presented on its own, players largely found it uninterpretable. Framed as a beach cleanup, players largely understood it.

thematic interpretations such as "people working together." But when the game was presented without the framing and players were asked to choose the intended theme from a multiple choice list a few minutes later, the players didn't do significantly better than if they were selecting randomly.

In other words, both our studies with Gemini and the work led by Anderson and Karzmark indicate that abstract games, without framing from other artforms, do not communicate their meanings effectively. On the other hand, it is also worth noting that our Gemini studies found players who had played other abstract games had an easier time understanding how to play our generated games. It could be that understanding abstract games is a relatively specific literacy, one that players can develop over time. And while we did not find that players who understood how the generated games operated were better at interpreting their meanings, we also found that some people are good at interpreting media even when the piece of media itself does little to support them.

It could be that, in time, we will find a growing group of players who are able to, like Ruberg, learn to play quite abstract games and provide interesting interpretations of them. But until then, those who wish to reach audiences with their messages cannot depend on broad understanding of the rhetorical affordances of logic structures or even entire game designs.

Logic Structures and Game Meaning

And so this chapter comes to a conclusion that resonates with the two previous chapters. Graphical logics and spatial models can be used to create compelling play experiences. And these can be used to communicate about topics that go beyond the obvious and beyond the currently conventional, which we can view in different ways.

One view focuses on a set of approaches to the communicative aspects of logics and models. There are alternative approaches, in which logics and models are used in currently conventional ways (for example, to represent space) but for less-conventional subjects (the space of a picket line). There are expansive approaches (the focus of the last two chapters) in which another, unconventional communicative role is added to logics within models, which run along a spectrum. One end of this spectrum is refinement, in which a logic can be used to communicate something that is understood as more specific, such as the once-unconventional move of collision's physical touch being used to communicate the physical act of collecting. The other end of the spectrum is doubling, when a second communicative role co-exists with the first, distinct from it. This is how we understand graphical logics when their spatial model is metaphorically overloaded as a model of something else.

This chapter has taken a different view, focused on logic structures. In particular, it has looked at how graphical logic structures can be identified as capable of communicating certain types of game activity (when their objects are appropriately skinned and arranged) and can be combined while retaining their meanings. This approach cuts across the other approach, but is sensitive to the level of complexity, as I will return to shortly.

As preparation, consider a game about "protection." Treanor's Democratic Party game sketch uses graphical logic structures to create a game on this topic—with something destructive moving toward potential victims and a player-controlled object capable of intercepting them. The objects could be skinned to suggest different readings: protection from bad policies (as in my interpretation of Treanor's sketch), protection from snowballs (a more literal option), protection from emotionally harmful internal ideas (a less literal option), and so on. The rhetorical affordances are present for any of these options.

These game ideas run from the alternative (the snowball game) to the doubled/overloaded (the harmful ideas game). Obviously, conventional games can also be made with this design—it is the original design of *Kaboom*, which sold more than a million copies by 1983,[55] making it one of the best-selling games for the Atari VCS. This is the sense in which logic structures cut across the spectrum from conventional to doubled—the same logic structure can communicate the same game activity across this spectrum. (Though for most players the meaning of protection is not present until the structure is appropriately skinned, which can be quite challenging to accomplish automatically.)

But this crosscutting is quite sensitive to the level of complexity, in two senses. One sense is the complexity of the game that uses the logic structure, while the other is the complexity with which logic structures are combined. Let's start with the complexity of the game. We could imagine skinning *Kaboom* so that a mean teenager is throwing snowballs at little kids waiting for the school bus, while a player-controlled kid tries to intercept them. But we could also use the same logic structures for much more complex games. Maybe the game could move into three dimensions. Maybe we can taunt the teenager to get her to throw snowballs at us, instead of the little kids, but then we take damage if the snowballs hit. Maybe there are snowbanks we can hide behind, when balls are aimed at us, to avoid that damage. And so on.

All of this works for the alternative approach of the snowball game. And it would all probably work if we used the same logic structure in a conventional game—for example, skinning it as a modern warfare game level with a group of civilians to protect.[56]

But as soon as we attempt to translate the same game into an expansive approach, we face all the problems of metaphorical complexity described in the previous chapter. If we're protecting ourselves from harmful internal thoughts, what does it mean to taunt the critical voice in our heads? What are the barriers that can be hidden behind when that voice targets the player character? It might be possible to find a consistent mapping, but it would be a creative leap worth admiring, rather than a straightforward (perhaps automatable) translation.

The other type of complexity is in the combination of logic structures, as discussed earlier in this chapter. In a snowball-fight game we might imagine adding in other logic structures to, for example, create a situation like *Pong*, in which the player is both trying to protect the kids on their side and hit something the teenager is trying to protect (such as her house, from which her parents will emerge to punish her after hearing a certain number of snowballs hit). Perhaps other logic structures could be added to create a safe zone to which non-player characters could be moved by the player character (perhaps the sheltered part of the bus stop, the equivalent of being behind a shield in a game like *Space Invaders*[57]).

Once again, we can imagine how all of this would work with alternative and conventional approaches to the logics and models. But once we move into expansive approaches, the complexity becomes problematic. Some of the problems are at the level of individual metaphors. Moving back into the policy domain, as in Treanor's game sketch, do the Democrats want to present themselves as also having policy ideas that could hurt someone? And what would it mean to move a member of the public beyond where Republicans can harm them—taking them to Canada? But other problems are with the complexity of the metaphorical space (as discussed with the Occupy games above). What does it mean when a donkey is moving toward the sheltered part of the game space, perhaps colliding with the shelter? If we added more logic structures, the meaning of any particular spatial movement, or position, or contact would become harder and harder to interpret in the overloading model (rather than in simply spatial terms).

This is not to say that graphical logics and spatial models cannot be used to make complex, powerful games that are about something other than physical objects moving through space. They have been and will continue to be. And I hope that the lenses of expansive approaches and logic structures will help us push further in how we make and understand such games.

But in the end, there are also severe limitations when we aim to use spatial models to communicate about things that aren't inherently spatial. If we wish to communicate about something else for which we have well-developed logics and models (such as resources), the best approach is to use them. If another set of logics and models is not available, this may inevitably send us down the path of inventive approaches. For example, in ideological or emotional domains, to make more complex games, we must do inventive work to develop ideological or emotional models if we wish to make complex games that enable play about them.

Of course, I say "inevitably" with the knowledge that it is anything but. Many game creators—wishing to create games about a topic for which there are not developed, ready-to-hand logics and models—instead place the topic within the game, but outside of play. They have characters speak fixed, cut-scene dialogue about the topic. Or they skin objects in the game with images that refer to the topic. In other words, they use the (effective) tools of other media to signal these topics, rather than using the tools of games to enable play that enacts these topics.

Considering this option, together with the others already explored in this book, is the topic of the next (and final) chapter.

Conclusion: What Games Are About

Many games are not about what they say they're about. At least, not as games.

Even as a child, you may begin to realize this. Your family might have a set of games in the cabinet that say they're about being part of a boy band, or going fishing, or acquiring high-flying Internet startups of the dot-com era. And these might all be versions of *Monopoly*.[1]

When you get one out of the cabinet and start setting it up, you see what the game says it's about. The members of One Direction are on the front of the box. Or the pieces you move include a tackle box, boat, and leaping fish. Or the names of the properties include Lycos, Ask Jeeves, and iVillage.com.

But then you start to play. And things stop making sense.

When you play the common version of *Monopoly*, the players are clearly competing property developers. They attempt to control neighborhoods, develop properties within them, and thereby drive up rents.

But who are we supposed to be when playing the One Direction edition? Some of the spaces are labeled with songs the band has recorded. Others with charity benefits they've played. Yet others with the reality show for which they separately auditioned. Are we members of the band, competing with one another? Are we agents and promoters, vying for portions of the band's money? Fans competing to control their legacy? There's no interpretation that makes the hodgepodge of labels make sense.

Playing the Bass Fishing edition might, at first, feel a little more sensible. If we imagine ourselves as anglers, we might encounter all the things on the board, which include different kinds of rods, reels, and bait, as well as competitions such as the Bass Masters Classic. But once we, for example, own all the different types of rods or contests, the game instructs us to develop them—building bait shops and marinas "on" things that clearly aren't physical locations.

Figure 11.1

In the ".com" edition of *Monopoly*, the properties are renamed after websites, the player pieces are representations of (or puns on) computing, and the currency denominations are in millions of dollars, but the gameplay is exactly like other forms of *Monopoly* sold by Hasbro in the same era. (Image courtesy of Jennifer K Mahal.)

The ".com" edition asks us to do something similarly nonsensical—I feel ridiculous putting a building down on top of Ask Jeeves, as though it were a plot of land (figure 11.1). Perhaps we could imagine this as further investment in the company, but Hasbro specifically suggests a less-sensible framing: "The game still has houses and hotels, but these now represent households and offices that are online."[2] Yes, please pay me more for a visit to my search engine, now that it has become an ISP.

Rather, the only sensible way to look at these games is that they are still the common version of *Monopoly*—still, as Hasbro puts it, the same "Property Trading Game." To think sensibly about our play, we need to imagine it in real estate terms, not those of music, or sports, or the 1990s World Wide Web.

In other words, these games—as games—aren't actually about what they say they're about.

And yet as something other than games—in every way other than in play—they are. As a sculpture, the tackle box player piece in the Bass Fishing edition of *Monopoly* is clearly about fishing. As a collage, the logo-festooned board of ".com" edition is clearly about the first Internet boom. As writing, the card text of the One Direction edition is clearly about the band.

When we look at a game, these are the aspects that are easiest to perceive—the pictures, the words, the shapes of the pieces—so we are taken in, over and over.

Skinning Games

I've talked about "skinning" games—the practice that gives us endless editions of *Monopoly*—throughout this book. But I've mostly focused on somewhat effective examples: Mary Flanagan's and Angela Ferraiolo's layoff-themed *Bejeweled*, Anna Anthropy's conversation-themed *Pong*, Mike Treanor's politically themed *Kaboom*.[3]

These work because the underlying operations are compatible with the new skin. We also see this with *Monopoly*—most clearly when it is re-skinned to represent property development in a different city. As of this writing, Wikipedia[4] lists more than forty US cities for which this has been done. It's also been done for US states and other geographic regions. I've played a couple of these, which usually retain exactly the same board layout with different property names, and I can attest that it feels just like playing the common *Monopoly*.

Yet as examples in earlier chapters have shown, skinning can also be more ambitious, while still remaining sensible. It is possible to change what a game is about through skinning—or to take a game that doesn't appear to be about anything and give it a clear, sensible theme. In chapter 3, for example, I discussed Raph Koster's thought experiment version of *Tetris*,[5] re-skinned to be about mass murder.[6]

We can remind ourselves of key points about skinning by looking at two additional examples, one from game designer Clint Hocking and one inspired by comedy group Monty Python.

Deadly *Tetris*

Koster's example demonstrates that abstract games like *Tetris*[7] can be skinned to present something specific. At another level, however, it is clear that the traditional feeling of playing *Tetris*, and traditional approach to playing it, is at odds with what is presented in Koster's reimagining.

From the point of view of Hocking, this tension is part of the point. His version of *Tetris*, presented in a talk at the 2011 Game Developers Conference,[8] takes inspiration from Brenda Romero's game *Train*.[9] It positions players as packing humans into box cars for the Nazi regime. When each line is "cleared" it represents a car that has left the station toward a death camp.

Hocking presents three ways to play the game. You can play as a dutiful servant of the Reich, which means playing *Tetris* in the normal, score-optimizing way (toward which both the game's design and its familiarity pulls). Or you could play in a role like Oskar Schindler's, optimizing the way you lose the game—carefully leaving one empty space in every row, so that the system backs up. Or you could play as a saboteur, stacking pieces as quickly as possible to reach "game over."

Hocking's point is that the latter two ways of playing would make no sense in the normal *Tetris*. By re-skinning the game, even though the underlying systems are the same, he's changed how it is meaningful to play—and made how to play into a meaningful choice. We could make a similar point with Anthropy's *Pong* skinning (discussed in chapter 9) of a conversation with her girlfriend. Choosing not to return the ball in *Pong*[10] is simply choosing to lose, whereas in Anthropy's version it is a choice to not engage what the girlfriend is saying, and avoid the inevitable weeping that will result, given Anthropy's vulnerable emotional state.

Of course, skinning doesn't have to leave every element of the original game system unchanged, as seen in *Monty Python & the Quest for the Holy Grail*.[11] In this 1996 title's "Drop Dead" minigame, we play a version of *Tetris* skinned as packing plague victims into a mass grave.[12] Most of the shapes act like normal *Tetris* pieces. But the "I" piece, in which four tiles are stacked in a line—the piece around which experienced *Tetris* players organize their play, in order to get the bonus that comes from clearing four lines simultaneously—rotates itself outside the player's control, while declaring, "I'm not dead!" This one small change makes traditional strategic *Tetris* play impossible, revealing the situation as ridiculous (and perhaps horrifying) even to players who have fallen under *Tetris*'s thrall. While *The Quest for the Holy Grail* plays its change of gameplay for laughs, Flanagan's and Ferraiolo's re-skinning of *Bejeweled* as *Layoff*[13] (discussed in chapter 3) shows how this approach can be used for critical ends.

More broadly, these examples together show that skinning doesn't have to lead to nonsense; they show how it instead can open up what a game can be about and how it is meaningful to play. Using this to grow what we can express through games, while building on player literacy developed through previous games, is a powerful aspect of expansive approaches to logics and models. The same is true when skinning and combining partial structures from games, as discussed in chapter 10.

At the same time—as I argued in chapter 3—there is a reason that *Tetris* has been re-skinned, repeatedly, as a game about mass death. There is a reason that *Layoff* is about disposing of workers, rather than creating a space for them to flourish. While we can make games appear to be about different things through re-skinning, we also cannot get away from what is fundamentally present in the logics and models. *Tetris* is a game about objects, and if we re-skin it to be about people, we will only be able to create games about situations in which people are treated like objects (see box 11.1, "People and Objects").

This is true not only because of its underlying logic but also its specific mechanics and game design, which a re-skinning leaves intact. The "filling spaces" pattern matching of Koster's or Hocking's re-skinned *Tetris* only says something about crimes against humanity on a momentary level—extended playing of the game might enable one of Hocking's strategies for losing, but the pattern matching becomes harder to perceive as what it is meant to portray (as Koster found,[14] when his thought experiment was realized). Similarly, while the "suit wearing" workers of Flanagan's and Ferraiolo's *Layoff* introduce additional commentary, fundamentally the "match three" pattern of their re-skinned *Bejeweled* has only the loosest connection to the motives or mechanisms of corporate layoffs. Such re-skinnings might actually make us more confused about their points if we try to take their gameplay seriously as saying something about their topics. Instead, their pattern matching is readable as being about something else only for a moment. As Treanor and Mateas have argued,[15] such re-skinnings function like political cartoons.

If we try to do something deeper or different through re-skinning, we will end up with the game system and its skin at odds, as happens with the nonsensical editions of *Monopoly*. And then, in order to play, players will have to increasingly "look past" the skin, so that they can effectively engage the game.[16] We won't actually have produced a game about what the skin proclaims.

Playable Models

Of course, skinning is only one way that a game can be based on another. For example—as touched on in chapter 2—the FPS game genre came to prominence with the runaway success of 1993's *DOOM*.[17] After this, its creators (id Software) had a significant business selling its underlying technology, and that of its successor titles, as an "engine" on which others could make games.

We could call these games "re-skins" of *DOOM*, but in most cases that would be misleading. Not only are the graphics changed, but also generally the geography of the levels, the behavior of enemies, the types of weapons, and so on. Rather, these games are building on *DOOM*'s implementations of a set of playable models (as defined in chapter 1

Box 11.1
People and Objects

When we move beyond thought experiments, we must be extremely careful creating games about situations in which people are treated like objects—especially games that put players in a position of power over those who are being treated this way and a position of being pulled by gameplay into seeing them in other-than-human terms. This was made particularly clear through the example of *Playing History 2: Slave Trade*,[18] which included another horrifically themed *Tetris* variation: having players enact the loading of a slave ship.[19] This proved controversial when the game was first proposed for distribution on Valve's Steam service, and the company defended the design in September 2014, saying it "really gets people to think about just how absurd and cruel it is."[20]

When the game launched on Steam in the summer of 2015, gaining greater attention, the creators got to see what a wider audience thought of that argument. For example, Dexter Thomas, writing in the *Los Angeles Times*, posed the question this way:

> Would a young player be able to grasp the inhumanity of the slave trade, all while being rewarded for stacking brick slaves efficiently or expertly navigating a slave ship?
>
> Allie Jane Bruce, a children's librarian at the Bank Street College of Education in New York, doesn't think so. I called her to ask if she would recommend a mini-game like "Slave *Tetris*" to teach kids, and before I could finish the question she interrupted me: "Slavery should not be fun."[21]

The overwhelmingly negative response led to the removal of that particular portion of the game—though as Thomas and others point out, it is not the only problematic element.

One could pose the question of why the *Tetris* piece microgames in *Dys4ia* are not also "treating people like objects." The difference is in the skinning. The *Tetris* pieces in *Dys4ia* remain skinned as abstract pieces, inviting us to see the gameplay metaphorically—for example, to see a metaphorical relationship between a *Tetris* piece trying to fit through an impossible spot and Anthropy's "feeling weird" about her body. If the *Tetris* piece were, instead, skinned with a contorted picture of Anthropy's body, it would raise the question of whether we are meant to literally interpret the game as moving Anthropy's body through some barrier, as *Playing History* literally asks us to stack the bodies of enslaved people. In other words, one operates expansively, while the other operates in an alternative mode. Further, *Dys4ia* removes the elements of gameplay that do not fit with its expansive approach—we are not trying to fit together bodies, and we are not trying to make rows of body parts disappear. While we are invited to contemplate the "fit" of a piece within/through a space, we are not treating it as one of a set of interchangeable objects in a spatial puzzle.

and most discussed in chapters 4, 6, and 7). In particular, they build on *DOOM's* models of spatial movement and combat, which are designed to complement each other.

From descriptions, you might think these games are quite different from each other. *Heretic*[22] is described as a dark fantasy game about the struggle between the magic-wielding Serpent Riders and the Sidhe elves. *Strife*[23] is described as a science fiction game about a ragtag resistance movement fighting The Order, a totalitarian regime that took power after a catastrophic comet impact. *Chex Quest*,[24] a game distributed in boxes of cereal, is described as presenting the Chex Warrior's heroic rescue of Chex people from the Flemoids, evil slime creatures.

But what makes these games work is that they are all about moving through constrained spaces and shooting at enemies. Whether one plays an elf, a resistance fighter on a distant planet, or a human encased in cereal armor, the skin/theme is carefully chosen to work with *DOOM's* particular implementations of its playable models. In short, while it might seem that a well-developed set of playable models are an invitation to make a game about anything, in fact they are an invitation only to make things that fit in with the gameplay those models enable. Building on the combination of models popularized by *DOOM* isn't a route to an effective game about romance, philosophy, prejudice, or most other things we might care about. In Treanor's terms (discussed in chapter 10) *DOOM's* combination of spatial and combat models lacks the "rhetorical affordances" for making games on such topics.

Which isn't to say people won't try, or at least say they're trying. Perhaps the most successful example of this being the work of game designer Ken Levine, his colleagues at studio Irrational Games, and the publicists who have promoted their work for publisher 2K Games.

Philosophical Shooters

Levine came to prominence as the creative lead for *BioShock*,[25] a game widely discussed as a critique of Ayn Rand-style Objectivist philosophy. *BioShock* builds on an approach to telling stories through spatial models often called *environmental storytelling*.[26] As players move through the game, they are exploring an underwater city, Rapture, designed as an Objectivist utopia. They can see—through structural collapses, broken-down equipment, graffiti, discarded protest signs, and more—that the experiment failed. As they move through the space, they can discover and listen to audio diaries that tell more of the story of the city and its inhabitants. In short, the spatial model of the FPS was successfully repurposed to reveal a story, through exploration, that portrays the failure of a set of economic/philosophical ideas (ones which are quite influential in US politics). As portrayed by the game's publicists, this was catnip for journalists and reviewers, especially those who had been waiting for games to "grow up" as a medium.[27]

But as anyone who has played the game knows, you don't spend much of your time thinking about Objectivism. *BioShock* is not a game about philosophical debate. It's a shooter—with the twist being that you can turn your player character into a weapon (through genetic modification) rather than only using regular weapons. It is the combat model that dominates gameplay. The spatial model serves primarily as its support, and only in the breaks between battles does the environmental storytelling have any prominence. But from most cultural comment on the game, you wouldn't know this.[28]

Leading up to the release of Levine's successor title, *BioShock Infinite*,[29] it seemed likely to get away with the same trick. The pre-release reviews were again stellar, and it was described as again dealing with difficult issues at the heart of the United States (this time, in particular, racism and xenophobia) as players navigate the game's airborne city of Columbia. But after release, when people really started to play it, the reception got a lot rockier. As Joe Bernstein summarized for *BuzzFeed News*: "While much of the enthusiast community has received the game as an unqualified triumph, the more thoughtful people who work in gaming have argued over every inch of it. People have pointed out problems with its politics, its violence, its racial politics, its plot, its gaminess, its metaphysics, the way it made them feel."[30]

While one might argue that problems with *BioShock Infinite* stem from issues such as being philosophically muddied, or placing less emphasis on the environmental storytelling that was key to the prior title's success, or many other things, I believe the core problem was its gameplay. Not that the gameplay was bad, but that FPS gameplay is as poor a fit for a theme of racism and xenophobia as *Monopoly* gameplay is for the theme of being a boy band.[31] Journalist, critic, and game developer Leigh Alexander experienced this, even though she had been particularly excited for the game after an interview with key studio staff at Irrational[32] (Levine, director of product development Tim Gerritsen, lead artist Shawn Robertson, and art director Nate Wells). Alexander describes her thoughts about the game this way:

> When does a supposed essay on the purposelessness of conflict simply become purposeless? Racism, corpses, endless slaughter—all the things that are supposed to remind me of how horrible Columbia is only make me think of how horrible games are. There are more dead bodies in this world than live people, and ever moreso as the game progresses.[33]

Or as Bernstein, who liked the game much better, puts it, "the rules of the genre are at odds with the very magnificence of Irrational's game . . . the very last thing I wanted to do as I played this game was to sprint around finding cover and chaining headshots."[34] This is not to say that games cannot be made about ideas. Rather, the ideas must be consonant with the playable models that enable the core gameplay. And the fact is that the combat model that dominates FPS gameplay is not compatible with a story about interacting with anything human, unless our role is to play a soldier, assassin, or psychopath.

This is why environmental storytelling often works better without the FPS combat model added to the spatial model, without "finding cover and chaining headshots." Art and indie game studios such as Tale of Tales, The Chinese Room, and Galactic Cafe have explored this in the genre sometimes called the "walking simulator." I discussed *Gone Home*,[35] an example of this genre from studio Fullbright, in chapter 2.

But there is also an issue with this approach. When traveling through a walking simulator, if the goal is to tell a story of a traditional shape, the space must be contorted to fit—as seen in the strange, circuitous route through the house of *Gone Home* and the spaces that wink in and out of existence in *The Beginner's Guide*.[36] If we actually want players to be able to use the spatial model for more open exploration, environmental storytelling is probably better suited to the kinds of experimental story shapes pioneered by the literary hypertext community, as seen in the town geography of *Marble Springs*[37] or the spaces of the body in *Patchwork Girl*.[38]

All that said—though FPS games are ill suited to human interaction, and walking simulators have more often focused on storytelling than philosophy—it is not impossible to make a successful game focused on philosophical issues. In fact, the common version of *Monopoly* is a rip-off of just such a game.

Playing Monopolist

What happens when you play *Monopoly*? You move your piece around the periphery of the board, using a simple model of space (a track) that you move down a randomly determined number of spaces (by rolling a die). In the early game the randomness feels harmless, and you have various decisions to make: Do you buy the properties on which you land? Do you bid on the properties other players don't buy (if your group follows the auction rule)? How much money do you save for future rounds, when players who land on owned properties will have to pay rent?

All of these, of course, are decisions about how much of one resource to convert (or plan to convert) into another. And it is these resources that are at the heart of all versions of *Monopoly*. That is the nature of its playable model.

This becomes more apparent in the middle game, as players begin to invest resources in developing their properties, so that landing on them becomes a much bigger resource drain. But to do this development, players have to own all the properties of a particular set (usually represented by color). This is the last of the main elements of

Monopoly's playable representation of real estate investment: a pattern-matching logic. Throughout the middle game, players negotiate over properties, trying to balance using resources to acquire complete sets (which are opportunities for development), using resources to develop these sets, and hoarding resources for potential rent payments to other players. The randomness, which previously felt harmless, now seems more consequential: whether you land on another player's property, or they land on yours, will now make or break your plans.

As the game enters its end phase, the resource model reveals the positive feedback that lies within it (see box 6.1, "Machinations and *Monopoly*"). One player lands on another player's highly developed property. The result is that they must mortgage some of their properties, or trade them away, reducing their opportunities to collect rent. Randomness becomes all—the positive feedback makes it likely that a player in the lead will win, but it plays out slowly and unpredictably as the rolls of the die determine who loses resources and who collects them.

And this is the point. *Monopoly* is based on *The Landlord's Game*,[39] which was created at the turn of the twentieth century as "a practical demonstration of the present system of land-grabbing with all its usual outcomes and consequences,"[40] as characterized by its designer, Elizabeth Magie. The best-known version of Magie's story is told by Mary Pilon in her book, *The Monopolists*. Pilon traces Magie's outlook back to the economic philosophy of Henry George, who argued that people should own the products of their labor, but everything natural—including land—should belong to everyone equally. According to Pilon, Magie taught classes about this philosophy after work and saw in games "a new medium—something more interactive and creative" for expressing these ideas.[41] In order to dramatize the difference between a Georgist approach and the current one, as Pilon reports:

> [Magie] created two sets of rules for her game: an anti-monopolist set in which all were rewarded when wealth was created, and a monopolist set in which the goal was to create monopolies and crush opponents. Her dualistic approach was a teaching tool meant to demonstrate that the first set of rules was morally superior.[42]

In its systems, the common version of *Monopoly* is based on the second of these rule sets. To put it another way, *Monopoly* is a rip-off of a game that was designed to ask a question: Do we really want a handful of wealthy people, chosen by chance, to drive the rest of us into desperation?

It is these systems, and their question, that shine through—which is why so many *Monopoly* games are never completed. It stops being fun when the realities of its resources and randomness confront us, when we experience its economic philosophy. And it doesn't matter what the supposed version is "about." It might be funny if someone is bankrupted by landing on a property bearing the logo of the long-dead AltaVista, but no one around the table thinks this makes it a fundamentally different game from the version with fish.

Instead, everyone around the table is learning (perhaps unconsciously) that one of the things it is possible to make a game about is *resources*. If they're feeling particularly thoughtful, or if they know the game's history, they may realize that it is possible to make a game about unfair resource systems, perhaps one that reflects those in our own society. Perhaps they may relate it to video games that do this, such as *Cart Life*,[43] a game about the precarious position of street vendors. Or perhaps they may relate it to the many, many games—both physical and digital—that present the avaricious accumulation of resources as the ultimate good (see box 11.2, "Historical Resources").

Human Resources

Just as with the playable models of space and combat that are at the heart of the FPS genre, there is a temptation to believe that the resource models that underlie games like *Monopoly* and *Cart Life* could be used to make a simulation of anything. For example, if we look at *The Sims*,[44] which launched one of the most successful game franchises of all time, we appear to see a game about middle-class, suburban life in the United States. Sometimes it has an obvious focus on resources, as when building, remodeling, and outfitting the homes that are key to maintaining the happiness for each group of Sims. Yet at other times it does not. In more recent entries in the series, Sim families grow up together, with children passing into adulthood and perhaps forming families of their own, while older family members enter old age and then pass away.

Thus, one could argue that *The Sims* titles are one of the few places that video games have taken on the deeply human topic of the passage of time. But at their cores, as discussed in chapter 6, the characters are collections of resource meters. A child Sim might feel sad after grandma has passed away, but neither the character nor the game knows or can say anything about that history.[45] Instead the child just goes to find something in the house to counteract the drag on her mood—perhaps watching TV. And she's not suppressing feelings she's going to have to deal with later. She's fully meeting what the game systems represent as her need to feel happier.

In short, *The Sims* games might be read as about the passage of time. But if we read them that way, they tend to say pretty awful things. They're probably better read as what they are—games about building dollhouses, using human-looking tokens to score our current creations and collect upgrade resources for the future. Which is why we don't feel too bad when we set the tokens on fire, or trap them in the pool, or do other

Box 11.2

Historical Resources

This book puts its focus on games in which spatial models are key. For this reason, games in which other models are primary have received less attention. But examining them through a logics and models lens is at least as important and revealing.

For example, it has become a relatively commonplace observation that resource-oriented games with historical themes, like *Civilization*,[46] are focused on what Alfie Bown calls "western capitalist empire-building."[47] While this is a broad statement, we can dig into these ideas specifically by using the tools of logics and models. We can see how the non-human objects and spaces that exist in these games are framed in terms of the resource model—they are there to be controlled, harvested/mined, built upon, or otherwise exploited. Meanwhile, the most developed model for dealing with the people in such games tends to be the combat model—people, especially the people of other civilizations, are there to be killed. In other words, what the game models, what it is possible to express through play, is in fact the avaricious and deadly drives of empire. It seems the "natural" way for a civilization to develop. Further, Paolo Pedercini points out that a similar approach characterizes the broader category of which these games are a part:

> In strategy and management games, the simulated world is presented as a collection of resources to extract. The landscape is often subdivided into spatial units by grids or cells, and the actors inhabiting it are defined by the function they perform. Historical games like *Civilization* even project this modern vision toward the past, portraying ancient societies functioning like imperialistic nation-states devoid of any tradition or system of values other than the drive toward expansion.[48]

This is not necessary for making a game about history or even about the development of nations, as Christopher Franklin argues in a video essay on *Civilization* for Errant Signal. Rather, it is a result of constructing the game from the perspective of "the civilization." As Franklin puts it, "In *Civilization* you don't play as Gandhi or George Washington or Catherine the Great. You're playing as the state—an ageless construct interested only in its own growth, power, and self-preservation that's as divorced from the people that make it up as you are from the cells that make you up."[49] There are other options, as Franklin demonstrates with a comparison to the *Crusader Kings* games. In these, we play from the perspective of individuals, and in *Crusader Kings II*[50] the social model for interacting with non-player characters is among the most developed in a mainstream commercial game. Even if our gameplay choices might still be focused on the perspective of an aristocratic family, it is a very different way of presenting acts of conquest—as growing out of human desires and relationships, rather than as the inevitable destiny of a state that has decided, before "it" even founds its first city, that it exists and must "explore, expand, exploit, and exterminate" (the words that form the basis of the "4X" nickname often given to this genre).[51]

Box 11.2 (continued)

To be clear, the issue here is not skinning. Both *Civilization IV*[52] and *Crusader Kings II*, for example, begin with the player selecting a leader from the past to play. But then, in *Civilization*, the "leader" has no actions to take, at the level of being a human being. Whereas in *Crusader Kings* the leader's early moves may involve actions such as arranging their own marriage or recruiting vassals. These parts of the game are presented as specific to the leader and taking place in a social environment. Arranging a marriage is influenced by how the potential spouse and her family feel about the player character, with players attending to how her personality traits will complement those of the leader, while the nature of the match itself will impact everything from external prestige to the likelihood of having children. Recruiting vassals is necessary because the leader can only directly control a small number of significant holdings, so other holdings must be indirectly controlled by vassals, with the nature of relationships with vassals shifting over time—both interpersonally and because there is always the danger of vassals shifting position in the larger social hierarchy (for example, by inheriting a title that supersedes the one granted by the leader). That is to say, Franklin is correct that the *Crusader Kings* games have a different perspective than the *Civilization* games—but what makes that perspective real for players is the addition of the social model, not the skinning of the genre's common resource, spatial, and combat models.

Primarily spatial models, on the other hand, can take a different approach to placing players within the perspectives of people from the past. For example, *Walden: A Game*,[53] created by Tracy Fullerton et al., puts players in the first-person perspective of Henry David Thoreau within a reconstruction of Walden Pond at his time. Walking through the space allows players to appreciate the natural beauty and changing seasons, as well as get a sense of the scale of the pond and its spatial relationship with the town and Thoreau's home. The world's beauty literally fades if it is not given enough attention by the player, the view becoming grayer and narrower. There are more traditional resource systems at work as well, from food growing and gathering to shelter construction—but these are also enacted through the spatial model, with the player seeing Thoreau's hands and arms carrying out berry picking and nail pounding, reinforcing that the world is being seen from his perspective. This is effective because there are aesthetic, logistic, and philosophical aspects of his relationship to space to which *Walden: A Game* seeks to draw our attention. Similarly, *Cassius*,[54] an in-process game by James Coltrain, seeks to communicate the scale of American slavery as an institution by putting players in the perspective of an escaped slave, moving through a Virginia plantation on which hundreds of Black people are enslaved by a single White family. The spatial model is used to try to make this scale visceral.

things it would be monstrous to do to actual humans, or even well-drawn fictional characters.

This is not to say that we can't imagine a version of *The Sims* that actually captured the bittersweet experience of the passage of time in an extended network of family and friends. But this would need to be a game in which the foundations of the playable model were made up of things like histories and emotions, rather than resources. Similarly, if we were to imagine a game about philosophical issues that are less economically focused than those in *The Landlord's Game*, its playable model would need a foundation other than resources. Which brings us to the question of whether it is possible to make such games, and why.

Operational Logics

As this book has described, the foundation of any playable model is a set of operational logics (as defined in chapter 1 and cataloged in chapter 4). For example, the primary foundation of *Monopoly*'s real estate investment model is its resource logics, though a pattern-matching logic determines which properties can be further developed, and a chance logic triggers resource flows. Similarly, the spatial models of shooters and walking simulators have logics such as control/navigation, movement physics, and collision as a foundation.

An important aspect of these logics—and one of the key points of this book—is that they cut across a divide in how we often talk about games. Many discussions of games, including the earlier sections of this chapter, make a division between what a game purports to communicate (its skin or theme or fiction) and how it operates and enables play (its rules or mechanics or models). But the foundational logics of games are both at the same time. We can only understand a logic such as "collision" by seeing it as something that communicates ("virtual objects can touch") and something that operates algorithmically ("when two entities overlap, do something").

From one perspective, operational logics are a site of remarkable flexibility and creativity. On a technical level, a logic such as collision can be implemented in many ways—from the 2-D hardware implementation of the Atari VCS to the 3-D quadtrees or raycasting that might be found in current software. And on a communicative level, collision might be used to represent a wall we can't pass through, a bullet hitting a body, or something more unexpected. Game designers have found a remarkable range of things to communicate with this logic, from Pac-Man's eating to the availability of life choices in Jason Rohrer's *Passage*.[55] This is the power of the expansive approach—from refinement through doubling—as discussed in chapters 3, 8, and 9.

But from another perspective, the very fact that logics communicate something in particular (for example, the virtual touch of collision detection) means that they can't arbitrarily communicate *anything*. At the furthest, they can communicate things we understand metaphorically, such as the "deflection" of a statement.

And while some would argue that, therefore, metaphor is the key to making games on a wide array of topics, the metaphorical approach actually has severe limitations, as I discuss in chapter 9. This is because of the nature of metaphor, as explored in Conceptual Metaphor Theory (CMT). My example, from that chapter, is the metaphor, "An idea is a building." For this metaphor, it makes sense to ask questions such as, "What is the foundation of this idea?" But it doesn't make sense to ask, "What is the HVAC system of this idea?" This is because the metaphorical mapping is to an idea of a building that is highly abstract and schematic,[56] without specifics such as HVAC systems.

On the other hand, when we are building a game, the metaphorical mapping is made to every specific element of the game. Getting all these specifics to work appropriately for the metaphor is very challenging, and can prove impossible, as recounted in the development stories in Doris C. Rusch's *Making Deep Games*.[57] This is what makes games that manage a complete metaphorical mapping, such as Rohrer's *Passage*—with each collision with a wall, chest, or person readable both as spatial movement and as a larger life event—so widely discussed. And this is why all such games tend to be quite short, whether they are Anthropy's *Dys4ia* microgames or *Passage* with its five-minute play time. As discussed in chapter 9, rather than looking for a way to expand the scope of such experiences, we might be better off considering these games in terms of another generally short, often-metaphoric form: the lyric poem.

Flexible Links

Looking at the landscape of games, one might find hope in a different direction: linking logics, which create networks of connections between game spaces, texts, and other objects. We see such logics in a wide variety of places: cave entrances in *The Legend of Zelda*,[58] dialogue trees in *The Elder Scrolls V: Skyrim*,[59] textual links in Twine titles such as *Howling Dogs*,[60] and so on. Because the communicative role of linking logics is so abstract—perhaps, "this is connected to that"—we can imagine using them for a game about nearly anything.

And, in fact, the literary hypertext community I mentioned earlier has shown how links can be used to tell stories about a vast number of things. But this is not the same as enabling play about these things. Rather, in most hypertext fiction the audience does not think of itself as taking action within the fictional world. Instead they are developing an understanding of the fiction (just as with a novel or film) with links allowing and shaping their explorations.[61] In addition, some hypertext works attempt an interesting hybrid—primarily telling a story, but using hand-created links (rather than a game system) to offer players key choices about what happens.

Going further, there are also more systematic elements of games implemented as links. A common example is movement—from the textual interactive fiction tradition founded by *Adventure*'s[62] cave system to the evocative island of *Myst*[63] or the world-spanning map of *80 Days*.[64] For this to be successful requires a very consistent use of links, both in how they are presented to players and in how they operate. A common beginner mistake is to implement link-based doors that, unintentionally, don't operate in both directions.

Of course, there are also other ways to implement movement in games. The problem comes when we try to use links to move beyond movement and beyond other experiences that other logics offer—such as toward broader ability to choose and take actions in the fictional world, of the sort we might imagine when truly playing a character, over a long period of gameplay. For example, many computer role-playing games offer the ability to pursue romantic relationships with non-player characters. We might imagine romance developing in many ways, over a significant period of time, ranging from a history of meaningful, shared experiences to momentary interactions of carefully chosen words, playful touches, and/or significant looks. But these games instead tend to include a constrained set of pre-authored "romance options" in their link-based dialogue trees, gated by simple progression logics. As one of the respondents in Heidi McDonald's survey of romance in games puts it, a satisfying romance is "not simply 'Here is five chocolates, Marry me?'"[65] And even providing relatively paltry options such as these is time-consuming for RPG creators to hand-author, so there tend to be only a small number of predetermined paths available.

A limited, predetermined path works better in a game like *Howling Dogs*, in which the player character is presented as imprisoned and transported into VR fantasies, with a route to potential agency that is barely hinted. Limited paths also work in situations like the vignettes of *80 Days*, in which we play a character constrained by servitude, etiquette, outsider status, and lack of knowledge of the surroundings (as I discuss further in the section of this chapter on alternatives to traditional agency) and the consequences for each choice are largely limited to the current vignette (beyond impacts on resource logics).[66] Such games offer opportunities for reflection and critical thinking, much like the literary hypertexts that preceded them. But they don't offer much of the opportunity to experiment and understand the world through actions that change it— through play—that is key to games from *DOOM* to *Layoff*.

Agency

This line of thinking about logics and models might be seen as another route to a core question about video games, one that has been asked repeatedly since they began to have significant cultural and economic impact: What does it mean for players to have agency within a game? Perhaps it seems that the idea of a game being "about something through play" is simply a long-winded synonym for agency. I think there is an important difference, but to explain it will require a closer consideration of the concept of agency.

A Chess player looks at (or imagines) the board, seeing possibilities for action and response deeply shaped by their experience of the game. A player of *The Sims* develops a feel for what actions might be possible, and desirable, in short moments before a Sim rushes off to work—and in their simulated week or month. A player of *Counter-Strike*[67] understands its spaces, how to move through them, how they create choke points, and how weapons behave differently when moving, or still, or crouched.

The actions these players perform are very different: capturing a piece, getting the dishes done, shooting an opposing soldier. Their goals are very different: trapping their opponent's King, creating a happy suburban life, performing an act of terrorism. Yet each of them understands the world of their game in such a way that their actions seem to fit, and feel engaging, and they can see a way to use them to pursue their goals.

And the players are correct. These actions can be used to change the world of the game. They do open a path to pursuing their goals. In fact, they open many paths, which they and other players can discover and refine and share. This experience is called *agency*.

A series of authors—including Brenda Laurel, Janet Murray, Doug Church, and Michael Mateas—have proposed and refined the core ideas for understanding agency.[68] These core ideas include:

- Agency is not just the ability to act in the game. Players of *Candy Land*[69] have no agency, because all decisions lie with the chance logic that determines the color to which their characters next move. Players enjoy enacting their moves, but the pleasure comes from sources other than agency.

- Agency is not simply the ability to choose things to do that end up having an impact on the game world. Players experience agency when they take action based on their understanding of the game world—and see a response to that action that is appropriate and can serve to further build their understanding of the game world.[70] Both the choice and the understanding, of course, can be embodied and unconscious by the player as much (or more) than consciously considered.

- Agency is not the ability to take arbitrary actions in the game world. Players of *The Sims* do not experience a lack of agency because Sims cannot gun down housemates, just as players of *Counter-Strike* do not lack agency because their characters cannot urinate. Rather, agency requires that the actions suggested by the world of the game are in balance with the actions available for players to take.

These are powerful design insights. But they bring along with them a hidden requirement: *something* must enable the game to respond to player actions appropriately, in a way that can continue to build player understanding of the game world.

For a player of *The Sims* making breakfast, it's a resource model. For a *Counter-Strike* player running down a hallway, it's a spatial model. For a player of Chess moving a piece, it's a different kind of spatial model (operating in discrete space and time) which may be executing as software or implemented with physical game pieces and human intelligence.

The experience of agency is only possible in games that can provide this kind of response. We might make a game that strongly suggests taking the kinds of actions that we see in romantic comedies. We might give the player the ability to take these actions—to choose clever words for their character, to make bad choices and then try to redeem themselves, to take the hands of other characters and look into their eyes. But if the game's other characters respond inappropriately, or with incomprehension, or not at all, we certainly don't have a game about romance (though we may have unintentional comedy).

One way to address this would be to make our romantic comedy a multi-player game, depending on other humans for romantic response, much as Chess can depend on humans for strategic response. In other words, we could make games that are primarily conduits for human communication and creativity, such as tabletop and live action RPGs. And it is true that these can offer powerful experiences about topics ranging from our understanding of history (*Microscope*[71]) to the workings of colonialism (*Dog Eat Dog*[72]).

It is only when we want a game that can be experienced by a single person (like most forms of media) or enjoyed without requiring extraordinary creativity on the part of players (like nearly all games that aren't RPGs) that this solution won't work. Which is, of course, most of the time.

And this, I believe, is the core reason for the conservatism of the mainstream game industry. While cultural issues are also a factor, the sad fact is that we can only provide the kinds of responses that agency requires in situations for which we have appropriate logics and models. We have those for creating playable representations of space, resource flows, combat, pattern matching, and a limited number of other areas (many discussed in this book). Trying to make a game outside of these areas (unless it is a relatively freeform multi-player game) has no clear path to providing player agency, which is a key element of what makes many games engaging and enjoyable.

Alternatives to Traditional Agency

This is not to say that agency is the only thing that makes games engaging or meaningful.

I've played *Candy Land* with my kids, and they're very engaged—and I'm engaged through their engagement. The *Candy Land* gameplay doesn't have any relationship to the theme of candy, but moving down a track (a simple, discrete spatial model) is not incompatible with the skin of moving through a fantasy kingdom. And the focus on the chance logic, with its results including occasional large jumps, so that different players' characters move dramatically in and out of the lead, reveals the primary source of engagement: *Candy Land* is a child's introduction to the pleasures of gambling.

Perhaps even further from an experience of agency, there are games we find pleasurable that not only dictate the actions players should take but do this based on a predetermined set of challenges (there's not even chance involved). Rhythm games are like this, including titles such as *Guitar Hero*,[73] *Rock Band*,[74] and *Dance Central*.[75] While players have no agency in the core gameplay, simply performing the challenges the games present can be quite engaging. And what's more, the games actually manage to be about topics like music and dance performance. This is because beginning performance in these fields can be understood as temporal pattern matching, which is the logic on which they are founded.

There are also games that are about a lack of agency, or possessing agency only in the wrong domain. For example, Dietrich Squinkifer's *Interruption Junction*[76] is a one-button conversation game. A single button is paltry means for engaging one of the most complex human activities, but that's the point. Three non-player characters engage in an endless conversation, generated using the recombinatory logic (grammars) at the heart of the Tracery[77] system, with shared variables between them making it appear that they are gossiping about the same people and events. If the player presses her button, the player character interrupts. For a single press, there will be a brief, substance-less interjection ("Wait . . ."). For multiple presses, there will begin a brief moment of engaging in the same social gossip, followed by a generated monologue (which is sustained, for as long as presses continue) about video games. When a monologue finishes, one of the NPCs offers a moment of acknowledgement ("You're really into that stuff . . .") before continuing the gossip conversation among the NPCs. If the player goes too long without pressing their button, the player character fades away and the game ends. If

Figure 11.2

In *Interruption Junction*, players can make their character speak, but have no control over what the character says. The other characters never offer any meaningful response to what the player character says, and vice versa. Extended talking will result in a generated monologue, while the other characters fade away. (Image taken by the author during play.)

the player character presses their button too much, the NPCs fade away and the game ends (figure 11.2).

As Squinkifer puts it:

> By not allowing a chance for the player character to meaningfully connect to the NPCs, I attempt to convey a sense that this is not a game one ought to attempt to master or win. Indeed, either outcome that ends the conversation is preferable to continuing an empty dialogue indefinitely.[78]

Brenda Romero's *Train* (noted earlier as the inspiration for Hocking's proposed *Tetris* skin) at first appears quite different in its approach to agency. It presents three *Candy Land*-like track games next to each other, created with toy boxcars and train tracks. The chance logic not only gives players cards they can use to move down the track but also ones that can be used for sabotage. Players may feel some agency as they try to move their car down the track and as they use cards to sabotage the other players, until the first player reaches the goal at the end of their track. At this point, the goal is revealed to be a Nazi death camp. The remaining players are then faced with the question of what to do. Some feel their only possible agency is to walk away from the game. Others continue to draw cards, working within the given logics, perhaps using cards to sabotage their own progress. Some expand beyond the given logics and unspoken rules, in the manner of an open-ended RPG—perhaps removing the human figures from broken-down train cars and telling other players they have escaped.

Both Squinkifer's and Romero's games succeed at being about their topics—uncomfortable conversation and confronting complicity—without having a logic or model that enables play in its terms. But they succeed by being about the inability to act in ways that would be desirable. They are about players coming to understand situations in which agency is impossible, or nearly so, much like the limited agency portrayed in the linking-logic games mentioned above.[79]

An alternative to this is to create games that attempt to fool players into thinking they have agency of a certain sort, while using logics and models that can't support it. A prominent set of examples for this are the products of former studio Telltale Games, such as episodic games *The Walking Dead*[80] and *The Wolf Among Us*.[81] These games begin with statements such as, "This game series adapts to the choices you make. The story is tailored by how you play." These statements create a strong extra-diegetic (outside the story) expectation that players will be able to alter the games' stories. Similarly, players control characters who should be able to take actions that significantly alter their fictional worlds, such as a member of a small group of survivors or a detective investigating a mystery. Player characters are constantly faced with consequential-seeming choices and given both diegetic (within the story) acknowledgement of their choices and extra-diegetic cues that they matter (most famously, the game system saying explicitly that NPCs "will remember" particular decisions). Yet the fact is that, in these games, player influence is mostly limited to momentary character reactions—the overall shape of the story and character journeys is fixed. This combination of an interface that emphasizes the importance of choice and a fundamentally linear underlying structure "violates the player's expectation and understanding of the design"[82]—as pointed out by Elin Carstensdottir, Erica Kleinman, and Magy Seif El-Nasr. For many players, this created a failure of agency. The realities of the system didn't match the dramatic probabilities suggested by the games, both within the game world and through the interface.

On the other hand, for some players the games proved quite satisfying. These players didn't focus on the story-changing potential that was promised, but rather on the ability to choose how characters would respond to a relatively fixed set of situations—primarily on the level of emotions and values—and the opportunity to see responses to those choices presented through high quality writing and cinematic animation. This affective engagement has been referred to as "emotional agency" (by Liting Kway and Alex Mitchell) and "the Telltale effect" (by John Thomas Murray) and more generally resembles the concept of "bounded agency" (from Theresa Jean Tanenbaum).[83] It is an experience that proved quite expensive to produce (with high production costs relative to sales, eventually leading to the studio's closure in 2018) while still not delivering agency at a story level.[84]

Another option is to make different promises. As noted above, the game *80 Days* offers players a dramatic situation in which they are meant to be planning and executing a trip around the world—and offers the player character a wide range of choices in how to spend resources on objects, accommodations, and travel (following links) to undertake journeys of many shapes. This aspect of the game produces a traditional experience of agency. At the same time, a choice-based story is also a key element of *80 Days*, but here the promises of the dramatic situation are not like those of *The Walking Dead* or *The Wolf Among Us*. Rather, most choices in *80 Days* are presented as relevant only to a bounded geographic setting in which the characters will spend a limited time.[85] Further, the dramatic situation of *80 Days* is deliberately anti-colonial, with the player character occupying a number of colonizer categories. Specifically, the story of *80 Days* is a retelling of Jules Verne's novel *Around the World in Eighty Days*,[86] set in a steampunk 1872, with valet Jean Passepartout (the male, White, French player character) attempting to succeed at a bet made by his (male, White, English) employer, Phileas Fogg, that they can accomplish the task named in the novel's title. As Meg Jayanth, lead writer for the game, puts it:

> Whiteness and masculinity make you an outsider in *80 Days* more often than [they allow] you within the circle. We remind players of Passepartout's social and cultural limitations. NPCs will often discuss their plans, goals, and ideas with Passepartout—but we very rarely allow Passepartout to make a choice for them. He gets involved in the revolutions, riots, plots, and adventures of the people he encounters but he does not drive them—yes, he can meet a beautiful revolutionary and shout alongside him in protest against a despot—but he can't lead the revolution. It was already happening without him—he wasn't the one oppressed, so he can't do the liberating—and often, the issues our NPCs struggle with are political and systemic—beyond the ability of one person to solve.[87]

Jayanth and her collaborators at Inkle managed to use linking and resource logics to create a story model in which the players are able to carry out the actions that are dramatically probable for Passepartout. But these simply aren't the actions to which most game players are accustomed. They aren't save-the-day actions. They aren't change-the-world actions. Yet they are actions that matter to Passepartout; they are actions that allow his character to be played—and for players who can see it, that's what the game promises. To put it another way, players who understand this dramatic situation should experience agency, of a very constrained form, because they are able to take the constrained actions the situation suggests and see responses that help them build their understanding of the situation. Personally, I greatly enjoyed playing the story of *80 Days*. (As Jayanth points out, the stories we enjoy most don't tend to be about characters who get everything they want, all the time.) I was engaged in learning about the world and learning about my own character's limitations—and as I learned them I turned to choosing the story options that fit my character's relationship with the world's people, focusing more on understanding than attempting to "solve" situations. I felt the story experiences paired well with the logistic problems for Passepartout and Fogg, emerging from the game's travel aspect (which I was pretty sure I could solve).

What makes the story situation of *80 Days* hard for some players to grasp and appreciate is not just our wider colonialist culture. It is also, in many cases, years of experience of games. Games have trained players to expect much less constrained agency. Players expect a dramatic situation in which their probable actions are the ones that allow every contest to be won, every puzzle to be solved. As Jayanth argues:

> It feels unfair to the player, to be shown a problem and not allowed to fix it. But it is important—we couldn't have done it any other way without completely undermining the story that we wanted to tell. We had to deny the player their fairness fantasy, their white saviour fantasy.

Jayanth argues that it is not only necessary to constrain player agency in order to tell the specific story of *80 Days*, but also that, more generally, we need to take power from player characters in order to allow non-player characters "power and space and depth and importance." On one level this is obviously true, as too many games are what might be called "entitlement simulators"[88]—giving players and their characters whatever they want, if only they can figure out how to get it.

But on another level, we can also imagine stories about peers. About the potential for solidarity, or value-based conflict, or romantic relationships between equals. At a story level we don't always need to make the player character a servant and outsider, like Passepartout, or someone similarly highly constrained, just so the non-player characters can take independent action. Both player and non-player characters could have opportunities for action, and constraints on their actions, and could choose what to do based on how the actions of other characters have changed the world. The problem is, of course, that supporting this kind of experience using a playable model of story based on linking and resource logics (as seen in *80 Days* and many story-based video games) would be exceedingly difficult. So, at this technological and design moment in the game industry, it likely is the case that agency in game stories will be highly constrained for either player or non-player characters.

Looking at this group of games—that are engaging and sometimes meaningful play experiences, while eschewing agency—four observations present themselves. First, even if agency is not a goal, these games still require appropriate logics and models to support their designs. Because of this, deeper understanding of logics and models can help us better analyze and create these games, as well as those that aim to provide agency.

Second, we can see clearly that games can be compellingly about something, through play, without providing agency. This is because they can be about situations in which we don't have agency. When learning a musical instrument, it can be a struggle just to play the right notes at the right time. Games like *Rock Band* simplify this and present it in the context of songs that audiences want to play, creating an engaging experience somewhere between actual musicianship and air guitar. Games can also present less comfortable situations in which agency is lacking, or severely constrained, such as *Interruption Junction*, *Train*, or the border agent game *Papers, Please*[89] (discussed in chapter 3). In these situations, logics and models are still required to support the activities that do exist (recombinant text in *Interruption Junction*, pattern matching in *Papers, Please*) unless they are supported through human communication and creativity (certain approaches to playing the end of *Train*). Games can also offer us traditional agency in one area of gameplay, while denying or severely restricting it in another—each area with its own playable model (*80 Days*).

We can also imagine other situations in which agency would be inappropriate. For example, we could imagine a game set in a world from a David Lynch production, such as *Twin Peaks*[90] or *Mulholland Drive*.[91] Because characters and viewers struggle to understand such worlds, agency may be available in some immediate areas (such as spatial movement) but impossible in others, because the players do not understand the world well enough to predict the results of their actions, at least for much of the game. But if interaction is to be meaningful in the context of the game, it must still operate by its own internal rules, and do so in a way that can support the different interpretations that different players bring to the game, or it will not succeed in delivering an interactive version of the pleasures of Lynch's worlds. That is to say, it must create a world that operates by models that embody its ideas, just as much as a world that aims to produce the experience of agency.

Third, our definitions of agency require a further refinement. Naive definitions of "high agency" experiences have focused on the player's ability to influence the game world. Many authors have corrected this. One aspect of these corrections has focused on the fact that influence does not provide agency if the actions that produce influence do not match the actions suggested by the game world. Another aspect of these corrections has emphasized that influential actions do not provide agency if the actions are not ones that players can choose based on, and can understand through, a developing mental model of the game. These have seemed like two sides of the same coin, with the world's suggestions being part of what builds the player's mental model of actions, possible goals, and possible responses.

But as games move away from a near-exclusive focus on player empowerment, it becomes clear that these two elements of agency are somewhat independent. A game world may suggest that the player character can take few actions that provoke differing consequences, making it unnecessary to build much of a mental model of the sort described. In short, a balance between the actions that games suggest and offer is a prerequisite for agency, but does not determine where a game's agency falls on the continuum from high to severely constrained. A game's place on this continuum is determined by the extent to which it provides the ability for players to define goals that are meaningful in terms of the world the game presents, to carry out (perhaps at a bodily level, rather than through conscious consideration) chosen actions, and to see responses that build further world understanding.[92] And as noted earlier, different aspects of a game may fall in different places on this continuum.

Finally, games can also produce the illusion of giving us agency, and thereby being about things through play, such as the emotional and moral choices presented as story-defining moments in Telltale games. But when further engagement through play, especially replay, reveals the illusion, it becomes clear that there is a fundamental mismatch between what players have been promised and what the implemented model supports.

Making Games about More

It can be difficult to talk about this topic. The fundamental things that shape what games can be about are generally beneath our notice. To talk about games with attention to their foundations is like Laurie Anderson saying, "With each step, you fall forward slightly, and then catch yourself from falling."[93] It generally doesn't come to mind unless someone says it, and once they've said it the tendency is for the conversation to return to higher level concerns, like what path we will walk down and what sights we will see along the way.[94]

When we look at a game like Chess or *Counter-Strike*, our tendency is to focus on things such as the different military situations they portray and strategies players enact.

We are less likely to think about how players learn to engage and understand the logics that create their models of space and combat. We're less likely to consider how both games involve projecting force across space, something that is possible because players understand their spatial models and how collision can be threatened at a distance. We're less likely to consider these things because they just work—they function as the foundation for the rest to be built upon.

If we start to consider the foundations of games, we start to notice when the logics and models are a poor fit with the game's presented skin or theme.[95] The mismatch examples discussed earlier—from fishing *Monopoly* to *BioShock Infinite*—provide, in a sense, an overview of ways the central logics and models of a game can fail to match what it presents itself as being about.

Beyond identifying mismatches, we can also attempt to be more precise about what is happening when there is not a mismatch.[96] When I say a game is "about something through play," I mean that the understanding built through engagement with the logics and models (in both their procedural and communicative aspects) is an appropriate match with the way we are meant to interpret our play activity. For some relatively abstract games, such as Go or *Bejeweled*, our interpretation is based entirely on the implemented logics and models, perhaps a small number of additional rules or scenario design elements, and the clues offered by the specific presentation of the abstract gameplay—from the smooth, simple feel of a traditional Go piece to the over-the-top animations and sounds that accompany special matches in *Bejeweled*.[97] (Of course, there are also the cultural and personal associations that games can accrue, but in this they are the same as anything else that is part of culture—from folk dances to famous paintings.) Our interpretations of such games often focus on our patterns of engagement with the logics and models and the situations and feelings that arise through this, as examined through approaches like the MDA (Mechanics, Dynamics, Aesthetics) framework discussed in chapters 4 and 6.

But games that are trying to be about something generally add another element. Using the tools of other artforms—language, sound, imagery, tactility—they present a larger situation in which we are meant to interpret our game activity as taking place. They augment and emphasize certain interactions with logics and models, while placing them within the larger situation. And it is the situation that is thereby signaled that can match, to a greater or lesser degree, the understanding built through the logics, models, additional rules, scenario design, and resulting gameplay. A spatial model can be a foundation for a game fundamentally about controlling space (such as Chess or *Counter-Strike*) or a game fundamentally about moving through space (in the tradition of *Adventure* or a platformer). But as discussed above, it can actively conflict with and undermine a game attempting to be about economic philosophy or racism—especially when paired with the combat model so often included in games with models of 3-D space.

The foundation provided by logics and models can give us opportunities for agency, as when players come to understand a resource model, such that they can deliberately gather and deploy resources to change the game world (for example, developing a neighborhood in *Monopoly*). But this foundation doesn't need to provide us agency. Short, often metaphorical, "lyric games" (discussed in chapter 9) aim to create a resonance between their use of logics and models and their themes, rather than to offer a way for players to use their understanding of the game world to meaningfully alter it. Also, the pattern-matching puzzles found in adventure games often don't provide agency, as there is often only one, relatively arbitrary solution, disconnected from players' world knowledge. But they can be as engaging as other kinds of pattern matching (such as crossword puzzles) and they can be themed to be appropriate to the world. Theming can also present the play activity enabled by the logics and models as the most important and positive one in the world (moving down the track in *Candy Land*), or as something secondary but complementary (many Twine games are primarily textual experiences, with complementary link-based play), or even something central that should not be done (moving down the track in *Train*).

Finally, we can extend, or move beyond, what logics and models can enable through forms of play built on human communication. Just as humans can have a conversation on any topic for which they are prepared, so they can be prompted to play in these terms. Appropriately prompting and scaffolding such play is as exciting and challenging as work with the logics and models described in this book. This represents another way that games can be about something through play.

And, of course, players can decide to play about things that are more or less loosely connected to the game's topic. It is in some ways similar to theater: a production of *Hamlet* can be about mental illness (something suggested by the play) or use the play as a starting point for a production on other topics (such as Rick Moranis's and Dave Thomas's *Strange Brew*[98]). Similarly, players can decide to play on topics other than those a game is about, or even counter-play in opposition to the intended topic. Even though this is a deliberate departure from what the game itself is about, it still often involves close engagement with the game's logics and models, as discussed in chapter 6.

To summarize, then, there are four ways we can make games about something. First, we can use logics and models as the foundation (both procedural and communicative) of a play experience that builds an understanding that matches well with undertaking the central activity in a wider situation portrayed through the tools of other artforms. Much of the power and popularity of this approach comes from the potential to provide players agency—but certainly not all. Second, we can use logics and models to create a play experience about the inability, or very limited ability, to engage in a central activity presented in the game world—denying players agency, or providing limited agency, or providing it only in one of the areas the game presents as key. Third, we can create a framework in which human communication and creativity enables play related to the game's central activity (as seen in tabletop RPGs) which, with skilled and willing players, can provide the most complete experience of agency. And finally, fourth, we can create an experience primarily through other artforms, but with logics and models enabling complementary (rather than unrelated or mismatched) play, giving the experience greater meaning, as often seen in hypertext fictions and interactive cinema. In this last category the centrality of play is diminished, and agency is quite difficult to provide, sometimes to the extent that the term "game" may feel inappropriate.[99]

When considering these options, we must acknowledge the difficulties of tabletop RPG-style play—such as finding and assembling a creative, energized group of players. And we are also faced with the presumably limited number of games we want to create about being disempowered, complicit, unheard, trapped, or otherwise lacking the ability to act. Given this, if we want to create games in which play is central and that are about something, we have no choice but to grapple with the limited number of well-developed operational logics and playable models—because these provide the foundations for the activities we can make games about.[100]

The ways we might grapple with this have been the focus of *How Pac-Man Eats*. My goal is not simply to explain what the common logics and models are, how some of them work, or where some of them came from—but to look at the strategies that we can use to make games that are about more than killing, greed, sport, and the other commonly encountered game themes.

The *alternative* strategy discussed in chapter 2 (of using well-understood logics and models to explore ideas that are uncommon in the world of games) is still a rich one, though we have had more than half a century of making video games. Nina Freeman et al.'s *How Do You Do It?*[101] uses well-understood spatial models to create a brief, humorous portrait of a young girl using her dolls to try to understand the physical aspects of human sexuality (figure 11.3). It is not only an engaging experience but also a reminder of how rarely games have addressed such topics. Yet the alternative approach has its limitations. Presumably we do wish to also be able to make games that are about more than the spatial aspects of sex and love.

Figure 11.3
The player character of *How Do You Do It?* gazes in fascination while different player-driven spatial arrangements of the dolls result in different thoughts (and embarrassment levels) from the character. (Image taken by the author during play.)

The *expansive* strategy discussed in chapters 3, 8, and 9 (of adding additional, unconventional communicative roles to existing logics and models) has had many successes, such as growing the collision logic to be broadly understood as representing nearly any kind of physical interaction, and preparing players to understand it even more broadly (as cued by the larger game). But the expansive strategy also has its pitfalls. Complex expansions are difficult to construct and maintain. And even simple ones can fail to hit their mark. The ZX Spectrum game *Sex Tetris*[102] could be seen as trying to address the same physical aspects of sex found in *How Do You Do It?*, but its attempt at an expansive use of a pattern-matching logic results in nonsense (figure 11.4). A disappearing line is difficult to read as a sex act—and the remaining bodies, after a line is matched, have to be turned into abstract blobs, so as to avoid horrifyingly dismembering its lovers as gameplay progresses.

There is urgent and exciting cultural work to be done through alternative and expansive approaches. But their limitations are why I have chosen to dedicate a significant amount of my work to the *inventive* strategy discussed in chapters 4, 5, and 7

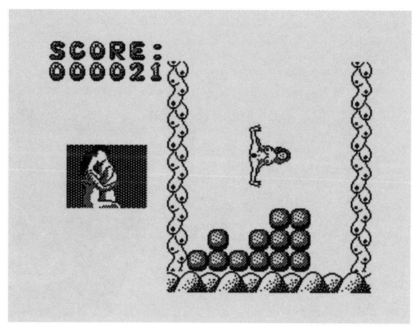

Figure 11.4
Sex Tetris attempts to use the spatial pattern matching of *Tetris* to also present something sexual—
but ends up nonsensical. (Image taken by the author during play on an emulator, https://zxart.ee/
eng/software/game/puzzle/sex-tetris1/.)

(of creating or adapting new logics and models for games, or new implementations of
them) as slow and difficult as it may be. Just as the social models described in chapter 5
can give players the opportunity to explore social possibilities and feel responsible for
their outcomes, in a variety of situations, I believe similar explorations could develop
models of romantic relationships that are about more than physical acts. And I believe
that the same is true of many other areas of human experience, from creative conversation to ideological belief and political resistance. Inventive approaches could make
these playable in new ways, on their own terms, rather than through the overloading
of models developed for quite different, arguably incompatible aims.

In addition, there are other areas of exciting work that this book has barely touched
on. One of the most promising is to apply inventive approaches to the limitations of
current game designs, rather than the more challenging road of developing highly
novel game designs around new logics and models. In chapter 10 I discussed this in
relation to generating microgames, so that their designs could be responsive to ongoing
play. But there are many other examples. For one, as this chapter describes, link-based

game designs have been successful at harnessing the power of other artforms and the experience of unfolding narrative. Yet as authors such as Chris Crawford have pointed out for decades, human authors find it intractable to create branches in the linking structure that reflect more than a few choices for any player.[103] This is why a number of research groups, our own included, are exploring inventive approaches to generating choice structures and dynamically adapting the contents of nodes within story graphs to reflect past choices.[104] I believe this research has the potential to open the door to Telltale-like experiences that say more about their stated topics through extended play, and replay, rather than revealing their promises of story flexibility to have been false.

In short, I believe it is important to understand how Pac-Man eats, and I hope this book has explained it clearly. But I also believe that games are well on their way to being about more than shooting, eating, collecting, and the other activities covered by well-understood logics and models. I hope this book inspires you to be part of the work that is to come.

Notes

Preface

1. Mojang, *Minecraft*. A note on citation: in this book, games with known authors (both digital games and physical games) are capitalized, italicized, and cited. Games without known authors (e.g., Go, Chess) and sports are capitalized, but not italicized or cited.

2. PopCap Games, *Bejeweled: Deluxe*.

3. Grow et al., "Crafting in Games."

Introduction

1. Namco Limited, *Pac-Man*.

2. Mojang, *Minecraft*.

3. MPS Labs, *Sid Meier's Civilization*.

4. BioWare Austin, *Star Wars: The Old Republic*.

5. Electronic Arts, *The Sims: Hot Date*.

6. Electronic Arts, *The Sims 2: Nightlife*.

7. 2K Boston and 2K Australia, *BioShock*.

8. Milton Bradley, *Twister*.

9. Crawford, *The Art of Computer Game Design*, 4.

10. Juul, *Half-Real: Video Games between Real Rules and Fictional Worlds*.

11. Bogost, *Persuasive Games: The Expressive Power of Videogames*.

12. Flanagan, *Critical Play*.

13. Harrell, *Phantasmal Media*.

14. Rusch, *Making Deep Games*.

15. Wardrip-Fruin, *Expressive Processing*.

16. At the same time, those books that do examine lower levels, such as the Platform Studies series, tend to be very specific to the particular lower-level examples being examined. As a result, it is difficult to use such work to find a set of core concepts for understanding what stretches across contexts.

17. Atari, *Pong*.

18. Atari, *Asteroids*.

19. Higinbotham, Dvorak, and Potter, *Tennis for Two*.

20. Stephen Russell et al., *Spacewar!*

21. For ease of reading, titles ending in an exclamation point (such as *Spacewar!*, *Pitfall!*, and *Kaboom!*) are given without their exclamation points after their first use in the text of this book. Exclamation points are retained in bibliography entries and quoted material. This note is included after the first mention of a title that ends in an exclamation point in each chapter.

22. Taito Corporation, *Space Invaders*.

23. Exidy, *Mouse Trap*.

24. Data East Corporation, *Lock 'n' Chase*.

25. Alpha Denshi, *Make Trax*.

26. Texas Instruments Incorporated, *Munch Man*.

27. Nintendo Co. and Systems Research & Development Co., *Super Mario Bros.*

28. Nintendo Co., *The Legend of Zelda*. Rather than attempt to cite a small sliver of the scholarship about these games, I will take the same route as Mia Consalvo's *Atari to Zelda* and simply note that they are widely discussed and (personally) I am more of the Atari VCS generation than the NES generation. See: Consalvo, *Atari to Zelda*.

29. Nintendo R&D1, *Devil World*.

30. Altice, *I Am Error*, 110.

31. In other Christian religions there are physical practices of touching crosses—such as "venerating the cross" with a kiss on Good Friday—so whether this part of the game makes sense literally or metaphorically is at least in part a personal theological question.

32. Rockstar North, *Grand Theft Auto IV*.

33. Syzygy, *Computer Space*.

34. Atari, *Adventure*.

35. Nintendo R&D1, *WarioWare, Inc.: Mega Microgame$!*

36. Dunhill Electronics, *Tax Avoiders*.

37. Anthropy, *Dys4ia*.

38. Atari, *Breakout*, 1976.

39. Activision, *Kaboom!*

40. For a discussion of historical "circuits" that connect technology, marketing, and play, see Stephen Kline, Nick Dyer-Witheford, and Greig de Peuter's *Digital Play: The Interaction of Technology, Culture and Marketing* (McGill-Queen's University Press, 2003).

41. Strachey, *M. U. C. Draughts*.

42. Pajitnov, *Tetris*.

43. Crowther and Woods, *Adventure*.

Chapter 1: Operational Logics and Playable Models

1. Rohrer, *Passage*.

2. Images of *Passage* from gameplay video taken by John Thomas Murray.

3. Richert, *Passage in 10 Seconds*.

4. Stephen Russell et al., *Spacewar!*

5. Crowther and Woods, *Adventure*.

6. For ease of reading, titles ending in an exclamation point (such as *Spacewar!*, *Pitfall!*, and *Kaboom!*) are given without their exclamation points after their first use in the text of this book. Exclamation points are retained in bibliography entries and quoted material. This note is included after the first mention of a title that ends in an exclamation point in each chapter.

7. Atari, *Pong*.

8. For more discussion of how *Passage* does this, and discussion of related work by other authors who have examined *Passage,* please see chapter 9.

9. Wardrip-Fruin, "Playable Media and Textual Instruments."

10. Jameson, *Postmodernism, Or, The Cultural Logic of Late Capitalism*.

11. Franklin, *Control*.

12. Lebra, *The Japanese Self in Cultural Logic*.

13. Comaroff and Roberts, *Rules and Processes*.

14. Enfield, "The Theory of Cultural Logic."

15. Baumbach, Young, and Yue, "Introduction: For a Political Critique of Culture."

16. Barthes, *The Fashion System*.

17. Sack, *The Software Arts*.

18. I am indebted to Soraya Murray, Jennifer González, and Warren Sack for personal communication about these arguments and their relations to my concerns here and to Sack for sharing a pre-publication draft of his book.

19. In earlier writing, Michael Mateas and I discussed the idea of higher-level logics being composed of lower-level ones. It was working with Joseph C. Osborn that convinced us that the notion of logics is most useful if limited to a foundational level. See: Mateas and Wardrip-Fruin, "Defining Operational Logics"; Osborn, Wardrip-Fruin, and Mateas, "Refining Operational Logics."

20. Osborn, Summerville, and Mateas, "Automated Game Design Learning"; Osborn, Summerville, and Mateas, "Automatic Mapping of NES Games with Mappy"; Summerville et al., "Gemini"; Summerville et al., "From Mechanics to Meaning."

21. It is also worth noting that computational media also has a long history—stretching back well before the modern computer. Just as an abacus is a non-digital computing device so, for example, are most tabletop games non-digital computational media works. Obviously digital and non-digital computational media have some differences from each other (for example, it's hard to hide what's going on from players if they have to carry out the computations themselves) and the spread of computers has made computational media much more pervasive, but the fact remains that the existence of computational media is not new.

22. While the workshop took place in 2010, the report was published in 2012. See: Boellstorff et al., "The Future of Research in Computer Games and Virtual World Environments: Workshop Report."

23. The idea of playable models has been further developed in a collaborative paper on combat in games and in Joseph C. Osborn's dissertation, which is reflected in this chapter, as well as chapters 4 and 7. See: Osborn et al., "Combat in Games"; Osborn, "Operationalizing Operational Logics."

24. Crowther and Woods, *Adventure*.

25. Blizzard Entertainment, *StarCraft*.

26. Maxis Software, *The Sims*.

27. Treyarch, *Call of Duty: Black Ops 4*.

28. However, as time goes on, algorithmic techniques (also called "procedural" or "generative" techniques) may shift the situation. Already, physics engines such as Havok are enabling animations to be produced on the fly that would once have had to be hand-crafted. As Chris Crawford noted in his influential 1987 essay "Process Intensity," it is well known that it is possible to shift between storing pre-created data and doing on-the-fly processing (as long as we know how to automatically produce the type of data). See: Crawford, "Process Intensity."

29. Atari, *Breakout*, 1976.

30. Nintendo and Systems Research & Development, *Super Mario Bros.*

31. I summarize Osborn's catalog of logics and three types of logic composition in chapter 4.

Chapter 2: Alternative Approaches

1. Neil, "How We Design Games Now and Why."

2. In between the era of hand-writing games in low-level languages and today's accessibility of tools was a period of expensive, less-capable game engines. Neil summarizes the situation:

> Take game engines, for example. In the early 2000s they were costly whether your studio developed one itself or licensed one from another company. The widely used game engine Renderware cost tens of thousands of dollars to use per title. Even the Torque game engine—the low-fi, "budget" option aimed at independent developers—would set you back $1,500. And if you wanted to include video in your cutscenes? Sound? Physics? Developers also needed to pay thousands in licensing fees for those technologies. A level or world-building tool? Build your own.

3. I discuss games that function like political cartoons in chapters 3 and 10. The serialized games of Telltale are discussed in the conclusion.

4. Stephen Russell et al., *Spacewar!*

5. Epic Games and People Can Fly, *Fortnite: Battle Royale.*

6. For ease of reading, titles ending in an exclamation point (such as *Spacewar!*, *Pitfall!*, and *Kaboom!*) are given without their exclamation points after their first use in the text of this book. Exclamation points are retained in bibliography entries and quoted material. This note is included after the first mention of a title that ends in an exclamation point in each chapter.

7. Dyment and Ahl, *Hamurabi.*

8. *Passage*, discussed in chapters 1 and 9, is (at least in part) about the fleeting nature of life. *Layoff*, discussed in chapter 3, is about callous layoffs driven by the financial industry. *Dys4ia*, discussed in chapter 9, is about beginning to take estrogen as a trans woman. *Cart Life*, about trying to get by doing precarious service work, is mentioned briefly in chapters 4 and 9, as well as the Conclusion. *Gone Home*, discussed in this chapter, is at least in part about wondering what has become of one's family.

9. The Fullbright Company, *Gone Home.*

10. As the game's reception indicates, I was far from alone in anticipating horror. Ian Bogost, in *How to Talk about Videogames*, writes, "Tropes from horror fiction are present in *Gone Home* from the start." Marty Sliva, reviewing the game for *IGN*, writes about an "ever-present sense of dread" and Patrick Klepek, writing for *Giant Bomb*, agrees, "*Gone Home* feels exceedingly creepy." Melissa Kagen, writing in "Walking Simulators, #GamerGate, and the Gender Of Wandering," notes that *Gone Home* is "Pervaded with . . . horror game tropes that convince the player of an impending jump scare that never arrives." However, Giancarlo Saldana, reviewing for *Edge* magazine, sees

this as a touch of reality, rather than a trope of horror: "Your fears will mimic real life when you enter a dark room to turn on the lights." Aaron A. Reed, John Murray, and Anastasia Salter suggest that beginning with a suggestion of supernatural horror is a foundation for where the story of *Gone Home* ends up: "The player's initial fear that they might need to act quickly to defend themselves from some lurking supernatural horror becomes transmuted, by the end of the story, into the inevitable realization that their character has already lost her chance to act, has arrived too late to intervene in her sister's story. All she can do now is understand it." See: Bogost, *How to Talk about Videogames*, 2015; Sliva, "Gone Home Review"; Klepek, "*Gone Home* Review"; Kagen, "Walking Simulators, #Gamergate, and the Gender of Wandering," 288; Saldana, "*Gone Home* Review"; Reed, Murray, and Salter, *Adventure Games*, 131.

11. Anderson, *Happy Accidents*.

12. Black Isle Studios, *Planescape: Torment*.

13. For more discussion, Dominic Arsenault's "Video Game Genre, Evolution and Innovation" provides a critical overview of how the notion of genre is employed in game studies and the industry—arguing that genre is defined by play experiences, rather than checklists of mechanics. See: Arsenault, "Video Game Genre, Evolution and Innovation."

14. Interplay Productions, *Fallout*.

15. In fact, *Planescape* is specifically based on rules and a world drawn from *D&D*.

16. Gary Gygax and Dave Arneson, *Dungeons & Dragons*.

17. Sandy Petersen, *Call of Cthulhu*.

18. Though Lessard does not use the language of logics and models, instead suggesting that game genres could be seen as "bodies of games sharing a stable foundation of [game design] patterns"—but that the concept of "patterns" could be substituted for others (he suggests "one can substitute it to 'formal element,' 'mechanics,' 'characteristic,' atoms, or 'ludèmes'"—so I don't think the substitution of logics and models does his work any violence). See: Lessard, "Game Genres and High-Level Design Pattern Formations."

19. There are, of course, exceptions to this—such as the horror game genre that *Gone Home* in some ways signals. The genre name is most strongly associated with "survival" or "stealth" horror games, in which movement through a dangerous space is central, such as the early *Resident Evil* games or *Amnesia* series. As Nick Junius argues, in these cases it is one of the few genres that is named for elements at every level of the "Mechanics, Dynamics, Aesthetics" framework—from horror mechanics to horror aesthetics. (Personal communication, April 16, 2018.) On the other hand, there are also horror-themed games, including ones focused on movement through space, that are not usually called "horror games." *DOOM*, the founder of the first-person shooter genre, is an obvious example. The difference might lie in Arsenault's focus on play experiences—while the spatial model is foundational for both, is the focus on fearfully moving through space, or on moving through like a hunter, in search of targets?

20. Zagal and Altizer, "Examining 'RPG Elements': Systems of Character Progression."

21. Bjork and Holopainen, *Patterns in Game Design*.

22. Not all reviewers praised *Gone Home* without qualification, of course. And the more critical reviews raised two important points for those who might want to pursue projects of this sort. First, the interaction is almost purely in terms of the spatial model, with "discovery of backstory-revealing objects" as the only meaningful story action the player can take. As Emily Short puts it, "The problem I have with it in *Gone Home* is that this interaction style enforces the distance and lack of agency that is backstory's chief defect, and it does so without offering much of value in exchange." Second, the story that is revealed through the exploration is very straightforward (one piece of information builds on another, rarely contradicting or complicating our early ideas) with characters and situations drawn more in the manner of young adult fiction than literary fiction. Ian Bogost argues that may simply mean *Gone Home* is doing for games what we've seen in cinema and print fiction: making what was once adolescent mainstream. He writes, "Just as Katie Greenbriar comes home to a home that isn't a home for anyone, so *Gone Home* reveals a secret that turns out to be an obvious one, and one much bigger than video games: today, narrative *writ large* is mired in a permanent adolescence that video games can now easily equal, the modest, subtle pleasures of the literary arts melting under Iron Man's turbines, impaled by Katniss Everdeen's arrow."

For Bonnie Ruberg, this is one of the key ways that *Gone Home* manages to be straight in form, even if it features queer content. Ruberg writes, "Much as the player must find the linear path designed into the seemingly twisting architecture of the house, these diary entries create a straight narrative line through Sam's queer experiences for the player to follow. In this way, *Gone Home* ultimately straightens the queer potential of its approach to storytelling. Rather than leaving its narrative elements in a jumble, allowing Sam and Lonnie's romance to remain messy and out of sync . . . the game ultimately tells a story that is strikingly straightforward in its form if not straight in its representational content." This is in notable contrast to scholars such as Shira Chess, who writes that *Gone Home* "denies both the expected hard-core action of many game worlds, but also the expected catharsis and release of hetero-narrative"—the player character has arrived too late to help in the narratives of other characters, and the player character's narrative climax comes through reading a book that we, as players, are not allowed to read.

See: Short, "Reading and Hypothesis"; Bogost, *How to Talk about Videogames*, 179–180; Ruberg, "Straight Paths through Queer Walking Simulators"; Chess, "The Queer Case of Video Games."

23. Riendeau, "*Gone Home* Review."

24. id Software, *DOOM*.

25. id Software, *Wolfenstein 3D*.

26. *Myst*, a puzzle-oriented game released the same year as *DOOM*, also allowed players to explore a 3-D space from a first-person perspective. However, this was not a real-time, continuous experience—though it did become one for later puzzle games, such as *Portal* and *The Witness*. Perhaps because the use of such models in puzzle games came later, the reception of *Gone Home* focused much more on its lack of combat (its differentiation from the FPS) than its lack of puzzles. See: Cyan, *Myst*; Valve Corporation, *Portal*; Thekla, *The Witness*.

27. That players see the absence of FPS models and conventions, not just what *Gone Home* makes present, can be seen in the game's reviews. Ludwig Kietzmann's review for *Joystiq* calls *Gone Home* a "First-Person Snooper" while Colin Campbell's early coverage for *IGN* is titled "*Gone Home*: Gentle Gaming Takes Aim at Shooters." Dale North, writing for *Destructoid*, notes it has "No jumping or shooting, and certainly no loadouts or stats." Patrick Klepek writes for *Giant Bomb*, "*Gone Home* is played from a first-person-perspective, and there is no combat. This is a game about exploration, though one not without its share of tension. But you will never pick up a gun." Danielle Riendeau writes for *Polygon*, "That there is no combat—or other mechanics aside from exploration and environmental manipulation—proves that you don't need to kill hordes of people to keep things interesting."

However, it is also worth noting that Elise Vist, in "Cyborg Games: Videogame Blasphemy and Disorientation," makes a compelling case that the genre *Gone Home* refuses is the horror game:

> The game tells you, over and over again, that you are in a horror story. It was prototyped in the *Amnesia* engine and its mechanics, narrative tropes, and sound design remind the player, over and over again, that what they're about to experience is terrifying, horrific. . . . For people expecting a horror game, expecting to reach out and find bloody bodies and psychopaths, not hair dye and mixtapes, *Gone Home* is a lesson in disorientation. . . . In fact, the more you know about horror games, the harder it will be for you to really play the game, because while Sam talks about coming to terms with being in love with her best friend Lonnie, you'll be peering into corners and trying to figure out if the great-uncle is going to come back from the dead to murder you. . . . *Gone Home* is a *cyborg game* because it is blasphemous to the tropes of the horror/survival game; it takes players who believe they know what to expect and gives them an entirely different story.

In a sense, Vist's comments point to a hybrid position: that by signaling horror through its environment and (to some) signaling shooting through genre expectation, but delivering neither, the result may have been a group of players perceiving *Gone Home* as refusing the "survival horror" genre (perhaps at the more action-oriented end of its spectrum). That said, *DOOM*, the most influential FPS, itself uses many horror tropes. So those who "returned" *Gone Home* to a DOOM-like form may also have been responding to both aspects.

See: Kietzmann, "*Gone Home* Review: First-Person Snooper"; Campbell, "*Gone Home*"; North, "Review"; Klepek, "*Gone Home* Review"; Riendeau, "*Gone Home* Review"; Vist, "Cyborg Games," 59–60.

28. 2K Boston and 2K Australia, *BioShock*.

29. Kagen, "Walking Simulators, #Gamergate, and the Gender of Wandering," 276.

30. The term "walking simulator" seems to have emerged as a negative one, but then was embraced by some creators and critics.

31. On August 21, 2013, less than a week after the August 15 release and highly positive reviews of *Gone Home*, user "Impse !!9/alULWmsW5" on the 4chan /vr/ "retro games" forum sought help from others to make *Gone Homo* more complete—asking for screenshots of the entire *Gone Home* house if they "really want this thing to be filled with feminism jabs and whatnot." In a post later the same day, the same user describes the final battle of *Gone Homo* as being against "tons of /pol/'s Shreks with the face being changed by the one from that bald feminist with black lipstick on her lips." A later post refers to the final battle as "a slaughtermap involved around 'checking your privilege.'"

4chan threads expire and then are deleted (Bernstein et al., "4chan and /b/: An Analysis of Anonymity and Ephemerality in a Large Online Community"). These posts are quoted from an archive at warosu.org.

32. As Christopher A. Paul observes, "Defining games and gamers in a specific manner rewards the investment that a certain subgroup of players has made over years. Seeing that cultural capital eroded is hard, making the status quo something worth desperately fighting for." Or as Melissa Kagen puts it, "Between its pleas to keep politics out of gaming and its association of feminist politics with walking sims, the #GamerGate faction tied together the fear that games were becoming unrecognizable to gamers with the fear that women were taking over nerdy male spaces."

One question that game creators have asked is how they, through their work, can help create a healthier gaming community. Writing from the tradition of theatrical dramaturgy, as applied to digital media, Michael Mark Chemers and Mike Sell make the following recommendations:

1. Recognize that, as in theatre, the content and mechanics of games have a real influence on the culture of gamers that create, consume, and support game development.

2. Recognize that, as in theatre, the work game developers do is impactful and important for real people and their lives.

3. Recognize that dramaturgs have a responsibility to our community to change the currency of the culture, and never stop asking this question: what can we do with THIS GAME, RIGHT NOW, that could potentially ameliorate suffering?

See: Paul, "A Toxic Culture," 89–90; Kagen, "Walking Simulators, #Gamergate, and the Gender of Wandering," 288; Chemers and Sell, *Systemic Dramaturgy: A Handbook for the Digital Age*.

33. Kyle Hilliard wrote for *Game Informer* about one of these: a Steam Workshop user by the name Nipper re-created the *Gone Home* house as a level for the multi-player FPS *Counter-Strike: Global Offensive*. Hillard tellingly comments: "I remember after playing *Gone Home*, I remarked to Jeff Cork that I would love to see the house appear as a map in a shooter. I wanted it to exist mostly because it would be hilariously ironic since *Gone Home* is nearly the polar opposite of a shooter, but I also wanted to see it because over the course of the game, you learn the layout of the home so well." See: Hilliard, "*Gone Home* House Becomes A Multiplayer Map in *Counter-Strike* Mod."

34. Dorkly, *Gun Home*.

35. Melissa Kagen writes, "With a gun in the player's hand and 8-bit Nazis to demolish, the parody implies, *Gone Home* would be a *real* game." Kagen, "Walking Simulators, #Gamergate, and the Gender of Wandering," 289.

36. This ranges from the relatively tame (for example, one *Joystiq* commenter writing, "Oh cool maybe this one will be a video game") to the unpublishable. ImSteevin, "Comment on 'Dorkly Unleashes a Trailer for *Gone Home*'s Ideal DLC, "Gun Home.""

37. Ruberg, "Straight Paths through Queer Walking Simulators."

38. Boluk and Lemieux, *Metagaming*.

39. It is also interesting to note that, somewhat ironically, the capacity for *Gone Home* speedrunning was actually discussed as a major shortcoming and motivation by the creator of *Gone Homo*. In one of the early posts about the project, Impse !!9/alULWmsW5 wrote:

> People on /v/ have been making threads all day about this, and they found out that you can skip almost the entire game by doing what this GIF displays, and it doesn't even take one and a half minute [sic] to do all of this. You can put some popcorn on the microwave, cook it, go back to play and finish the game, and you can calmly go back to the microwave and see that it's still cooking 'em
>
> Okay, so based on this I've been preparing what could be called GoneHome.wad (or GoneHomo.wad, heh), which is the entire game done in Doom with stock textures, and done in ZDoom in Hexen format.

40. Patrick LeMieux also points out that there are many other types of playful engagement found in the *Gone Home* play community, such as collecting every object in a single room to slow or crash the program. (Personal communication, September 23, 2019.) See: Wiggins, *Gone Home— Every Item (No Audio)*.

41. Steam Hunters, "*Gone Home* Achievements."

42. Giant Sparrow, *What Remains of Edith Finch*.

43. Naughty Dog, *The Last of Us: Left Behind*.

44. The Chinese Room, *Dear Esther*.

45. Campo Santo Productions, *Firewatch*.

Chapter 3: Expansive Approaches

1. The addition of a second communicative role to an existing logic can be experienced in a variety of ways. In some cases, the second role can be thought of (at least, by some audiences) as a more specific case of the first. When the second communicative role gives us a more specific way of interpreting the first, I characterize the experience of expansion as "refinement," which is discussed further in chapter 8. Of course, there are many cases in which the second role is clearly not a more specific version of the first, as with the second role collision detection plays in *Passage* (indicating a life choice is unavailable). In these cases, I characterize the addition of a second communicative role as "doubling"—both roles are still present. Chapter 9 further discusses doubling's power and its relationship to metaphor. Of course, many cases are somewhere between the polar ends of refinement and doubling and, as I also discuss in chapter 9, our perception of this can shift.

2. Milton Bradley, *Connect Four*.

3. If there were computational support for the more specific communicative role, the approach would be an inventive one (if creating a new logic for the second role, perhaps within an existing family), simply the use of a more specific logic in the family (if this support was well established), or the use of a model. The *dialogue tree* model employed in many role-playing games, for example, has a more complex abstract process than the basic linking logic, including computational support for its more specific communicative role. As discussed in chapter 4, it is the additions

provided by a progression logic that accomplish this and, in doing so, move it from being a logic to a model.

4. inkle, *80 Days.*

5. Of course, this confusion can be pursued deliberately, as part of the overall theme of the work, as demonstrated by some early hypertext projects from the electronic literature community.

6. 3909, *Papers, Please.*

7. Though the creator, apparently, would not agree, as Leigh Alexander reports in *Gamasutra:*

> Pope's been a little disappointed by reviews that emphasize the "not-fun-ness" of *Papers, Please* with its demanding tasks and depressing subject matter. "I hope that people simply enjoy playing," he says. "After that, I'm not sure . . . if players come away with a little more balance in how they perceive the intentions of others, that'd be okay, too."

See: Alexander, "Designing the Bleak Genius of *Papers, Please.*"

8. Harmonix Music Systems, *Rock Band.*

9. The 2009 iPhone game *Jetset: A Game for Airports,* designed by Ian Bogost and developed by Persuasive Games, puts players in the position of an airport security line worker. It uses a pattern-matching logic in a manner similar to *Papers, Please.* Players must search passenger bags and bodies, removing prohibited items and avoiding two game-ending conditions—making five confiscation errors (failing to confiscate prohibited items or mistakenly confiscating allowed items) or allowing the line of passengers to reach the door. This is made more difficult by continual changes to the list of prohibited items. As the game's instructions say: "Like real airport security policy, **the rules change frequently.**" (Emphasis in original.) Persuasive Games, *Jetset: A Game for Airports.*

10. Another such logic is *temporal pattern matching,* as seen in childhood play (such as Simon Says and hand-clapping games) and video games (such as quick-time events and music and dance games). But interestingly, I know of no examples of temporal patterns being used to place the player in disturbing circumstances such as those described later in this chapter.

11. Juul, *A Casual Revolution.*

12. Juul, 84.

13. Moribe, *Chain Shot.*

14. Pajitnov, *Tetris.*

15. PopCap Games, *Bejeweled: Deluxe.*

16. Koster, *A Theory of Fun for Game Design.*

17. Koster, "ATOF *Tetris* Variant Comes True."

18. Koster is not alone (or even first) in imagining re-skinning *Tetris* as a horrifying act, with some having actually carried it out, as discussed in the conclusion.

19. Flanagan et al., *LAYOFF.*

20. Tiltfactor, "Tiltfactor | *LAYOFF.*"

21. Tiltfactor, "Tiltfactor | *LAYOFF* — 1 Million Players in the First Week; at GDC."

22. McWhertor, "Layoffs."

23. Perman, "Layoffs: The Videogame."

24. Mawhorter, "Artificial Intelligence as a Tool for Understanding Narrative Choices"; Mawhorter et al., "Choice Poetics by Example."

25. Paul Formosa, Malcolm Ryan, and Dan Staines draw our attention to how such choices arise out of the game's systems, rather than being pre-scripted, as is common for games that focus on morality. They also go into some detail in describing how *Papers, Please* engages four moral themes: dehumanization, privacy, fairness, and loyalty. Formosa, Ryan, and Staines, *"Papers, Please* and the Systemic Approach to Engaging Ethical Expertise in Videogames."

26. Mawhorter et al., "Towards a Theory of Choice Poetics"; Mawhorter, Mateas, and Wardrip-Fruin, "Generating Relaxed, Obvious, and Dilemma Choices with Dunyazad"; Mawhorter, Mateas, and Wardrip-Fruin, "Intentionally Generating Choices in Interactive Narratives."

27. Mawhorter, "Artificial Intelligence as a Tool for Understanding Narrative Choices."

28. *Papers, Please* also doesn't let players off the hook by giving them a well-defined character to play, so that they can choose to do "what the character would do" rather than making a more personal choice. The tendency of players with well-defined characters to choose what they believe that character would do has been termed the "Mimesis Effect" by Ignacio X. Domínguez, Rogelio E. Cardona-Rivera, James K. Vance, and David L. Roberts. See: Domínguez et al., "The Mimesis Effect."

29. Hart and Case, *Parable of the Polygons.*

30. The concept of explorable explanations is fluently described by Brett Victor in a 2011 essay of the same name. Victor is well aware that this work is in a tradition that stretches back to before the advent of personal computing (such as Ted Nelson's 1970 essay in *Computer Decisions*) and helped to inspire the development of personal computing (such as the work of Doug Engelbart and Bill English at Stanford Research Institute, or Alan Kay and Adele Goldberg at Xerox PARC) and even formed the basis of earlier educational interventions (Seymour Papert's *Mindstorms* and the Logo programming language, both aimed at spreading the idea of learning through explorable, alterable microworlds). However, a number of those who have taken up the explorable explanations banner seem unfortunately unaware of this early history—and even of later work such as Kay's research under the term "active essays." See: Nelson, "No More Teachers' Dirty Looks"; Douglas C. Engelbart and William K. English, "A Research Center for Augmenting Human Intellect"; Kay and Goldberg, "Personal Dynamic Media"; Papert, *Mindstorms*; Yamamiya, Warth, and Kaehler, "Active Essays on the Web."

31. Gardner, "Mathematical Games: The Fantastic Combinations of John Conway's New Solitaire Game 'Life.'"

32. Maxis Software, *SimCity*.

33. The foundation of *Parable of the Polygons* is mathematical social science work that had previously applied spatial pattern matching to the workings of segregation. But creators Hart and Case do the key work of turning a simulation model into a playable model: making it learnable and actionable through their design. Though the original author, Thomas Schelling, also made some gestures in this direction, such as writing, of the model used by Hart and Case, "The reader can check this for himself in about ten minutes if he has a roll of pennies, a roll of nickels, and a sheet of paper big enough for 16 columns of one-inch squares." He also wrote, of a different model described in the same paper, "the linear experiment can be replicated by any reader in five minutes; variants can readily be devised, and any reader with a spare half hour can change the hypotheses to suit himself." Of course, using automatic computation, Hart and Case can make it much easier for the model to be learned, altered, and played. For Schelling's original work (which also includes two other models), see: Schelling, "Dynamic Models of Segregation," 149, 156.

34. Treanor, "Investigating Procedural Expression and Interpretation in Videogames," 59–61.

35. Molleindustria, *Kosmosis—a Communist Space Shooter*.

36. Pedercini, "Videogames and the Spirit of Capitalism."

37. This possibility is also considered in the mathematical social science on which their work is founded, but not given the same "happy ending" status. See: Schelling, "Dynamic Models of Segregation," 165, 166, 180.

38. As with any metaphor, it's not perfect (bias is not equally distributed in populations), but it offers us a way to think about these issues from the perspective of small, local choices, rather than top-down, which could be a useful reframing.

39. Of course, understanding how games can function as political cartoons, and finding effective design and technology strategies for enabling the creation of them by non-specialists, is itself a fascinating topic—as is the broader topic of how games can engage the news. See: Treanor, "Newsgames—Procedural Rhetoric Meets Political Cartoons"; Bogost, Ferrari, and Schweizer, *Newsgames: Journalism at Play*.

Chapter 4: Six Questions about Logics and Models

1. Midway Mfg., General Computer Corporation, *Ms. Pac-Man*.

2. Rohrer, *Passage*.

3. Firaxis Games, *XCOM: Enemy Unknown*.

4. Naughty Dog, *Uncharted 2: Among Thieves*.

5. For more on models of combat, see chapter 7.

6. The foundation of *Kriegsspiel* was also built upon by *Dungeons & Dragons* (and other tabletop role-playing games) in eventually quite different directions. For an introduction to the history of tabletop war simulation in Europe, see Peterson, "A Game Out of All Proportions: How a Hobby Miniaturized War." For the foundations of tabletop RPGs, see Peterson, *Playing at the World*. For reflections on RAND in particular, see Ghamari-Tabrizi, "Wargames as Writing Systems"; Losh, "Playing Defense: Gender, Just War, and Game Design."

7. These ongoing connections are discussed in Dyer-Witheford and de Peuter, *Games of Empire*.

8. Pathfinding logics are probably a specific subset, used in spatial models, of a more general AI logic family. But the theory of AI logics is not yet well-developed enough for me to say. One possibility might be that pathfinding logics are part of a *planning* family. Logics in this candidate family would communicate that an entity can pursue a goal (such as a location, in a spatial model) over multiple steps (such as moving efficiently around multiple objects in the way). The abstract process might be that an entity takes steps to alter the game state progressively toward an objective until it is achieved, abandoned, or superseded (perhaps temporarily).

9. Though with very different implementations, given their different models and platforms.

10. Reynolds, "Flocks, Herds, and Schools"; Reynolds, "Steering Behaviors for Autonomous Characters."

11. Reynolds, "OpenSteer: Steering Behaviors for Autonomous Characters."

12. Fray, "Steering Behaviours Are Doing It Wrong."

13. Zubek writes, in personal communication:

> The difficulty with steering is that it operates on too low of a cognitive level—steering is the spatial cognition of insects, which respond to things in their vicinity, but get confused by obstacles in their way.
>
> But something like A* pathfinding is more akin to what human-level (or animal-level) cognition is capable of—we all can figure out how to get from point A to point B without too much work. Sure, the method is different (humans don't run A*), but what we expect from NPCs in games is this kind of high-level spatial cognition.
>
> So while I wouldn't say pathfinding was inevitable, it does seem like a much better fit for the problem at hand, for games filled with people and smart animals. And sometimes both get used—we've seen agents use A* or similar for path-finding, plus a few basic steering behaviors to avoid running into nearby obstacles while path-following.

(Personal communication, November 25, 2018.)

14. As Joris Dormans suggests, in response to an earlier draft of this chapter, pathfinding and steering are "different solutions to different problems, and frequently co-exist within the same game." (Personal communication, January 4, 2019.) This is certainly correct. What I'm trying to point out, however, is not that the two are incompatible, but rather that one approach is much more readily available to game creators, and this is not necessary or inevitable.

15. One framing is to think of the implementation of an abstract process as what must be preserved across versions of the same game on different platforms. If porting a Famicom game to

Unity, the details of how particular abstract processes are realized might be substantial, from how collision functions to how the player's camera appears to move across a game level. Similarly, a game might be ported from a database-driven hypertext system to one that does a search for a matching title when a link is clicked. But each concrete implementation strategy works to make the game function in terms of the abstract process (and if it doesn't, a particular game port will be considered "broken" in that way).

Another framing might be to think of an operational logic as a bridge concept. On one side of the bridge are many possible technical implementations that all satisfy the abstract process. On the other side of the bridge are many specific things that can be communicated, using a range of media forms. (And different communication approaches, through their details, can change player perceptions of gameplay possibilities, even when the processes are held steady, as discussed in endnote 86 of this chapter.) The ongoing presentation of game state (and changes to that state) help the player understand the significance of the logic and the opportunities for play it offers within the context of a playable model. If we wanted to catalog some of the major members of a particular logic family, we could choose different aspects to drive the catalog—such as the ways the logic is implemented on major platforms, the major things the logic is used to communicate, or the major types of playable models within which it is integrated.

16. Adams and Dormans, *Game Mechanics*.

17. Swink, *Game Feel*.

18. And this, in turn, is part of the challenge that faces the different communities seeking to move forward the possibilities of video games. The difficult, uncertain process of invention, as discussed in the next chapter, is one that independent and art game creators often lack the resources to pursue. But the reward structures of technology research are often arranged such that the creation of a complete game is difficult to justify. And even as new work is created, neither type of context rewards the careful consideration of the results that is necessary to see the cultural impact of new works, understand what we have learned, and guide future creation. This is why a number of us have dedicated significant portions of our lives toward the creation of new contexts, in which invention, creation, and analysis are all valued.

That said, the creation process for exploring new logics and models, and new uses of them, can be undertaken at different scales. Just as story structure for cinema can be explored using storyboards, logics can be explored with prototypes—as long as the domain is well-developed enough for playful interaction, experimentation, and communication. For example, Melanie Dickinson's exploration of the strengths and limitations of current social interaction models in the context of activist meetings is still illuminating, even without being a complete game (though of course more could be learned by creating a complete game based on it). See: Dickinson, Wardrip-Fruin, and Mateas, "Social Simulation for Social Justice."

19. Lederle-Ensign and Wardrip-Fruin, "What Is Strafe Jumping?"

20. id Software, *Quake*.

21. id Software, *Quake III Arena*.

22. Robert Zubek, one of the authors of the first scholarly publication on MDA, has proposed a reformulation in his book *Elements of Game Design*. His new categories are "mechanics and systems," "gameplay," and "player experience." He argues that there are two advantages to the reformulation. First, in game creation circles, his new terms will be more easily understood (for example, in game development practice, "aesthetics" is usually a term for visual aesthetics, not experiential aesthetics). Second, the "dynamics" term, in the original MDA formulation, attempts to contain both how mechanics work together in systems and how players interact with the game. Zubek's new formulation puts game mechanics and systems together, with player interaction separate—rather than placing player interaction and game systems together, with game mechanics separate. See: Zubek, *Elements of Game Design*.

23. Hunicke, LeBlanc, and Zubek, "MDA: A Formal Approach to Game Design and Game Research."

24. There are also more unusual approaches, such as Miguel Sicart's, which describes mechanics as the actions available both to the player and to other "agents" involved in the game ("methods invoked by agents, designed for interaction with the game state"). This last, while widely cited, has actually been specifically attacked by its own author, who writes seven years later, "Sicart's concepts do not scale up properly when trying to analyze more complex relations between game mechanics and the intended play experience they are designed to create." Sicart particularly criticizes his conception of mechanics for not accounting for system response and connection to other mechanics, both of which are addressed in this book by situating mechanics within the larger context of logics and models. That said, Sicart's focus on loops and metagames (as context for mechanics and play) is complementary to my approach.

Some scholars also employ the term "mechanics" very broadly. For example, Stephanie Boluk and Patrick LeMieux write: "game *mechanics* (and especially *video game mechanics*) typically refer to the involuntary processes of a game (or game engine) not freely chosen by the player. The Earth's gravity, the material composition of a baseball bat, the display rate of a CRT screen, and the conditional logic of a video game are game mechanics native to the given field, equipment, platform, or code and cannot be altered at will." They use mechanics this way in order to contrast it with "rules" which are "voluntary constraints or social contracts" in their argument.

See: Sicart, "Defining Game Mechanics"; Sicart, "Loops and Metagames: Understanding Game Design Structures"; Boluk and Lemieux, *Metagaming*.

25. Neil, "Game Design Tools: Can They Improve Game Design Practice?"

26. Cousins, "Selfconscious and Unselfconscious Cultures."

27. Cousins, "Elementary Game Design."

28. Personal communication, Raph Koster, December 11, 2018.

29. Koster, "An Atomic Theory of Fun Game Design."

30. Koster, "A Grammar of Gameplay: Game Atoms: Can Games Be Diagrammed?"

31. Cook, "The Chemistry of Game Design."

32. While not specific to games, a chapter from Crawford's *Art of Interactive Design* offers a clear explanation of his concept of verbs. Also worth noting are influential early calls for a more developed language for discussing games from Greg Costikyan and Doug Church. See: Crawford, "Chapter 8: Guidelines"; Costikyan, "I Have No Words & I Must Design"; Church, "Formal Abstract Design Tools."

33. Cook does provide a look "inside" the skill atom of "jump"—which contains three elements: "Press a button," "Jump and collide," and "Animation on screen." For Cook these correspond to broader categories of what makes up skill atoms: "Player action," "Simulation," and "Feedback." From an operational logics perspective, these same elements exist, but are only part of the picture and are organized differently. The button pressing and its corresponding animation are communication elements of a control logic (which also has a process element—and potentially other communication elements, such as sound). The simulation elements of jump and collide, together with their corresponding animations (and sounds, vibrations, etc.), are a physics and collision logic, respectively. (The entity-state logic noted in the operational logics account of a jumping mechanic is not noted in Cook's approach.)

In any case, as Cook does not provide a name for the elements inside a skill atom, we can't draw an alternative to "operational logics" from Cook's work. That said, we may still be able to learn more about operational logics in the future by looking at work that builds upon the skill atoms approach, such as Deterding, "The Lens of Intrinsic Skill Atoms."

34. Russell et al., *Spacewar!*

35. Rather than directly shaping gameplay, the *Spacewar* starfield provides skinning for the playable spatial model, contributing to the suggestion (which also comes from the skinning of the objects controlled by the players, the name of the game, and so on) that we interpret the play area as outer space.

For ease of reading, titles ending in an exclamation point (such as *Spacewar!, Pitfall!,* and *Kaboom!*) are given without their exclamation points after their first use in the text of this book. Exclamation points are retained in bibliography entries and quoted material. This note is included after the first mention of a title that ends in an exclamation point in each chapter.

36. Alex Zook, for example, suggests a category of "interactional logics" that flow from a focus on player experience, rather than the dual system-and-author focus of early writings on operational logics. Some of his critique has, I believe, been addressed by further development of the core ideas presented in this book (e.g., the previous absence of discussion of data structures and state in operational logics is, here, addressed by discussion of these in the context of the implementation of playable models). But other aspects will likely remain disagreements—given the differences in what we hope to use the tool of logics to analyze and understand—which is perfectly appropriate. See: Zook, "Expanding Operational Logics."

37. Osborn, Wardrip-Fruin, and Mateas, "Refining Operational Logics"; Osborn, "Operationalizing Operational Logics."

38. Osborn, Lambrigger, and Mateas, "HyPED: Modeling and Analyzing Action Games as Hybrid Systems"; Osborn, Summerville, and Mateas, "Automatic Mapping of NES Games with Mappy"; Summerville et al., "Gemini."

39. Dormans, "Engineering Emergence."

40. For more detail, I recommend Osborn's insightful and elegantly written dissertation. In particular, for those planning to do technical research, Osborn's dissertation identifies mathematical formalisms that not only capture the abstract process of the logic but also are modeled in a manner consistent with the logic's communicative role (making them appropriate for representing the logic in software that reasons about games). See: Osborn, "Operationalizing Operational Logics."

41. Osborn, "Operationalizing Operational Logics," 49.

42. Osborn, 50.

43. Konami Computer Entertainment Japan, *Metal Gear Solid.*

44. Osborn, "Operationalizing Operational Logics," 52.

45. Osborn, 52.

46. Osborn, 52.

47. id Software, *DOOM.*

48. Maxis Software, *SimCity.*

49. Gary Gygax and Dave Arneson, *Dungeons & Dragons.*

50. Milton Bradley, *Candy Land.*

51. Björk and Juul, "Zero-Player Games, Or: What We Talk about When We Talk about Players."

52. Moon, *Ticket to Ride.*

53. Quinn, *Depression Quest.*

54. Tosca, "A Pragmatics of Links."

55. inkle, *80 Days.*

56. PopCap Games, *Bejeweled: Deluxe.*

57. Mojang, *Minecraft.*

58. Quantic Dream SA, *Heavy Rain.*

59. Capcom, *Street Fighter.*

60. Parker Brothers, *Monopoly.*

61. Harmonix Music Systems, *Dance Central.*

62. 3909, *Papers, Please.*

63. Harmonix Music Systems, *Guitar Hero.*

64. Harmonix Music Systems, *Rock Band.*

65. inkle, *Heaven's Vault.*

66. Valve Corporation, *Portal.*

67. Atari, *Pong.*

68. Leduc, *Momentum.*

69. Bethesda Game Studios, *The Elder Scrolls V: Skyrim.*

70. Toy, Wichman, and Arnold, *Rogue.*

71. Blizzard Entertainment Inc. and Blizzard North, *Diablo.*

72. Compton, Kybartas, and Mateas, "Tracery," 2015.

73. Ryan et al., "Expressionist."

74. Márquez Segura et al., "Designing Future Social Wearables with Live Action Role Play (LARP) Designers."

75. Dormans, "Engineering Emergence."

76. Take Action Games, *Darfur Is Dying.*

77. In addition, simple "logic structures" (discussed further in chapter 10), with their differing rhetorical affordances, each involve connections between multiple logics combined with spatial relationships.

78. Osborn, Wardrip-Fruin, and Mateas, "Refining Operational Logics"; Osborn, "Operationalizing Operational Logics."

79. Osborn gives the example of an inventory system with objects of different shapes (a collision logic prevents objects for which there is not a space of the right shape being added) but allowing stacking of multiple items of the same type (a resource logic) containing the necessary ingredients for an item to be crafted (also governed by resources). When the inventory is full, an object of an existing type could be created—because it will stack—but not an object of a new type, because there is not an appropriate space for the new item to reside in the inventory (as determined by collision). This isn't a case of a resource logic acting on a fact established by a collision logic, but rather a case of their two different sorts of representations being understood as referring to the same entity.

80. BioWare Corporation, *Mass Effect.*

81. Wardrip-Fruin, *Expressive Processing.*

82. BioWare Corporation, *Star Wars: Knights of the Old Republic.*

83. Weizenbaum, "ELIZA: A Computer Program for the Study of Natural Language Communication between Man and Machine."

84. Studio Mountains, *Florence*.

85. Aytemiz, Junius, and Altice, "Exploring How Changes in Game Systems Generate Meaning."

86. Though the goal of this book is to focus on logics and models, the importance of their implementation should not be underestimated. For example, we took the underlying conversational model of the game *Façade* (which is not a dialogue tree) and gave it three different interfaces: its original natural language understanding interface (allowing players to type what they like), a full-sentence selection interface (familiar from dialogue tree-driven games like *Planescape: Torment*), and a short-answer selection interface (familiar from other dialogue tree-driven games, such as the *Mass Effect* series). Though the underlying processes were the same, and nothing else about the game was changed, we found that players had quite different experiences with these different implementations of the communicative aspect of the model. Players felt most involved in the story, and more motivated to move it forward, when using the interface offering them full sentences for their character to say. Players felt the most in control, and most able to influence the game, when using the short answer interface. And players felt most engaged (though most out of control) in the natural language interface.

These findings help emphasize the fact that there is no right answer when implementing logics and models—the question is which experience best serves the project's goals. A similar point is made by Alex Zook, via an analysis of Pokémon games: "Operational logics emphasize how processes execute and are intertwined. But ignoring the strategies for visualizing results downplays crucial aspects that influence player experience." While the lens of logics and models allows us to see the fundamental vocabulary of games, and how that vocabulary is commonly composed and employed, it can also disguise the importance of the decisions made in particular implementations.

See: Sali et al., "Playing with Words"; Zook, "Expanding Operational Logics."

87. I believe that Osborn's image is helpful—of players climbing a ladder of understanding operational logics, in order to reach understanding of the broader playable model(s). However, I think it is also important to note that travel on this ladder flows both directions. This is most obvious, perhaps, in the case of doubling, the subject of chapter 9. I believe it is the overloading of playable models that helps players understand that they should interpret the logics at play in an additional way.

88. Osborn, "Operationalizing Operational Logics," 110.

89. Cyan, *Myst*.

90. Thiel and Houshmand, *Beyond Manzanar*.

91. Demruth, *Antichamber*.

92. Will and Game Yarouze!, *Echochrome*.

93. Play can also reveal interactions between the rules and structures that game designers did not intend. In competitive combat games—ranging from collectible card games to first-person shooters—players can discover dominant strategies that reduce the fun and variety of play, leading to designers changing the behavior of cards/weapons in future iterations, or removing them entirely from the game.

94. Hofmeier, *Cart Life*.

95. Pedercini, "Videogames and the Spirit of Capitalism."

96. Molleindustria, *Unmanned*.

Chapter 5: Inventive Approaches

1. Rohrer, *Passage*.

2. I discuss such approaches, which I call expansive, in chapters 3, 8, and 9.

3. Inventive approaches can also bring an existing logic or model to a new type of game or platform or show a new way of formulating or using a logic or model.

4. McCoy et al., *Prom Week*.

5. Maxis Software, *The Sims*.

6. BioWare Edmonton, *Dragon Age: Origins*.

7. Aaron Reed notes (in personal communication, January 18, 2018) that ChoiceScript's "fair math" operates something like this, scaling addition and subtraction, so the change in 10 + 10 is much larger than the change in 80 + 10. See: Choice of Games, "Important ChoiceScript Commands and Techniques."

8. Creating *Prom Week,* and other games in this area, is walking down a path blazed by influential game designer (and founder of the Game Developers Conference) Chris Crawford. While *Façade* built on the interactive drama research pioneered by universities (including work led by Joe Bates at Carnegie Mellon University, Ken Perlin and Athomas Goldberg at New York University, Barbara Hayes-Roth at Stanford University, and Bruce Blumberg at MIT), it is Crawford, without institutional support, who pioneered thinking about general models of social interaction for games. He left the mainstream game industry to pursue this vision, published a number of influential writings on the subject (including the book *Chris Crawford on Interactive Storytelling*), and developed remarkable tools that embody his insights. Unfortunately, despite a successful early career in game design (including the seminal *Balance of Power*), Crawford has developed few games using his social interaction ideas, with only one game (as of this writing) released after 1991 (which has since been withdrawn from circulation). Even more unfortunately, in the summer of 2018 Crawford announced his retirement from the field, depriving us of the chance of future games that will embody his vision and knowledge. The one remaining hope seemed to be that his move to open source his software (announced the same summer) would inspire others to fruitful experimentation with his approaches.

However, a little over a year later, Crawford began to write about a new approach to interactive storytelling: retaining his language for character interaction but making encounters central to the experience. As he writes:

> I have already shown that a standard language could be used for statements of perceptions. That is, we already have a language system for statements as to how much a person likes, trusts, and dominates another person. So here's the issue: could we interleave a very detailed encounter system with a standard language system to permit a workable interactive storyworld?

As of this writing, Crawford's work in this direction has only begun. But it is exciting to have him active in the field again.

See: Kelso, Weyhrauch, and Bates, "Dramatic Presence"; Perlin and Goldberg, "Improv: A System for Scripting Interactive Actors in Virtual Worlds"; Hayes-Roth et al., "Directed Improvisation with Animated Puppets"; Blumberg and Galyean, "Multi-Level Direction of Autonomous Creatures for Real-Time Virtual Environments"; Crawford, *Chris Crawford on Interactive Storytelling*; Crawford, *Balance of Power: Geopolitics in the Nuclear Age*; Crawford, "Why I Am Ending Further Work on Interactive Storytelling"; Maya, "The Once and Future Storytron"; Crawford, "A New Approach."

9. Mateas and Stern, *Façade*.

10. In taking this approach to playable models of social volition, the project that became *Prom Week* was following the methods of "AI-based game design." See: Eladhari and Mateas, "Semi-Autonomous Avatars in World of Minds"; Eladhari, Sullivan, Smith, and McCoy, "AI-Based Game Design"; Treanor et al., "AI-Based Game Design Patterns."

11. McCoy and Mateas, "The Computation of Self in Everyday Life: A Dramaturgical Approach for Socially Competent Agents"; McCoy, Mateas, and Wardrip-Fruin, "Comme il Faut."

12. Goffman, *The Presentation of Self in Everyday Life*.

13. Berne, *Games People Play: The Psychology of Human Relationships*.

14. Gleicher, "Retargetting Motion to New Characters."

15. A fuller account of the design evolution of *Prom Week* can be found in the paper *"Prom Week*: Designing Past the Game/Story Dilemma." More details of the underlying AI system can be found in the journal article "Social Story Worlds with Comme il Faut." Much more detailed information (ranging from source code to internal development email messages) is available in the archive and oral history developed by Eric Kaltman, found in the University of California's Merritt digital archive. A fuller discussion of Kaltman's methodology and lessons learned for archival practice can be found in the report "A Unified Approach to Preserving Cultural Software Objects and Their Development Histories." See: McCoy et al., *"Prom Week*: Designing Past the Game/Story Dilemma"; McCoy et al., "Social Story Worlds With *Comme il Faut*"; Kaltman, "UC3 Merritt: Collection—UCSC Library *Prom Week* Development Archive"; Kaltman et al., "A Unified Approach to Preserving Cultural Software Objects and Their Development Histories."

16. Reiss, *The Normal Personality: A New Way of Thinking about People*.

17. As Mike Treanor puts it in his dissertation:

> Through the development process and playtesting, we discovered that social exchanges solely driven by psychological needs were unintuitive and hard to communicate or justify to players. Particularly, the abstracted social exchanges performed by the characters did not match the exchanges that were anticipated by the play testers given the characters' basic needs. For example, having a need to be embarrassed resulting in a desire to engage in a flirt action was unintuitive.

See: Treanor, "Investigating Procedural Expression and Interpretation in Videogames," 101.

18. McCoy et al., "Comme il Faut 2."

19. McCoy et al., "Social Story Worlds with *Comme il Faut.*"

20. I believe the potential for a family of "ranked-choice" logics was suggested by Joseph C. Osborn. Turning to rule evaluation, there are, of course, many AI approaches that depend on the evaluation of rules. But if we posit a category of rule-evaluation logics, the key is that they must operate both in terms of process and communication. In other words, simply having something operate in the background of a game that evaluates rules (like a production system) is not enough. There must also be a way that players come to understand this as part of the game: a way to understand that rules are being evaluated and what goes into that evaluation.

The names and scopes of these logics might become clearer as the theory of AI logics is developed, but this chapter presents my current thinking.

21. Choosing among them randomly is, in fact, the default approach of James Ryan's Hennepin system, described further in endnote 35 in this chapter.

22. Another addition to the system, as we developed our understanding through the process of creating *Prom Week,* was the creation of "microtheories" of different areas of social life—so that these rules could be applied to all exchanges for which these theories were relevant. See: McCoy et al., "Comme il Faut."

23. Waters, *Mean Girls.*

24. Star, *Sex and the City.*

25. McCoy et al., "Authoring Game-Based Interactive Narrative Using Social Games and *Comme Il Faut.*"

26. Specifically, as Mike Treanor writes:

> Each relevant microtheory rule that was relevant to a character's intent or hypothetical response was broken down by predicate, and presented in order of significance to the player as text that represented the predicate. The predicates were sorted by bucket and given a weight by evenly divid[ing] the weight of the overall microtheory rule (or social consideration). (Personal communication, October 4, 2018.)

27. Our play testers had shown that there were many satisfyingly different ways to shape the social world to achieve combinations of the goals we had authored, which were then reflected in different, dynamically constructed endings at that level's version of the prom. But even more excitingly, they had shown it was possible to imagine and achieve social goals we hadn't foreseen. For example, one player reported feeling angered by the actions of Monica, one of the leaders of

the school's popular clique. He manipulated the social world so that two of the goth students—Edward and Mave—became friends with the popular students, imparting additional social power to themselves and all their friends. Then he destroyed the friendships of the once-popular clique, turning them into loner outsiders. As Reed puts it in his dissertation, "The sequence culminated with Monica the cheerleader desperately asking Edward, the now-popular goth, to be her date to the prom—and Edward rejecting her for not being popular enough. The player had gained enough of an understanding of the dynamics of the social simulation to manipulate it to turn the tables, creating a delightful power-play story about one clique overthrowing another that none of the designers had anticipated." See: Reed, "Changeful Tales," 197.

28. Pearson, "Impressions."

29. Stephens, "*Prom Week*."

30. Some players also told us stories of feeling bad initially, then feeling better. For example, I was a guest speaker in Kimberly Lau's undergraduate class at UC Santa Cruz in spring 2013, and the students played *Prom Week* in anticipation of my visit. During the conversation I was particularly struck by one student's story of playing the game. I wrote to the *Prom Week* team about it, saying:

> She chose to play a character's story because the description reminded her of herself in high school. But then the experience of play really didn't go the way she wanted—she ended up feeling backed into a corner, in a relationship with Buzz that she couldn't make better. It felt unfortunately close to her actual experience of high school and she found herself wondering, "Is that it, then? Is this inevitable?" (Personal communication, June 2, 2013.)

But then she told the class about going back to the game and trying again. She experimented with different choices and discovered different potential directions for the character's life. She told us how finding that those options were there and pursuing them in different directions removed the feeling of oppressive inevitability and brought her joy—which to me was moving to hear. As I wrote to the team, "Playing *Prom Week* seemed to genuinely provide her an emotionally deep way of engaging with a character's situation, thinking back on her own life, and re-seeing both of them through the possibilities of the system." This kind of system-enabled self-reflection is part of what I find exciting about the future potential of social simulation, interactive storytelling, and new genres of games.

31. The Tiniest Shark, *Redshirt*.

32. Roddenberry, *Star Trek*.

33. Reed, "Changeful Tales," 210.

34. Some felt Khandaker was unnecessarily shaving the sharp edges from her satire. She explained that her goal was not to create further discomfort for those who have experienced sexism and racial fetishization and that the bigotry slider had always been present. See: Alexander, "Learning about Community and Inclusiveness with *Redshirt*."

35. Another approach, which currently requires using a simplified social model, is that of simulating large casts of characters, rather than focusing on the experience of a small number of

characters. James Ryan's Hennepin system uses a volition model that makes it possible to choose actions for each character with less computational cost by focusing only on these elements: eliminating inappropriate actions, unlocking actions when necessary conditions are met, and queuing and prioritizing key actions. And by sifting through the intersecting actions of large casts of characters, Ryan is certainly able to discover compelling dramatic situations. But Ryan's aesthetic is also one that is willing to sacrifice some individual character believability in exchange for efficiencies that enable much larger casts and timescales. For example, in this system he is willing to accept one character searching for another at a place that they should know does not exist, which would only be acceptable for scatterbrained, demented, or highly distressed characters in a more "zoomed in" social simulation. See: Ryan, "Curating Simulated Storyworlds," 628–629.

36. Flanagan et al., *LAYOFF*.

37. Monolith Productions, *Middle-Earth: Shadow of Mordor*.

38. Little Story People, *Blood & Laurels*.

39. *Blood & Laurels* was not the first game created with Versu. A small collection was released in 2013 (at the same time the tools were announced) in a "Jane-Austen-esque Regency England" setting, and other small episodes were created in other settings. But *Blood & Laurels* was by far the most ambitious game released using Versu. See: Evans and Short, "Versu—A Simulationist Storytelling System."

40. Though it is also interesting to note, as Reed does in his dissertation, that all three of the (quite different) game designs of *Prom Week, Redshirt,* and *Blood & Laurels* lead to experiences that have much in common with a particular tradition of fiction. As Reed argues, "Since most content for social simulations is written for patterns of interaction, rather than specific characters, what arises perhaps unsurprisingly tends to be stories more about a particular social milieu than specific characters within it. In fact, social simulation's focus on rules, large casts of characters (to best show off the system), and primarily social actions gives it much in common with the existing dramatic tradition of the comedy of manners." See: Reed, "Changeful Tales," 224–225.

41. Another interesting technical difference is that Versu forward-simulates (making the game's world take a step forward) as part of its evaluation of actions, while CiF characters evaluate solely based on their own desires—making them more likely to take actions that go wrong for them. We might see this as the integration of an additional logic into the social volition model. For a more detailed comparison, see Reed, "Changeful Tales," especially section 5.3.2.

42. Short argues that, in retrospect, *Blood & Laurels* needed to do more to communicate to players, noting that "a lot of what didn't work was about communicating world state." This has informed her work on Character Engine at Spirit AI, which can employ both highly dynamic text output (to communicate through performance) and dynamically suggested menu options (to communicate through interface).

Conversely, as Alex Mitchell notes, there is a consequence of our focus on communication and enabling strategic play in *Prom Week*. Specifically, the framing of *Prom Week* as a set of levels, each with goals, and with a foregrounding of the social knowledge needed to take action results in the feel of a puzzle game (we called it a "social strategy game"), rather than the feeling of ongoing narrative flow in *Blood & Laurels*. As Mitchell puts it, "What I was beginning to understand was the correspondence between character actions and changes in character relationships within the social simulation, changes that lead towards achievement of the goals set by the system. There is, however, no modelling or representation here of any *story* structure."

See: Short, "Conversation as Gameplay (Talk)"; Mitchell, "Reflective Rereading and the *SimCity* Effect in Interactive Stories."

43. Oliveira and Santos, "A Model for Socially Intelligent Merchants."

44. Morais, Dias, and Santos, "From Caveman to Gentleman."

45. Evans and Short, "Versu—A Simulationist Storytelling System."

46. Sullivan et al., "The Design of Mismanor"; Sullivan, "The Grail Framework: Making Stories Playable on Three Levels in CRPGs."

47. Samuel et al., "The Ensemble Engine."

48. Treanor, McCoy, and Sullivan, "A Framework for Playable Social Dialogue."

49. The open source Ensemble release uses the BSD-4-Clause (University of California-Specific) license and is currently located at https://github.com/ensemble-engine/ensemble.

Chapter 6: Understanding Games through Logics and Models

1. Rockstar North, *Grand Theft Auto IV*.

2. Wardrip-Fruin, *Expressive Processing*.

3. BioWare Corporation, *Star Wars: Knights of the Old Republic*.

4. As a general rule, player choices in *GTA IV* do not have an impact on the plot. See: Taylor, "*Grand Theft Auto IV*—Plot Guide."

5. Mateas, "A Preliminary Poetics for Interactive Drama and Games."

6. Frasca, "Sim Sin City—Some Thoughts about *Grand Theft Auto 3*."

7. DMA Design Limited, *Grand Theft Auto III*.

8. Rockstar North, *Grand Theft Auto: Vice City*.

9. Rockstar North, *Grand Theft Auto: San Andreas*.

10. Bogost, *Persuasive Games: The Expressive Power of Videogames*.

11. Bogost, 114.

12. Bogost, 13.

13. Leonard, "Young, Black (& Brown) and Don't Give a Fuck," 267.

14. Leonard, 251.

15. Dyer-Witheford and de Peuter, *Games of Empire*, 156.

16. Dyer-Witheford and de Peuter, 163.

17. Harrell, *Phantasmal Media*.

18. Dizikes, "Building Culture in Digital Media."

19. Munroe, "*My Trip to Liberty City*."

20. Malaby, "Beyond Play," 103.

21. Sicart, "Against Procedurality."

22. Grand Theft Wiki, the GTA wiki, "Swingset Glitch."

23. This computational nature, and its relation to rule breaking, is also foregrounded in McKenzie Wark's *Gamer Theory*—which takes the *GTA* franchise entry *Vice City* as the focus of its chapter "Atopia." Wark writes of *Vice City* as a game in which, though it appears to be about transgression, it is not possible to break the rules. For Wark, it is a game in which every move to break the rules is merely a move into a different game, which might be seen as another way of calling attention to the inescapability of the game's logics and models, but it is not simply that. Wark's interpretation of *Vice City* runs along similar lines to Frasca's of *GTA III*—focusing on it as an algorithmic simulation. But for Wark this is the starting point for connecting *Vice City* to politics and culture in a particular way. For Wark, just as utopic writing points to what has power to remake the world of its time, so does the atopian game in our time. By pointing to the increasingly computational, gamelike nature of the world in which we live when not explicitly playing a game (which she calls "gamespace"), and by offering "a safe haven in which to enact the problem of being" in our contemporary world, *Vice City* points to something culturally urgent.

In order to engage this, Wark points us toward something beyond the rather simple framing of defying designer-imposed rules. Instead, she suggests a "subjective, intuitive, particular" approach to play and theory that engages the contemporary world through games. Wark's book might be seen as her example of how to do this as a trained critical theorist. Turning (in the next section) away from the *GTA* games, looking at another game series and its broader context, will help show how everyday players, even children, have long engaged in analogous approaches to play.

See: Wark, *Gamer Theory*, 118, 123, 124.

24. Murray, "High Art/Low Life," 97.

25. Maxis Software, *The Sims*.

26. Flanagan, *Critical Play*.

27. Forman-Brunell, *Made to Play House: Dolls and the Commercialization of American Girlhood, 1830–1930*.

28. Flanagan, *Critical Play*, 32.

29. Flanagan, 33.

30. Machinima is the practice of using games, or game engines, to produce video that may or may not be eventually presented as taking place in a game. Fan fiction is the practice of writing (or otherwise creating) fiction set in the world of, and sometimes featuring the characters of, a fiction of which one is a fan.

31. Flanagan, *Critical Play*, 333.

32. Burkinshaw, "Alice and Kev."

33. The Sims Studio, *The Sims 3*.

34. This is different from the "social volition" model discussed for *Prom Week* (in chapter 5) in two respects. First, most obviously, it is not focused on social behavior. Second, while it includes logics from the same families (rule evaluation and ranked choice) it operates over a much simpler structure (primarily focused on the state of a handful of needs, and notably missing detailed history) in order to select simpler actions (which cannot, for example, include third parties).

35. *The Sims 4* primarily changed the AI system by enabling characters to carry out multiple simultaneous actions and transition between actions more naturally, rather than through deepening of how actions are selected. See: Ingebretson and Rebuschatis, "Concurrent Interactions in *The Sims 4*."

36. Burkinshaw, "Selflessness."

37. At the same time, this moment also poses the question of whether Burkinshaw will let the experiment continue—letting the systems of *The Sims 3* determine most of what happens to the characters (beyond the initial setup). As Mirjam Palosaari Eladhari puts it:

> Burkinshaw expresses in the text how his role as author/player becomes dramatic by the need to make a choice—he doesn't want Alice to give the money away, but lets her anyway, allowing her to act according to her character. Readers of Burkinshaw's text who have also played *The Sims 3* know what Burkinshaw is alluding to when Alice is "as exhausted as it is possible to be," and what it means within the game rules that Alice has a wish. This adds to the degree of enjoyment when comparing and discussing the unique narrative experiences from the same game.

This observation ties in with Max Kreminski's investigations of how games like *The Sims 3*—with large, generative possibility spaces—can be engaged as storytelling partners, helping address a number of traditional barriers to creative work.

See: Eladhari, "Re-Tellings"; Kreminski and Wardrip-Fruin, "Generative Games as Storytelling Partners."

38. Returning to the *GTA* games, complicity is also a useful approach to understanding their structure and play, especially as the series has progressed. We can see the erosion of avenues for critical play over time—for example, the re-skinning that Munroe exploits so well in *GTA III* is removed as a supported option by *GTA IV* (instead requiring a player-created game modification). We can also see the developers increasingly emphasizing the inflexible story logic of the mission system. By *GTA V*, the most recent game as of this writing (which I have decided not to play), the

only major story choice is between three endings, and opting out of the mission logic is strongly discouraged. Players are steered toward the missions by the way the game is positioned culturally, with marketing focused on the story of its three playable characters. They are similarly steered systemically, with the money resource hard to come by in the game's initial state, a situation they can change by beginning to progress along the path of the missions. And the acts that must be committed to continue this progression appear aimed toward cheap shock and disgust. The most attention has been given to the mission featuring torture, but more broadly one of the characters the player controls is now explicitly, violently mentally unstable. As Leigh Alexander writes:

> For a game defined by its attitude to freedom and openness, it gives you very little liberty to escape its structure. You can go for a drive, or play tennis or do yoga, but you're delaying the inevitable.
> To make progress, you eventually submit . . .

The *GTA* games are discussed as though they hold up a mirror for the souls of players. But a mirror allows for making many expressions—something that past *GTAs* did on a level closer to the *Sims* games. Now the *GTA* games appear to have devolved into something closer to a clown makeup version of Milgram's compliance experiments. Like Burkinshaw's play of *The Sims 3*, the question is one of complicity. But the question isn't what you might do to stop suffering over which you have power. Rather, it is how far you will go along with inflicting suffering on behalf of a bully who claims it is all in good fun.

This is not just a matter of what happens in the *GTA V* story. *GTA V* could arrange its logics and models differently and achieve a very different effect. Games like *Skyrim* also balance a simulated world and a relatively linear story progression. But *Skyrim* not only uses a different story logic (akin to that of *Star Wars: Knights of the Old Republic*), which makes it possible to offer the player more meaningful choices—it also makes living in the world, without pursuing the story or the core linear thread of the story, a more viable option.

See: *Grand Theft Auto IV* Message Board for PC, "Player Selector Mod / Play as Pedestrian Mod"; Franich, "Entertainment Geekly"; *GTA 5* Wiki Guide, "How to Make Money in *GTA 5*"; Alexander, "Opinion."

39. In addition to those who have contributed directly to these ideas, there are also those who have pursued related ideas—and even similar terms for different ideas. An example of the last of these, from outside my field, is James K. Feibleman's chapter "Of Operational Logic," which uses this similar term to name the elements of logic necessary to make computation possible. Within discussions of computational media, similar terms have also been used for different concepts. In Jeremy Douglass's 2007 dissertation he writes: "When I say that implied code models 'operational logic' I mean a set of behaviors on the part of software, whether perceived by the user as tendencies, rules, or laws." In Sarah T. Roberts's 2018 article "Digital Detritus" she writes, "Obfuscation and secrecy work together to form an operating logic of opacity around social media moderation." I highly recommend the work of Douglass and Roberts, even if our use of similar terminology for different concepts may produce some confusion.

See: Feibleman, "Of Operational Logic"; Douglass, "Command Lines"; Roberts, "Digital Detritus."

40. Something similar can be seen in models of computational media that are not specific to games. For example, in *Cybertext,* Espen Aarseth proposes that we attend to the "textual machine" as a triangle, with the operator, medium, and verbal sign each at a corner. While the analogy is not exact, we could think of the game player(s), system, and media data (models, animations, sounds, text, etc.) as occupying the corners of a similar triangle. See: Aarseth, *Cybertext: Perspectives on Ergodic Literature.*

41. Juul, *Half-Real: Video Games between Real Rules and Fictional Worlds.*

42. Hunicke, LeBlanc, and Zubek, "MDA: A Formal Approach to Game Design and Game Research."

43. Koster, "A Grammar of Gameplay: Game Atoms: Can Games Be Diagrammed?"

44. For example, his presentations at PAX Dev 2015 and the 2017 Game UX Summit. See: Koster, "Game Grammar"; Koster, "(Dis)Assembling Experience."

45. There are also a variety of other ways that Koster's atoms differ from operational logics, not all of which are worth enumerating here. For example, the operational logics approach breaks out direct player control into a separate logic. Players can see and understand logics at work (for example, collision) without being able to control any of the entities involved at the time.

46. Koster, *A Theory of Fun for Game Design.*

47. Koster writes, in discussing his work relative the MDA framework, "We're especially leaving out aesthetics." Nis Bojin, in 2010, argued for attention to the uses of Koster's game design atoms, rather than simply cataloging them divorced from their conventional uses, which nicely complements the operational logics approach. See: Koster, "A Grammar of Gameplay: Game Atoms: Can Games Be Diagrammed?"; Bojin, "Ludemes and the Linguistic Turn."

48. Dormans, "Engineering Emergence."

49. Dormans, 208.

50. Bura, "Emotion Engineering."

51. Lazzaro, "Why We Play: Affect and the Fun of Games."

52. Bura, "Emotion Engineering," 4.

53. Parker Brothers, *Monopoly.*

54. Adams and Dormans, *Game Mechanics.*

55. Magie, *The Landlord's Game.*

56. Galloway, *Gaming: Essays on Algorithmic Culture*, 91.

57. Wark, *Gamer Theory*, 30–32.

58. Bogost, *Unit Operations: An Approach to Videogame Criticism.*

59. Specifically, Mike Treanor's semiotics-inspired method of analyzing games that depend on graphical logics, particularly collision detection, is discussed in chapter 10.

60. Huber, "The Foundations of Videogame Authorship," 32.

61. Kreimeier, "The Case for Game Design Patterns"; Bjork and Holopainen, *Patterns in Game Design*.

62. Perhaps the closest previous work is Ian Bogost's on "unit operations"—which he was developing at the same time as my initial work on operational logics. But Bogost's concept is much broader. As Michael Mateas and I argued in 2009:

> Operational logics are more specific to computational systems than concepts such as Bogost's of the "unit operation," which creates a foundation for "any medium—poetic, literary, cinematic, computational" to be "read as a configurative system, an arrangement of discrete, interlocking units of expressive meaning" (2006, ix).

See: Bogost, *Unit Operations: An Approach to Videogame Criticism*; Wardrip-Fruin, "Playable Media and Textual Instruments"; Mateas and Wardrip-Fruin, "Defining Operational Logics."

63. Murray, *On Video Games*.

64. This initially prompted legal action from the game's publisher, before a slew of online complaints from players (and a dramatic lowering of the game's online ratings) led to a walkback. See: Wehner, "*Grand Theft Auto 5* Publisher Rockstar Learns What Happens When You Mess with PC Gamers." (I am indebted to Jacob Garbe and Melanie Dickinson for drawing my attention to the *GTA V* role-playing scene.).

65. Sometimes they're also ex-cabbies, posing as journalists but acting as criminals, as Joe Donnelly reports for *PC Gamer*. See: Donnelly, "I Robbed a String of Banks Unarmed by Posing as a Journalist in a *GTA 5* Roleplaying Server."

66. Some players attempt to role-play situations that aren't supported by *GTA V*'s existing models and logics, but this requires leaning harder into the interpersonal aspects of role-playing. Players who already have role-playing experience from other contexts may be more likely to do this successfully. For example, James Dator, in *Polygon*, tells the story of Chris Cone, who reports, "I've been consistently role-playing since I was seven years old." Cone played enough on the "Legacy RP" server to be able to create an opportunity to move beyond the logics and models of *GTA V*.

> He joined the Legacy RP police force, and quickly dedicated himself to the RP like a full-time job. Cone, a student with aspirations of becoming a full-time streamer, worked eight- to twelve-hour shifts five times per week, handing out traffic citations, trying to arrest drug runners, and occasionally being called to armed robberies.
> The dedication led to a promotion, and Cone became a junior detective. The switch came with a new host of challenges. The system wasn't built for evidence gathering and case building, which forced him to use an imperfect system of collaborating with other players, rather than traditional *Grand Theft Auto* mechanics, to play out intense criminal investigations.

Cone's full story is fascinating to read, as he and other players attempt to negotiate this hybrid form of role-play. Cone is ambushed and shot—something *GTA V*'s logics and models handle easily. He attempts to investigate and build a case, which works out serendipitously, via role-play. Then he and other members of the police force raid the location of those responsible, which again is well-supported by *GTA V*. After this, however, they attempt to press charges, only to realize the planned charges would come with penalties that would ruin the role-playing of a whole group of other players. This draws in the importance of the metagame, where anything not supported by *GTA V*'s logics and models can become subject to debate. See: Dator, "The Life of a *Grand Theft Auto* Role-Player."

67. Boluk and LeMieux suggest that it is not only possible to approach video games as though they are not games (in order to make metagames) but that video games (without accompanying metagames) lack a key element necessary for games:

> Despite their colloquial designation and sale as games, video games do not have rules. Rules are voluntary constraints and social contracts. They are pacts between players not to peek or move outside invisible boundaries. Mechanics, on the other hand, are ontological operations. Players have no choice but to work within the limitations of these involuntary systems. Whereas rules can be broken at a moment's notice, mechanics cannot be turned off.

See: Boluk and Lemieux, *Metagaming*.

68. Webb, "*GTA V* RP is the Hottest Thing on Twitch Right Now."

Chapter 7: Inventing Graphical Logics

1. Sudnow, *Pilgrim in the Microworld*.

2. Sudnow, 37.

3. Sudnow, *Pilgrim in the Microworld*, 121–122.

4. Jon Robson and Aaron Meskin argue that just thinking in these terms (of the actions we wish to take, rather than the actions we wish to control the game in order to have characters or objects take) is evidence that most video games should be considered through the lens of their term "Self-Involving Interactive Fictions" (SIIFs). They write:

> Gamers typically make a variety of first-person claims concerning the games they are playing ("I defeated the dragon," "I was killed by the creeper," and so on), and this is reflected in the use of the generic second-person in much video-game criticism. We argue that this talk should be taken seriously; the player's actions genuinely make things *about the player* true in the fiction of the video game.

A number of objections have been raised to this position. For example, Stephanie Patridge has pointed out that we freely mix language that refers to the game with language that refers to the game's fictional world:

> For example, in playing *Monopoly* players might say "I've landed on Park Place, and now I'm bankrupt." Notice that we use the term "landed" here, rather than, say, "arrived." "Landed" is a game concept that refers explicitly to the piece stopping on a particular board space; it is not a concept that has a place in the imaginative world of *Monopoly*.

Robson and Meskin have argued that this is not incompatible with their position, as we see such mixtures in games of childhood make-believe, which are understood to be self-involving.

Picking up the example of childhood play, Nele Van de Mosselaer seeks to complicate the account of fictionality offered by Robson and Meskin:

> Imagine a child who is playing with a doll, imagining it to be a toddler, but not imagining herself to be part of the fictional world she imagines. She might imagine, for example, that the toddler can walk on its own, by pushing the doll forward. The girl thus pushes the representation of the toddler, imagining it to be a real toddler, but she does not fictionally push the toddler: fictionally, the toddler is walking on its own.

From the perspective of logics and models, on the other hand, we can set aside the question of what is fictional. Whether they view the actions in part through a fictional frame or not, players actually take actions through mechanics (as argued by Jesper Juul in *Half-Real,* and others). These actions are supported by logics and embedded in models. This is true of games that are not usefully considered in fictional terms—as Robson and Meskin write, "Insofar, then, as chess is not a fiction, it is not a SIIF." But players still say "I took his Queen" while playing chess. In short, when players say "I" did something in the game, it seems likely that this is because they took action, in addition to whatever possible fictional projection took place. The phenomenon of that action feeling natural, because the model has been deeply learned, is what Sudnow describes.

See: Robson and Meskin, "Video Games as Self-Involving Interactive Fictions," 167, 173; Patridge, "Video Games and Imaginative Identification," 182; Van de Mosselaer, "Fictionally Flipping Tetrominoes?"; Juul, *Half-Real: Video Games between Real Rules and Fictional Worlds.*

5. This is in contrast to other ways that the topic of space in games might be approached, without a focus on logics and models. To further specify what these chapters will discuss, all of them focus primarily on two-dimensional spatial models, rather than three-dimensional ones. They also focus almost exclusively on space as represented within the game, rather than wider spatial contexts (such as where players are located in the everyday world). And, finally, they also focus on general issues regarding spatial models and graphical logics, rather than the specifics of how space is used in particular genres or design patterns. For treatment of other issues, there is a wide history of work on game space, much of which has focused on 3-D space—though it also includes some treatment of special issues such as glitch spaces and the spaces of the "connection game" genre. Some places to begin include: Murray, *Hamlet on the Holodeck;* Aarseth, "Allegories of Space: The Question of Spatiality in Computer Games"; Wolf, *The Medium of the Video Game;* von Borries, Walz, and Böttger, *Space Time Play;* Nitsche, *Video Game Spaces;* Pearce, "Spatial Literacy: Reading (and Writing) Game Space"; Juul, *A Casual Revolution;* Huber, "Epic Spatialities: The Production of Space in *Final Fantasy* Games"; Pinchbeck, *DOOM.*

6. I am using the phrase *"just so" story* to describe a story that appears to explain what we observe, but attributes it to causes that are of unprovable, partial, or false validity.

7. Syzygy, *Computer Space.*

8. Atari, *Pong.*

9. While *Computer Space* is often referred to as a "failure," this is only true in comparison to the massive success of *Pong.* As Benj Edwards writes, "The game sold fairly well for the first commercial video game–estimates range from 500 to 1,000 units–but it was no blockbuster." See Edwards, "*Computer Space* and the Dawn of the Arcade Video Game."

10. Strachey described this work in multiple publications, including at the 1952 ACM National Conference. But to my knowledge he never gave a name to the resulting game, which may contribute to its relative obscurity. I have named it *M. U. C. Draughts* for purposes of this book, a name I welcome others to use. See: Strachey, "Logical or Non-Mathematical Programmes"; Strachey, "The 'Thinking' Machine."

11. Stephen Russell et al., *Spacewar!*

12. For ease of reading, titles ending in an exclamation point (such as *Spacewar!*, *Pitfall!*, and *Kaboom!*) are given without their exclamation points after their first use in the text of this book. Exclamation points are retained in bibliography entries and quoted material. This note is included after the first mention of a title that ends in an exclamation point in each chapter.

13. We experience these models as continuous, though, for modern games, at the level of implementation this is illusory, just as the continuity of movement in film is an illusion created by the use of many discrete frames. This distinction between discrete and continuous spatial models is different from the distinction between discrete screens of game content and continuous, scrolling screens of game content, as discussed by Clara Fernández-Vara, José Pablo Zagal, and Michael Mateas in "Evolution of Spatial Configurations in Videogames" and Mark J. P. Wolf in *The Medium of the Video Game*. The importance of this distinction is certainly not unique to video games. For example, as Jon Peterson describes in *Playing at the World*, differing spatial models is one of the primary distinguishing factors between miniatures-based war simulation games (continuous space) and those based on boards and counters (discrete space).

   The distinction is also not unique to spatial models. For example, Ernest Adams and Joris Dormans, in their discussion of discrete and continuous mechanics, note that physics and timing mechanics are often continuous, while internal economies (considered broadly) are generally discrete. You generally cannot pick up half a power-up.

   See: Fernández-Vara, Zagal, and Mateas, "Evolution of Spatial Configurations in Videogames"; Wolf, *The Medium of the Video Game*, 55–61; Peterson, *Playing at the World*; Adams and Dormans, *Game Mechanics*.

14. Activision, *Pitfall!*

15. Of course, playable models of space need not fall neatly into one of these two categories. In fact, spatial models need not even be presented as images. For example, they can be organized as graphs and presented as text, as in the original *Adventure* and the tradition of interactive fiction, which is discussed in the next chapter. In such games players type commands to move between spaces (which may be connected to an arbitrary number of other spaces) and to take actions within spaces. In terms of the core spatial model, in such games jumping (the example mechanic discussed with the other games, earlier) is an action performed in the undifferentiated space within a node of the graph.

16. Rovio Mobile, *Angry Birds*.

17. Higinbotham, Dvorak, and Potter, *Tennis for Two*.

18. Guins, *Game After*, 310.

19. Guins, 97–98.

20. In this case, "M. U. C." is for "Manchester University Computer." Strachey's love letter generator, which I believe is the first piece of electronic literature (and digital art of any kind) signed its creations "M. U. C." See: Wardrip-Fruin, "Digital Media Archaeology: Interpreting Computational Processes"; Wardrip-Fruin, "Christopher Strachey: The First Digital Artist?"

21. Higinbotham is generally credited with the game's design. He is also notable for being first chair of the Federation of American Scientists and a lobbyist for nuclear non-proliferation. He had previously done work (at the MIT Radiation Laboratory) on radar displays—the kinds of interactive screens that also inspired computing pioneers such as Douglas Engelbart. See: Brookhaven National Laboratory, "BNL | History: The First Video Game?"

22. The Vladar Company, *When Games Went Click.*

23. Guins, *Game After*, 272.

24. The logics in this section were first discussed in my "Playable Media and Textual Instruments," which did not formally name or define them. The full definitions were first introduced in "Defining Operational Logics," by Michael Mateas and myself, but have since been revised. One key revision is the removal of the notion of a "coordinate space" when discussing collision. As Nathan Altice pointed out, many early games and platforms that clearly implemented these logics did not do so using a coordinate space. Other changes include the collapsing of continuous movement and physics into one logic, the categorization of navigation as a type of control logic, and the removal of the notion of hierarchical logics. All of these changes are inspired (for Mateas and me) by work with Joseph C. Osborn. See: Wardrip-Fruin, "Playable Media and Textual Instruments"; Mateas and Wardrip-Fruin, "Defining Operational Logics"; Osborn, Wardrip-Fruin, and Mateas, "Refining Operational Logics."

25. Personal communication, June 30, 2017.

26. To be clear, I mean to indicate that *Tennis for Two* marks a still-incomplete version of this game design. I do not mean to suggest, however, that later games such as *Pong* were directly inspired by *Tennis for Two*, which was only rediscovered after the work of the Sanders team.

27. These mechanics depend on a general control logic, but neither provides the specific experience we associate with the "navigation" version of this logic.

28. Of course, gravity itself can be implemented at many levels of complexity and with varying relationships to everyday world phenomena. A more complex approach to gravity might use an abstract process in which all physical bodies attract one another. More complex approaches are uncommon, though not unheard of, in the spatial models of video games.

29. Brookhaven National Laboratory, "BNL | History: The First Video Game?"

30. Montfort and Bogost, *Racing the Beam.*

31. Brookhaven National Laboratory, "BNL | History: The First Video Game?"

32. Nelson, *Computer Lib/Dream Machines*.

33. Graetz, "The Origin of *Spacewar*," 56.

34. Computer History Museum, "Jack Dennis."

35. On the TX-0, for example, interactive computing pioneer Ivan Sutherland had just been getting the feel of working with a display and light pen the previous winter—setting the stage for his groundbreaking Sketchpad system. As Sutherland puts it, while working on the TX-0's display, "the idea began to grow in my mind that application of computers to making line drawings would be exciting and might prove fruitful." See: Sutherland, "Sketchpad, a Man-Machine Graphical Communication System," 24.

36. Digital Equipment Corporation, "PDP-1 Story"; Levy, *Hackers*.

37. Graetz, "The Origin of *Spacewar*," 61.

38. Supporting interaction is necessary, but not sufficient, for supporting playability.

39. *Spacewar* is also notable for most likely being the first game to include all three of the key elements that Steve Swink has identified for "game feel." Like *Tennis for Two*, it has Swink's "spatial simulation." The addition of the navigation logic contributes Swink's "real-time control." Finally, *Spacewar* has what Swink calls "polish": "any effect that artificially enhances interaction without changing the underlying simulation." We see polish, for example, when flames emerge from the back of the ships during thrusting. This is just a signal to the player and an enhancement of the visual presentation, as opposed to "interactions such as collisions, which feed back into the underlying simulation." You can't attack another player using the flames from your thruster. See: Swink, *Game Feel*, 5–6.

40. When it can't do what we want, however, the identification tends to break down. I say things like, "I went into the room and tried to open the connecting door, without a key, but you can't do that" (rather than "but I couldn't," which would have been the natural continuation if identification was maintained). Sudnow also describes how this identification does not exist before we learn how to play: "Then, with no sense that I was playing a game, not knowing who 'I' was among the various moving objects on screen, not even sure 'I' was there—without the slightest idea whether, why, or when whatever was happening would end, it was all over." As chapter 8 discusses, part of what is interesting about the *WarioWare* games is how they build on this phenomenon. See: Sudnow, *Pilgrim in the Microworld*, 5.

41. Keogh, *A Play of Bodies*, 14. For treatment of wider questions of embodiment, cognition, computational media, and the arts, see Penny, *Making Sense*.

42. Graetz, "The Origin of *Spacewar*," 64.

43. For more on the shape of *Spacewar*'s gravity well (and its shifts between versions) see Norbert Landsteiner's remarkable "Inside *Spacewar!*" Especially "Part 6: Fatal Attraction—Gravity." See: Landsteiner, "Inside *Spacewar!*—A Software Archeological Approach to the First Video Game."

44. Graetz, "The Origin of *Spacewar*," 64.

45. In addition to Edwards' contribution, *Spacewar* also benefited from Graetz adding a "hyper-space" capability (jumping players to a random location), Peter Samson adding a set of stars showing a section of the night sky as seen from Earth, and Alan Kotok and Robert A. Saunders creating custom controllers.

46. Graetz, "The Origin of *Spacewar*," 66.

47. Lowood, "Videogames in Computer Space," 7.

48. Brand, "*Spacewar*: Fanatic Life and Symbolic Death Among the Computer Bums"; Brand, *II Cybernetic Frontiers*.

49. Brand's article also describes some of the results of those who had created modifications and extensions to the original *Spacewar* in its first decade of release.

50. Graetz, "The Origin of *Spacewar*," 62.

51. Osborn et al., "Combat in Games."

52. There are many excellent discussions of game combat within game genres. This includes the wisdom of game designers in genres as old as tabletop war simulations and genres as comparatively new as first-person shooters. It also includes very detailed analyses by player communities, such as the "theorycrafting" of massively multiplayer online (MMO) game players and the training tools (from move databases to hitbox visualizers) of fighting game enthusiasts. But these discussions almost invariably take the specifics of their genre as given, then discuss combat within them—leaving aside any discussion of what "combat" in games is more generally, across genres.

53. Capcom, *Super Street Fighter II*.

54. Square, *Final Fantasy*.

55. Molleindustria, *Unmanned*.

56. Lowood, "Videogames in Computer Space."

57. While many accounts suggest Bushnell first encountered *Spacewar* at the University of Utah, Alexander Smith argues that this is highly unlikely:

> So, when did Nolan Bushnell first see the *Spacewar!* game? According to my own interview with Bushnell, when he relocated to the San Francisco area, he began attending several *Go* clubs, as he had recently become fascinated by the game in his later years at the University of Utah. At the Stanford University *Go* club, Bushnell met Jim Stein, who worked at the Artificial Intelligence Laboratory. In both our interview and the book *High Score*, Bushnell recounted how one day in 1969 Stein told him about the cool games available at the lab, where, as we saw previously, *Spacewar!* was an incredibly popular pastime. Bushnell states that he told his friend that he already knew of *Spacewar!*, but would love to play it again. Note how this recollection so closely mirrors the story in his deposition that a friend with the first name Jim with whom he played chess told him about all the cool games in the Utah computer center. I believe there is a high degree of likelihood that Bushnell took the true story of how he was introduced to the game at Stanford and tweaked it to take place earlier at Utah instead in order to show that his ideas predated those of Ralph Baer.

Smith's conclusion is in part based on research by Martin Goldberg, which Goldberg discusses at length in a blog post and also writes about briefly in footnote 13 of an article with

Devin Monnens. See: Smith, "The Book of Nolan"; Goldberg, "Nolan Bushnell and Digging up *Spacewar!*"; Monnens and Goldberg, "Space Odyssey: The Long Journey of *Spacewar!* from MIT to Computer Labs Around the World."

58. Lowood, "Videogames in Computer Space," 9.

59. Lowood, 12.

60. Wolf, "Abstraction in the Video Game," 49.

61. Price, "Social Science Research on Video Games," 114.

62. Montfort and Bogost, *Racing the Beam*, 7–9

63. Wolf, *Encyclopedia of Video Games*, 81.

64. Lowood, "Videogames in Computer Space," 10.

65. Kent, *The Ultimate History of Video Games*, 34.

66. Sito, *Moving Innovation: A History of Computer Animation*, 107–8.

67. Guins, *Atari Design: Impressions on a Cultural Form, 1972 - 1979*.

68. Glaser, "Before the Big Bang; The Space Age Game That Set the Stage."

69. Barton, *Vintage Games 2.0: An Insider Look at the Most Influential Games of All Time*, 9.

70. Cinematronics and Vectorbeam, *Space Wars*.

71. Barton and Loguidice, "The History of *Spacewar!*"

72. Baer, *Videogames: In the Beginning*, 18.

73. The Odyssey is a fascinating machine, with different games selected by the activation (or not) of different components on the board. In one version manufactured, these components can also be physically removed from the board, allowing (as Nathan Altice demonstrated during a talk at an Expressive Intelligence Studio meeting) the games to be altered during play. For example, the removal of a particular component removes a game's collision logic. The games are also designed to be both physical and electronic, with physical overlays meant to be placed on the television set and many games employing objects such as tokens, money, cards, and so on.

74. Lowood, "Videogames in Computer Space," 16.

Chapter 8: Refinement

1. Higinbotham, Dvorak, and Potter, *Tennis for Two*.

2. Stephen Russell et al., *Spacewar!*

3. For ease of reading, titles ending in an exclamation point (such as *Spacewar!*, *Pitfall!*, and *Kaboom!*) are given without their exclamation points after their first use in the text of this

book. Exclamation points are retained in bibliography entries and quoted material. This note is included after the first mention of a title that ends in an exclamation point in each chapter.

4. Atari, *Pong*.

5. Namco Limited, *Pac-Man*.

6. Crowther and Woods, *Adventure*.

7. For more on the original *Adventure* and its roots, see Jerz, "Somewhere Nearby Is Colossal Cave."

8. Montfort, *Twisty Little Passages: An Approach to Interactive Fiction*.

9. As well as one of the first doctoral dissertations on computer games, by Mary Ann Buckles, completed in 1985 at UC San Diego. The only earlier dissertation I know of is Thomas Malone's, completed in 1980 at Stanford University. See: Buckles, "Interactive Fiction"; Malone, "What Makes Things Fun to Learn?"

10. Synapse Software Corporation, *Mindwheel*.

11. For the story of this game, see Reith, "When Robert Pinsky Wrote a Video Game."

12. Montfort and Bogost, *Racing the Beam*.

13. Syzygy, *Computer Space*.

14. Kee Games, *Tank*.

15. Of course, the support that platform creators provide for particular logics may not be sufficient in all cases. And such support is also, itself, a technical resource, which game creators may use for purposes other than intended. Nathan Altice writes about such phenomena with the ColecoVision's VPD and Famicom/Nintendo Entertainment System's sprite 0:

> Finally, bit 5 of the VDP status register recorded the "Coincidence Flag," a catch-all collision detection that triggered if any two sprites onscreen shared an overlapping pixel. This limited functionality worked for only a small range of gameplay types where coincidence events were discrete. In cases where multiple collisions might happen simultaneously, its use was less practical.
>
> The Famicom had a coincidence flag of a different sort, governed by the status of sprite 0, the first entry in Object Attribute Memory. When a non-transparent pixel of sprite 0 overlapped with a non-transparent pixel of a background tile, bit 6 of $2002 set. Like the VDP's limited collision detection, sprite 0 had little practical import for conventional object collisions but proved useful for scanline timing and raster effects.

See: Altice, *I Am Error*, 357–358.

16. Montfort and Bogost, *Racing the Beam*, 48.

17. Montfort and Bogost, 49–50.

18. Atari, *Adventure*.

19. Atari, Consumer Division, *Adventure Game Program Instructions*, 3.

20. Namco Limited, *Dig Dug*.

21. Dunhill Electronics, *Tax Avoiders*.

22. Nintendo R&D1, *WarioWare, Inc.: Mega Microgame$!*

23. The "microgames" referred to in the title are the primary content of the game. Each presents a small scenario in which the player is asked to accomplish a simple goal, with limited available actions, in a small amount of time. However, the first time a microgame (or variant) is presented, it may be a challenge to understand the goal, the available actions, and/or the mappings of actions to on-screen entities.

24. Bally Midway Mfg., *Tapper*.

25. Gingold, "What *WarioWare* Can Teach Us about Game Design."

26. Intelligent Systems and Nintendo R&D1, *WarioWare: Touched!*

27. Intelligent Systems and Nintendo SPD, *WarioWare: Smooth Moves*.

28. The novel interactions would be experienced as alternative by players who have come to understand collision's communicative role very broadly, perhaps as "some physical interaction takes place" (after long exposure to once-expansive uses of collision). What can become conventional is further discussed in chapter 9.

Chapter 9: Doubling

1. Atari, *Pong*.

2. Atari, *Adventure*.

3. Rohrer, *Passage*.

4. Sterne, *Tristram Shandy: Authoritative Text, Contexts, Criticism*.

5. Dunhill Electronics, *Tax Avoiders*.

6. Bogost, *Persuasive Games: The Expressive Power of Videogames*.

7. Bogost, 3.

8. Bogost, 52.

9. Stephen Russell et al., *Spacewar!*

10. For ease of reading, titles ending in an exclamation point (such as *Spacewar!*, *Pitfall!*, and *Kaboom!*) are given without their exclamation points after their first use in the text of this book. Exclamation points are retained in bibliography entries and quoted material. This note is included after the first mention of a title that ends in an exclamation point in each chapter.

11. Mattie Brice describes something similar in *Passage*, and as a broader strategy for games, as players "drawing from the emergent narrative to extract meaning from their experience." See: Brice, "Alternate Ending."

12. These could be seen in general terms or through the specifically autobiographical framing Rohrer offers. If choosing the former, as Patrick Jagoda points out, one must contend with the fact that "the options for modes of living are here limited by parameters of White heteronormativity." In either case, the tradeoffs between activities, like other aspects of the game, may not be (through play, or in code) as described in Rohrer's widely cited artist's statement. See: Montfort, "PvP: *Portal* versus *Passage*"; Jagoda, "*Passage*," 27; Lederle-Ensign et al., "A Software Studies Approach to Interpreting *Passage*."

13. Rusch, *Making Deep Games*.

14. Rusch's book is not the only one to take on this topic, certainly. For example, the subject of chapter 3 of Bogost's *Persuasive Games* is metaphor in games and draws on Lakoff's work in particular. However, Bogost's chapter is strongly focused on the issue of ideological frames in games, while Rusch's book approaches metaphor more generally.

15. Minority Media, *Papo & Yo*.

16. SCE Studio Santa Monica, *God of War II*.

17. Rovio Mobile, *Angry Birds*.

18. Rusch, *Making Deep Games*, xxv.

19. Lakoff, "The Contemporary Theory of Metaphor."

20. Though Rusch often uses the language of simulation theory, which instead terms the real-world phenomenon being simulated the "source." For clarity, I will consistently use the CMT meaning of "source" here.

21. Humble, *The Marriage*.

22. Team Aha!, *Akrasia*.

23. Rusch, *Making Deep Games*, 59.

24. Rusch, 61.

25. Gibbs, "Evaluating Conceptual Metaphor Theory," 535–536.

26. In the particular case of "Theories are buildings," Gibbs notes that it can also be seen as a complex metaphor (combining "Persisting is remaining erect" and "Structure is physical structure") which motivates metaphorical inferences such as needing support, while not motivating those about HVAC, windows, and many other aspects of buildings. See: Gibbs, 537.

27. Or we may see someone moving beyond the bounds of normal metaphor use as creative, playful, and interesting. See: Gibbs, "Words Making Love Together."

28. Nintendo R&D1, *WarioWare, Inc.: Mega Microgame$!*

29. Anthropy, *Dys4ia*.

30. The major way that *Passage* departs from this tradition, as Rusch and Weise point out, is in the unusual shape and composition of the window in which we see the game. Of the window's shape, they write, "At all times you can only perceive a very limited section of the game world. Moving left and right, up and down allows you to explore it, but your perspective stays restricted. The effect is quite profound: you realize that you will never know what you are missing unless you go and find out." Of the window's composition, particularly its edges, they write:

> In *Passage,* LIFE is represented by a spatial metaphor. This space is visually restricted by "blurry edges," i.e. the pixels at the left and right edge of the screen appear to be scrambled. As you move, all the landscapes, obstacles, and objects you encounter seem to unscramble out of the blur in front of you and scramble again into the blur behind you. One reading that suggests itself: the scrambled left and right edges of the screen are a visual metaphor for the human cognitive experience of life, one in which a hazy future and a hazy past are expressed in scrambled pixels.

The effect of these visual metaphors is to help the presentation of the game work in tandem with both models created through the expansive approach. If the visual presentation was more traditional, it would be working to support only the spatial navigation model.

See: Rusch and Weise, "Games about LOVE and TRUST?," 93.

31. Rusch and Weise, "Games about LOVE and TRUST?"

32. Toy, Wichman, and Arnold, *Rogue.*

33. Adams and Adams, *Dwarf Fortress.*

34. Harrell, *Phantasmal Media.*

35. Harrell is building on the work of Joseph Goguen, whose semiotic work bridges the traditions of Saussure and Peirce.

36. Harrell, *Phantasmal Media,* 165.

37. thatgamecompany, *Journey.*

38. And there is yet another sense in which games can appear metaphorical, but not operate metaphorically at the level of playable models. For example, we might characterize the spaces of the game *Psychonauts* as "metaphorical," just as we have with the space of *Passage.* But because of the differences between alternative and expansive approaches to spatial models, they are not metaphorical in the same way.

In *Psychonauts* there is a framing space—a summer camp for psychics populated by campers, counselors, wildlife, and so on. But by far the most memorable spaces are game levels set inside the minds of characters who exist in the framing space. For example, a level set inside the mind of a security guard, "The Milkman Conspiracy," is a literally twisted suburban landscape (folding back on itself) populated by mysterious figures who require the player to don disguises to move into different areas. A rather different level, "Lungfishopolis," is set inside the mind of a mutated lungfish, with the player character taking on the role of a giant, city-destroying monster along the lines of Godzilla. In these levels, moving through them progressively reveals information about the mental problems of the characters in the framing space (a hypnotically induced personality with paranoid delusions in the first case, a mind control implant in the second) and completing the level brings resolution to the framing character's issues. The alternative uses of spatial models are inventive and funny, with metaphorical spaces providing an engaging way of uncovering and resolving fictional elements of the game. But even though these spaces are clearly metaphorical representations of the mental problems of characters (much more clearly metaphorical than *Journey*'s evocative but seemingly literal spaces) *Psychonauts*, like *Journey*, never builds a second interpretation of its spatial model through metaphor. Spatial movement and action do not correspond to different ways of engaging the underlying issues of its characters. So, while moving between two walls in *Passage* can be understood both spatially and as a life choice, and running into a wall can be understood both spatially and as a life impossibility, moving between two skyscrapers in Lungfishopolis is simply a spatial movement.

See: Double Fine Productions, *Psychonauts*.

39. Rusch, *Making Deep Games*.

40. Hofmeier, *Cart Life*.

41. Blizzard Entertainment, *Overwatch*.

42. Gingold, "What *WarioWare* Can Teach Us about Game Design."

43. Chew and Mitchell, "Bringing Art to Life," 13–14.

44. Anthropy and Clark, *A Game Design Vocabulary*, 170.

45. Quotation marks appear around "feminists" after the last verbal volley has been launched.

46. These expansive portions of *Dys4ia* use comparatively abstract graphics—Anthropy/the player is represented by a shield, rather than a humanoid figure. This helps turn the attention of players to the activity that is represented in the overloaded model, rather than to unhelpful questions such as, "Do people actually absorb speech with that part of their bodies?" It also gets around potential issues with representations of people that are treated as objects, as discussed in chapter 3 and the conclusion.

47. Pajitnov, *Tetris*.

48. Atari, *Breakout*, 1976.

49. Vist, "Cyborg Games," 64.

50. Flanagan et al., *LAYOFF*.

51. Othenin-Girard, "Bodies, Games, and Systems: Towards an Understanding of Embodiment in Games," 18–19.

52. Magnuson, "Playing and Making Poetic Videogames," 73.

53. Magnuson's approach resonates with Alex Mitchell's writing on "poetic gameplay," which Mitchell describes as "the structuring of the actions the player takes within a game, and the responses the game provides to those actions, in a way that draws attention to the form of the game, and by doing so encourages the player to reflect upon and see that structure in a new way."

At the same time, Magnuson's work is different in focus from Mitchell's in two ways. In one sense it is narrower, focusing on the lyric specifically, rather than the poetic more broadly. In another sense it is broader, focusing on ways of looking at poetic effects widely, rather than specifically focusing on those that produce defamiliarization. In further work, Mitchell and collaborators have gone definitively broader than Magnuson's focus on the lyric, including identifying an expanding number of poetic devices that operate not only in short, lyric experiences but also in narrative and other modes. See: Mitchell, "Making the Familiar Unfamiliar: Techniques for Creating Poetic Gameplay," 2; Mitchell, Sim, and Kway, "Making It Unfamiliar in the 'Right' Way"; Chew and Mitchell, "Bringing Art to Life."

54. dino (formerly nina), *Seasonal Mixtape*.

55. Namco Limited, *Pac-Man*.

56. Mateas and Wardrip-Fruin, "Defining Operational Logics," 7.

Chapter 10: Logic Structures

1. Atari, *Pong*.

2. Activision, *Kaboom!*; For ease of reading, titles ending in an exclamation point (such as *Spacewar!*, *Pitfall!*, and *Kaboom!*) are given without their exclamation points after their first use in the text of this book. Exclamation points are retained in bibliography entries and quoted material. This note is included after the first mention of a title that ends in an exclamation point in each chapter.

3. Treanor, Mateas, and Wardrip-Fruin, "*Kaboom!* is a Many-Splendored Thing."

4. Anthropy, *Dys4ia*.

5. Siecke, *Conversation Pong 1.0*.

6. Alexander et al., *Pongversation*.

7. Bookchin, *The Intruder*.

8. It is possible to argue that *Pong* is the design template for *BIT.TRIP BEAT*, in which players control a *Pong*-like paddle, moving up and down the screen to collide with a pattern of moving dots arranged to create a temporal pattern—therefore making it an example of *Pong* as a pattern-matching game. However, because there is no "opponent" paddle, careful examination reveals that *BIT.TRIP BEAT* is actually more similar to the design of *Kaboom*, simply with its orientation rotated into the *Pong* position. See: Gaijin Games, *BIT.TRIP BEAT*.

9. Barr, *PONGS*.

10. Pajitnov, *Tetris*.

11. Ruberg, *Video Games Have Always Been Queer*, 49.

12. Treanor, "Investigating Procedural Expression and Interpretation in Videogames," 21.

13. Frasca, *Kabul Kaboom!*

14. Bogost, *Persuasive Games: The Expressive Power of Videogames*, 43.

15. Sedgwick, *Between Men: English Literature and Male Homosocial Desire.*

16. Ruberg, *Video Games Have Always Been Queer*, 47–48.

17. Nintendo R&D1, *WarioWare, Inc.: Mega Microgame$!*

18. Gingold, "What *WarioWare* Can Teach Us about Game Design."

19. Taito Corporation, *Space Invaders.*

20. Namco Limited, *Galaxian.*

21. Nelson and Mateas, "Towards Automated Game Design"; Nelson and Mateas, "An Interactive Game-Design Assistant."

22. Miller, "WordNet."

23. Speer and Havasi, "Representing General Relational Knowledge in ConceptNet 5."

24. Nelson and Mateas, "An Interactive Game-Design Assistant."

25. Sullivan, Mateas, and Wardrip-Fruin, "QuestBrowser: Making Quests Playable with Computer-Assisted Design."

26. Toy, Wichman, and Arnold, *Rogue.*

27. Treanor et al., "Game-O-Matic"; Treanor et al., "The Micro-Rhetorics of Game-o-Matic."

28. Treanor, "Investigating Procedural Expression and Interpretation in Videogames," 49–54.

29. Treanor, 54.

30. Treanor, 37.

31. Konami Industry, *Frogger.*

32. Treanor, "Investigating Procedural Expression and Interpretation in Videogames," 52.

33. Summerville et al., "From Mechanics to Meaning"; Summerville et al., "Gemini." As of the completion of this book, most of these postdocs and students have moved on to assistant professor positions: Martens at North Carolina State University, Samuel at University of New Orleans, Summerville at Cal Poly Pomona, Osborn at Pomona College, and Harmon at Bowdoin College. Dickinson continues working with newer lab member Max Kreminski on further Gemini projects.

34. We are building on a new game description language called Cygnus (also developed by our project) and the "proceduralist readings" approach spearheaded by Treanor—which itself attempts to formalize aspects of the "mechanics, dynamics, aesthetics" framework (discussed in chapter 4) and approaches to computational expression developed by Bogost, Mateas, and me. Some of the reasoning that Gemini does about pairs of entities would have been possible in

Game-o-Matic. But Gemini's rules can also encode arbitrary readings about any set of entities, variables, or the game as a whole that were not previously expressible by any game generation system. See: Summerville et al., "From Mechanics to Meaning"; Treanor et al., "Proceduralist Readings"; Hunicke, LeBlanc, and Zubek, "MDA: A Formal Approach to Game Design and Game Research"; Bogost, *Persuasive Games: The Expressive Power of Videogames*; Mateas, "Interactive Drama, Art and Artificial Intelligence"; Wardrip-Fruin, *Expressive Processing*; Mateas and Wardrip-Fruin, "Defining Operational Logics."

35. And when multiple encounters with Wall Street must be won, or multiple Occupiers must be jailed, something non-spatial is obviously key.

36. Humble, "Game Rules as Art."

37. Humble, *The Marriage*.

38. Bogost, *Persuasive Games: The Expressive Power of Videogames*, ix.

39. Juul, "A Certain Level of Abstraction," 512.

40. The importance of the title of *The Marriage* is not an artistic problem, merely a problem for those who subscribe to what I am calling the "strong" version of procedural rhetoric. Many creators of largely abstract games (and other forms of abstract art) are comfortable with titles doing significant work to signal appropriate interpretations to readers. For example, as Jordan Magnuson writes of his game *Loneliness*:

> People have sometimes told me that *Loneliness* is a failure of a game because people cannot make sense of its central meaning without knowing the game's title. I think such comments are misguided because they seem to suggest that an abstract-platonic-mechanical-universal game about loneliness could exist somehow: that is, a kind of metaphoric game consisting only of figure, with no ground (or only ground, with no figure). In my mind it is the game's title that serves as the central ground for *Loneliness*'s intended meaning, producing a metaphor to the effect of, "loneliness is like this." That grounding is what allows the subsequent experience of playing the game, with its ambiguous symbolic representations and mechanics, to be interpreted and considered in a particular light. ("If this game is loneliness, then what are these squares? What is the meaning of these movements?" etc.) In other words, I believe that it is precisely *Loneliness*'s concrete title that allows it to succeed as a metaphoric game, rather than flounder as a mostly abstract one.

See: Magnuson, "Playing and Making Poetic Videogames," 67.

41. Begy, "Experiential Metaphors in Abstract Games."

42. Anderson, Karzmark, and Wardrip-Fruin, "The Psychological Reality of Procedural Rhetoric."

43. Frasca et al., *September 12th: A Toy World*.

44. k, *LIM*.

45. Vollmer et al., *Threes JS*.

46. Cirulli, "2048, Success and Me."

47. Adams, "Interview—Merritt Kopas."

48. Allen, "Video Games as Feminist Pedagogy," 71.

49. Porpentine, "Live Free, Play Hard."

50. Chess, "The Queer Case of Video Games."

51. Anderson, Karzmark, and Wardrip-Fruin, "The Psychological Reality of Procedural Rhetoric."

52. While merritt k has explicitly expressed support for players who interpret the game in light of their experiences of other kinds of passing (as in situations of disability or race), this is quite different from interpreting the game as encouraging conformity.

53. Osborn et al., "Is Your Game Generator Working?"

54. Samuel et al., "Leveraging Procedural Narrative and Gameplay to Address Controversial Topics."

55. Buchanan, "Top 10 Best-Selling Atari 2600 Games."

56. Though some care would need to be taken to explain what the enemy is throwing and how the player character deals with it. Perhaps grenades that can be dropped into a container that defuses them?

57. Taito Corporation, *Space Invaders*.

Chapter 11: Conclusion

1. Parker Brothers, *Monopoly*.

2. Hasbro Games, "Rule Book," 2.

3. Flanagan's and Ferraiolo's game is *Layoff*, discussed in chapter 3. Anthropy's *Pong* variant is included in *Dys4ia*, discussed in chapter 9. Treanor's *Kaboom* design sketches are discussed in chapter 10. For ease of reading, titles ending in an exclamation point (such as *Spacewar!*, *Pitfall!*, and *Kaboom!*) are given without their exclamation points after their first use in the text of this book. Exclamation points are retained in bibliography entries and quoted material. This note is included after the first mention of a title that ends in an exclamation point in each chapter.

4. Wikipedia, "List of Licensed and Localized Editions of *Monopoly*."

5. Koster, *A Theory of Fun for Game Design*, 167–169.

6. Koster's game was used as an example of an expansive approach to logics and models. But not all skinning is expansive. Many skinnings, not moving beyond what is commonly done, are simply conventional.

7. Pajitnov, *Tetris*.

8. Hocking, "Dynamics."

9. Romero, *Train*.

10. Atari, *Pong*.

11. 7th Level, *Monty Python*.

12. I am indebted to Barrett Anderson and Dylan Lederle-Ensign for bringing this example to my attention. (Personal communication, January 28, 2015.)

13. Flanagan et al., *LAYOFF*.

14. Koster, "ATOF *Tetris* Variant Comes True."

15. Treanor, "Newsgames—Procedural Rhetoric Meets Political Cartoons."

16. The possibility of "looking past" or "looking through" a game's theme or skinning raises a high-stakes issue in game studies. To consider one example, relatively early in the field's development Espen Aarseth wrote, "the dimensions of Lara Croft's body, already analyzed to death by film theorists, are irrelevant to me as a player, because a different-looking body would not make me play differently. When I play, I don't even see her body, but see through it and past it." Aarseth wrote this in an essay included in the volume *First Person* and also published online in a dedicated "First Person" section of the journal *electronic book review* (both of which Pat Harrigan and I coedited). Stuart Moulthrop responded in the same venues:

> Aarseth claims the pneumatic Lara Croft could be traded for a less salacious anatomy, leaving the game intact. . . . The player's engagement with the rule system—the "gaming situation"—matters far more than incidental details of the "gameworld."
>
> If these claims seem indisputable at face value it is only because they are alarmingly narrow. . . . Certainly one could swap Lara Croft for a digitized Rowan Atkinson without technically changing the feedback loop between player and program. It seems unlikely, though, that *Mr. Bean: Tomb Raider* would sell nearly as well to its primary audience. Lara Croft's physique may consist of raw data but it cannot be treated as such for critical purposes. While one may look past or through the avatar body during play, the significance of games as cultural forms goes beyond the player's time in the loop.

In time, Aarseth's claim of "looking through" came to be seen as a telling moment for the field. Brendan Keogh writes of it, in 2014, as an artifact of game studies' "purity complex" that manifests in part as a "historical hostility to critical and textual readings." Keogh argues that this leads to interpretations that fail to account for how players actually understand games:

> Claims . . . that Lara Croft's depiction in *Tomb Raider* as a human female matters less than what her body allows the player to do ignore the very fact that the player only considers "walk," or "run," or "jump" as viable options because Lara Croft is represented as a human being capable of such actions. Further, Lara Croft's representation as a human being suggests that the player should jump over the bottomless pit rather than fall into or float over it. . . . Audiovisual design, those elements of video game design that explicitly overlap with attributes of other media and which apparently mar the purity of video games, is fundamental to the player's comprehension of what actions a game affords.

For Keogh, one issue with the idea of "looking through" is that it points away from the engagement with video games and their players that he advocates, in which we adopt "a conception of the video game text as a hybrid of semiotics, actions, and systems." But beyond issues of scholarly insight, Keogh also argues that there is something destructive to the field in formalist approaches that imagine "looking through" audiovisual representations to focus on game systems:

> These critiques of Lara Croft are also significant for their implication that the gender of one of video games' most popular woman characters should be ignored. Formalist claims to a "purity" of the video game form

are inevitably hegemonic. To make sweeping, authoritative, a priori claims as to what a video game is at its core is only ever an act of exclusion, of determining that certain works and experience of those works are invalid.

Amanda Phillips (in 2020) takes Aarseth's discussion of Croft, and his "doubling down" response to Moulthrop's critique, as one of the key moments she analyzes in constructing an affective history of the game studies field. Specifically, she writes of it as part of an "emphatic rejection of the political under the guise of representation":

> [Aarseth's argument] merges the rejection of film theorists (established by *Game Studies* 1, no. 1) with a rejection of the political critique implicit when invoking Lara Croft's measurements, which were a source of early criticism by feminist (including feminist game studies) critics. When pressed on the inextricability of representation and game play in the case of Lara Croft, the author doubles down on the strict separation between representation and game play in an early instance of asserting what Brendan Keogh calls the "purity complex of game studies." We may attribute this purity to a real concern with theoretical rigor, as the ludologists consistently claimed, but it is impossible to separate this from the political context of video games in larger society.

As Phillips convincingly argues, such attitudes from voices widely regarded as foundational in game studies—aired most strongly during the "ludology/narratology debate" that *First Person* in part documents—have served to create a pervasive sense that the field is, and should be, quite narrow. Not only narrow methodologically, but in terms of who is welcome within it. As a result, while some of the impact of this debate may be methodological,

> the affective structures it has embedded in the field imaginary are arguably more lasting, and more detrimental. From Vossen's interview subjects expressing reluctance to do feminist work in the field to the generalized sense of anxiety and exasperation still expressed in private circles by scholars of marginalized identities, most of which cannot and will never be published or citable in the official record of the field, many of us feel the effects on our work and our embodied positions in the academy every single day.

In short, while players at times may feel as though they "look through" a game's skin or theme, perhaps particularly when it is nonsensical or highly familiar, as those who seek to understand and design games we must find ways to consider games as wholes (as procedural representations that are embedded in cultures and operated and interpreted by players). We must also find ways to broaden the methodologies, games, and people that we take as important to the field.

See: Aarseth, "Genre Trouble: Narrativism and the Art of Simulation"; Aarseth, "Genre Trouble"; Moulthrop, "From Stuart Moulthrop's Online Response"; Moulthrop, "Stuart Moulthrop's Response"; Keogh, "Across Worlds and Bodies"; Phillips, "Negg(at)Ing the Game Studies Subject."

17. id Software, *DOOM*.

18. Serious Games Interactive, *Playing History 2*.

19. I am indebted to Espen Aarseth, Michael Debus, Pawel Grabarcyk, and José Pablo Zagal for drawing my attention to the example of *Playing History 2* and that of *Sex Tetris*, discussed in the main text. (Personal communication, May 24, 2018.)

20. Egenfeldt-Nielsen, "Clarifications on the Game."

21. Thomas, "I Played 'Slave *Tetris*' so Your Kids Don't Have To."

22. Raven Software, *Heretic*.

23. Rogue Entertainment, *Strife*.

24. Digital Cafe, *Chex Quest*.

25. 2K Boston and 2K Australia, *BioShock*.

26. While "environmental storytelling" is the more common term, I find Clara Fernández-Vara's concept of "indexical storytelling" a more useful one—both because it is broader and because it moves beyond the assumption (borrowed from theme park design) that the audience's role is almost purely interpretive. As she writes in "Game Spaces Speak Volumes: Indexical Storytelling":

> Indices, however, can be more than sheer markers pointing the player towards what she has to do, but encourage her to interpret and reconstruct the events that have taken place in the space. Moreover, players can also leave their own indices on the space, creating opportunities not only for storytelling, but also for narrative gameplay.

See: Fernández-Vara, "Game Spaces Speak Volumes: Indexical Storytelling," 5.

27. For an account of *BioShock*'s elevation to the status of "important game," see Parker, "Canonizing *Bioshock*."

28. Even Hocking, who offered a then-rare critique of the fit between its elements—"*Bioshock* seems to suffer from a powerful dissonance between what it is about as a game, and what it is about as a story"—and coined the term "ludonarrative dissonance" in his critique, doesn't mention how much more it focuses on shooting than storytelling. Likely due to how (sadly) common this is.

One of the few exceptions is Ian Bogost. Writing later (in a review of *Gone Home*) Bogost points out: "The problem is, *Bioshock* never really deserved the praise it received. It posed as a serious, hard science fiction take-down of the doomed hubris of technophilic selfishness, but in truth the game was just a spruced-up first-person shooter. Its engagement with morality and politics was window dressing, its apparent critique of Randian Objectivism mostly allegorical hand-waving."

Or as Brendan Keogh puts it:

> In 2007, the very presence of themes made *Bioshock* a relatively "smart" game to an audience of players who had never had to deal with these things before. Stuff like objectivism and the idea of being financially rewarded if you are mean to people and not being rewarded if you are nice really felt like a big leap in maturity for games to make. *Bioshock* convinced a lot of people that games could be smart not because it was the smartest game ever made, but because it was the smartest game a lot of us had ever played. *Bioshock Infinite*'s biggest problem is that it is not 2007 anymore.

See: Hocking, "Ludonarrative Dissonance in *Bioshock*"; Bogost, *How to Talk about Videogames*, 173; Keogh, "Notes on *Bioshock Infinite*."

29. Irrational Games, *BioShock Infinite*.

30. Bernstein, "Why We Can't Talk about *BioShock Infinite*."

31. For example, as Brendan Keogh observes, when the underground movement of oppressed minorities turns into a group of crazed killers, "*Bioshock Infinite* says, intentionally or not, that

Columbia—that America—is right to fear and oppress the non-white person because these people are naught but savage beasts. *Bioshock Infinite* says that Columbia's racism, built upon a fear of the Other, is justified." This design decision is not excused by the requirement that FPS games continually provide new waves of enemies to kill. But it is partially explained by it.

Further, unlike some action games, *BioShock Infinite* does not make it possible to explore its spaces (in which many of its story elements are embedded) while avoiding killing through its FPS combat model. As Amy M. Green notes, "*BioShock Infinite* offers no stealth mechanism for sneaking by enemies or avoiding combat. At best, a player could try to run past enemies in certain areas, but in many cases, all enemies must be defeated before Booker and Elizabeth can move on. Booker remains a killer."

See: Keogh, "Some Preliminary Thoughts on *Bioshock Infinite*'s Racism"; Green, "The Play Versus Story Divide in Game Studies."

32. Alexander, "Irrational Games, Journalism, and Airing Dirty Laundry."

33. Alexander, "*BioShock Infinite*."

34. Bernstein, "Why Is *Bioshock Infinite* A First-Person Shooter?"

35. The Fullbright Company, *Gone Home*.

36. Everything Unlimited, Ltd., *The Beginner's Guide*. Alternatively, one could argue that the spaces of walking simulators, with their limited and sometimes odd spatial exploration, are not using spatial models to enable broader play in spatial terms. They might, instead, be seeking something like a form of interactive cinema in which the audience is given control of the camera within scenes, but it is still the screenplay that determines the shape of the experience, often through blocked or forced links between the scene locations. As Aaron Reed suggests, in response to an earlier draft of this chapter:

> You mention the unnatural, circuitous routes in environmental storytelling games: but to a certain extent you can say that this now reads to fans of this genre purely as a pacing technique rather than as an unrealistic instantiation of an explorable environment. *Everybody's Gone to the Rapture* had a much more open-ended, hypertext-like structure than *Dear Esther*, but was less successful in part because, to many (including myself), it felt . . . directionless and disconnected . . . perhaps because players of these games now expect simulations of space to encode not explorable worlds but curated mappings of movements through environments to movements through connected story beats. (Personal communication, October 21, 2018.)

37. Larsen, *Marble Springs*.

38. Jackson, *Patchwork Girl*.

39. Magie, *The Landlord's Game*.

40. Pilon, *The Monopolists*, 30.

41. Pilon, 30.

42. Pilon, "Monopoly's Inventor."

43. Hofmeier, *Cart Life*.

44. Maxis Software, *The Sims*.

45. The issue of mourning in *The Sims* titles is an odd one. Different titles in the series have taken different approaches, and these approaches have sometimes been altered through software patches. As Kenzie Cartwright wrote after the release of *The Sims 4*:

> There was a time when Sims ignored the death of anyone who didn't die in their presence. Players complained, so game makers tried to make Sims care more about their dearly departed. Now, Sim mourning is in overdrive.

This sense of overdrive led to players sharing knowledge about how to overwhelm the negative "moodlet" from mourning with positive moodlets such as happy, energized, and flirty. It also led players to create unofficial "mods" to reflect their own ideas about mourning. The description of one of these ("Reduced Mourning from Death Notifications") suggests:

> Sims are getting phone calls advising them of the death of a sim with which they have some sort of relationship. A very long mourning period with a very strong *sad buff* is then applied to the sim. This seems fine if the relationship is for a parent or spouse. However, a *sad +3* buff that lasts for *2 days* just because some random sim with a *friend* relationship level has died seems wrong.

To my knowledge, none of the various approaches to mourning in *The Sims* games have involved actually showing mourning as anything but an abstract, negative feeling. No Sim ever remembers particular experiences with Sims that have passed on, or associates them with objects other than an urn or tombstone, a reminisces about them with another Sim that knew them. The death of a loved one is like sitting in a messy room: it's a drag on the mood of the Sims involved, to be overcome or waited out.

    See: Cartwright, "*The Sims 4* Guide"; cyclelegs, "Reduced Mourning from Death Notifications."

46. MPS Labs, *Sid Meier's Civilization*.

47. Bown, "Video Games Are Political. Here's How They Can Be Progressive."

48. Pedercini, "Videogames and the Spirit of Capitalism."

49. Franklin, "*Civilization*."

50. Paradox Development Studio, *Crusader Kings II*.

51. On the other hand, by portraying warfare primarily as a matter of resources, games like the *Civilization* series avoid some of the pitfalls of the big-budget military FPS. As Robert Yang observes:

> No AAA FPS currently depicts "modern warfare." The war they present, of roughly symmetrical forces meeting each other on battlefields in trenched combat, is an antique of World War II and the Korean War. . . .
>   *Civilization IV* probably does the best job of depicting modern warfare as it exists today: in it, war is when you change your civic priorities, build more jails, shift the economies in all your cities, and begin planning the logistics of transporting dozens (if not many more) of platoons across vast continents and oceans.

    See: Yang, "On the First Person Military Manshooter and the Shape of Modern Warfare."

52. Firaxis Games East, *Sid Meier's Civilization IV*.

53. USC Game Innovation Lab, *Walden: A Game*.

54. Coltrain, *Cassius*.

55. Rohrer, *Passage*.

56. Gibbs, "Evaluating Conceptual Metaphor Theory."

57. Rusch, *Making Deep Games*.

58. Nintendo, *The Legend of Zelda*.

59. Bethesda Game Studios, *The Elder Scrolls V: Skyrim*.

60. Porpentine, *Howling Dogs*.

61. Various distinctions between an emphasis on exploration/interpretation/spectation (on one hand) and construction/configuration/play (on the other) have been made in conversations around computational media. The most influential discussion in the hypertext literature community of the 1980s and 1990s was probably that of Michael Joyce, who described "exploratory" and "constructive" hypertexts. In the game studies discourse of the 2000s, likely the most influential was that of Markku Eskelinen, who wrote in the first issue of the journal *Game Studies* (with a later variation in the volume *First Person*):

> Another quick look at Espen Aarseth's typology of cybertexts (Aarseth 1997, 62–65) should make us see that the dominant user function in literature, theatre, and film is interpretative, but in games it is the configurative one. To generalize: in art we might have to configure in order to be able to interpret, whereas in games we have to interpret in order to be able to configure, and proceed from the beginning to the winning or some other situation.

See: Joyce, "Siren Shapes: Exploratory and Constructive Hypertexts"; Eskelinen, "The Gaming Situation"; Eskelinen, "Towards Computer Game Studies."

62. Crowther and Woods, *Adventure*.

63. Cyan, *Myst*.

64. inkle, *80 Days*.

65. McDonald, "Romance in Games."

66. To put it another way, link-based choices in games, like metaphorical approaches to games, face challenges when we try to use them to produce long-form experiences. But for shorter experiences (or encapsulated experiences, like the largely independent vignettes of *80 Days*) they are powerful for representing, and making playable, things for which we don't have game systems, especially the nuances of life choices. For example, our group at UC Santa Cruz was challenged to make a game about such nuanced choices by Jim Moore and Tyrus Miller (then the Assistant Dean and Dean of the Division of Graduate Studies at UCSC). Specifically, they asked if we could make a game about the difficult choices graduate students face around what is called "Responsible Conduct of Research" (RCR). This includes issues such as authorship attribution, conflict of interest, and mentoring—which are often embedded in power differentials, desires for success, sometimes-murky moral reasoning, and more. We created a link-based game, using short vignettes, each exploring a particular issue from both the perspective of a graduate student and that of their

advisor. As of this writing we have begun to evaluate the game's efficacy, through comparisons with a traditional RCR curriculum from the University of Utah. As one might expect, our game so far appears to be more engaging than the traditional curriculum and shows equal or better traditional learning outcomes (as measured by quizzes from the Utah curriculum). While many game forms could have supported such traditional learning, what particularly excites me is that the nuanced choices enabled by a link-based game seem to have led to significant improvements (over the Utah curriculum) in ability to 1) analyze a moral problem, 2) consider the viewpoints of all individuals involved, and 3) propose solutions and anticipate their possible short- and long-term consequences. See: Melcer et al., "Teaching Responsible Conduct of Research Through an Interactive Storytelling Game"; Melcer et al., "Getting Academical: A Choice-Based Interactive Storytelling Game for Teaching Responsible Conduct of Research."

67. Valve Corporation, *Half-Life: Counter-Strike.*

68. To tell the history of the evolution of the idea of agency in video games would require a book of its own. Such a book could begin with some of the first academic studies of video games, such as the idea of "effectance" in Thomas W. Malone's dissertation—and how it was taken up in the dissertation of Mary Ann Buckles, moving from the domain of arcade-style games into the broader world of the original *Adventure.*

An essential topic for a thorough treatment would be the writing of Brenda Laurel, who presented influential ideas about meaningful interaction in her PhD dissertation and multiple editions of her book *Computers as Theatre.* Two of the key ideas are:

- First-person interaction. This is when "the user feels himself to be present and participating in the action—a first-person experience." (This is not necessarily presented from a first-person visual perspective.)

- Dramatic probability. Players are not enabled or encouraged to do "anything," but rather the things that it would be meaningful for a character in a similar dramatic situation to do.

While comparatively little has been written about the contributions of Malone, Buckles, and Laurel (including, unfortunately, in my own writing about agency), there has been much better coverage of the work of Janet Murray and Doug Church. The most academically influential conception of agency comes from Murray's *Hamlet on the Holodeck,* as "the satisfying power to take meaningful action and see the results of our decisions and choices." Shortly after (and apparently without knowledge of Murray's writing) in the world of game development, Doug Church considered the concept through a pair of terms. The first, "intention," he discusses as a "process of accumulating goals, understanding the world, making a plan, and then acting on it." The second, "perceived consequence," he describes as a "clear reaction from the game world to the action of the player."

Michael Mateas united the conceptualizations of Laurel and Murray, developing the idea that agency requires a balance between the "formal affordances" of the game (what actions are suggested by the game world and situation) and the "material affordances" available to the player (what actions are supported by the game interface and systems). Mateas's conception has implicit within it the requirement for computational models that provide appropriate response. We made this explicit in a joint publication with Steven Dow and Serdar Sali—which also wrapped together a number of refinements and extensions to the concept, ranging from discussion of the influence of interface modalities to the necessity (suggested by Hocking) of moving toward a conception of agency that includes improvisational action.

There have been many further considerations of the topic. Some authors that have influenced my thinking include D. Fox Harrell and Jichen Zhu (who, among other contributions, differentiate models of agency that focus on the player's actions as a character in a dramatic situation from those that do not), Stacey Mason (whose contributions include a vocabulary for the key modes of diegetic agency, extra-diegetic agency, and "affect"—the experience of being present and taking immediate action in the game world), and Isaac Karth (whose contributions include connecting the player's developing agency to Aarseth's discussion of aporia and epiphany in *Cybertext*). These thinkers also usefully take the discussion of agency explicitly beyond a focus on fictional worlds, as when Mason discusses taking extra-diegetic actions motivated by extra-diegetic desires.

See: Malone, "What Makes Things Fun to Learn?"; Buckles, "Interactive Fiction"; Laurel, "Toward the Design of a Computer-Based Interactive Fantasy System," 90; Laurel, *Computers as Theatre*; Murray, *Hamlet on the Holodeck*, 126; Church, "Formal Abstract Design Tools," 4; Mateas, "A Preliminary Poetics for Interactive Drama and Games"; Wardrip-Fruin et al., "Agency Reconsidered"; Harrell and Zhu, "Agency Play"; Mason, "On Games and Links"; Karth, "Ergodic Agency."

69. Milton Bradley, *Candy Land*.

70. Unfortunately, even in academic contexts, there can be a failure to understand that agency is not simply the ability to take actions that impact the world (but requires that player actions emerge from, and game responses potentially contribute to, an understanding of the world). A particularly stark example is the paper "Achieving the Illusion of Agency," which suggests it is a significant finding that "in a text-based story with forced-choice points there were in most cases no significant difference in players' reported feelings of agency when they experience a branching story vs. a linear story with explicit acknowledgement of their choices." But in the experiment reported in the paper, players would not be expected to experience agency in any of the three conditions—because they had no way of understanding the potential significance of their choices in the game world before making the choices and no basis for evaluating any consequences.

For example, one of the choices is between going to the forest or mountains, with no indication of what will be found there. Another is between types of weapons, with no indication of how this may shape the experience of combat. Neither provides consequences that help build player knowledge of the world that can be used later—the first results in different obstacles, of sorts never encountered again, and the second is a false choice that leads to the same next node after an acknowledgement.

Only a misunderstanding of agency could lead one to expect any difference between the conditions. The authors say they are using Janet Murray's definition of agency, but she explicitly describes such a situation as not providing agency: "The players' actions have effect, but . . . the effects are not related to the players' intentions." What the study actually reveals, rather than anything about agency, is the power of acknowledging player decisions.

See: Fendt et al., "Achieving the Illusion of Agency"; Murray, *Hamlet on the Holodeck*, 128.

71. Robbins, *Microscope: A Fractal Role-Playing Game of Epic Histories*.

72. Burke, *Dog Eat Dog*.

73. Harmonix Music Systems, *Guitar Hero*.

74. Harmonix Music Systems, *Rock Band*.

75. Harmonix Music Systems, *Dance Central*.

76. Squinkifer, *Interruption Junction*.

77. Compton, Kybartas, and Mateas, "Tracery," 2015.

78. Squinkifer, "Well, This Is Awkward . . ." 37.

79. I am certainly not the first to note that some games use the denial of agency to powerful effect. Harrell and Zhu argue that, rather than always seeking to maximize agency, the goals of a work can be served by "dynamically changing the scope, nature, and degree of user agency" and that an "equally expressive use is to limit or even temporarily eliminate user agency to convey a certain message, such as the sense of confinement or helplessness."

More specifically, in the context of the initial "walking home" minigame of *Dys4ia*, Evelyn C. Chew and Alex Mitchell write of the potential poetic effects of such denials of agency:

> The expectation and the ability to act are present, but the only course of action presented is not desirable. By thwarting this aspect of agency, the player feels forced and not entirely free. Unwilling cooperation is demanded of the player, who wants the game to progress but does not relish the only option presented. The setup is calculated to produce internal tension and dissonance as an aesthetic response that also serves a narrative purpose.

See: Harrell and Zhu, "Agency Play," 47; Chew and Mitchell, "Bringing Art to Life," 14.

80. Telltale, *The Walking Dead*.

81. Telltale, *The Wolf Among Us*.

82. Carstensdottir, Kleinman, and El-Nasr, "Player Interaction in Narrative Games."

83. Writing about *Balloon Diaspora* (a short game from *Kentucky Route Zero* creators Cardboard Computer) Gregory Weir coined the term "emotional agency" in 2011 as a description of how the game "presents the player with questions that carry emotional weight and visible consequences that paradoxically have little to no effect on the events of the game." In 2018, Liting Kway and Alex Mitchell took up the term and looked carefully at how the experience was produced in three games: *Kentucky Route Zero*, Telltale's *The Wolf Among Us*, and Night School Studio's *Oxenfree*, finding it is sometimes correlated with what Mateas and Andrew Stern have termed "local agency"—but at times simply with opportunities to reflect on character backgrounds and relationships.

Also in 2018, John Thomas Murray defended a dissertation in which *The Wolf Among Us* served as the primary case study. Murray discussed a closely related phenomenon, observed through detailed annotation of playthroughs and analysis of player reactions. His results led to an emphasis on how interactions prompt players to make value-oriented choices: "The Telltale effect is the emotional response elicited from players by the integration of value-based choices in a charged cinematic context without the presence of significant agency within the story."

In a sense, these players are enjoying the experience of transforming into a character and performing their role, rather than shaping a story. This is what Theresa Jean Tanenbaum, while not discussing Telltale games specifically, has called "bounded agency": "The result of this shift away from unrestricted agency to bounded agency is that it supports a participatory model of narrative gameplay in which the actions of the player are constrained to a small set of communicatively meaningful choices, rather than a large set of meaningless capabilities."

See: Weir, "Analysis"; Kway and Mitchell, "Emotional Agency in Storygames"; Mateas and Stern, "Structuring Content in the *Façade* Interactive Drama Architecture"; Murray, "Telltale Hearts"; Tanenbaum, "Being in the Story."

84. In August 2019 a new company announced that it would begin doing business under the Telltale name, after buying the original company's intellectual property following the shutdown. See: Campbell, "Telltale Games Is Being Revived."

85. In a presentation at the 2018 Game Developers Conference, Jon Ingold suggests that the playable stories of games like *80 Days* should be understood as specifically not trying to provide player agency. Rather, they provide forms of freedom that are appropriate to the fictional situation, without providing players the ability to build and strategically use a mental model of the world. Ingold is the Narrative Director of inkle, the studio behind *80 Days* and a number of other titles that combine episodic, choice-driven narrative with resource logics. Ingold observes:

> To me, agency suggests that players can strategize to achieve a particular outcome, and in our games that's very rarely true. We work within highly contextual environments where what happens one moment might not be available in the next moment, so strategy can be quite difficult. (What I'm saying is our games are inherently very unfair, and I'm good with that.) But what we do try to offer is—we try to offer a sense of freedom. That in any given moment in this story you can behave in the sort of way you might want to behave, given the limitations of the interface, or whatever. So you shouldn't feel that you're stuck on a track, you shouldn't feel that you're pressing the only button that the author gave you to press, you shouldn't feel that you're just tapping through options. That's high player freedom, but I wouldn't go so far as to say that it was agency.

The limits of this approach are more apparent in some games than others. For *80 Days*, in which characters spend a brief period in a series of previously-unfamiliar situations (and in which the player character is limited by his background and station in several ways), Ingold's "player freedom" arguably provides the constrained agency that the fictional situation suggests. On the other hand, in inkle's *Sorcery!* series (adapted from Steve Jackson's gamebook series) the player character is an adventurer with a spellbook. The player learns the secret words that allow different spells to be cast—but finds there are arbitrary limits on when different spells can be used. From an authoring perspective, the reason for this is obvious: it's not tractable to hand-write a reaction to every possible spell in every fictional situation the game presents. But from a player experience perspective, it's clearly a long way from agency, occupying a frustrating position: the player actually builds something of a mental model of actions and their world impact (from when the spells can be used) but the fictional world's presentation of constraints (suggesting reasons that spells cannot be used at all times) feels arbitrary and unconvincing. This leads to a mismatch between what it feels like we should be able to do, as a spell-casting fantasy adventurer, and what the game world affords. See: Ingold, "Heaven's Vault," 3:05 to 3:50; inkle, *Steve Jackson's Sorcery!*

86. Verne, *Around the World in Eighty Days*.

87. Jayanth, "Forget Protagonists," June 5, 2016; Jayanth, "Forget Protagonists," March 2016. I am indebted to Cyril Focht for bringing Jayanth's argument to my attention.

88. Boch, "GDC Microtalks 2015."

89. 3909, *Papers, Please*.

90. Frost and Lynch, *Twin Peaks*.

91. Lynch, *Mulholland Drive*.

92. In teaching, Mateas has discussed this continuum using Marie-Laure Ryan's distinction between exploratory and ontological interaction. (Ryan's distinction, in turn, is related to Espen Aarseth's typology of user functions and perspectives in cybertexts, Markku Eskelinen's interpretive and configurative user functions, and Michael Joyce's exploratory and constructive hypertexts, as discussed in an earlier note.) See Ryan, "Beyond Myth and Metaphor: The Case of Narrative in Digital Media."

93. Anderson, *Walking and Falling*. Lyric reproduced with permission from Laurie Anderson.

94. And, of course, it is possible to step even further back. Human attention can turn almost any situation playful. In *Play Matters* Miguel Sicart discusses playfulness as "a way of engaging with particular contexts and objects that is similar to play but respects the purposes and goals of that object or context." The title of Ian Bogost's *Play Anything* is also its thesis—everything has play in it, and if we pay attention and treat its structures and limitations as reasonable (as we do with the arbitrary structures of games), we can find a way to operate it in a satisfying way. From the perspective of Stephanie Boluk's and Patrick LeMieux's *Metagaming*, we can use almost anything as equipment for a game, including a game.

We can bring a playful attitude even to things that seem non-interactive, such as watching a traditional television program or attending a conference panel with no question and answer period. We could also give our play some structure, perhaps taking a drink every time the televised characters enact a well-worn trope (or simply imagining doing so). Or someone else could give it structure, as with the "Ally Bingo" cards distributed by the Union of Concerned Feminists at the all-male plenary panel for the 2014 Grace Hopper Celebration of Women in Computing—with squares containing phrases such as "I am related to a woman" and "Quotes woman he has power over in the workplace." This can change the personal experience and social meaning of an experience, for example surfacing the expectation of repeated patterns (as through a bingo card's pattern-matching logic) and turning it from a dull inevitability into something to engage playfully.

From this zoomed-out perspective, we can see a piece of playable media, like a video game, as something that embeds the logics and models that invite and structure play within itself, rather than depending on them being provided from the outside—though players obviously also bring their own play approaches to their experiences of games and other playable forms.

See: Sicart, *Play Matters*, 21; Bogost, *Play Anything*; Boluk and Lemieux, *Metagaming*; Honeywell, "Bingo and Beyond."

95. To add another example to those above, I had always thought of *Chutes and Ladders* (also known as *Snakes and Ladders*) as being yet another childhood game about a simple spatial model and the hand of fate moving us across it—like *Candy Land,* it's a track game driven by a chance logic. But then game designer Heather Logas pointed out to me that the theme, the skin, is actually childhood decision making. Only then did I really notice that every "ladder" shows a child making a good decision (such as eating healthy food at the bottom and being taller at the top) while every "chute" shows a bad one (such as pretending to study at the top and sitting with a dunce cap at the bottom). The chance logic that we experience through play either undermines this or takes it in an unexpectedly complicated direction—given that it determines all the actions that player characters take. Maybe the game's theme is that what appears to be good or bad judgement in children's lives is actually an accident of happenstance?

96. A range of designers and scholars have talked about the "non-mismatch" between game systems and subjects. One common approach is through an inversion of Hocking's "ludonarrative dissonance." Mattie Brice talks about "ludonarrative resonance" as "when the emergent qualities echo and strengthen the embedded narrative (or the overall design)." Chew and Mitchell, reflecting on previous scholarship, write, "Interactions can and should *contribute positively* to enhancing the player's experience of the story or game by promoting ludonarrative resonance or harmony." See: Brice, "Alternate Ending"; Chew and Mitchell, "Bringing Art to Life."

97. And for multiplayer games, we also look at how the relationship between players is structured, as with the competitive relationship in Go. As Katherine Isbister and others have discussed, multiplayer games are shared human activities, like tandem rock climbing, like being on a basketball team, like competitive debate, like escape rooms. Activities can be structured to bring out different types of experiences and feelings toward other people, and in games this is commonly by connecting their activities through logics and models. *Monopoly* connects players competitively through its resource model, with players paying out currency resources primarily to other players (the amounts paid to the game's bank are trivial) and based on the resource-development actions of other players, with resource loss removing players from play. But these kinds of connections can also create collaboration, as with the spatial model of cooperative platformer *ibb & obb* or the combat model through which groups of players cooperatively attack powerful enemies (and heal damage from those enemies) in *World of Warcraft.*

This kind of relationship-building can also be extended to non-player characters, as long as the models involved are ones the NPCs can understand well enough to play their relationship roles. This can have remarkable nuance, as seen in games like *Papo & Yo*. And when all the players involved are humans, you can play on human feelings without modeling them, such as the relationship-damaging focus on trust and betrayal seen in the tabletop game *Diplomacy*. In short, you can make games, in part, about different kinds of relationships by setting up those relationships among entities engaging in the activity. But this is not specific to games—it is something they have in common with other shared human activities, from formal dance to spontaneously throwing and catching a ball.

See: Isbister, "Social Play"; Codeglue B. V. and Sparpweed, *ibb & obb*; Blizzard Entertainment, *World of Warcraft*; Minority Media, *Papo & Yo*.

98. Moranis and Thomas, *Strange Brew*.

99. Such experiences are still clearly quite different from linear media experiences, even in technologically limited forms such as the *Choose Your Own Adventure* books. As for whether they are games, I think that is similar to asking whether a piece of text is a poem. It changes how we engage a text to consider it as a poem—and our most obvious guide to whether we should do so is any indication given by the author (or other presenter) of the text. If these are not found, we can look for signals in the work itself. But given the huge changes we have seen in, for example, video games—with games like *World of Warcraft* and *80 Days* being quite distant from early arcade games—it would be foolish to attempt a limiting definition focused on our current moment.

Instead we need to be broadly open to works that are presented, or present themselves, as games. As Bonnie Ruberg puts it, for the case of video games, "video games are defined as any designed, interactive experience that operates primarily through a digital interface and understands itself as a video game." At the same time, if these experiences wish to be about something through play, their logics and models must not conflict with their themes or be unrelated, but rather must provide deeper resonance through player engagement.

Finally, a much more detailed discussion of the topic of "real games," is found in the book of the same name by Mia Consalvo and Christopher A. Paul.

See: Ruberg, *Video Games Have Always Been Queer*, 8; Consalvo and Paul, *Real Games*.

100. This is part of the significance of the project of "platform studies" (as seen in the MIT Press series of the same name). Some versions of logics and models are provided by particular platforms, or made easy to implement by them, but those platforms do not provide other logics and models or other implementations of the ones they do provide. In this book I discuss the importance of platform and implementation in cases such as those of *Spacewar* and *Computer Space* in chapter 7. But the issues are more general, as the platform studies project helps reveal.

101. Freeman et al., *How Do You Do It?*

102. Russian Soft, *Sex Tetris*.

103. Crawford has pointed to this issue at least since 1984, writing in his seminal *The Art of Computer Game Design*:

> Hard branching must be hand-wired by the game designer. This restricts the total amount of branching in the game to the amount the designer has time to hand-wire. The problem cannot be solved with high-capacity storage media like optical disks, for the limitation is not in the storage medium but in the designer's inability to anticipate every case and condition and to provide proper branches to deal with all allowed cases.

See: Crawford, *The Art of Computer Game Design*, 56.

104. Mawhorter, Mateas, and Wardrip-Fruin, "Generating Relaxed, Obvious, and Dilemma Choices with Dunyazad"; Garbe et al., "StoryAssembler"; Mason et al., "Lume."

Bibliography

2K Boston and 2K Australia. *BioShock*. Microsoft Windows. Ken Levine, Jonathan Chey, Alyssa Finley, Tony Oakden, Scott Sinclair, Shawn Robertson, Paul Hellquist, William Gardner, Christopher Kline, Rowan Wyborn, John Abercrombie, et al. 2K Games, 2007.

7th Level. *Monty Python: The Quest for the Holy Grail*. Microsoft Windows. Robert Alan Ezrin, Eric Idle, Steve Martino, Charles Otte, Hollis Leech, Bert Jennett, Patrick Deupree, George Grayson, Trent M. Wyatt, Jon M. Greenwood, Alex Yevgenyev, et al. 7th Level, 1996.

3909. *Papers, Please*. Microsoft Windows. Lucas Pope. 3909, 2013.

Aarseth, Espen J. "Allegories of Space: The Question of Spatiality in Computer Games." In *Cybertext Yearbook 2000*, edited by Markku Eskelinen and Raine Koskimaa, 152–171. Finland: University of Jyväskylä, 2001.

Aarseth, Espen J. *Cybertext: Perspectives on Ergodic Literature*. Baltimore: Johns Hopkins University Press, 1997.

Aarseth, Espen J. "Genre Trouble." *electronic book review*, May 21, 2004. https://electronicbookreview.com/essay/genre-trouble/.

Aarseth, Espen J. "Genre Trouble: Narrativism and the Art of Simulation." In *First Person: New Media as Story, Performance and Game*, edited by Noah Wardrip-Fruin and Pat Harrigan, 45–55. Cambridge, MA: MIT Press, 2004.

Activision. *Kaboom!* Atari 2600. Larry Kaplan and David Crane. Activision, 1981.

Activision. *Pitfall!* Atari 2600. David Crane. Activision, 1982.

Adams, Ernest, and Joris Dormans. *Game Mechanics: Advanced Game Design*. Thousand Oaks, CA: New Riders Publishing, 2012.

Adams, Meghan Blythe. "Interview—Merritt Kopas—Part I: Feminist Porn, Games, & Capital." *First Person Scholar*, June 25, 2014. http://www.firstpersonscholar.com/interview-merritt-kopas/.

Adams, Tarn, and Zach Adams. *Slaves to Armok: God of Blood Chapter II: Dwarf Fortress*. Microsoft Windows. Bay 12 Games, 2006.

Alexander, Leigh. "*BioShock Infinite*: Now Is the Best Time." *Leigh Alexander: On the Art, Culture & Business of Interactive Entertainment, Social Media and Stuff* (blog), April 11, 2013. https://leighalexander.net/bioshock-infinite-now-is-the-best-time/ (no longer available).

Alexander, Leigh. "Designing the Bleak Genius of *Papers, Please*." *Gamasutra*, September 3, 2013. https://www.gamasutra.com/view/news/199383/Designing_the_bleak_genius_of_Papers_Please.php.

Alexander, Leigh. "Irrational Games, Journalism, and Airing Dirty Laundry." *Gamasutra*, February 19, 2014. https://www.gamasutra.com/view/news/211139/Irrational_Games_journalism_and_airing_dirty_laundry.php.

Alexander, Leigh. "Learning about Community and Inclusiveness with *Redshirt*." *Gamasutra*, January 17, 2014. https://www.gamasutra.com/view/news/208555/Learning_about_community_and_inclusiveness_with_Redshirt.php.

Alexander, Leigh. "Opinion: The Tragedy of *Grand Theft Auto V*." *Gamasutra*, September 20, 2013. https://www.gamasutra.com/view/news/200648/Opinion_The_tragedy_of_Grand_Theft_Auto_V.php.

Alexander, Nick, David H. Turpin, Katherine Prendergast, Anna Huerta, Filippo Beck Peccoz, and Leon Neilson. *Pongversation*. Adobe Flash. University of Southern California, 2010. See gameplay here: https://vimeo.com/13426225.

Allen, Samantha Leigh. "Video Games as Feminist Pedagogy." *Loading . . .* 8, no. 13 (November 17, 2014). http://journals.sfu.ca/loading/index.php/loading/article/view/135.

Alpha Denshi. *Make Trax*. Arcade. Masashi Yamaguchi. Williams Electronics, 1981.

Altice, Nathan. *I Am Error: The Nintendo Family Computer / Entertainment System Platform*. Platform Studies. Cambridge, MA: MIT Press, 2015.

Anderson, Barrett, Christopher Karzmark, and Noah Wardrip-Fruin. "The Psychological Reality of Procedural Rhetoric." Presented at the 14th International Conference on the Foundations of Digital Games (FDG), San Luis Obispo, CA, USA, August 26–30, 2019. https://doi.org/10.1145/3337722.3337751.

Anderson, Brad, dir. *Happy Accidents*. 2001; New York: IFC Films, 2001.

Anderson, Laurie. "Walking and Falling." Track 4 on *Big Science*. Warner Bros., 1982, LP record.

Andrews, Jim. "Videogames as Literary Devices." In *Videogames and Art*, edited by Grethe Mitchell and Andy Clarke. Bristol: Intellect Books, 2007.

Anthropy, Anna (Auntie Pixelante). *Dys4ia*. Adobe Flash. 2012. https://www.newgrounds.com/portal/view/591565 (no longer available).

Anthropy, Anna, and Naomi Clark. *A Game Design Vocabulary: Exploring the Foundational Principles Behind Good Game Design*. Boston: Addison-Wesley Professional, 2014.

Arsenault, Dominic. "Video Game Genre, Evolution and Innovation." *Eludamos: Journal for Computer Game Culture* 3, no. 2 (October 26, 2009): 149–176.

Atari. *Adventure*. Atari 2600. Warren Robinett. Sears, Roebuck, 1979.

Atari. *Asteroids*. Arcade. Ed Logg, Lyle V. Rains, Howard Delman. Atari, 1979.

Atari. *Breakout*. Arcade. Nolan Bushnell, Steve Bristow, Steve Wozniak, Steve Jobs. Atari, 1976.

Atari. *Breakout*. Atari 2600. Bradley G. Stewart. Atari, 1978. [Based on Atari's arcade game of the same name.]

Atari. *Pong*. Arcade. Alan Alcorn. Atari, 1972.

Atari, Inc., Consumer Division. *Adventure Game Program Instructions*. Sunnyvale, CA: Warner Communications, 1979.

Aytemiz, Batu, Nick Junius, and Nathan Altice. "Exploring How Changes in Game Systems Generate Meaning." Presented at the 2019 DiGRA International Conference: Game, Play and the Emerging Ludo-Mix, Kyoto, Japan, August 6–10 2019. http://www.digra.org/wp-content/uploads/digital-library/DiGRA_2019_paper_195.pdf.

Baer, Ralph H. *Videogames: In the Beginning*. Springfield Township, NJ: Rolenta Press, 2005. http://archive.org/details/VideogamesInTheBeginningRalphH.Baer.

Bally Midway Mfg. *Tapper*. Arcade. Steven E. Meyer, R. Scott Morrison, Rick Hicaro, Elaine Hodgson, and Richard A. Ditton. Bally Midway Mfg., 1983.

Barr, Pippin. *PONGS*. Adobe Flash. 2012. https://www.pippinbarr.com/2012/04/11/pongs/.

Barthes, Roland. *The Fashion System*. Translated by Matthew Ward and Richard Howard. Berkeley, CA: University of California Press, 1990.

Barton, Matt. *Vintage Games 2.0: An Insider Look at the Most Influential Games of All Time*. Boca Raton, FL: Taylor & Francis, 2017.

Barton, Matt, and Bill Loguidice. "The History of *Spacewar!*: The Best Waste of Time in the History of the Universe." *Gamasutra*, June 10, 2009. https://www.gamasutra.com/view/feature/132438/the_history_of_spacewar_the_best_.php.

Baumbach, Nico, Damon R. Young, and Genevieve Yue. "Introduction: For a Political Critique of Culture." *Social Text* 34, no. 2 (127) (June 1, 2016): 1–20. https://doi.org/10.1215/01642472-3467942.

Begy, Jason. "Experiential Metaphors in Abstract Games." *Transactions of the Digital Games Research Association* 1, no. 1 (April 5, 2013). https://doi.org/10.26503/todigra.v1i1.3.

Berne, Eric. *Games People Play: The Psychology of Human Relationships*. New York: Grove Press, 1964.

Bernstein, Joseph. "Why Is *Bioshock Infinite* a First-Person Shooter?" *BuzzFeed News*, April 1, 2013. https://www.buzzfeed.com/josephbernstein/why-is-bioshock-infinite-a-first-person-shooter.

Bernstein, Joseph. "Why We Can't Talk about *BioShock Infinite*." *BuzzFeed News*, April 15, 2013. https://www.buzzfeed.com/josephbernstein/why-we-cant-talk-about-bioshock-infinite.

Bernstein, Michael S., Andrés Monroy-Hernández, Drew Harry, Paul André, Katrina Panovich, and Greg Vargas. "4chan and /b/: An Analysis of Anonymity and Ephemerality in a Large Online Community." Presented at the 5th International AAAI Conference on Weblogs and Social Media, Barcelona, Spain, July 17–21, 2011. https://www.aaai.org/ocs/index.php/ICWSM/ICWSM11/paper/view/2873.

Bethesda Game Studios. *The Elder Scrolls V: Skyrim*. Microsoft Windows. Todd Howard, Guy Carver, Matthew Carofano, Bruce Nesmith, Kurt Kuhlmann, Ashley Cheng, Craig Lafferty, Mark Lampert, et al. Bethesda Softworks, 2011.

BioWare Austin. *Star Wars: The Old Republic*. Microsoft Windows 7. Richard Vogel, James Ohlen, Jeff Dobson, Arnie Jorgensen, Thomas Boyd, Chad Robertson, Daniel Erickson, Brad Prince, Emmanuel Lusinchi, Dallas Dickinson, et al. Electronic Arts, 2011.

BioWare Corporation. *Mass Effect*. Microsoft Xbox 360. Casey Hudson, Preston Watamaniuk, Drew Karpyshyn, Derek Watts, David Falkner, Jonathan K. Cooper, Shane Welbourn, Mike Spalding, Michael Trottier, Adrien Cho, Shareef Shanawany, Ken Thain, Dusty Everman, Yanick Roy, Darren Wong, et al. Microsoft Game Studios, 2007.

BioWare Corporation. *Star Wars: Knights of the Old Republic*. Microsoft Xbox. David Falkner, Steven Gilmour, Casey Hudson, Drew Karpyshyn, James Ohlen, Preston Watamaniuk, Derek Watts, et al. LucasArts, 2003.

BioWare Edmonton. *Dragon Age: Origins*. Microsoft Windows. Dan Tudge, Mark Darrah, Brent Knowles, Mike Laidlaw, James Ohlen, Dean Andersen, Ross Gardner, Benoit Houle, et al. Electronic Arts, 2009.

Björk, Staffan, and Jussi Holopainen. *Patterns in Game Design*. Needham Heights, MA: Charles River Media, 2004.

Björk, Staffan, and Jesper Juul. "Zero-Player Games, or: What We Talk about When We Talk about Players." Presented at the 6th International Conference on the Philosophy of Computer Games, Madrid, Spain, January 29–31, 2012. http://gamephilosophy.org/wp-content/uploads/confmanuscripts/pcg2012/Bjor%20Juul%202012%20-Zero-player-games-Exploring-the-distinction-between-Games-as-Artifacts-and-Games-as-Activities.pdf.

Black Isle Studios. *Planescape: Torment*. Microsoft Windows. Chris Avellone, Dan Spitzley, Timothy Donley, Guido Henkel, Kenneth Lee, et al. Interplay Entertainment, 1999.

Blizzard Entertainment. *Overwatch*. Microsoft Windows. Frank Pearce Jr., Ray Gresko, Jeffrey Kaplan, Chris Metzen, William Petras, Mike Elliott, et al. Blizzard Entertainment, 2016.

Blizzard Entertainment. *StarCraft*. Microsoft Windows. Ayman Adham, Michael Morhaime, James Phinney, Bill Roper, Chris Metzen, Bob Fitch, Sam Didier, Duane Stinnett, et al. Blizzard Entertainment, 1998.

Blizzard Entertainment. *World of Warcraft.* Microsoft Windows. Michael Morhaime, Mark E. Kern, William Petras, Chris Metzen, Kevin Beardslee, Justin Thavirat, Brandon Idol, Robert Pardo, Ayman Adham, Johnny Cash, Kyle Harrison, Shane Dabiri, Carlos Guerrero, et al. Blizzard Entertainment, 2004.

Blizzard Entertainment and Blizzard North. *Diablo.* Microsoft Windows. David Brevik, Erich Schaefer, Sam Didier, Ayman Adham, Bill Roper, Matt Uelmen, Chris Metzen, et al. Blizzard Entertainment, 1996.

Blumberg, Bruce M., and Tinsley A. Galyean. "Multi-Level Direction of Autonomous Creatures for Real-Time Virtual Environments." In *SIGGRAPH '95: Proceedings of the 22nd Annual Conference on Computer Graphics and Interactive Techniques,* 47–54. New York: ACM, 1995. https://doi.org/10.1145/218380.218405.

Boch, Matt. "GDC Microtalks 2015: One Hour, Ten Speakers, Games and Play, and Us." Presented at the 29th Game Developers Conference, San Francisco, CA, USA, March 2–6, 2015. https://www.gdcvault.com/play/1022011/GDC-Microtalks-2015-One-Hour.

Boellstorff, Tom, Mic Bowman, Jody Clarke-Midura, Mia Consalvo, Hamid Ekbia, Magda El Zarki, Wu-Chi Feng, et al. "The Future of Research in Computer Games and Virtual World Environments: Workshop Report." Walt Scacchi, ed. Institute for Software Research, University of California Irvine, July 2012. http://www.isr.uci.edu/tech_reports/UCI-ISR-12-8.pdf.

Bogost, Ian. *How to Talk about Videogames.* Minneapolis: University of Minnesota Press, 2015.

Bogost, Ian. *Persuasive Games: The Expressive Power of Videogames.* Cambridge, MA: MIT Press, 2007.

Bogost, Ian. *Play Anything: The Pleasure of Limits, the Uses of Boredom, and the Secret of Games.* New York: Basic Books, 2016.

Bogost, Ian. *Unit Operations: An Approach to Videogame Criticism.* Cambridge, MA: MIT Press, 2006.

Bogost, Ian, Simon Ferrari, and Bobby Schweizer. *Newsgames: Journalism at Play.* Cambridge, MA: MIT Press, 2010.

Bojin, Nis. "Ludemes and the Linguistic Turn." In *Futureplay '10: Proceedings of the International Academic Conference on the Future of Game Design and Technology,* 25–32. New York: ACM, 2010. https://doi.org/10.1145/1920778.1920783.

Boluk, Stephanie, and Patrick Lemieux. *Metagaming.* Minneapolis: University of Minnesota Press, 2017.

Bookchin, Natalie. *The Intruder.* Macromedia Shockwave. 1999. https://bookchin.net/projects/the-intruder/.

Borries, Friedrich von, Steffen P. Walz, and Matthias Böttger. *Space Time Play: Computer Games, Architecture and Urbanism: The Next Level.* Basel, Switzerland: Walter de Gruyter GmbH, 2007.

Bown, Alfie. "Video Games Are Political. Here's How They Can Be Progressive." *The Guardian*, August 13, 2018. https://www.theguardian.com/games/2018/aug/13/video-games-are-political -heres-how-they-can-be-progressive.

Brand, Stewart. *II Cybernetic Frontiers*. New York: Random House / The Bookworks, 1974. http:// archive.org/details/iicyberneticfront00bran.

Brand, Stewart. "*Spacewar*: Fanatic Life and Symbolic Death Among the Computer Bums." *Rolling Stone*, December 7, 1972.

Brice, Mattie. "Ludonarrative Resonance." *Alternate Ending* (blog), September 15, 2011. http:// xgalatea.blogspot.com/2011/09/ludonarrative-resonance.html.

Brookhaven National Laboratory. "BNL | History: The First Video Game?" Brookhaven National Laboratory, n.d. https://www.bnl.gov/about/history/firstvideo.php.

Buchanan, Levi. "Top 10 Best-Selling Atari 2600 Games." IGN, August 26, 2008. https://www.ign .com/articles/2008/08/26/top-10-best-selling-atari-2600-games.

Buckles, Mary Ann. "Interactive Fiction: The Computer Storygame *Adventure*." PhD diss., University of California, San Diego, 1985. http://search.proquest.com/docview/303372594/ abstract/8A289AE6BF884CD1PQ/1.

Bura, Stephane. "Emotion Engineering: A Scientific Approach for Understanding Game Appeal." *Gamasutra*, July 29, 2008. https://www.gamasutra.com/view/feature/132135/emotion _engineering_a_scientific_.php.

Burke, Liam. *Dog Eat Dog*. Tabletop Role Playing Game. Liwanag Press, 2012.

Burkinshaw, Robin. "Alice and Kev: The Story of Being Homeless in *The Sims 3*." *Alice and Kev* (blog), 2009. https://aliceandkev.wordpress.com/.

Burkinshaw, Robin. "Selflessness." *Alice and Kev* (blog), June 16, 2009. https://aliceandkev .wordpress.com/2009/06/16/selflessness/.

Campbell, Colin. "*Gone Home*: Gentle Gaming Takes Aim at Shooters." *IGN*, July 18, 2012. https:// www.ign.com/articles/2012/07/18/gone-home-gentle-gaming-takes-aim-at-shooters.

Campbell, Colin. "Telltale Games Is Being Revived." *Polygon*, August 28, 2019. https://www .polygon.com/2019/8/28/20835854/telltale-games-return-walking-dead-lcg-entertainment.

Campo Santo. *Firewatch*. Microsoft Windows. Chris Remo, James Nicholas Benson, Nels Anderson, Ben Burbank, Paolo Surricchio, William W. Armstrong, Jake Rodkin, Olly Moss, Sean Vanaman, et al. Campo Santo Productions, 2016.

Capcom. *Street Fighter*. Arcade. Takashi Nishiyama, Hiroshi Matsumoto, Hiroshi Koike, Crusher Ichi, Dabada Atsushi, Bonsoir Yuko, Ocan Miyuki, Bravo Oyu, Innocent Saicho, Yoshihiro Sakaguchi, Takashi Kubozono, Strong Take, Radish Kamin. Capcom, 1987.

Capcom. *Super Street Fighter II*. Super Nintendo Entertainment System. Yoshito Ito, Hisashi Kuramoto, Jun Takeuchi, et al. Capcom USA., 1994.

Carstensdottir, Elin, Erica Kleinman, and Magy Seif El-Nasr. "Player Interaction in Narrative Games: Structure and Narrative Progression Mechanics." Presented at the 14th International Conference on the Foundations of Digital Games (FDG), San Luis Obispo, CA, USA, August 26–30, 2019. https://doi.org/10.1145/3337722.3337730.

Cartwright, Kenzie. "*The Sims 4* Guide: How to Snap Sims out of Sadness After a Death." Level-Skip, July 17, 2019. https://levelskip.com/simulation/The-Sims-4-Guide-How-to-Snap-Your-Sims-Out-of-Mourning-Fast.

Chemers, Michael Mark, and Mike Sell. *Systemic Dramaturgy: A Handbook for the Digital Age*. Carbondale, IL: Southern Illinois University Press, forthcoming.

Chess, Shira. "The Queer Case of Video Games: Orgasms, Heteronormativity, and Video Game Narrative." *Critical Studies in Media Communication* 33, no. 1 (January 1, 2016): 84–94. https://doi.org/10.1080/15295036.2015.1129066.

Chew, Evelyn C., and Alex Mitchell. "Bringing Art to Life: Examining Poetic Gameplay Devices in Interactive Life Stories." *Games and Culture* (June 3, 2019). https://doi.org/10.1177/1555412019853372.

Chinese Room. *Dear Esther*. Microsoft Windows. Robert Briscoe, Dan Pinchbeck, Ben Andrews, Nigel Carrington, Samuel Justice, Jack Morgan, et al. Chinese Room, 2012. [Commercial remake of a *Half-Life 2* modification of the same name first released in 2007.]

Choice of Games. "Important ChoiceScript Commands and Techniques." Choice of Games, April 26, 2013. https://www.choiceofgames.com/make-your-own-games/important-choicescript-commands-and-techniques/.

Church, Doug. "Formal Abstract Design Tools." *Gamasutra*, July 16, 1999. https://www.gamasutra.com/view/feature/131764/formal_abstract_design_tools.php.

Cinematronics and Vectorbeam. *Space Wars*. Arcade. Larry Rosenthal. Amutech, 1977.

Cirulli, Gabriele. "2048, Success and Me." Medium, May 20, 2017. https://medium.com/@gabrielecirulli/2048-success-and-me-7dc664f7a9bd.

Codeglue B. V. and Sparpweed. *ibb & obb*. Sony PlayStation 3. Richard Boeser, Eva Nieuwdorp, Roland Ijzermans, Kevin Geers, Peter de Jong, Harald Maassen, Tom Rutjens, Reimer Eising, et al. Sparpweed, 2013.

Coltrain, James. *Cassius*. Microsoft Windows, forthcoming.

Comaroff, John L., and Simon Roberts. *Rules and Processes: The Cultural Logic of Dispute in an African Context*. Chicago: University of Chicago Press, 1981.

Compton, Kate, Ben Kybartas, and Michael Mateas. "Tracery: An Author-Focused Generative Text Tool." In *Interactive Storytelling*, edited by Henrik Schoenau-Fog, Luis Emilio Bruni, Sandy Louchart, and Sarune Baceviciute, 154–161. Lecture Notes in Computer Science. Berlin: Springer International Publishing, 2015. https://doi.org/10.1007/978-3-319-27036-4_14. [See http://www.tracery.io/.]

Computer History Museum. "Jack Dennis." PDP-1 Restoration Project, n.d. https://www .computerhistory.org/pdp-1/jack-dennis/.

Consalvo, Mia. *Atari to Zelda: Japan's Videogames in Global Contexts*. Cambridge, MA: MIT Press, 2016. https://doi.org/10.7551/mitpress/8853.001.0001.

Consalvo, Mia, and Christopher A. Paul. *Real Games: What's Legitimate and What's Not in Contemporary Videogames*. Cambridge, MA: MIT Press, 2019.

Cook, Daniel. "The Chemistry of Game Design." *Gamasutra*, July 19, 2007. https://www.gamasutra .com/view/feature/129948/the_chemistry_of_game_design.php.

Costikyan, Greg. "I Have No Words & I Must Design." Reprinted from *Interactive Fantasy* 2, (1994). http://www.costik.com/nowords.html (unavailable as of this writing, new version at http://www .digra.org/wp-content/uploads/digital-library/05164.51146.pdf).

Cousins, Ben. "Elementary Game Design." *Develop*, October 2004.

Cousins, Ben. "Selfconscious and Unselfconscious Cultures." *Ben Cousins* (blog), April 1, 2014. https://benjaminjcousins.wordpress.com/2014/04/01/selfconscious-and-unselfconscious-cultures/.

Crawford, Chris. "A New Approach." Erasmatazz, September 2, 2019. http://www.erasmatazz.com/ library/interactive-storytelling/a-new-approach.html.

Crawford, Chris. *Balance of Power: Geopolitics in the Nuclear Age*. Apple Macintosh System Software. Mindscape, 1985.

Crawford, Chris. "Chapter 8: Guidelines." In *Art of Interactive Design: A Euphonious and Illuminating Guide to Building Successful Software*. San Francisco: No Starch Press, 2002.

Crawford, Chris. *Chris Crawford on Interactive Storytelling*. Berkeley, CA: New Riders Games, 2004.

Crawford, Chris. "Process Intensity." *Journal of Computer Game Design* 1, no. 5 (1987).

Crawford, Chris. *The Art of Computer Game Design*. New York: Osborne/McGraw-Hill, 1984.

Crawford, Chris. "Why I Am Ending Further Work on Interactive Storytelling." Erasmatazz, June 13, 2018. http://www.erasmatazz.com/library/interactive-storytelling/why-i-am-ending-further .html.

Crowther, William, and Donald Woods. *Adventure*. Digital Equipment Corporation PDP-10. Bolt, Beranek, and Newman & Stanford University, 1975–1977.

Cyan. *Myst*. Apple System 7. Rand K. Miller, Robyn Miller, Chuck Carter, Christopher Brandkamp, Laurie Strand, et al. Brøderbund Software, 1993.

cyclelegs. "Reduced Mourning from Death Notifications." Mod the Sims, September 10, 2018. http://modthesims.info/d/617829/reduced-mourning-from-death-notifications.html.

Data East Corporation. *Lock 'n' Chase*. Arcade. Taito America Corporation, 1981.

Dator, James. "The Life of a *Grand Theft Auto* Role-Player." Polygon, June 25, 2018. https://www.polygon.com/features/2018/6/25/17494836/grand-theft-auto-5-role-play-chris-cone.

Demruth. *Antichamber.* Microsoft Windows. Alexander Bruce, Robin Arnott, Siddhartha Barnhoorn, Julian Bruce, and Mike Blackney. 2013.

Deterding, Sebastian. "The Lens of Intrinsic Skill Atoms: A Method for Gameful Design." *Human–Computer Interaction* 30, no. 3–4 (May 1, 2015): 294–335. https://doi.org/10.1080/07370024.2014.993471.

Dickinson, Melanie, Noah Wardrip-Fruin, and Michael Mateas. "Social Simulation for Social Justice." Presented at the 13th AAAI Conference on Artificial Intelligence and Interactive Digital Entertainment (AIIDE), Snowbird, UT, USA, October 5–9, 2017. https://www.aaai.org/ocs/index.php/AIIDE/AIIDE17/paper/view/15917.

Digital Cafe. *Chex Quest.* Microsoft Windows. Dean Hyers, Mike Koenigs, Scott Holman, Davis Brus, Charles Jacobi, Josh Storms, Andrew Benson, Mike Koenigs, Mary Bregi, et al. Ralston-Purina, 1996.

Digital Equipment Corporation. "The Story of . . . PDP-1." Documenting DIGITAL, 1995–1998. https://gordonbell.azurewebsites.net/digital/timeline/pdp-1story.htm. CD-ROM preserved by Gordon Bell.

dino (formerly nina). *Seasonal Mixtape.* Browser (Bitsy). 2018. https://mome.itch.io/seasonalmixtape.

Dizikes, Peter. "Building Culture in Digital Media." MIT News, October 23, 2013. http://news.mit.edu/2013/fox-harrell-phantasmal-media-1023.

DMA Design Limited. *Grand Theft Auto III.* Sony PlayStation 2. Leslie Benzies, Dan Houser, Jamie King, Renaud Sebbane, Aaron Garbut, Adam Fowler, Obbe Vermeij, Craig Filshie, William Mills, Chris Rothwell, James Worrall, et al. Rockstar Games, 2001.

Domínguez, Ignacio X., Rogelio E. Cardona-Rivera, James K. Vance, and David L. Roberts. "The Mimesis Effect: The Effect of Roles on Player Choice in Interactive Narrative Role-Playing Games." In *Proceedings of the 2016 CHI Conference on Human Factors in Computing Systems*, 3438–3449. New York: ACM, 2016. https://doi.org/10.1145/2858036.2858141.

Donnelly, Joe. "I Robbed a String of Banks Unarmed by Posing as a Journalist in a *GTA 5* Role-playing Server." PC Gamer, March 7, 2018. https://www.pcgamer.com/i-robbed-a-string-of-banks-unarmed-by-posing-as-a-journalist-in-a-gta-5-roleplaying-server/.

Dorkly. "Gun Home: The Ultimate *Gone Home* DLC." *Dorkly*, 2014. Video. http://www.dorkly.com/video/58404/gun-home (no longer available).

Dormans, Joris. "Engineering Emergence: Applied Theory for Game Design." PhD diss., University of Amsterdam, 2012. https://dare.uva.nl/search?identifier=40b1a42a-4291-48a3-80a1-c85dfe927f50.

Double Fine Productions. *Psychonauts.* Microsoft Xbox. Tim Schafer, Dave Dixon, Scott Campbell, Erik Robson, Sandra B. Christensen, Eric P. Ingerson, David Russell, Matthew Franklin, Caroline Esmurdoc, Jonathan Stone, et al. Majesco Entertainment, 2005.

Douglass, Jeremy. "Command Lines: Aesthetics and Technique in Interactive Fiction and New Media." PhD diss., University of California, Santa Barbara, 2007. http://search.proquest.com/docview/304880875/abstract/DA9D678575BD4BF3PQ/1.

Dunhill Electronics. *Tax Avoiders*. Atari 2600. John Simonds, Todd Clark Holm, Darrell Wagner. American Videogame, 1982. Played on Stella emulator, v4.7, from ROM file "Taxavoid.bin" SHA1: 7aaf6be610ba6ea1205bdd5ed60838ccb8280d57.

Dyer, Jason. "Review: Blood and Laurels." *Renga in Blue* (blog), June 13, 2014. https://bluerenga.blog/2014/06/12/review-blood-and-laurels/.

Dyer-Witheford, Nick, and Greig de Peuter. *Games of Empire: Global Capitalism and Video Games*. Minneapolis: University of Minnesota Press, 2009.

Dyment, Doug, and David H. Ahl. *Hamurabi*. BASIC computer language. 1968–1973. [Originally developed under the name *King of Sumeria* or *The Sumer Game* by Doug Dyment in 1968 at Digital Equipment Corporation, it was popularized when David H. Ahl released the 1973 book *BASIC Computer Games*. This book included an expanded version of the game, ported to the BASIC language, under the name *Hamurabi*.]

Edwards, Benj. "Computer Space and the Dawn of the Arcade Video Game." Technologizer by Harry McCracken, December 12, 2011. https://www.technologizer.com/2011/12/11/computer-space-and-the-dawn-of-the-arcade-video-game/.

Egenfeldt-Nielsen, Simon. "Clarifications on the Game." Steam Community: Discussions: *Playing History 2: Slave Trade*, September 6, 2014. https://steamcommunity.com/sharedfiles/filedetails/updates/310110691/1410023000.

Eladhari, Mirjam Palosaari. "Re-Tellings: The Fourth Layer of Narrative as an Instrument for Critique." In *Interactive Storytelling*, edited by Rebecca Rouse, Hartmut Koenitz, and Mads Haahr, 11318:65–78. Cham, Switzerland: Springer International Publishing, 2018. https://doi.org/10.1007/978-3-030-04028-4_5.

Eladhari, Mirjam Palosaari, and Michael Mateas. "Semi-Autonomous Avatars in World of Minds: A Case Study of AI-Based Game Design." In *Proceedings of the 2008 International Conference on Advances in Computer Entertainment Technology*, 201–208. New York: ACM, 2008. https://doi.org/10.1145/1501750.1501798.

Eladhari, Mirjam Palosaari, Anne Sullivan, Gillian Smith, and Josh McCoy. "AI-Based Game Design: Enabling New Playable Experiences." Technical Report. Jack Baskin School of Engineering, University of California, Santa Cruz, December 7, 2011. https://www.soe.ucsc.edu/research/technical-reports/UCSC-SOE-11-27.

Electronic Arts. *The Sims 2: Nightlife*. Microsoft Windows. Tim LeTourneau, Margaret Ng, Shannon Copur, Mary Beth Haggerty, Kevin Hogan, Frank Simon, Ed Nanale, David Patch, Goopy Rossi, Robert Kauker, Rod Humble, Brian Deppiesse, et al. Electronic Arts, 2005. Expansion for *The Sims 2*.

Electronic Arts. *The Sims: Hot Date*. Microsoft Windows. Tim LeTourneau, Patrick J. Barrett III, Eric Hedman, Sean Baity, Claire Curtin, Brooke Harris, Michael McCormick, Todd Reamon, Roxana Wolosenko, Chris Wren, Waylon Wilsonoff, Virginia Ellen McArthur, et al. Electronic Arts, 2001. Expansion for *The Sims*.

Enfield, Nick J. "The Theory of Cultural Logic: How Individuals Combine Social Intelligence with Semiotics to Create and Maintain Cultural Meaning." *Cultural Dynamics* 12, no. 1 (March 1, 2000): 35–64. https://doi.org/10.1177/092137400001200102.

Engelbart, Douglas C., and William K. English. "A Research Center for Augmenting Human Intellect." In *AFIPS '68 (Fall, Part I): Proceedings of the Fall Joint Computer Conference*, 395–410. New York: ACM, 1968. https://dl.acm.org/doi/10.1145/1476589.1476645.

Epic Games and People Can Fly. *Fortnite: Battle Royale*. Microsoft Windows. Epic Games, 2017.

Eskelinen, Markku. "The Gaming Situation." *Game Studies* 01, no. 01 (July 2001). http://www.gamestudies.org/0101/eskelinen/.

Eskelinen, Markku. "Towards Computer Game Studies." In *First Person: New Media as Story, Performance, and Game*, edited by Noah Wardrip-Fruin and Pat Harrigan. Cambridge, MA: MIT Press, 2004.

Evans, Richard, and Emily Short. "Versu—A Simulationist Storytelling System." *IEEE Transactions on Computational Intelligence and AI in Games* 6, no. 2 (June 2014): 113–130. https://doi.org/10.1109/TCIAIG.2013.2287297.

Everything Unlimited Ltd. *The Beginner's Guide*. Microsoft Windows. Davey Wreden, 2015.

Exidy. *Mouse Trap*. Arcade. Howell Ivy, Larry W. Hutcherson Sr., Dave Staugas. Exidy, 1981.

Feibleman, James K. "Of Operational Logic." In *Assumptions of Grand Logics*, edited by James K. Feibleman, 119–132. Dordrecht, Netherlands: Springer, 1979. https://doi.org/10.1007/978-94-009-9278-8_8.

Fendt, Matthew William, Brent Harrison, Stephen G. Ware, Rogelio E. Cardona-Rivera, and David L. Roberts. "Achieving the Illusion of Agency." In *Interactive Storytelling*, edited by David Oyarzun, Federico Peinado, R. Michael Young, Ane Elizalde, and Gonzalo Méndez, 114–125. Lecture Notes in Computer Science. Berlin: Springer Berlin Heidelberg, 2012.

Fernández-Vara, Clara. "Game Spaces Speak Volumes: Indexical Storytelling." Presented at the 2011 DiGRA International Conference: Think Design Play, Hilversum, the Netherlands, September 14–17, 2011. http://www.digra.org/wp-content/uploads/digital-library/Game-Spaces-Speak-Volumes.pdf.

Fernández-Vara, Clara, José P. Zagal, and Michael Mateas. "Evolution of Spatial Configurations in Videogames." Presented at the 2005 DiGRA International Conference: Changing Views—Worlds in Play, Vancouver, BC, Canada, June 16–20, 2005. http://www.digra.org/wp-content/uploads/digital-library/06278.04249.pdf.

Firaxis Games East. *Sid Meier's Civilization IV*. Microsoft Windows. Soren Johnson, Mustafa Thamer, Steve Ogden, Barry Caudill, Jesse Smith, Dan Magaha, Alex Mantzaris, Bart Muzzin, Dan McGarry, Eric MacDonald, Brian Busatti, Mark Shahan, Dorian Newcomb, et al. 2K Games, 2005.

Firaxis Games. *XCOM: Enemy Unknown*. Microsoft Windows. Jacob Solomon, Ananda Gupta, Todd Broadwater, Casey O'Toole, Justin Boswell, Gregory Foertsch, Dennis Moellers, Roland J. Rizzo, Garth DeAngelis, Clint McCaul, Amber Hinden, et al. 2K Games, 2012.

Flanagan, Mary. *Critical Play: Radical Game Design*. Cambridge, MA: MIT Press, 2009. https://doi.org/10.7551/mitpress/7678.001.0001.

Flanagan, Mary, Angela Ferraiolo, Greg Kohl, Grace Ching-Yung, Peng, Jennifer Jacobs, and Paul Orbell. *LAYOFF*. Adobe Flash. Tiltfactor Lab and the Rochester Institute of Technology (RIT) Game Design and Development Program. Tiltfactor, 2009. http://www.tiltfactor.org/game/layoff/.

Forman-Brunell, Miriam. *Made to Play House: Dolls and the Commercialization of American Girlhood, 1830–1930*. New Haven, CT: Yale University Press, 1993.

Formosa, Paul, Malcolm Ryan, and Dan Staines. "*Papers, Please* and the Systemic Approach to Engaging Ethical Expertise in Videogames." *Ethics and Information Technology* 18, no. 3 (September 1, 2016): 211–225. https://doi.org/10.1007/s10676-016-9407-z.

Franich, Darren. "Entertainment Geekly: *Grand Theft Auto V*'s Depressing Endings." EW.com, October 10, 2013. https://ew.com/article/2013/10/10/grand-theft-auto-v-ending/.

Franklin, Christopher. "*Civilization*." *Errant Signal* (blog), May 26, 2014. http://www.errantsignal.com/blog/?p=638.

Franklin, Seb. *Control: Digitality as Cultural Logic*. Cambridge, MA: MIT Press, 2015.

Frasca, Gonzalo. *Kabul Kaboom!* Macromedia Shockwave. ludology.org, 2010. http://ludology.org/games/kabulkaboom.html (no longer available).

Frasca, Gonzalo. "Sim Sin City—Some Thoughts about *Grand Theft Auto 3*." *Game Studies* 3, no. 2 (December 2003). http://www.gamestudies.org/0302/frasca/.

Frasca, Gonzalo, Sofia Battegazzore, Nicolas Olhaberry, Pepe Infantozzi, Fabian Rodriguez, and Federico Balbi. *September 12th: A Toy World*. Macromedia Shockwave. Newsgaming.com, 2003. http://www.newsgaming.com/games/index12.htm.

Fray, Andrew. "Steering Behaviours Are Doing It Wrong." *Andrew Fray* (blog), February 20, 2013. https://andrewfray.wordpress.com/2013/02/20/steering-behaviours-are-doing-it-wrong/.

Freeman, Nina, Emmett Butler, Joni Kittaka, and Decky Coss. *How Do You Do It?* Adobe Flash (Flixel). 2014. http://ninasays.so/howdoyoudoit/.

Fries, Ed. "Fixing *Computer Space*." *EDFRIES: The Game Is Not Over* (blog), March 13, 2015. https://edfries.wordpress.com/2015/03/13/fixing-computer-space-3/.

Frost, Mark, and David Lynch. *Twin Peaks*. CBS Television Distribution, ABC, 1990–1991.

Fullbright Company. *Gone Home*. Microsoft Windows. Steve Gaynor, Karla Zimonja, Johnnemann Nordhagen, Kate Craig, Chris Remo, and Emily Carroll. Fullbright Company, 2013.

Gaijin Games. *BIT.TRIP BEAT*. Nintendo Wii. Alex Neuse, Chris Osborn, and Mike Roush. Aksys Games Localization, 2009.

Galloway, Alexander R. *Gaming: Essays on Algorithmic Culture*. Minneapolis: University of Minnesota Press, 2006.

Garbe, Jacob, Max Kreminski, Ben Samuel, Noah Wardrip-Fruin, and Michael Mateas. "StoryAssembler: An Engine for Generating Dynamic Choice-Driven Narratives." Presented at the 14th International Conference on the Foundations of Digital Games (FDG), San Luis Obispo, CA, USA, August 26–30, 2019. https://doi.org/10.1145/3337722.3337732.

Gardner, Martin. "Mathematical Games: The Fantastic Combinations of John Conway's New Solitaire Game 'Life.'" *Scientific American*, October 1970. https://doi.org/10.1038/scientificamerican1070-120.

Ghamari-Tabrizi, Sharon. "Wargames as Writing Systems." In *Zones of Control: Perspectives on Wargaming*, edited by Pat Harrigan and Matthew G. Kirschenbaum. Cambridge, MA: MIT Press, 2016.

Giant Sparrow. *What Remains of Edith Finch*. Microsoft Windows. Ian Dallas, Joshua M. Sarfaty, Chelsea Hash, Brandon Martynowicz, Chris Bell, et al. Annapurna Interactive, 2017.

Gibbs, Raymond W. "Evaluating Conceptual Metaphor Theory." *Discourse Processes* 48, no. 8 (October 27, 2011): 529–562. https://doi.org/10.1080/0163853X.2011.606103.

Gibbs, Raymond W. "Words Making Love Together: Dynamics of Metaphoric Creativity." In *Cultures and Traditions of Wordplay and Wordplay Research*, edited by Esme Winter-Froemel and Verena Thaler, 23–46. Berlin: De Gruyter, 2018.

Gingold, Chaim. "What *WarioWare* Can Teach Us about Game Design." *Game Studies* 5, no. 1 (October 2005). http://www.gamestudies.org/0501/gingold/.

Glaser, Mark. "Before the Big Bang; The Space Age Game That Set the Stage." *New York Times*, August 9, 2001. https://www.nytimes.com/2001/08/09/technology/before-the-big-bang-the-space-age-game-that-set-the-stage.html.

Gleicher, Michael. "Retargetting Motion to New Characters." In *SIGGRAPH '98: Proceedings of the 25th Annual Conference on Computer Graphics and Interactive Techniques*, 33–42. New York: ACM, 1998. https://doi.org/10.1145/280814.280820.

Goffman, Erving. *The Presentation of Self in Everyday Life*. New York: Anchor Books, 1959.

Goldberg, Martin. "Nolan Bushnell and Digging Up *Spacewar!*" Atari Inc.—Business Is Fun, January 11, 2014. http://ataribook.com/book/nolan-digging-spacewar/ (currently available at: https://web.archive.org/web/20160303213731/http://ataribook.com/book/nolan-digging-spacewar/).

Graetz, J. M. "*Spacewar!* Real-Time Capability of the PDP-1." In *DECUS Proceedings 1962: Papers and Presentations of the Digital Equipment Computer Users Society*, 37–39. Maynard, MA: Digital Equipment Computer Users Society, 1962. http://bitsavers.org/pdf/dec/decus/confProceedings/ DECUS_1962.pdf.

Graetz, J. M. "The Origin of *Spacewar!*" *Creative Computing*, August 1981.

Grand Theft Auto IV Message Board for PC. "Player Selector Mod / Play as Pedestrian Mod." GameFAQs. Accessed September 27, 2019. https://gamefaqs.gamespot.com/boards/952150 -grand-theft-auto-iv/47583324.

Grand Theft Wiki. "Swingset Glitch." GTA Wiki. Updated August 9, 2012. https://www .grandtheftwiki.com/Swingset_Glitch.

Green, Amy M. "*Bioshock Infinite*: The Search for Redemption and the Repetition of Atrocity." In *The Play Versus Story Divide in Game Studies: Critical Essays*, edited by Matthew Wilhelm Kapell, 125–144. Jefferson, NC: McFarland, 2015.

Greenberg, Diane. "Celebrating *Tennis for Two* with a Video Game Extravaganza." *The Bulletin, Brookhaven National Laboratory*, October 31, 2008. https://www.bnl.gov/bnlweb/pubaf/bulletin/ 2008/bb103108.pdf.

Grow, April, Melanie Dickinson, Johnathan Pagnutti, Noah Wardrip-Fruin, and Michael Mateas. "Crafting in Games." *Digital Humanities Quarterly* 011, no. 4 (December 22, 2017).

GTA 5 Wiki Guide. "How to Make Money in *GTA 5*." IGN, 2014. https://www.ign.com/wikis/ gta-5/How_to_Make_Money_in_GTA_5.

Guins, Raiford. *Atari Design: Impressions on a Cultural Form, 1972–1979*. London: Bloomsbury Press, 2020.

Guins, Raiford. *Game After: A Cultural Study of Video Game Afterlife*. Cambridge, MA: MIT Press, 2014. https://doi.org/10.7551/mitpress/9289.001.0001.

Guins, Raiford. "*Tennis for Two* at the NY Historical Society Museum." *Raiford Guins* (blog), November 19, 2015. https://raifordguins.com/2015/11/19/tennis-for-two-at-the-ny-historical -society-musuem/.

Gygax, Gary, and Dave Arneson. *Dungeons & Dragons*. Lake Geneva, WI: Tactical Studies Rules, 1974.

Harmonix Music Systems. *Dance Central*. Microsoft Xbox 360. Kasson Crooker, Naoko Takamoto, Jason Kendall, Marc Flury, Dean Tate, Marcos Aguirre, Francisca Hernandez, Helen McWilliams, Dare Matheson, Riseon Kim, et al. MTV Games, 2010.

Harmonix Music Systems. *Guitar Hero*. Sony PlayStation 2. Greg LoPiccolo, Daniel Sussman, Philip Winston, Ryan Lesser, Rob Kay, Eric Brosius, John Tam, et al. RedOctane, 2005.

Harmonix Music Systems. *Rock Band*. Microsoft Xbox 360. Greg LoPiccolo, Tracy Rosenthal-Newsom, Josh Randall, Rob Kay, Dan Teasdale, Eran Egozy, James Wiley Fleming, Ryan Lesser, Jason Arnone, et al. MTV Games, 2007.

Harrell, D. Fox. *Phantasmal Media: An Approach to Imagination, Computation, and Expression*. Cambridge, MA: MIT Press, 2013.

Harrell, D. Fox, and Jichen Zhu. "Agency Play: Dimensions of Agency for Interactive Narrative Design." In *AAAI Spring Symposium: Intelligent Narrative Technologies II*, 44–52. Palo Alto, CA: AAAI, 2009. http://www.aaai.org/Papers/Symposia/Spring/2009/SS-09-06/SS09-06-008.pdf.

Hart, Vi, and Nicky Case. "Parable of the Polygons." Parable of the Polygons, 2014. http://ncase.me/polygons.

Hasbro Games. "Rule Book." In *Monopoly Brand Property Trading Game from Parker Brothers: The .Com Edition*, edited by Parker Brothers. Pawtucket, RI: Hasbro, 2000.

Hayes-Roth, Barbara, Erik Sincoff, Lee Brownston, Ruth Huard, and Brian Lent. "Directed Improvisation with Animated Puppets." In *Conference Companion on Human Factors in Computing Systems* (CHI '95), 79–80. New York: ACM, 1995. https://doi.org/10.1145/223355.223438.

Higinbotham, William, Robert V. Dvorak, and David Potter. *Tennis for Two*. Custom hardware. Brookhaven National Laboratory, 1958. Retrospectively named.

Hilliard, Kyle. "*Gone Home* House Becomes a Multiplayer Map in Counter-Strike Mod." Game Informer, September 17, 2014. https://www.gameinformer.com/b/news/archive/2014/09/17/gone-home-house-becomes-a-multiplayer-map-in-counter-strike-mod.aspx.

Hocking, Clint. "Dynamics: The State of the Art." Presented at the 25th Game Developers Conference, San Francisco, CA, USA, February 28–March 4, 2011. http://www.gdcvault.com/play/1014597/Dynamics-The-State-of-the.

Hocking, Clint. "Ludonarrative Dissonance in *Bioshock*." *Click Nothing* (blog), October 7, 2007. http://www.clicknothing.com/click_nothing/2007/10/ludonarrative-d.html.

Hofmeier, Richard. *Cart Life*. Microsoft Windows. 2011.

Honeywell, Leigh. "Bingo and Beyond." *Hypatia Dot Ca* (blog), September 23, 2015. https://hypatia.ca/2015/09/23/bingo-and-beyond/.

Huber, William Humberto. "Epic Spatialities: The Production of Space in *Final Fantasy* Games." In *Third Person: Authoring and Exploring Vast Narratives*, edited by Pat Harrigan and Noah Wardrip-Fruin. Cambridge, MA: MIT Press, 2009.

Huber, William Humberto. "The Foundations of Videogame Authorship." PhD diss., University of California, San Diego, 2013. http://escholarship.org/uc/item/96x08750.

Humble, Rod. "Game Rules as Art | Can a Game Make You Cry?" *Escapist*, April 18, 2006. https://v1.escapistmagazine.com/articles/view/video-games/issues/issue_41/247-Game-Rules-as-Art.2.

Humble, Rod. *The Marriage*. Microsoft Windows. 2007. https://www.rodvik.com/rodgames/marriage.html.

Hunicke, Robin, Marc LeBlanc, and Robert Zubek. "MDA: A Formal Approach to Game Design and Game Research." In *Proceedings of the AAAI Workshop on Challenges in Game AI*, San Jose, CA, July 25–26, 2004. Menlo Park, CA: AAAI, 2004.

id Software. *DOOM*. MS-DOS. John Romero, John Carmack, Sandy Petersen, Tom Hall, Dave Taylor, et al. id Software, 1993.

id Software. *Quake*. MS-DOS. John Romero, John Carmack, Adrian Carmack, American McGee, Michael Abrash, Sandy Petersen, Tim Willits, John Cash, Kevin Cloud, Paul Steed, Trent Reznor, et al. GT Interactive, 1996.

id Software. *Quake III Arena*. Microsoft Windows. Graeme J. Devine, John Carmack, John Cash, Adrian Carmack, Kevin Cloud, Kenneth Scott, Paul Steed, Christian Antkow, Martin Cluney, Brandon James, Jennell Jaquays, Tim Willits, et al. Activision, 1999.

id Software. *Wolfenstein 3D*. MS-DOS. John Romero, John Carmack, Tom Hall, Adrian Carmack, Robert Prince, et al. Apogee Software, 1992.

ImSteevin. January 16, 2014. Comment on Prell, "Dorkly Unleashes a Trailer for *Gone Home*'s Ideal DLC, 'Gun Home.'" http://www.joystiq.com/2014/01/16/dorkly-unleashes-a-trailer-for-gone -homes-ideal-dlc-gun-home/ (no longer available).

Ingebretson, Peter, and Max Rebuschatis. "Concurrent Interactions in *The Sims 4*." Presented at the 28th Game Developers Conference, San Francisco, CA, USA, March 17–21, 2014. https:// www.gdcvault.com/play/1020413/Concurrent-Interactions-in-The-Sims.

Ingold, Jon. "Heaven's Vault: Creating a Dynamic Detective Story." Virtual presentation at the 34th Game Developers Conference, San Francisco, CA, USA, March 16–20, 2020. https://www .youtube.com/watch?v=o02uJ-ktCuk.

inkle. *80 Days*. Apple iOS. Meg Jayanth, Joseph Humfrey, Jon Ingold, Jaume Fabregat, Laurence Chapman, et al. Profile Books, 2014.

inkle. *Heaven's Vault*. Microsoft Windows. Jon Ingold, Joseph Humfrey, Tom Kail, Laura Dillo- way, Piran Tremethick, Thomas Blunden, Sarah Hefford, Anastasia Wyatt, Laurence Chapman, et al. inkle, 2019.

inkle. *Steve Jackson's Sorcery!* (Part 1). Apple iOS. Jon Ingold, Graham Robertson, Joseph Hum- frey, Mike Schley, Eddie Shaarm, Ara Carrasco, Laurence Chapman, Dave Wise, et al. inkle, 2013. [Based on a 1983 gamebook of the same title.]

Intelligent Systems and Nintendo R&D1. *WarioWare: Touched!* Nintendo DS. Yoshio Sakamoto, Ryouichi Kitanishi, Katsuya Yamano, Toshio Sengoku, Kouichi Kawamoto, Ryuichi Nakada, Goro Abe, Taku Sugioka, Teruyuki Hirosawa, et al. Nintendo of America, 2005.

Intelligent Systems and Nintendo SPD. *WarioWare: Smooth Moves*. Nintendo Wii. Yoshio Saka- moto, Ryouichi Kitanishi, Osamu Yamauchi, Katsuya Yamano, Toshio Sengoku, Kouichi Kawa- moto, Goro Abe, Taku Sugioka, Hideo Hatayama, Ko Takeuchi, et al. Nintendo of America, 2007.

Interplay Productions. *Fallout*. Microsoft Windows. Christopher Taylor, Timothy Cain, Chris Jones, Leonard Boyarsky, Charles Deenen, et al. Interplay Entertainment Corp., 1997.

Irrational Games. *BioShock Infinite*. Microsoft Windows. Ken Levine, Rod Fergusson, Leonie Manshanden, Adrian Murphy, Scott Sinclair, Shawn Robertson, Forrest Dowling, Andres Elias Gonzalez Tahhan, Jordan Thomas, Christopher Kline, John Abercrombie, Steven Ellmore, Scott Haraldsen, et al. 2K Games, 2013.

Isbister, Katherine. "Social Play." In *How Games Move Us: Emotion by Design*. Cambridge, MA: MIT Press, 2016. https://doi.org/10.7551/mitpress/9267.003.0005.

Jackson, Shelley. *Patchwork Girl*. Apple System 6. Eastgate Systems, 1995.

Jagoda, Patrick. *"Passage."* In *The Game Worlds of Jason Rohrer*, by Michael Maizels and Patrick Jagoda. Wellesley, MA: Davis Museum; Cambridge, MA: MIT Press, 2016.

Jameson, Fredric. *Postmodernism, Or, The Cultural Logic of Late Capitalism*. Durham, NC: Duke University Press, 1991.

Jayanth, Meg. "Forget Protagonists: Writing NPCs with Agency for *80 Days* and Beyond." Presented at the Game Narrative Summit, 30th Game Developers Conference, San Francisco, CA, USA, March 14–18, 2016. https://gdcvault.com/play/1023393/Forget-Protagonists-Writing-NPCs-with.

Jayanth, Meg. "Forget Protagonists: Writing NPCs with Agency for *80 Days* and Beyond." Medium, June 5, 2016. https://medium.com/@betterthemask/forget-protagonists-writing-npcs -with-agency-for-80-days-and-beyond-703201a2309.

Jerz, Dennis G. "Somewhere Nearby Is Colossal Cave: Examining Will Crowther's Original *Adventure* in Code and in Kentucky." *Digital Humanities Quarterly* 1, no. 2 (2007). http://www .digitalhumanities.org/dhq/vol/001/2/000009/000009.html.

Joyce, Michael T. "Siren Shapes: Exploratory and Constructive Hypertexts." *Academic Computing* 3 (1988).

Juul, Jesper. *A Casual Revolution: Reinventing Video Games and Their Players*. Cambridge, MA: MIT Press, 2009.

Juul, Jesper. "A Certain Level of Abstraction." Presented at the 2007 DiGRA International Conference: Situated Play, Tokyo, Japan, September 24–28, 2007. http://www.digra.org/wp-content/ uploads/digital-library/07312.29390.pdf.

Juul, Jesper. *Half-Real: Video Games between Real Rules and Fictional Worlds*. Cambridge, MA: MIT Press, 2005.

k, merritt (formerly Merritt Kopas). *LIM*. Browser (HTML5). 2012. https://merrittk.com/files/Lim (no longer available).

Kagen, Melissa. "Walking Simulators, #Gamergate, and the Gender of Wandering." In *The Year's Work in Nerds, Wonks, and Neocons*, edited by Jonathan P. Eburne and Benjamin Schreier, 275–300. Bloomington, IN: Indiana University Press, 2017. https://doi.org/10.2307/j.ctt20060h2.15.

Kaltman, Eric. "UC3 Merritt: Collection—UCSC Library *Prom Week* Development Archive." Merritt Digital Archive: University of California Curation Center (UC3) at the California Digital Library (CDL), 2014. https://merritt.cdlib.org/m/ucsc_lib_promweek?page=1.

Kaltman, Eric, Noah Wardrip-Fruin, Henry Lowood, and Christy Caldwell. "A Unified Approach to Preserving Cultural Software Objects and Their Development Histories," November 20, 2014. https://escholarship.org/uc/item/0wg4w6b9.

Karth, Isaac. "Ergodic Agency: How Play Manifests Understanding." In *Engaging with Videogames: Play, Theory and Practice*, edited by Dawn Stobbart and Monica Evans, 205–216. Oxford: Inter-Disciplinary Press, 2014. http://manuel.boutet.free.fr/EngagingWithVideogames.pdf#page=220.

Kay, Alan, and Adele Goldberg. "Personal Dynamic Media." *Computer* 10, no. 3 (March 1977): 31–41. https://doi.org/10.1109/C-M.1977.217672.

Kee Games. *Tank*. Arcade. Steve Bristow, Lyle V. Rains, et al. Kee Games, 1974. ["Kee Games" was an initially unacknowledged subsidiary of Atari.]

Kelso, Margaret Thomas, Peter Weyhrauch, and Joseph Bates. "Dramatic Presence." *Presence: Teleoperators and Virtual Environments* 2, no. 1 (January 1, 1993): 1–15. https://doi.org/10.1162/pres.1993.2.1.1.

Kent, Steve L. *The Ultimate History of Video Games: From Pong to Pokémon and beyond: The Story behind the Craze That Touched Our Lives and Changed the World*. Roseville, CA: Prima Pub, 2001.

Keogh, Brendan. *A Play of Bodies: How We Perceive Videogames*. Cambridge, MA: MIT Press, 2018. https://doi.org/10.7551/mitpress/10963.001.0001.

Keogh, Brendan. "Across Worlds and Bodies: Criticism in the Age of Video Games." *Journal of Games Criticism* 1, no. 1 (January 22, 2014). http://gamescriticism.org/articles/keogh-1-1.

Keogh, Brendan. "Some Preliminary Thoughts on *Bioshock Infinite*'s Racism." *Critical Damage* (blog), April 19, 2013. http://critdamage.blogspot.com/2013/04/some-preliminary-thoughts-on -bioshock.html.

Keogh, Brendan. "Notes on *Bioshock Infinite*." *Critical Damage* (blog), April 22, 2013. http:// critdamage.blogspot.com/2013/04/notes-on-bioshock-infinite.html.

Kietzmann, Ludwig. "*Gone Home* Review: First-Person Snooper." Joystiq, August 15, 2013. https:// www.engadget.com/2013/08/15/gone-home-review/ (original URL no longer available).

Klepek, Patrick. "*Gone Home* Review." Giant Bomb, August 15, 2013. https://www.giantbomb .com/reviews/gone-home-review/1900-591/.

Kline, Stephen, Nick Dyer-Witheford, and Greig de Peuter. *Digital Play: The Interaction of Technology, Culture, and Marketing*. Montreal; London: McGill–Queen's University Press, 2003.

Konami Computer Entertainment Japan. *Metal Gear Solid*. Sony PlayStation. Hideo Kojima, Yoji Shinkawa, Tomokazu Fukushima, Yoji Shinkawa, Kazuki Muraoka, Yoshikazu Matsuhana, et al. Konami of America, 1998.

Konami Industry. *Frogger*. Arcade. Sega/Gremlin, 1981.

Koster, Raph. "A Grammar of Gameplay: Game Atoms: Can Games Be Diagrammed?" Presented at the 19th Game Developers Conference, San Francisco, CA, USA, March 7–11, 2005.

Koster, Raph. *A Theory of Fun for Game Design*. Scottsdale, AZ: Paraglyph, 2004.

Koster, Raph. "An Atomic Theory of Fun Game Design." Raph Koster's blog, January 24, 2012. https://www.raphkoster.com/2012/01/24/an-atomic-theory-of-fun-game-design/.

Koster, Raph. "ATOF *Tetris* Variant Comes True." Raph Koster's blog, February 13, 2009. https://www.raphkoster.com/2009/02/13/atof-tetris-variant-comes-true/.

Koster, Raph. "(Dis)Assembling Experience." Presented at the 2nd Game UX Summit, Toronto, ON, Canada, October 4–6, 2017. https://www.raphkoster.com/games/presentations/disassembling-games/.

Koster, Raph. "Game Grammar." Presented at PAX Dev 2015, Seattle, WA, USA, August 26–27, 2015. https://www.raphkoster.com/games/presentations/game-grammar/.

Kreimeier, Bernd. "The Case for Game Design Patterns." Gamasutra, March 13, 2002. http://www.gamasutra.com/view/feature/132649/the_case_for_game_design_patterns.php.

Kreminski, Max, and Noah Wardrip-Fruin. "Generative Games as Storytelling Partners." Presented at the 14th International Conference on the Foundations of Digital Games (FDG), San Luis Obispo, CA, USA, August 26–30, 2019. https://doi.org/10.1145/3337722.3341861.

Kway, Liting, and Alex Mitchell. "Emotional Agency in Storygames." Presented at the 13th International Conference on the Foundations of Digital Games (FDG), Malmö, Sweden, August 7–10, 2018. https://doi.org/10.1145/3235765.3235777.

Lakoff, George. "The Contemporary Theory of Metaphor." In *Metaphor and Thought*, edited by Andrew Ortony. Cambridge: Cambridge University Press, 1993.

Landsteiner, Norbert. "Inside *Spacewar!*—A Software Archeological Approach to the First Video Game." mass:werk media environments, 2014–2015. https://www.masswerk.at/spacewar/inside/.

Larsen, Deena. *Marble Springs*. Apple System 6. Eastgate Systems, 1993.

Laurel, Brenda. "Toward the Design of a Computer-Based Interactive Fantasy System." PhD diss., The Ohio State University, 1986. https://etd.ohiolink.edu/pg_10?0::NO:10:P10_ACCESSION_NUM:osu1240408469.

Laurel, Brenda. *Computers as Theatre*. Boston: Addison-Wesley Publishing, 1991.

Laurel, Brenda. *Computers as Theatre*. 2nd ed. Boston: Addison-Wesley Publishing, 2013.

Lazzaro, Nicole. "Why We Play: Affect and the Fun of Games." In *Human-Computer Interaction: Designing for Diverse Users and Domains* 155. Edited by Andrew Sears and Julie A. Jacko. Boca Raton, FL: CRC Press, 2009.

Lebra, Takie Sugiyama. *The Japanese Self in Cultural Logic*. Honolulu: University of Hawaii Press, 2004.

Lederle-Ensign, Dylan, William Robinson, Johnathan Pagnutti, and Michael Mateas. "A Software Studies Approach to Interpreting Passage." Presented at the 10th International Conference on the Foundations of Digital Games (FDG), Pacific Grove, CA, USA, June 22–25, 2015. http://fdg2015.org/papers/fdg2015_paper_46.pdf.

Lederle-Ensign, Dylan, and Noah Wardrip-Fruin. "What Is Strafe Jumping? IdTech3 and the Game Engine as Software Platform." *Transactions of the Digital Games Research Association* 2, no. 2 (April 5, 2016). https://doi.org/10.26503/todigra.v2i2.35.

Leduc, Phillip L. *Momentum*. Tabletop game. nestorgames, 2010. https://nestorgames.com/#momentum_detail.

Leonard, David. "Young, Black (& Brown) and Don't Give a Fuck: Virtual Gangstas in the Era of State Violence." *Cultural Studies ↔ Critical Methodologies* 9, no. 2 (April 1, 2009): 248–272. https://doi.org/10.1177/1532708608325938.

Lessard, Jonathan. "Game Genres and High-Level Design Pattern Formations." Presented at the 3rd Workshop on Design Patterns in Games (DPG), colocated with the 9th International Conference on the Foundations of Digital Games, Fort Lauderdale, FL, USA, April 3–7, 2014.

Levy, Steven. *Hackers: Heroes of the Computer Revolution*. New York: Anchor Press/Doubleday, 1984.

Little Story People. *Blood & Laurels*. Apple iOS. Emily Short, Richard Evans, Graham Nelson, et al. Linden Research, 2014.

Losh, Elizabeth. "Playing Defense: Gender, Just War, and Game Design." In *Zones of Control: Perspectives on Wargaming*, edited by Pat Harrigan and Matthew G. Kirschenbaum. Cambridge, MA: MIT Press, 2016.

Lowood, Henry. "Videogames in Computer Space: The Complex History of *Pong*." *IEEE Annals of the History of Computing* 31, no. 3 (2009): 5–19.

Lynch, David, dir. *Mulholland Drive*. Universal City, CA: Universal Pictures, 2001.

Magie, Elizabeth. *The Landlord's Game*. Tabletop. 1906.

Magnuson, Jordan. "Playing and Making Poetic Videogames." MFA thesis, University of California, Santa Cruz, 2019.

Malaby, Thomas M. "Beyond Play: A New Approach to Games." *Games and Culture* 2, no. 2 (April 1, 2007): 95–113. https://doi.org/10.1177/1555412007299434.

Malone, Thomas Wendell. "What Makes Things Fun to Learn? A Study of Intrinsically Motivating Computer Games." PhD diss., Stanford University, 1980. http://search.proquest.com/docview/303047451/abstract/5715E3B2BB5D4F44PQ/1.

Márquez Segura, Elena, James Fey, Ella Dagan, Samvid Niravbhai Jhaveri, Jared Pettitt, Miguel Flores, and Katherine Isbister. "Designing Future Social Wearables with Live Action Role Play (LARP) Designers." In *Proceedings of the 2018 CHI Conference on Human Factors in Computing Systems—CHI '18*. New York: ACM, 2018. https://doi.org/10.1145/3173574.3174036.

Mason, Stacey. "On Games and Links: Extending the Vocabulary of Agency and Immersion in Interactive Narratives." In *Interactive Storytelling*, edited by Hartmut Koenitz, Tonguc Ibrahim Sezen, Gabriele Ferri, Mads Haahr, Digdem Sezen, and Güven Çatak, 25–34. Lecture Notes in Computer Science. Berlin: Springer International Publishing, 2013.

Mason, Stacey, Ceri Stagg, Noah Wardrip-Fruin, and Michael Mateas. "Lume: A System for Procedural Story Generation." Presented at the 14th International Conference on the Foundations of Digital Games (FDG), San Luis Obispo, CA, USA, August 26–30, 2019. https://doi.org/10.1145/3337722.3337759.

Mateas, Michael. "A Preliminary Poetics for Interactive Drama and Games." In *First Person: New Media as Story, Performance and Game*, edited by Noah Wardrip-Fruin and Pat Harrigan. Cambridge, MA: MIT Press, 2004.

Mateas, Michael. "Interactive Drama, Art and Artificial Intelligence." PhD diss., Carnegie Mellon University, 2002. https://www.cs.cmu.edu/~dgroup/papers/CMU-CS-02-206.pdf.

Mateas, Michael, and Andrew Stern. *Façade*. Microsoft Windows. Procedural Arts, 2005.

Mateas, Michael, and Andrew Stern. "Structuring Content in the Façade Interactive Drama Architecture." Presented at the 1st AAAI Conference on Artificial Intelligence and Interactive Digital Entertainment (AIIDE), Marina del Rey, CA, USA, June 1–3, 2005. https://www.aaai.org/Papers/AIIDE/2005/AIIDE05-016.pdf.

Mateas, Michael, and Noah Wardrip-Fruin. "Defining Operational Logics." In *Proceedings of the Digital Games Research Association*. DiGRA, London, 2009.

Mawhorter, Peter Andrew. "Artificial Intelligence as a Tool for Understanding Narrative Choices." PhD diss., University of California, Santa Cruz, 2016. https://escholarship.org/uc/item/1tn22145.

Mawhorter, Peter Andrew, Michael Mateas, and Noah Wardrip-Fruin. "Intentionally Generating Choices in Interactive Narratives." Presented at the 6th International Conference on Computational Creativity, Park City, UT, USA, June 29–July 2, 2015.

Mawhorter, Peter Andrew, Michael Mateas, and Noah Wardrip-Fruin. "Generating Relaxed, Obvious, and Dilemma Choices with Dunyazad." Presented at the 11th AAAI Conference on Artificial Intelligence and Interactive Digital Entertainment (AIIDE), Santa Cruz, CA, USA, November 14–18, 2015. https://www.aaai.org/ocs/index.php/AIIDE/AIIDE15/paper/view/11550.

Mawhorter, Peter Andrew, Michael Mateas, Noah Wardrip-Fruin, and Arnav Jhala. "Towards a Theory of Choice Poetics." Presented at the 9th International Conference on the Foundations of Digital Games, Fort Lauderdale, FL, USA, April 3–7, 2014.

Mawhorter, Peter Andrew, Carmen Zegura, Alex Gray, Arnav Jhala, Michael Mateas, and Noah Wardrip-Fruin. "Choice Poetics by Example." *Arts* 7, no. 3 (September 2018). https://doi.org/10.3390/arts7030047.

Maxis Software. *SimCity*. Apple System 6. Will Wright, Jeff Braun, Robert Strobel, Brian Witt, Don Bayless, Steve Hales, et al. Broderbund Software, 1989.

Maxis Software. *The Sims*. Microsoft Windows. Will Wright, Kana Ryan, Charles London, Jamie Doornbos, Eric Bowman, et al. Electronic Arts, 2000.

Maya, Bill. "The Once and Future Storytron." Medium, November 11, 2018. https://medium.com/storytron/the-once-and-future-storytron-9579efd8d81b.

McCoy, Josh, Mike Treanor, Ben Samuel, Aaron A. Reed, Michael Mateas, and Noah Wardrip-Fruin. "Social Story Worlds with *Comme Il Faut*." *IEEE Transactions on Computational Intelligence and AI in Games* 6, no. 2 (June 2014): 97–112. https://doi.org/10.1109/TCIAIG.2014.2304692.

McCoy, Josh, and Michael Mateas. "The Computation of Self in Everyday Life: A Dramaturgical Approach for Socially Competent Agents." Presented at the AAAI Spring Symposium, Palo Alto, CA, USA, March 23–25, 2009.

McCoy, Josh, Mike Treanor, Ben Samuel, Aaron A. Reed, Michael Mateas, and Noah Wardrip-Fruin. "*Prom Week*: Designing Past the Game/Story Dilemma." Presented at the 8th International Conference on the Foundations of Digital Games, Chania, Crete, Greece, May 14–17, 2013. http://www.fdg2013.org/program/papers/paper13_mccoy_etal.pdf.

McCoy, Josh, Mike Treanor, Ben Samuel, Aaron A. Reed, Michael Mateas, Noah Wardrip-Fruin, Kathleen Kralowec, et al. *Prom Week*. Adobe Flash. UC Santa Cruz Expressive Intelligence Studio, 2012. https://promweek.soe.ucsc.edu/.

McCoy, Josh, Mike Treanor, Ben Samuel, Brandon Tearse, Michael Mateas, and Noah Wardrip-Fruin. "Authoring Game-Based Interactive Narrative Using Social Games and *Comme Il Faut*." Presented at the 4th International Conference & Festival of the Electronic Literature Organization: Archive & Innovate, Providence, RI, USA, June 3–6, 2010.

McCoy, Josh, Mike Treanor, Ben Samuel, Brandon Tearse, Michael Mateas, and Noah Wardrip-Fruin. "*Comme Il Faut 2*: A Fully Realized Model for Socially Oriented Gameplay." In *Proceedings of the Intelligent Narrative Technologies III Workshop*. INT3 '10. New York: ACM, 2010. https://doi.org/10.1145/1822309.1822319.

McCoy, Joshua, Michael Mateas, and Noah Wardrip-Fruin. "Comme Il Faut: A System for Simulating Social Games Between Autonomous Characters." Presented at the 8th Digital Arts and Culture Conference, Irvine, CA, USA, December 12–15, 2009. https://escholarship.org/uc/item/6x5933cw.

McCoy, Joshua, Mike Treanor, Ben Samuel, Noah Wardrip-Fruin, and Michael Mateas. "*Comme Il Faut*: A System for Authoring Playable Social Models." Presented at the 7th AAAI Conference on

Artificial Intelligence and Interactive Digital Entertainment (AIIDE), Palo Alto, CA, USA, October 11–14, 2011. https://www.aaai.org/ocs/index.php/AIIDE/AIIDE11/paper/view/4080.

McDonald, Heidi. "Romance in Games: What It Is, How It Is, and How Developers Can Improve It." *QED: A Journal in GLBTQ Worldmaking* 2, no. 2 (2015): 32–63. https://doi.org/10.14321/qed .2.2.0032.

McWhertor, Michael. "Layoffs: The Video Game Is Depressing Fun." Kotaku, March 16, 2009. https://kotaku.com/5170770/layoffs-the-video-game-is-depressing-fun.

Melcer, Edward, James Ryan, Nick Junius, Max Kreminski, Dietrich Squinkifer, Brent Hill, and Noah Wardrip-Fruin. "Teaching Responsible Conduct of Research Through an Interactive Story-telling Game." In *CHI EA '20: Extended Abstracts of the 2019 CHI Conference on Human Factors in Computing Systems*. New York: ACM, 2020.

Melcer, Edward, Katelyn Grasse, James Ryan, Nick Junius, Max Kreminski, Dietrich Squinkifer, Brent Hill, and Noah Wardrip-Fruin. "Getting Academical: A Choice-Based Interactive Storytell-ing Game for Teaching Responsible Conduct of Research." In *FDG '20: Proceedings of the Fifteenth International Conference on the Foundations of Digital Games*. New York: ACM, 2020.

Midway Mfg., General Computer Corporation. *Ms. Pac-Man*. Arcade. Douglas B. Macrae, John Tylko, Phil Kaaret, Kevin Curran, Chris Rode, Mike Horowitz, et al. Midway Mfg., 1982.

Miller, George A. "WordNet: A Lexical Database for English." *Commun. ACM* 38, no. 11 (Novem-ber 1995): 39–41. https://doi.org/10.1145/219717.219748.

Milton Bradley. *Candy Land*. Tabletop. Eleanor Abbott. 1949.

Milton Bradley. *Connect Four*. Tabletop (vertical). 1974.

Milton Bradley. *Twister*. Floor game. Charles Foley and Neil Rabens. 1966.

Minority Media. *Papo & Yo*. Sony PlayStation 3. Vander Caballero, Julien Barnoin, Paul Di Marco, Frédéric Hamel, Antonio Maiorano, Simon Lallement, Carol Bertrand, Stéphanie Landry, Yann Penno, Carlos Hidalgo, Ruben Farrus Beso, et al. Minority Media, 2012.

Mitchell, Alex. "Making the Familiar Unfamiliar: Techniques for Creating Poetic Gameplay." Presented at the 1st International Joint Conference of DiGRA and FDG, Dundee, Scotland, UK, August 1–6, 2016. http://www.digra.org/wp-content/uploads/digital-library/paper_272.pdf.

Mitchell, Alex. "Reflective Rereading and the *SimCity* Effect in Interactive Stories." In *Interac-tive Storytelling*, edited by Henrik Schoenau-Fog, Luis Emilio Bruni, Sandy Louchart, and Sarune Baceviciute, 27–39. Lecture Notes in Computer Science. Berlin: Springer International Publishing, 2015.

Mitchell, Alex, Yuin Theng Sim, and Liting Kway. "Making It Unfamiliar in the 'Right' Way." Presented at the 2017 DiGRA International Conference, Melbourne, Victoria, Australia, July 2–6, 2017.

Mojang. *Minecraft*. Browser. Markus Persson, Daniel Rosenfeld, Kristoffer Zetterstrand, Paul Spooner. Mojang, 2010.

Molleindustria. *The Free Culture Game*. Adobe Flash. 2008. http://www.molleindustria.org/en/ freeculturegame/.

Molleindustria. *Kosmosis—a Communist Space Shooter*. Adobe Flash. 2009. http://www .molleindustria.org/kosmosis/kosmosis.html.

Molleindustria. *Unmanned*. Adobe Flash. Paolo Pedercini, Jim Munroe, and Jesse Stiles. 2012. http://unmanned.molleindustria.org/.

Monnens, Devin, and Martin Goldberg. "Space Odyssey: The Long Journey of *Spacewar!* from MIT to Computer Labs Around the World." *Kinephanos: Journal of Media Studies and Popular Culture* (June 2015): 124–147.

Monolith Productions. *Middle-Earth: Shadow of Mordor*. Microsoft Windows. Michael de Plater, Philip Straub, Matthew T. Allen, Matthew Rice, Michael David Forgey, et al. Warner Bros. Interactive Entertainment, 2014.

Montfort, Nick. "PvP: *Portal* versus *Passage*." Grand Text Auto, February 24, 2008. https:// grandtextauto.soe.ucsc.edu/2008/02/24/pvp-portal-versus-passage/.

Montfort, Nick. *Twisty Little Passages: An Approach to Interactive Fiction*. Cambridge, MA: MIT Press, 2003.

Montfort, Nick, and Ian Bogost. *Racing the Beam: The Atari Video Computer System*. Cambridge, MA: MIT Press, 2009.

Moon, Alan R. *Ticket to Ride*. Tabletop game. Days of Wonder, 2004.

Morais, Luís, João Dias, and Pedro A. Santos. "From Caveman to Gentleman: A CiF-Based Social Interaction Model Applied to Conan Exiles." Presented at the 14th International Conference on the Foundations of Digital Games (FDG), San Luis Obispo, CA, USA, August 26–30, 2019. https:// doi.org/10.1145/3337722.3337746.

Moranis, Rick, and Dave Thomas, dirs. *Strange Brew*. Beverly Hills, CA, MGM/UA Entertainment, 1983.

Moribe, Kuniaki. *Chain Shot*. Fujitsu FM-7. 1985.

Moulthrop, Stuart. "From Stuart Moulthrop's Online Response." In *First Person: New Media as Story, Performance, and Game*, edited by Noah Wardrip-Fruin and Pat Harrigan, 47–48. Cambridge, MA: MIT Press, 2004.

Moulthrop, Stuart. "Stuart Moulthrop's Response." *electronic book review*, May 21, 2003. https:// electronicbookreview.com/essay/stuart-moulthrops-response/.

MPS Labs. *Sid Meier's Civilization*. MS-DOS. Sid Meier, Bruce Campbell Shelley, Michael Haire, Harry E. Teasley, Barbara Miller, Todd Brizzi, Stacey Clark, Brian Martel, Erroll Roberts, Nicholas J. Rusko-Berger, Chris Soares, Jeffery L. Briggs, et al. MicroProse Software, 1991.

Munroe, Jim. "My Trip to Liberty City." No Media Kings, 2003. Video, 8:49. https://archive.org/details/My_Trip_to_Liberty_City.

Murray, Janet H. *Hamlet on the Holodeck: The Future of Narrative in Cyberspace*. New York: The Free Press, 1997.

Murray, John Thomas. "Telltale Hearts: Encoding Cinematic Choice-Based Adventure Games." PhD diss., University of California, Santa Cruz, 2018. https://escholarship.org/uc/item/1n02n02z.

Murray, Soraya. "High Art/Low Life: The Art of Playing *Grand Theft Auto*." *PAJ: A Journal of Performance and Art* 27, no. 2 (May 2005): 91–98. https://doi.org/10.1162/1520281053850866.

Murray, Soraya. *On Video Games: The Visual Politics of Race, Gender and Space*. London: I. B. Tauris, 2017.

Namco Limited. *Dig Dug*. Arcade. Masahisa Ikegami, Shigeichi Ishimura, Toshio Sakai, Shōichi Fukatani, and Yuriko Keino. Atari, 1982.

Namco Limited. *Galaxian*. Arcade. Kazunori Sawano, Shigeichi Ishimura, Kouichi Tashiro, and Shigeichi Ishimura. Namco Limited, 1979.

Namco Limited. *Pac-Man*. Arcade. Toru Iwatani, Shigeichi Ishimura, Shigeo Funaki, Shigeichi Ishimura, Toshio Kai. Namco Limited, 1980.

Naughty Dog. *The Last of Us: Left Behind*. Sony PlayStation 3. Bruce Straley, Neil Druckmann, Erick Pangilinan, Michael Hatfield, Travis McIntosh, Jason Gregory, Michael Yosh, Christian Nakata, Jacob Minkoff, et al. Sony Computer Entertainment America, 2014. Expansion for *The Last of Us*.

Naughty Dog. *Uncharted 2: Among Thieves*. Sony PlayStation 3. Bruce Straley, Amy Hennig, Erick Pangilinan, Robh Ruppel, Pål-Kristian Engstad, Travis McIntosh, Dan Liebgold, Tate Mosesian, Bruce Swanson, Josh Scherr, Jeremy Yates, Michael Yosh, Eric Baldwin, Richard Lemarchand, Neil Druckmann, et al. Sony Computer Entertainment America, 2009.

Neil, Katharine. "Game Design Tools: Can They Improve Game Design Practice?" PhD diss., National Conservatory of Arts and Crafts (CNAM); Flinders University, 2015. https://tel.archives-ouvertes.fr/tel-01344638/document.

Neil, Katharine. "How We Design Games Now and Why." Medium, February 17, 2017. First published in the book *Critical Hits: An Indie Gaming Anthology*, ed. Zoë Jellicoe (self-pub., 2016). https://medium.com/@haikus_by_KN/how-we-design-games-now-and-why-bcbc1deb7559.

Nelson, Mark J., and Michael Mateas. "An Interactive Game-Design Assistant." In *Proceedings of the 13th International Conference on Intelligent User Interfaces*, 90–98. New York: ACM, 2008. https://doi.org/10.1145/1378773.1378786.

Nelson, Mark J., and Michael Mateas. "Towards Automated Game Design." In *AI*IA 2007: Artificial Intelligence and Human-Oriented Computing*, edited by Roberto Basili and Maria Teresa Pazienza, 626–637. Lecture Notes in Computer Science. Berlin: Springer Berlin Heidelberg, 2007.

Nelson, Theodor Holm. *Computer Lib/Dream Machines*. Self-published, 1974.

Nelson, Theodor Holm. "No More Teachers' Dirty Looks." In *Computer Lib / Dream Machines*, by Ted Nelson, 309–338. Self-published, 1974. Originally published in *Computer Decisions* (1970).

Nintendo. *The Legend of Zelda*. Nintendo Entertainment System. Shigeru Miyamoto, Takashi Tezuka, Toshihiko Nakago, Yasunari Soejima, I. Marui, Kōji Kondō, and Hiroshi Yamauchi. Nintendo of America, 1987.

Nintendo and Systems Research & Development. *Super Mario Bros.* Nintendo Entertainment System. Shigeru Miyamoto, Takashi Tezuka, Koji Kondo, Hiroshi Ikeda, Hiroshi Yamauchi, Toshihiko Nakago, and Kazuaki Morita. Nintendo of America, 1985.

Nintendo R&D1. *Devil World*. Nintendo Family Computer. Shigeru Miyamoto, Takashi Tezuka, Hiroyuki Yukami, Kōji Kondō, Yukio Kaneoka, Mikio Kakiuchi, and Akito Nakatsuka. Nintendo, 1984. As played on emulator at https://www.retrogames.cz/play_363-NES.php?language=EN.

Nintendo R&D1. *WarioWare, Inc.: Mega Microgame$!* Game Boy Advance. Takehiro Izushi, Hirofumi Matsuoka, Kouichi Kawamoto, Hirofumi Matsuoka, Ko Takeuchi, et al. Nintendo of America, 2003.

Nitsche, Michael. *Video Game Spaces: Image, Play, and Structure in 3D Worlds*. Cambridge, MA: MIT Press, 2008. https://doi.org/10.7551/mitpress/9780262141017.001.0001.

North, Dale. "Review: *Gone Home*." Destructoid, October 1, 2013. https://www.Destructoid.com/review-gone-home-262626.phtml.

Oliveira, Miguel, and Pedro A. Santos. "A Model for Socially Intelligent Merchants." Presented at the 14th International Conference on the Foundations of Digital Games (FDG), San Luis Obispo, CA, USA, August 26–30, 2019. https://doi.org/10.1145/3337722.3337729.

Osborn, Joseph C. "Operationalizing Operational Logics." PhD diss., University of California, Santa Cruz, 2018. https://escholarship.org/uc/item/67g658wb.

Osborn, Joseph C., Melanie Dickinson, Barrett Anderson, Adam Summerville, Jill Denner, David Torres, Noah Wardrip-Fruin, and Michael Mateas. "Is Your Game Generator Working? Evaluating Gemini, an Intentional Generator." Presented at the 15th AAAI Conference on Artificial Intelligence and Interactive Digital Entertainment (AIIDE), Atlanta, GA, USA, October 8–12, 2019. https://www.aaai.org/ojs/index.php/AIIDE/article/view/5225.

Osborn, Joseph C., Brian Lambrigger, and Michael Mateas. "HyPED: Modeling and Analyzing Action Games as Hybrid Systems." Presented at the 13th AAAI Conference on Artificial Intelligence and Interactive Digital Entertainment (AIIDE), Snowbird, UT, USA, October 5–9, 2017. https://aaai.org/ocs/index.php/AIIDE/AIIDE17/paper/view/15900/15170.

Osborn, Joseph C., Dylan Lederle-Ensign, Noah Wardrip-Fruin, and Michael Mateas. "Combat in Games." Presented at the 10th International Conference on the Foundations of Digital Games (FDG), Pacific Grove, CA, USA, June 22–25, 2015. http://fdg2015.org/papers/fdg2015_paper_53.pdf.

Osborn, Joseph C., Adam Summerville, and Michael Mateas. "Automated Game Design Learning." In *2017 IEEE Conference on Computational Intelligence and Games (CIG)*, 240–247. Piscataway, NJ: IEEE, 2017. https://doi.org/10.1109/CIG.2017.8080442.

Osborn, Joseph C., Adam Summerville, and Michael Mateas. "Automatic Mapping of NES Games with Mappy." Presented at the 12th International Conference on the Foundations of Digital Games, Cape Cod, MA, USA, August 14–17, 2017. https://doi.org/10.1145/3102071.3110576.

Osborn, Joseph C., Noah Wardrip-Fruin, and Michael Mateas. "Refining Operational Logics." Presented at the 12th International Conference on the Foundations of Digital Games, Cape Cod, MA, USA, August 14–17, 2017. https://doi.org/10.1145/3102071.3102107.

Othenin-Girard, Alexei. "Bodies, Games, and Systems: Towards an Understanding of Embodiment in Games." Master's thesis, University of California, Santa Cruz, 2012.

Pajitnov, Alexey. *Tetris*. Electronika 60. Soviet Academy of Sciences, 1984.

Papert, Seymour. *Mindstorms: Children, Computers, and Powerful Ideas*. New York: Basic Books, 1980.

Paradox Development Studio. *Crusader Kings II*. Microsoft Windows. Johan Andersson, Henrik Fåhraeus, Christopher King, Linda Kiby, Henrik Fåhraeus, Johan Lerström, Fredrik Zetterman, Fredrik Toll, Sara Wendel-Örtqvist, et al. Paradox Interactive, 2012.

Parker Brothers. *Monopoly*. Tabletop game. Charles Darrow. Parker Brothers, 1935. Rip off of *The Landlord's Game,* created by Elizabeth Magie, self-published beginning in 1906.

Parker, Felan. "Canonizing *Bioshock*: Cultural Value and the Prestige Game." *Games and Culture* 12, no. 7–8 (November 1, 2017): 739–763. https://doi.org/10.1177/1555412015598669.

Patridge, Stephanie. "Video Games and Imaginative Identification." *The Journal of Aesthetics and Art Criticism* 75, no. 2 (2017): 181–184. https://doi.org/10.1111/jaac.12355.

Paul, Christopher A. "A Toxic Culture: Studying Gaming's Jerks." In *The Toxic Meritocracy of Video Games: Why Gaming Culture Is the Worst*, 63–90. Minneapolis: University of Minnesota Press, 2018. https://doi.org/10.5749/j.ctt2204rbz.5.

Pearce, Celia. "Spatial Literacy: Reading (and Writing) Game Space." In *Proceedings of Future and Reality of Gaming (FROG)*, 19. Vienna, 2008.

Pearson, Craig. "Impressions: *Prom Week*." *Rock, Paper, Shotgun*, February 16, 2012. https://www.rockpapershotgun.com/2012/02/16/impressions-prom-week/.

Pedercini, Paolo. "Videogames and the Spirit of Capitalism." Molleindustria, February 14, 2014. http://www.molleindustria.org/blog/videogames-and-the-spirit-of-capitalism/.

Penny, Simon. *Making Sense: Cognition, Computing, Art, and Embodiment*. Cambridge, MA: MIT Press, 2017.

Perlin, Ken, and Athomas Goldberg. "Improv: A System for Scripting Interactive Actors in Virtual Worlds." In *SIGGRAPH '96: Proceedings of the 23rd Annual Conference on Computer Graphics and Interactive Techniques*. New York: ACM, 1996. http://dx.doi.org/10.1145/237170.237258.

Perman, Cindy. "Layoffs: The Videogame." CNBC, March 20, 2009. https://www.cnbc.com/id/29775890.

Persuasive Games. *Jetset: A Game for Airports*. Apple iOS. Ian Bogost et al. Persuasive Games, 2009. Based on *Airport Security*, Persuasive Games, 2006.

Petersen, Sandy. *Call of Cthulhu*. Tabletop Role Playing Game. Chaosium, 1981.

Peterson, Jon. "A Game Out of All Proportions: How a Hobby Miniaturized War." In *Zones of Control: Perspectives on Wargaming*, edited by Pat Harrigan and Matthew G. Kirschenbaum, 3–31. Cambridge, MA: MIT Press, 2016.

Peterson, Jon. *Playing at the World: A History of Simulating Wars, People and Fantastic Adventures, from Chess to Role-Playing Games*. San Diego, CA: Unreason Press, 2012.

Phillips, Amanda. "Negg(at)Ing the Game Studies Subject: An Affective History of the Field." *Feminist Media Histories* 6, no. 1 (January 1, 2020): 12–36. https://doi.org/10.1525/fmh.2020.6.1.12.

Pilon, Mary. "Monopoly's Inventor: The Progressive Who Didn't Pass 'Go.'" *New York Times*, February 13, 2015. https://www.nytimes.com/2015/02/15/business/behind-monopoly-an-inventor-who-didnt-pass-go.html.

Pilon, Mary. *The Monopolists: Obsession, Fury, and the Scandal Behind the World's Favorite Board Game*. London: Bloomsbury, 2015.

Pinchbeck, Dan. *DOOM: SCARYDARKFAST*. Ann Arbor, MI: University of Michigan Press, 2013. http://hdl.handle.net/2027/spo.11878639.0001.001.

Plutte, Jon. "Story of *Spacewar!*" Computer History Museum, 2011. Video, 4:15. https://www.computerhistory.org/revolution/computer-games/16/189/2213.

PopCap Games. *Bejeweled: Deluxe*. Microsoft Windows 98. Jason Kapalka, Brian Fiete, Josh Langley, Peter Hajba. PopCap Games, 2000.

Porpentine. *Howling Dogs*. Browser (Twine). 2012. http://slimedaughter.com/games/twine/howlingdogs/.

Porpentine. "Live Free, Play Hard: The Week in Free Indie Games." *Rock, Paper, Shotgun*, September 9, 2012. https://www.rockpapershotgun.com/2012/09/09/live-free-play-hard-the-week-in-free-indie-games-3/.

Price, John A. "Social Science Research on Video Games." *Journal of Popular Culture* 18, no. 4 (Spring 1985): 111–125.

Quantic Dream SA. *Heavy Rain*. Sony PlayStation 3. David Cage, Guillaume de Fondaumière, Charles Coutier, Sophie Buhl, Caroline Marchal, Jean-Charles Perrier, Thierry Prodhomme, Clément Castanier, et al. Sony Computer Entertainment America, 2010.

Quinn, Zoë. *Depression Quest*. Browser (Twine). 2013. http://www.depressionquest.com.

Raven Software. *Heretic*. MS-DOS. Brian Raffel, Ben Gokey, Chris Rhinehart, Shane Gurno, Steve Raffel, Brian Pelletier, James Sumwalt, Michael Raymond-Judy, Eric C. Biessman, Timothy Moore, Kevin Schilder, et al. id Software and GT Interactive, 1994.

Reed, Aaron A. "Changeful Tales: Design-Driven Approaches Toward More Expressive Storygames." PhD diss., University of California, Santa Cruz, 2017. https://escholarship.org/uc/item/8838j82v.

Reed, Aaron A., John Murray, and Anastasia Salter. *Adventure Games: Playing the Outsider*. London: Bloomsbury Academic, 2020.

Reiss, Steven. *The Normal Personality: A New Way of Thinking about People*. Cambridge: Cambridge University Press, 2008.

Reith, James. "When Robert Pinsky Wrote a Video Game." *The New Yorker*, January 21, 2016. https://www.newyorker.com/books/page-turner/when-robert-pinsky-wrote-a-video-game.

Reynolds, Craig W. "Flocks, Herds, and Schools: A Distributed Behavioral Model." In *SIGGRAPH '87: Proceedings of the 14th Annual Conference on Computer Graphics and Interactive Techniques*, 25–34. New York: ACM, 1987. https://doi.org/10.1145/37401.37406.

Reynolds, Craig W. "OpenSteer: Steering Behaviors for Autonomous Characters." OpenSteer. Updated October 25, 2004. http://opensteer.sourceforge.net/. Updated version at https://github.com/meshula/OpenSteer.

Reynolds, Craig W. "Steering Behaviors for Autonomous Characters." Presented at the Game Developers Conference, San Jose, CA, USA, March 15–19, 1999.

Richert, Marcus. *Passage in 10 Seconds*. Adobe Flash. Raitendo, 2010. http://www.kongregate.com/games/raitendo/passage-in-10-seconds.

Riendeau, Danielle. "*Gone Home* Review: Living Room." Polygon, August 15, 2013. https://www.polygon.com/2013/8/15/4620172/gone-home-review-if-these-walls-could-talk.

Robbins, Ben. *Microscope: A Fractal Role-Playing Game of Epic Histories*. Tabletop Role Playing Game. Lame Mage Productions, 2011.

Roberts, Sarah T. "Digital Detritus: 'Error' and the Logic of Opacity in Social Media Content Moderation." *First Monday* 23, no. 3 (March 1, 2018). https://doi.org/10.5210/fm.v23i3.8283.

Robson, Jon, and Aaron Meskin. "Video Games as Self-Involving Interactive Fictions." *The Journal of Aesthetics and Art Criticism* 74, no. 2 (2016): 165–177. https://doi.org/10.1111/jaac.12269.

Rockstar North. *Grand Theft Auto IV*. Microsoft Xbox 360. Leslie Benzies, Aaron Garbut, Alexander Roger, Imran Sarwar, William Mills, Dan Houser, Rupert Humphries, Craig Filshie, Keith McLeman, Simon Lashley, Alwyn Roberts, Andrew Duthie, Barry Clark, Brenda Carey, Chris McMahon, Dave Bruce, David R. Watson, James Arthur, Jim McMahon, John Haime, Kevin Wong, Lawrence Kerr, Neil Ferguson, Neil Meikle, Paul Green, Robert Bray, Ross Wallace, Ryan Baker, Steve Taylor, Thomas French, Ray Tran, John Whyte, Alex Hadjadj, Andrzej Madajczyk,

Mark Nicholson, Phil Hooker, Adam Croston, Chris Swinhoe, Jack Potter, James Broad, Jonathon Ashcroft, Michael Garry, Mike Diskett, Alexander Illes, Derek Payne, Derek Ward, Graeme Williamson, Matthew Shepcar, Miguel Freitas, Greg Smith, David Muir, Luke Openshaw, et al. Rockstar Games, 2008.

Rockstar North. *Grand Theft Auto: San Andreas*. Sony PlayStation 2. Sam Houser, Dan Houser, Jamie King, Alex Horton, Leslie Benzies, Aaron Garbut, Adam Fowler, Obbe Vermeij, Alexander Roger, et al. Rockstar Games, 2004.

Rockstar North. *Grand Theft Auto: Vice City*. Sony PlayStation 2. Sam Houser, Dan Houser, Jeremy Pope, Jamie King, Leslie Benzies, Aaron Garbut, Obbe Vermeij, Adam Fowler, et al. Rockstar Games, 2002.

Roddenberry, Gene. *Star Trek*. Paramount Television Sales, NBC, 1966–1969.

Rogue Entertainment. *Strife*. MS-DOS. Susan G. McBride, Jim Molinets, Sean Patten, Nicholas Earl, Gary Lake-Schaal, Tim Willits, Michael Kaplan, John Sanborn, James Monroe, Peter Mack, Rich Fleider, Steven Maines, et al. Velocity, 1996.

Rohrer, Jason. *Passage*. Microsoft Windows. 2007. http://hcsoftware.sourceforge.net/passage/.

Romero, Brenda. *Train*. Tabletop. 2009. http://brenda.games/train/.

Rovio Mobile. *Angry Birds*. Apple iOS. Niklas Hed, Mikael Hed, Raine Mäki, Harro Grönberg, Jaakko Iisalo, Tuomo Lehtinen, Tuomas Erikoinen, Ari Pulkkinen, et al. Clickgamer Technologies, 2009.

Ruberg, Bonnie. "Straight Paths through Queer Walking Simulators: Wandering on Rails and Speedrunning in *Gone Home*." *Games and Culture*, March 7, 2019. https://doi.org/10.1177/1555412019826746.

Ruberg, Bonnie. *Video Games Have Always Been Queer*. Postmillennial Pop. New York: New York University Press, 2019.

Rusch, Doris C. *Making Deep Games: Designing Games with Meaning and Purpose*. Boca Raton, FL: Focal Press, 2016.

Rusch, Doris C., and Matthew J. Weise. "Games about LOVE and TRUST?: Harnessing the Power of Metaphors for Experience Design." In *Proceedings of the 2008 ACM SIGGRAPH Symposium on Video Games*, 89–97. Sandbox '08, Los Angeles, CA, USA, August 9–10, 2008. New York: ACM, 2008. https://doi.org/10.1145/1401843.1401861.

Russell, Stephen, Peter Samson, Dan Edwards, Martin Graetz, Alan Kotok, Steve Piner, and Robert A. Saunders. *Spacewar!* Digital Equipment Corporation PDP-1. Massachusetts Institute of Technology, 1962.

Russian Soft. *Sex Tetris*. Version 1.2. ZX Spectrum. S. Tkachev and O. Kudinski. Orenburg: Russian Soft, 1993.

Ryan, Marie-Laure. "Beyond Myth and Metaphor: The Case of Narrative in Digital Media." *Game Studies* 1, no. 1 (July 2001). http://www.gamestudies.org/0101/ryan/.

Ryan, James. "Curating Simulated Storyworlds." PhD diss., University of California, Santa Cruz, 2018. https://escholarship.org/uc/item/1340j5h2.

Ryan, James, Ethan Seither, Michael Mateas, and Noah Wardrip-Fruin. "Expressionist: An Authoring Tool for In-Game Text Generation." In *Interactive Storytelling*, edited by Frank Nack and Andrew S. Gordon, 221–233. Lecture Notes in Computer Science. Berlin: Springer International Publishing, 2016.

Sack, Warren. *The Software Arts*. Cambridge, MA: MIT Press, 2019.

Saldana, Giancarlo. "*Gone Home* Review." Edge Online, August 15, 2013. https://www.gamesradar.com/gone-home-review/ (original URL no longer available).

Sali, Serdar, Noah Wardrip-Fruin, Steven Dow, Michael Mateas, Sri Kurniawan, Aaron A. Reed, and Ronald Liu. "Playing with Words: From Intuition to Evaluation of Game Dialogue Interfaces." In *Proceedings of the Fifth International Conference on the Foundations of Digital Games*, 179–186. New York: ACM, 2010. https://doi.org/10.1145/1822348.1822372.

Samuel, Ben, Jacob Garbe, Adam Summerville, Jill Denner, Sarah Harmon, and Gina Lepore. "Leveraging Procedural Narrative and Gameplay to Address Controversial Topics." Presented at the 8th International Conference on Computational Creativity, Atlanta, GA, USA, June 19–23, 2017.

Samuel, Ben, Aaron A. Reed, Paul Maddaloni, Michael Mateas, and Noah Wardrip-Fruin. "The Ensemble Engine: Next-Generation Social Physics." Presented at the 10th International Conference on the Foundations of Digital Games (FDG), Pacific Grove, CA, USA, June 22–25, 2015. http://www.fdg2015.org/papers/fdg2015_paper_07.pdf.

SCE Studio Santa Monica. *God of War II*. Sony PlayStation 2. Cory Barlog, Steve Caterson, Tim Moss, Stig Asmussen, Charlie Wen, David Jaffe, Shannon Studstill, et al. Sony Computer Entertainment America, 2007.

Schelling, Thomas C. "Dynamic Models of Segregation." *The Journal of Mathematical Sociology* 1, no. 2 (July 1, 1971): 143–186. https://doi.org/10.1080/0022250X.1971.9989794.

Sedgwick, Eve Kosofsky. *Between Men: English Literature and Male Homosocial Desire*. Gender and Culture. New York: Columbia University Press, 1985.

Serious Games Interactive. *Playing History 2: Slave Trade*. Microsoft Windows. Serious Games Interactive, 2013.

Short, Emily. "Conversation as Gameplay (Talk)." *Emily Short's Interactive Storytelling* (blog), January 20, 2019. https://emshort.blog/2019/01/20/conversation-as-gameplay-talk/.

Short, Emily. "Reading and Hypothesis." *Emily Short's Interactive Storytelling* (blog), January 9, 2014. https://emshort.blog/2014/01/09/reading-and-hypothesis/.

Sicart, Miguel. "Against Procedurality." *Game Studies* 11, no. 3 (December 2011). http://gamestudies.org/1103/articles/sicart_ap.

Sicart, Miguel. "Defining Game Mechanics." *Game Studies* 8, no. 2 (December 2008). http://gamestudies.org/0802/articles/sicart.

Sicart, Miguel. "Loops and Metagames: Understanding Game Design Structures." Presented at the 10th International Conference on the Foundations of Digital Games (FDG), Pacific Grove, CA, USA, June 22–25, 2015.

Sicart, Miguel. *Play Matters*. Cambridge, MA: MIT Press, 2014.

Siecke, Hanna Fidelis. *Conversation Pong 1.0*. Java. 2010. See gameplay here: https://vimeo.com/20825992.

Sims Studio. *The Sims 3*. Microsoft Windows. Benjamin Bell, Shannon Copur, JoAnna Lio, Lyndsay Pearson, Darren Gyles, Brian M. Bell, Peter Ingebretson, Avery Lee, Jon Parise, Nick Schipano, Bruce Wilkie, Morgan Godat, Chris Trimble, John Brown, Marion Gothier, et al. Electronic Arts, 2009.

Sito, Tom. *Moving Innovation: A History of Computer Animation*. Cambridge, MA: MIT Press, 2013.

Sliva, Marty. "*Gone Home* Review." IGN, August 15, 2013. https://www.ign.com/articles/2013/08/15/gone-home-review.

Smith, Alexander. "The Book of Nolan." *They Create Worlds* (blog), December 19, 2014. https://videogamehistorian.wordpress.com/2014/12/19/the-book-of-nolan/.

Speer, Robert, and Catherine Havasi. "Representing General Relational Knowledge in ConceptNet 5." Presented at the 8th International Conference on Language Resources and Evaluation, Istanbul, Turkey, May 21–27, 2012. http://www.lrec-conf.org/proceedings/lrec2012/pdf/1072_Paper.pdf.

Square. *Final Fantasy*. Nintendo Entertainment System. Hironobu Sakaguchi, Yoshitaka Amano, Nasir Gebelli, Kenji Terada, Nobuo Uematsu, et al. Nintendo of America, 1990.

Squinkifer, Dietrich. *Interruption Junction*. Browser. 2015. https://squinky.me/2015/01/18/interruption-junction/.

Squinkifer, Dietrich. "Well, This Is Awkward . . . A Radically Inclusive, Queer Theory-Inspired Approach to Game Design." MFA thesis, University of California, Santa Cruz, 2015.

Star, Darren, showrunner. *Sex and the City*. United States: Home Box Office, 1998–2004.

Steam Hunters. "*Gone Home* Achievements." Steam Hunters. Accessed September 24, 2019. https://steamhunters.com/stats/232430/achievements.

Stephens, Alastair. "*Prom Week*." Alastair Stephens, 2012. http://alastairstephens.com/prom-night/ (no longer available).

Sterne, Laurence. *Tristram Shandy: Authoritative Text, Contexts, Criticism*. Edited by Judith Hawley. Norton Critical Editions. New York: W. W. Norton, 2019.

Strachey, Christopher. "Logical or Non-Mathematical Programmes." In *Proceedings of the 1952 ACM National Meeting (Toronto)*, 46–49. ACM '52, Pittsburgh, PA, USA, May 2–3, 1952. New York: ACM, 1952. https://doi.org/10.1145/800259.808992.

Strachey, Christopher. *M. U. C. Draughts*. Manchester Mark I. Manchester University, 1951. Retrospectively named.

Strachey, Christopher. "The 'Thinking' Machine." *Encounter* 3, no. 4 (October 1954): 25–31.

Studio Mountains. *Florence*. Apple iOS. Kamina Vincent, Tony Coculuzzi, Sam Crisp, Kenneth Wong, Kevin Penkin, Fabian Malabello, Mat Dwyer, Brooke Maggs, Jason Pammet, et al. Annapurna Interactive, 2018.

Sudnow, David. *Pilgrim in the Microworld*. New York: Warner Books, 1983.

Sullivan, Anne Margaret. "The Grail Framework: Making Stories Playable on Three Levels in CRPGs." PhD diss., University of California, Santa Cruz, 2012. https://escholarship.org/uc/item/004129jn.

Sullivan, Anne, April Grow, Michael Mateas, and Noah Wardrip-Fruin. "The Design of *Mismanor*: Creating a Playable Quest-Based Story Game." In *Proceedings of the International Conference on the Foundations of Digital Games*, 180–187. New York: ACM, 2012. https://doi.org/10.1145/2282338.2282374.

Sullivan, Anne, Michael Mateas, and Noah Wardrip-Fruin. "QuestBrowser: Making Quests Playable with Computer-Assisted Design." Presented at the 8th Digital Arts and Culture Conference, Irvine, CA, USA, December 12–15, 2009. https://escholarship.org/uc/item/2tk0h882.

Summerville, Adam, Chris Martens, Sarah Harmon, Michael Mateas, Joseph Osborn, Noah Wardrip-Fruin, and Arnav Jhala. "From Mechanics to Meaning." *IEEE Transactions on Games* 11, no. 1 (March 2019): 69–78. https://doi.org/10.1109/TCIAIG.2017.2765599.

Summerville, Adam, Chris Martens, Ben Samuel, Joseph C. Osborn, Noah Wardrip-Fruin, and Michael Mateas. "Gemini: Bidirectional Generation and Analysis of Games via ASP." Presented at the 14th AAAI Conference on Artificial Intelligence and Interactive Digital Entertainment (AIIDE), Edmonton, AB, Canada, November 13–17, 2018. https://www.aaai.org/ocs/index.php/AIIDE/AIIDE18/paper/view/18086.

Sutherland, Ivan Edward. "Sketchpad, a Man-Machine Graphical Communication System." PhD diss., Massachusetts Institute of Technology, 1963. https://dspace.mit.edu/handle/1721.1/14979.

Swink, Steve. *Game Feel*. Amsterdam; Boston: Routledge, 2008.

Synapse Software Corporation. *Mindwheel*. MS-DOS. Robert Pinsky, Steve Hales, Cathryn Mataga, Richard Sanford, et al. Brøderbund Software, 1985.

Syzygy. *Computer Space*. Arcade. Nolan Bushnell and Ted Dabney. Nutting Associates, 1971.

Taito Corporation. *Space Invaders*. Arcade. Tomohiro Nishikado. Midway Mfg., 1978.

Take Action Games. *Darfur Is Dying*. Adobe Flash. Susana Ruiz, Ashley York, Huy Truong, Ramiro Cazaux, Corey Jackson, Mike Stein, and Alexander Tarr. University of Southern California: mtvU, 2006.

Tanenbaum, Theresa Jean. "Being in the Story: Readerly Pleasure, Acting Theory, and Performing a Role." In *Interactive Storytelling*, edited by Mei Si, David Thue, Elisabeth André, James C. Lester, Theresa Jean Tanenbaum, and Veronica Zammitto, 55–66. Lecture Notes in Computer Science. Berlin: Springer, 2011.

Taylor, Brian. "*Grand Theft Auto IV*—Plot Guide." GameFAQs, May 19, 2008. https://gamefaqs .gamespot.com/xbox360/933037-grand-theft-auto-iv/faqs/52853.

Team Aha! *Akrasia*. Microsoft Windows. Doris C. Rusch, Louis Teo, Paul Yang, Alexander Luke Chong, Shawn Dominic Loh Han Yi, Xinru Zou, Law Kok Chung, Stephie Wu, Erik Sahlström, et al. Singapore-MIT GAMBIT Game Lab, 2008. http://gambit.mit.edu/loadgame/akrasia.php.

Telltale. *The Walking Dead*. Microsoft Windows. Sean Vanaman, Jake Rodkin, Carl Muckenhoupt, Derek Sakai, Peter Tsaykel, Eric Parsons, Jonathon Banks, et al. Telltale, 2012.

Telltale. *The Wolf Among Us*. Microsoft Windows. Pierre Shorette, Ryan Kaufman, Joe Pinney, Matt LoPresti, Nick Herman, Dennis Lenart, David Bogan, Jared Emerson-Johnson, Keenan Patterson, Jeffrey Sarre, Vahram Antonian, Kim Lyons, Jason Findley, et al. Telltale, 2013.

Texas Instruments Incorporated. *Munch Man*. TI-99/4A. James E. Dramis. 1982.

thatgamecompany. *Journey*. Sony PlayStation 3. Chris Bell, Jenova Chen, Nicholas Clark, John Edwards, Robin Hunicke, Aaron Jessie, Martin Middleton, Matt Nava, John Nesky, Kellee Santiago, Bryan S. Singh, et al. Sony Computer Entertainment America, 2012.

Thekla. *The Witness*. Microsoft Windows. Jonathan Blow, Ignacio Castaño, Salvador Bel Murciano, Andrew Smith, Luis Antonio, Orsi Spanyol, Eric A. Anderson, et al. Thekla, 2016.

Thiel, Tamiko, and Zara Houshmand. *Beyond Manzanar*. Large screen virtual reality projection. 2000.

Thomas, Dexter. "I Played 'Slave *Tetris*' so Your Kids Don't Have To." *Los Angeles Times*, September 7, 2015. https://www.latimes.com/entertainment/herocomplex/la-et-hc-played-slave-tetris-kids -20150904-htmlstory.html.

Tiltfactor. "Tiltfactor | *LAYOFF*." Tiltfactor. Accessed March 29, 2018. http://www.tiltfactor.org/ game/layoff/.

Tiltfactor. "Tiltfactor | *LAYOFF* —1 Million Players in the First Week; at GDC." Accessed March 29, 2018. http://www.tiltfactor.org/layoff-1-million-players-in-the-first-week-at-gdc/.

Tiniest Shark. *Redshirt*. Microsoft Windows. Mitu Khandaker. Positech Games, 2013.

Tosca, Susana P. "A Pragmatics of Links." In *HYPERTEXT '00: Proceedings of the Eleventh ACM on Hypertext and Hypermedia*. New York: ACM, 2000. http://dx.doi.org/10.1145/336296.336327.

Toy, Michael, Glenn Wichman, and Ken Arnold. *Rogue*. BSD Unix 4.x. University of California Santa Cruz & Berkeley, 1980.

Treanor, Mike. "Investigating Procedural Expression and Interpretation in Videogames." PhD diss., University of California, Santa Cruz, 2013. https://escholarship.org/uc/item/1mn3x85g.

Treanor, Mike. "Newsgames—Procedural Rhetoric Meets Political Cartoons." Presented at the 2009 DiGRA International Conference: Breaking New Ground: Innovation in Games, Play, Practice and Theory, London, England, UK, September 1–4, 2009. http://www.digra.org/wp-content/uploads/digital-library/09300.09505.pdf.

Treanor, Mike, Bryan Blackford, Michael Mateas, and Ian Bogost. "Game-O-Matic: Generating Videogames That Represent Ideas." In *Proceedings of the Third Workshop on Procedural Content Generation in Games*, 11:1–8. New York: ACM, 2012. https://doi.org/10.1145/2538528.2538537.

Treanor, Mike, Michael Mateas, and Noah Wardrip-Fruin. "*Kaboom!* is a Many-Splendored Thing: An Interpretation and Design Methodology for Message-Driven Games Using Graphical Logics." In *Proceedings of the Fifth International Conference on the Foundations of Digital Games*, 224–231. New York: ACM, 2010. https://doi.org/10.1145/1822348.1822378.

Treanor, Mike, Josh McCoy, and Anne Sullivan. "A Framework for Playable Social Dialogue." Presented at the 12th AAAI Conference on Artificial Intelligence and Interactive Digital Entertainment (AIIDE), San Francisco, CA, USA, October 8–12, 2016. https://www.aaai.org/ocs/index.php/AIIDE/AIIDE16/paper/view/14018.

Treanor, Mike, Bobby Schweizer, Ian Bogost, and Michael Mateas. "Proceduralist Readings: How to Find Meaning in Games with Graphical Logics." In *Proceedings of the 6th International Conference on Foundations of Digital Games*, 115–122. New York: ACM, 2011. https://doi.org/10.1145/2159365.2159381.

Treanor, Mike, Bobby Schweizer, Ian Bogost, and Michael Mateas. "The Micro-Rhetorics of Game-o-Matic." In *Proceedings of the International Conference on the Foundations of Digital Games*, 18–25. New York: ACM, 2012. https://doi.org/10.1145/2282338.2282347.

Treanor, Mike, Alexander Zook, Mirjam P. Eladhari, Julian Togelius, Gillian Smith, Michael Cook, Tommy Thompson, Brian Magerko, John Levine, and Adam Smith. "AI-Based Game Design Patterns." Presented at the 10th International Conference on the Foundations of Digital Games (FDG), Pacific Grove, CA, USA, June 22–25, 2015. http://www.fdg2015.org/papers/fdg2015_paper_23.pdf.

Treyarch. *Call of Duty: Black Ops 4*. Microsoft Windows. Jason Blundell, Dan Bunting, Bruce Hall, Dave Anthony, Craig Houston, Jack Wall, et al. Activision, 2018.

USC Game Innovation Lab. *Walden: A Game*. Microsoft Windows. Tracy Fullerton, Todd Furmanski, Lucas Peterson, Logan Ver Hoef, Alex Mathew, Michael Sweet, et al. 2017. https://www.waldengame.com.

Valve Corporation. *Half-Life: Counter-Strike*. Microsoft Windows. Minh Le, Jess Cliffe, Chris Ashton, Ido Magal, et al. Sierra On-Line, 2000.

Valve Corporation. *Portal*. Microsoft Windows. Kim Swift, Erik Wolpaw, Chet Faliszek, Kelly Bailey, Mike Morasky, et al. Valve Corporation, 2007. Published as part of *The Orange Box*.

Van de Mosselaer, Nele. "Fictionally Flipping Tetrominoes? Defining the Fictionality of a Video-game Player's Actions." *Journal of the Philosophy of Games* 1, no. 1 (December 30, 2018). https://doi.org/10.5617/jpg.6035.

Verne, Jules. *Around the World in Eighty Days*. Translated by George Makepeace Towle. Philadelphia: Porter & Coates, 1873.

Vist, Elise. "Cyborg Games: Videogame Blasphemy and Disorientation." *Loading . . .* 9, no. 14 (November 15, 2015). http://journals.sfu.ca/loading/index.php/loading/article/view/153.

The Vladar Company. "When Games Went Click: The Story of *Tennis for Two*." Stony Brook University, 2013. Video, 17:57. https://www.youtube.com/watch?v=6QSHZ20MQfE.

Vollmer, Asher, Greg Wohlwend, Jimmy Hinson, and Angela Li. *Threes JS*. Browser. 2014. http://threesjs.com/.

Wardrip-Fruin, Noah. "Beyond Shooting and Eating: Passage, Dys4ia, and the Meanings of Collision." *Critical Inquiry* 45, no. 1 (Autumn 2018): 137–167. https://doi.org/10.1086/699587.

Wardrip-Fruin, Noah. "Christopher Strachey: The First Digital Artist?" *Grand Text Auto* (blog), August 1, 2005. https://grandtextauto.soe.ucsc.edu/2005/08/01/christopher-strachey-first-digital-artist/.

Noah Wardrip-Fruin. "De passagem por *Passage*." In *Jogador de Mil Fases*, edited by Arthur Protasio and Guilherme Xavier. Brasilia, Brazil: Novas Ideias, 2014.

Wardrip-Fruin, Noah. "Digital Media Archaeology: Interpreting Computational Processes." In *Media Archaeologies*, edited by Erkki Huhtamo and Jussi Parikka. Berkeley, CA: University of California Press, 2011.

Wardrip-Fruin, Noah. *Expressive Processing: Digital Fictions, Computer Games, and Software Studies*. Cambridge, MA: MIT Press, 2009.

Wardrip-Fruin, Noah. "Gravity in Computer Space." *ROMchip: A Journal of Game Histories* 1, no. 2 (December 2019). https://romchip.org/index.php/romchip-journal/article/view/91.

Wardrip-Fruin, Noah. "Playable Media and Textual Instruments." *Dichtung Digital*, 2005. http://www.dichtung-digital.de/2005/1/Wardrip-Fruin/index.htm.

Wardrip-Fruin, Noah. "You Can't Make Games About Much." In *Your Computer Is on Fire: The Politics of Computing and New Media*, edited by Thomas S. Mullaney, Benjamin Peters, Mar Hicks, and Kavita Philip. Cambridge, MA: MIT Press, 2021.

Wardrip-Fruin, Noah, Michael Mateas, Steven Dow, and Serdar Sali. "Agency Reconsidered." Presented at the 2009 DiGRA International Conference: Breaking New Ground: Innovation in Games, Play, Practice and Theory, London, England, UK, September 1–4, 2009. http://www.digra.org/digital-library/publications/agency-reconsidered/.

Wark, McKenzie. *Gamer Theory*. Cambridge, MA: Harvard University Press, 2007.

Waters, Mark S., dir. *Mean Girls*. Los Angeles: Paramount Pictures Corporation, 2004.

Webb, Dan. "*GTA V* RP Is the Hottest Thing on Twitch Right Now." VideoGamer.com, April 28, 2017. https://www.videogamer.com/features/gta-v-rp-is-the-hottest-thing-on-twitch-right-now.

Wehner, Mike. "*Grand Theft Auto 5* Publisher Rockstar Learns What Happens When You Mess with PC Gamers." BGR, June 26, 2017. https://bgr.com/2017/06/26/grand-theft-auto-5-mods-pc-ban/.

Weir, Gregory. "Analysis: Incidental Character Choices in *Balloon Diaspora*." Gamasutra, May 2, 2011. https://www.gamasutra.com/view/news/124604/Analysis_Incidental_Character_Choices_in_Balloon_Diaspora.php.

Weizenbaum, Joseph. "ELIZA: A Computer Program for the Study of Natural Language Communication between Man and Machine." *Communications of the ACM* 9, no. 1 (1966).

Wiggins, John. "*Gone Home*—Every Item (No Audio)." YouTube, 2013. Video, 1:02. https://www.youtube.com/watch?v=pcD-85NvXAM.

Wikipedia. "List of Licensed and Localized Editions of Monopoly: USA," September 21, 2019. https://en.wikipedia.org/w/index.php?title=List_of_licensed_and_localized_editions_of_Monopoly:_USA&oldid=916872775.

Will and Game Yarouze! *Echochrome*. Sony PlayStation 3. Jun Fujiki, Tatsuya Suzuki, Tatsuo Masuda, Satoru Imamura, Kashin Hodotsuka, Kenichiro Hatada, Tomokazu Ohki, Hideki Sakamoto, Takashi Noshiro, Takanori Kikuchi, Kenichiro Obara, Hironori Tsuruya, et al. Sony Computer Entertainment America, 2008.

Wolf, Mark J. P. "Abstraction in the Video Game." In *The Video Game Theory Reader*. New York: Routledge, 2003.

Wolf, Mark J. P. *Encyclopedia of Video Games: The Culture, Technology, and Art of Gaming*. Westport, CT: ABC-CLIO, 2012.

Wolf, Mark J. P. *The Medium of the Video Game*. Austin, TX: University of Texas Press, 2001.

Yamamiya, Takashi, Alessandro Warth, and Ted Kaehler. "Active Essays on the Web." In *2009 Seventh International Conference on Creating, Connecting and Collaborating through Computing*, 3–10. Piscataway, NJ: IEEE, 2009. https://doi.org/10.1109/C5.2009.10.

Yang, Robert. "On the First Person Military Manshooter and the Shape of Modern Warfare." *Radiator Design Blog* (blog), November 18, 2011. https://www.blog.radiator.debacle.us/2011/11/on-first-person-military-manshooter-and.html.

Zagal, José P., and Roger Altizer. "Examining 'RPG Elements': Systems of Character Progression." Presented at the 9th International Conference on the Foundations of Digital Games, Fort Lauderdale, FL, USA, April 3–7, 2014.

Zook, Alex. "Expanding Operational Logics." *Alexzook* (blog), January 11, 2013. https://alexzook.wordpress.com/2013/01/11/expanding-operational-logics/.

Zubek, Robert. *Elements of Game Design*. Cambridge, MA: MIT Press, 2020.

Index